NORTH WORLD

VOL. 1: THE EPIC OF CONRAD

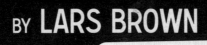

BY **LARS BROWN**

DEDICATED TO MOM AND DAD, I WOULD HA

DESIGN BY STEVEN BIRCH AT

EDITED BY JA

PUBLISHED BY ONI PRESS, INC.
JOE NOZEMACK, PUBLISHER
RANDAL C. JARRELL, MANAGING EDITOR
DOUGLAS E. SHERWOOD, EDITORIAL ASSISTANT

ONI PRESS, INC., 1305 SE MARTIN LUTHER KING JR. BLVD., SUITE A, PORTLAND, OR 97214

WWW.ONIPRESS.COM • NORTHWORLDONLINE.COM

FIRST EDITION: MARCH 2008
ISBN 978-1-932664-91-1
1 3 5 7 9 10 8 6 4 2

PRINTED IN CANADA

CHAPTER 1

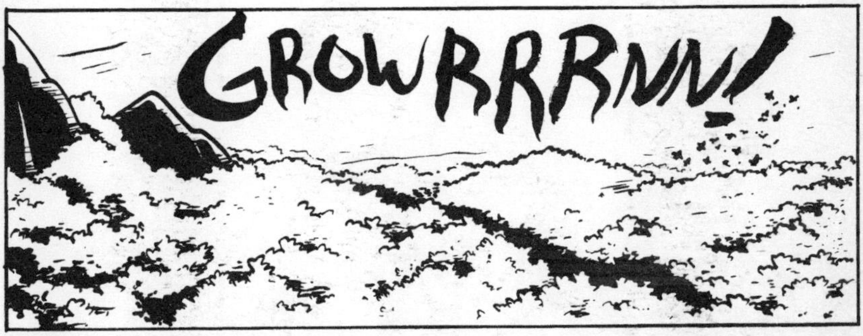
GROWRRRNN!

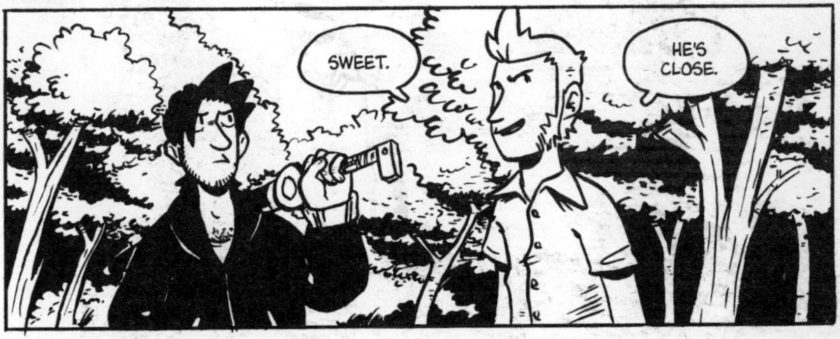
SWEET.
HE'S CLOSE.

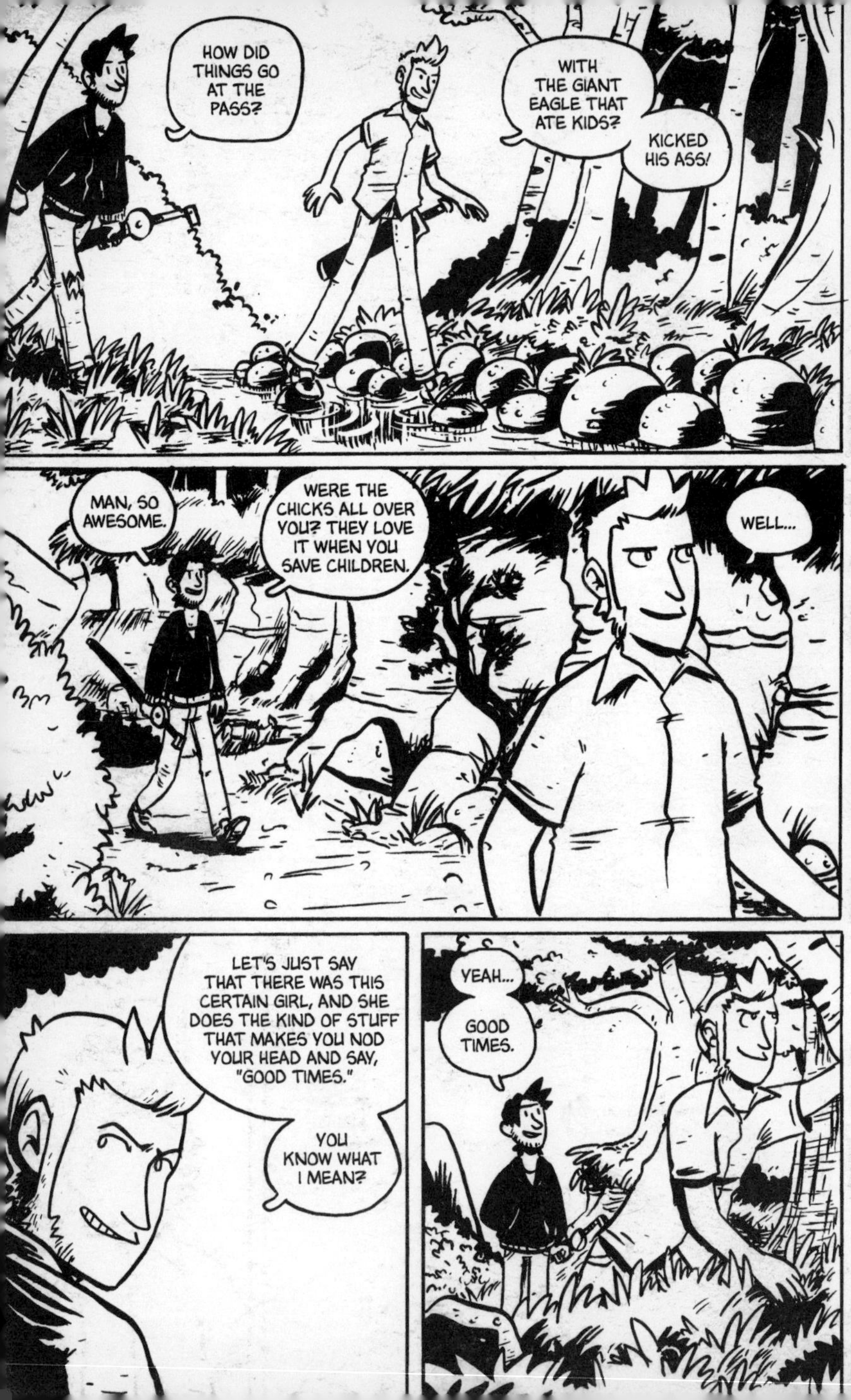
HOW DID THINGS GO AT THE PASS?
WITH THE GIANT EAGLE THAT ATE KIDS?
KICKED HIS ASS!
MAN, SO AWESOME.
WERE THE CHICKS ALL OVER YOU? THEY LOVE IT WHEN YOU SAVE CHILDREN.
WELL...
LET'S JUST SAY THAT THERE WAS THIS CERTAIN GIRL, AND SHE DOES THE KIND OF STUFF THAT MAKES YOU NOD YOUR HEAD AND SAY, "GOOD TIMES."
YOU KNOW WHAT I MEAN?
YEAH...
GOOD TIMES.

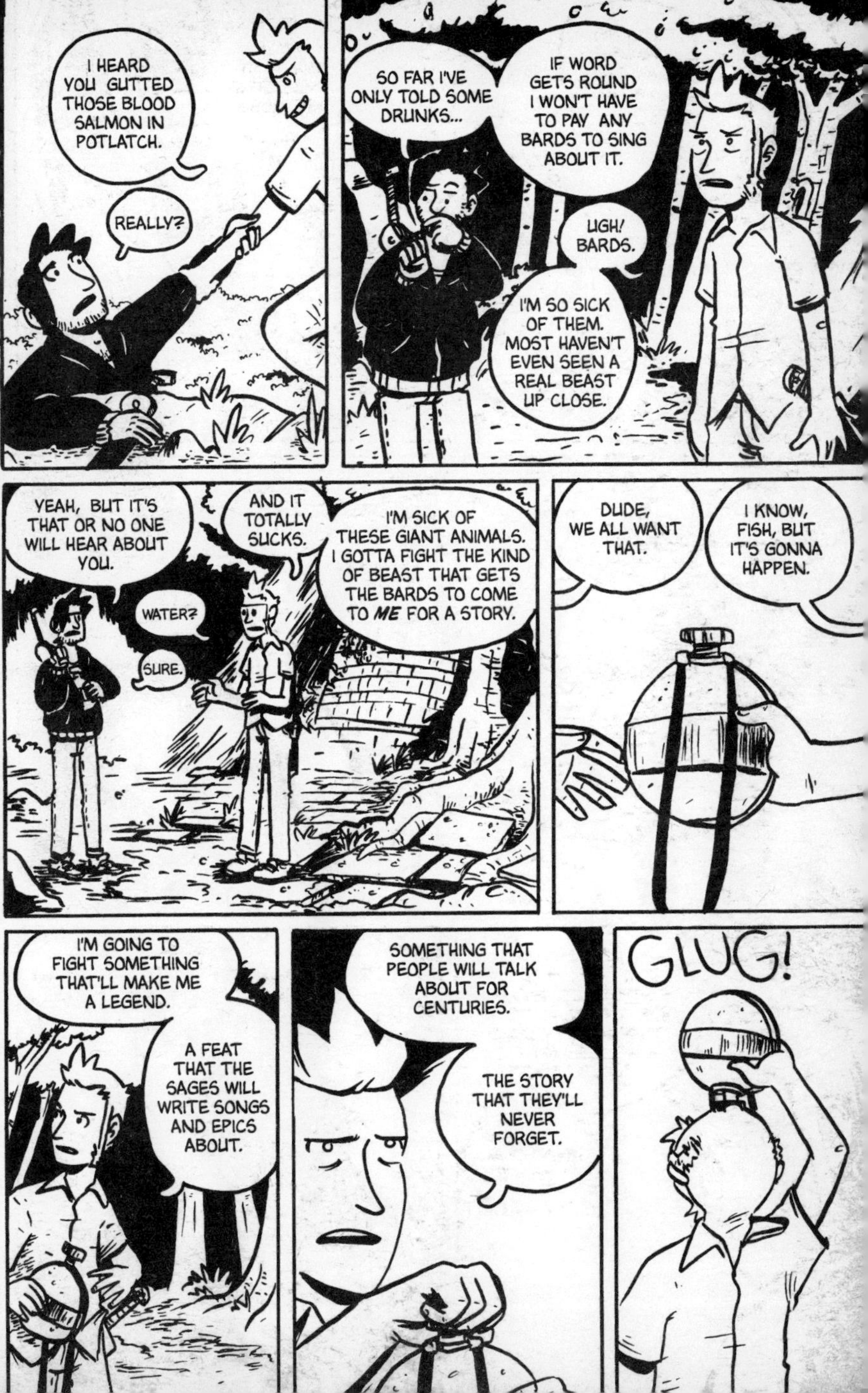
I HEARD YOU GUTTED THOSE BLOOD SALMON IN POTLATCH.
REALLY?
SO FAR I'VE ONLY TOLD SOME DRUNKS...
IF WORD GETS ROUND I WON'T HAVE TO PAY ANY BARDS TO SING ABOUT IT.
UGH! BARDS.
I'M SO SICK OF THEM. MOST HAVEN'T EVEN SEEN A REAL BEAST UP CLOSE.
YEAH, BUT IT'S THAT OR NO ONE WILL HEAR ABOUT YOU.
AND IT TOTALLY SUCKS.
WATER?
SURE.
I'M SICK OF THESE GIANT ANIMALS. I GOTTA FIGHT THE KIND OF BEAST THAT GETS THE BARDS TO COME TO *ME* FOR A STORY.
DUDE, WE ALL WANT THAT.
I KNOW, FISH, BUT IT'S GONNA HAPPEN.
I'M GOING TO FIGHT SOMETHING THAT'LL MAKE ME A LEGEND.
A FEAT THAT THE SAGES WILL WRITE SONGS AND EPICS ABOUT.
SOMETHING THAT PEOPLE WILL TALK ABOUT FOR CENTURIES.
THE STORY THAT THEY'LL NEVER FORGET.
GLUG!

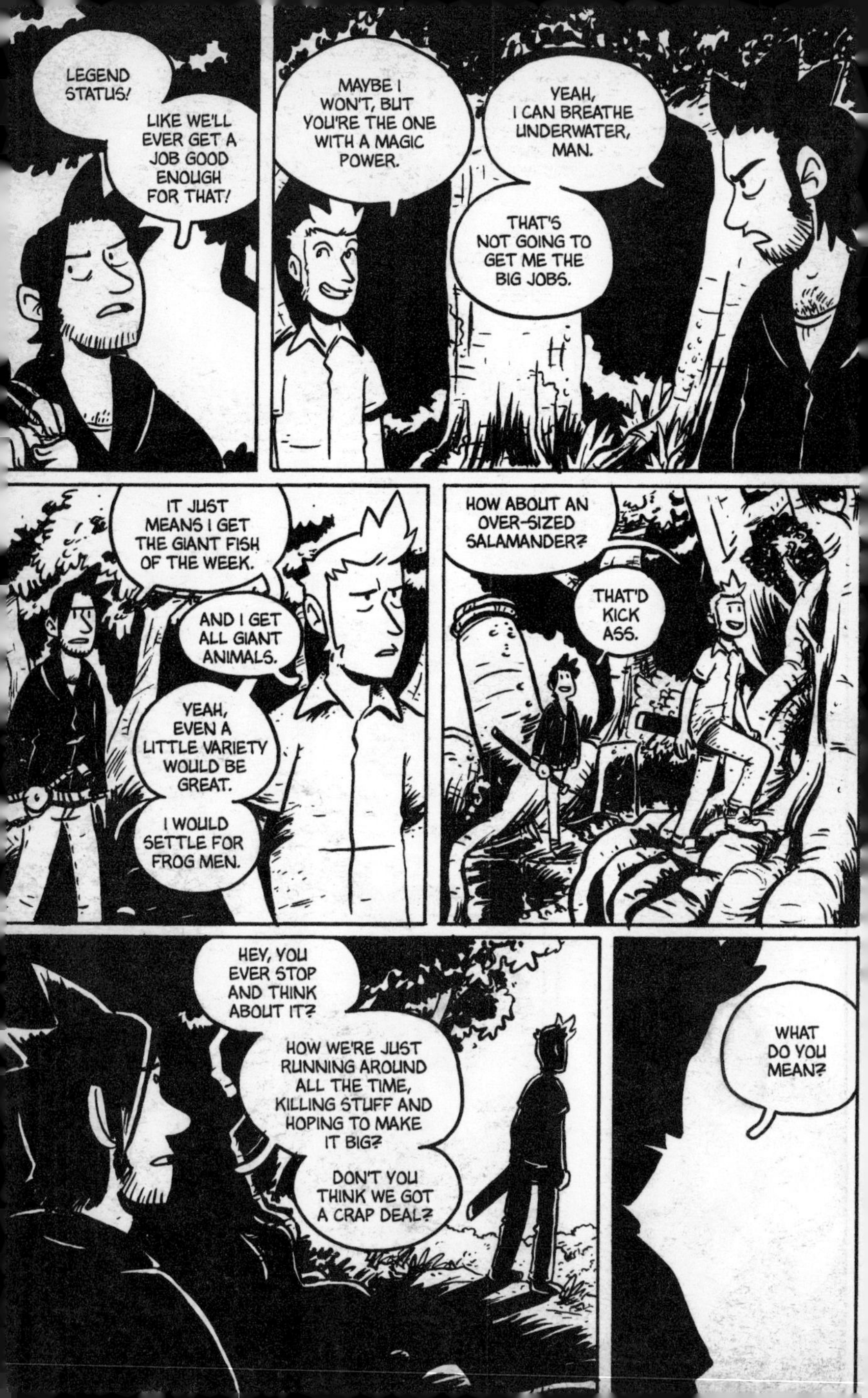

LEGEND STATUS!
LIKE WE'LL EVER GET A JOB GOOD ENOUGH FOR THAT!
MAYBE I WON'T, BUT YOU'RE THE ONE WITH A MAGIC POWER.
YEAH, I CAN BREATHE UNDERWATER, MAN.
THAT'S NOT GOING TO GET ME THE BIG JOBS.
IT JUST MEANS I GET THE GIANT FISH OF THE WEEK.
AND I GET ALL GIANT ANIMALS.
YEAH, EVEN A LITTLE VARIETY WOULD BE GREAT.
I WOULD SETTLE FOR FROG MEN.
HOW ABOUT AN OVER-SIZED SALAMANDER?
THAT'D KICK ASS.
HEY, YOU EVER STOP AND THINK ABOUT IT?
HOW WE'RE JUST RUNNING AROUND ALL THE TIME, KILLING STUFF AND HOPING TO MAKE IT BIG?
DON'T YOU THINK WE GOT A CRAP DEAL?
WHAT DO YOU MEAN?

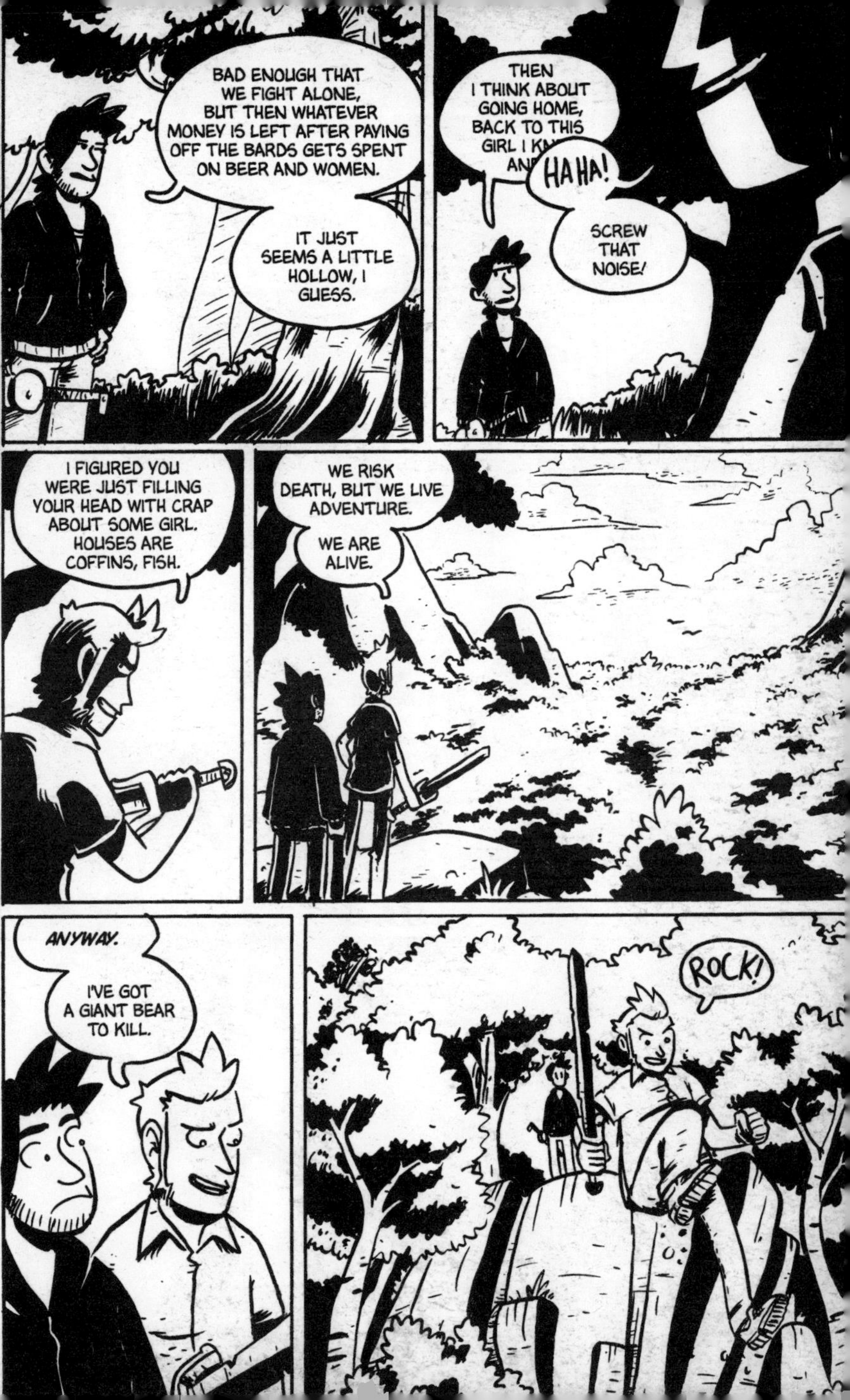
BAD ENOUGH THAT WE FIGHT ALONE, BUT THEN WHATEVER MONEY IS LEFT AFTER PAYING OFF THE BARDS GETS SPENT ON BEER AND WOMEN.
IT JUST SEEMS A LITTLE HOLLOW, I GUESS.
THEN I THINK ABOUT GOING HOME, BACK TO THIS GIRL I KN
AN
HAHA!
SCREW THAT NOISE!
I FIGURED YOU WERE JUST FILLING YOUR HEAD WITH CRAP ABOUT SOME GIRL. HOUSES ARE COFFINS, FISH.
WE RISK DEATH, BUT WE LIVE ADVENTURE.
WE ARE ALIVE.
ANYWAY.
I'VE GOT A GIANT BEAR TO KILL.
ROCK!

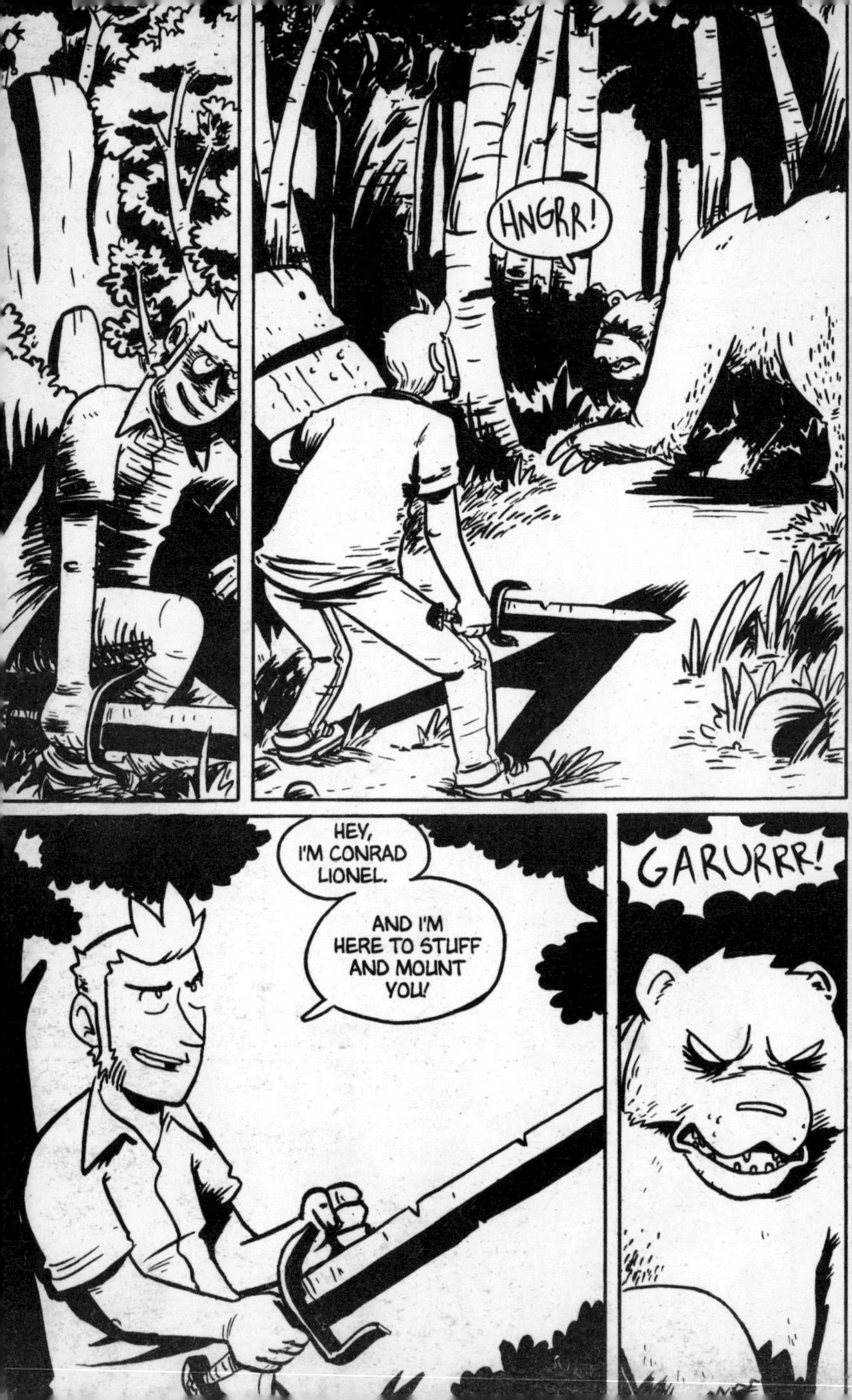
HNGRR!
HEY, I'M CONRAD LIONEL.
AND I'M HERE TO STUFF AND MOUNT YOU!
GARURRR!

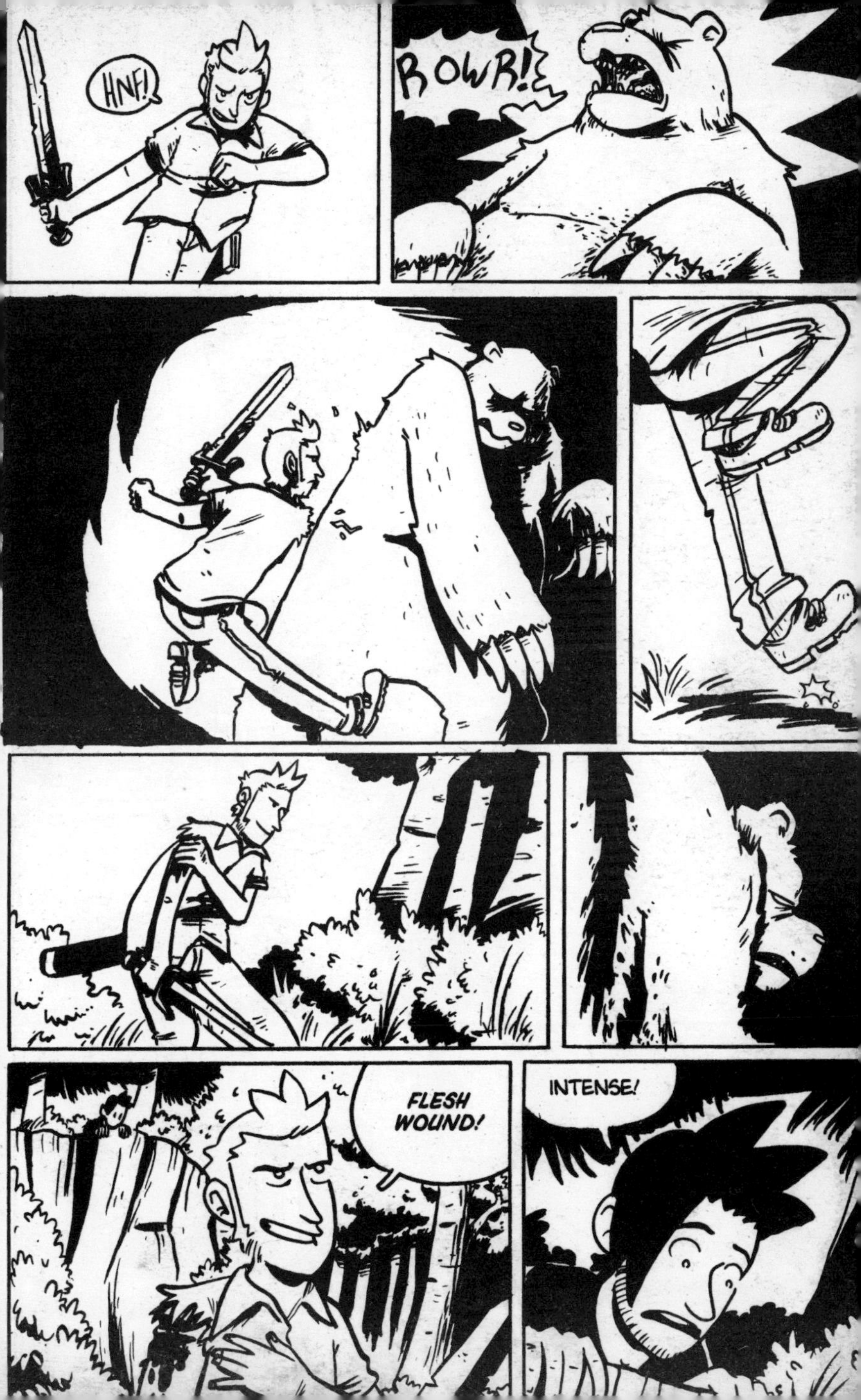
HNF!
ROWR!
FLESH WOUND!
INTENSE!

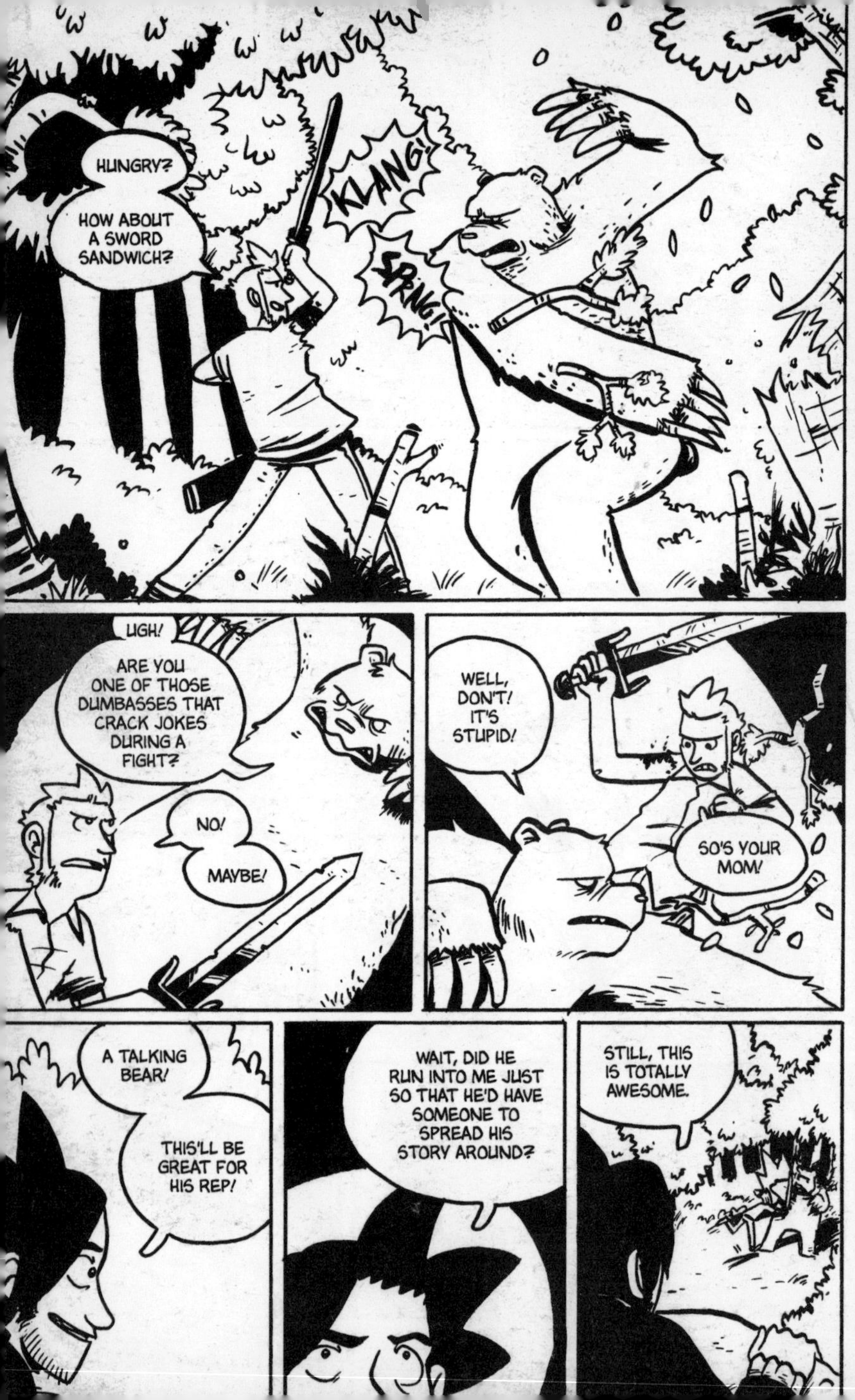

HUNGRY?
HOW ABOUT A SWORD SANDWICH?
KLANG!
SPRING!
UGH!
ARE YOU ONE OF THOSE DUMBASSES THAT CRACK JOKES DURING A FIGHT?
NO!
MAYBE!
WELL, DON'T! IT'S STUPID!
SO'S YOUR MOM!
A TALKING BEAR!
THIS'LL BE GREAT FOR HIS REP!
WAIT, DID HE RUN INTO ME JUST SO THAT HE'D HAVE SOMEONE TO SPREAD HIS STORY AROUND?
STILL, THIS IS TOTALLY AWESOME.

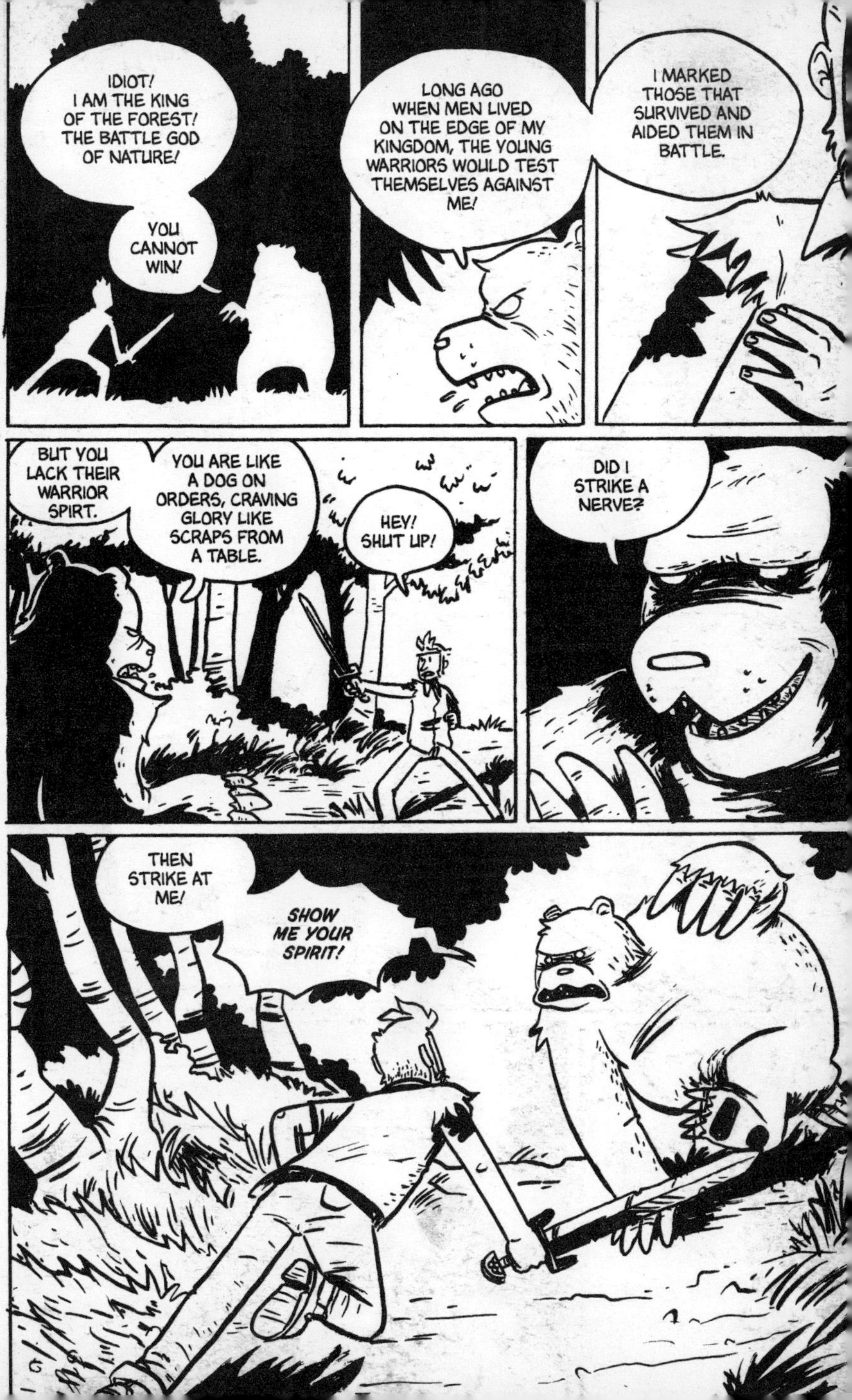
IDIOT! I AM THE KING OF THE FOREST! THE BATTLE GOD OF NATURE!
YOU CANNOT WIN!
LONG AGO WHEN MEN LIVED ON THE EDGE OF MY KINGDOM, THE YOUNG WARRIORS WOULD TEST THEMSELVES AGAINST ME!
I MARKED THOSE THAT SURVIVED AND AIDED THEM IN BATTLE.
BUT YOU LACK THEIR WARRIOR SPIRT.
YOU ARE LIKE A DOG ON ORDERS, CRAVING GLORY LIKE SCRAPS FROM A TABLE.
HEY! SHUT UP!
DID I STRIKE A NERVE?
THEN STRIKE AT ME!
SHOW ME YOUR SPIRIT!

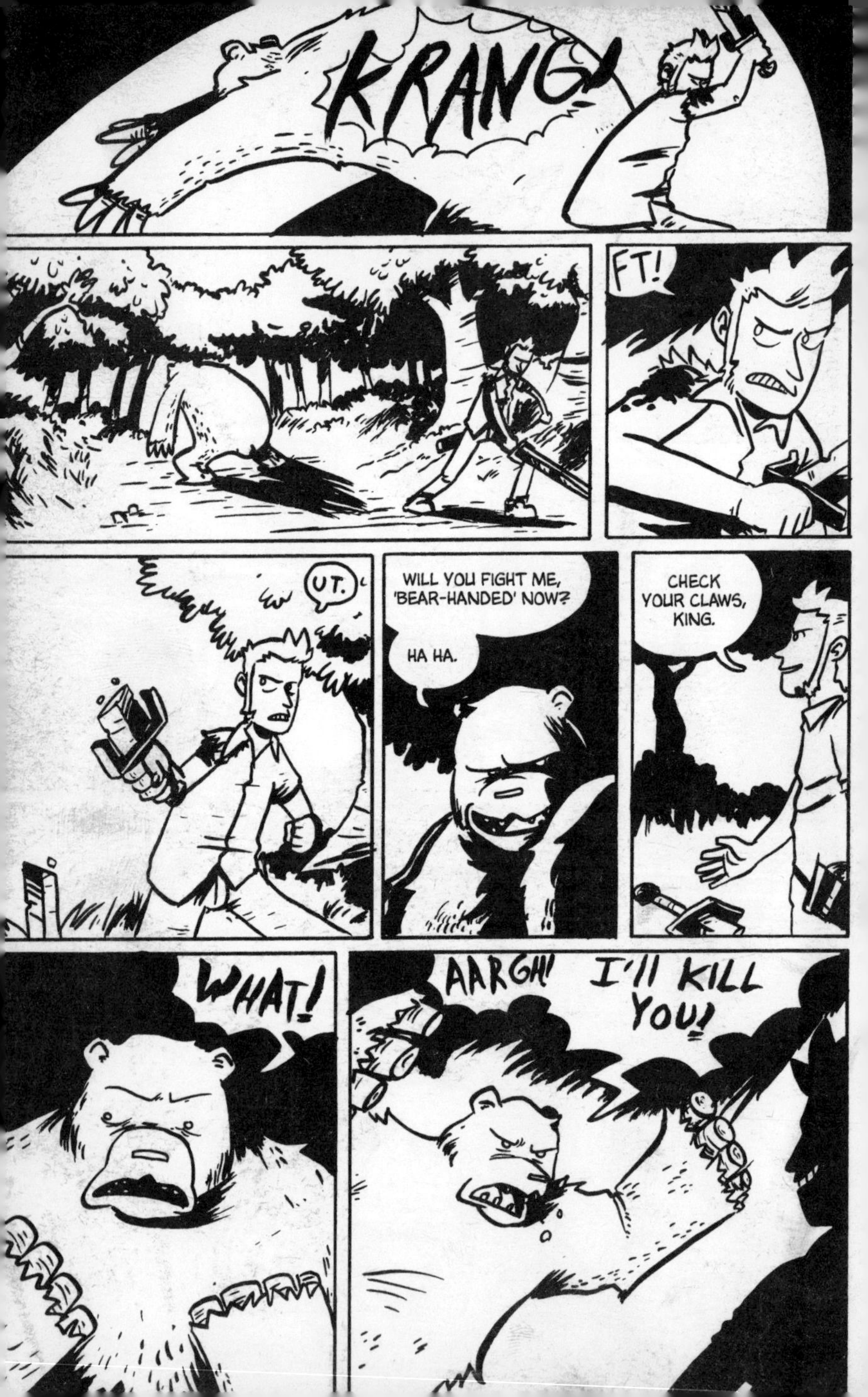
KRANG!
FT!
UT.
WILL YOU FIGHT ME, 'BEAR-HANDED' NOW?
HA HA.
CHECK YOUR CLAWS, KING.
WHAT!
AARGH!
I'll KILL YOU!

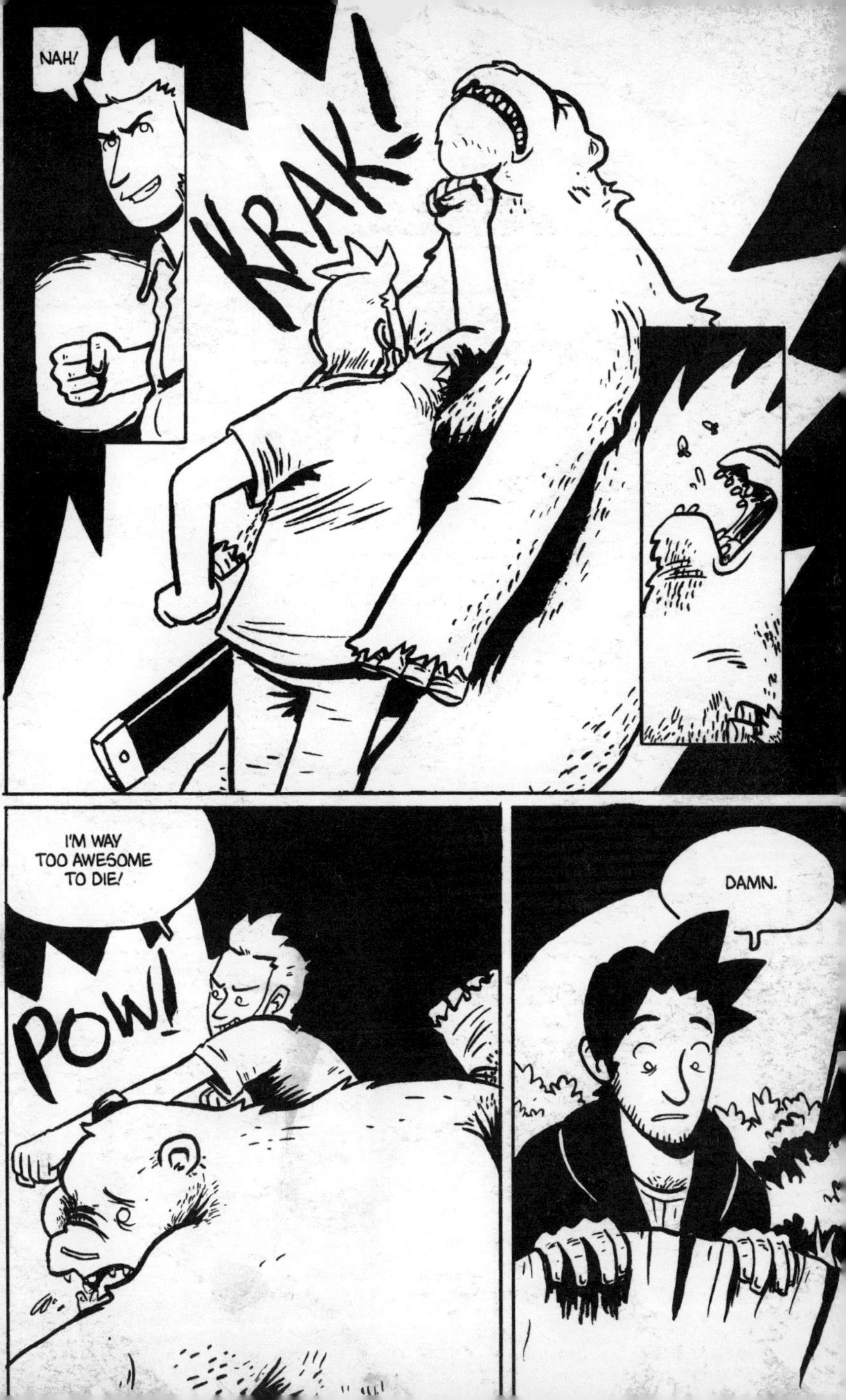
NAH!
KRAK!
I'M WAY TOO AWESOME TO DIE!
POW!
DAMN.

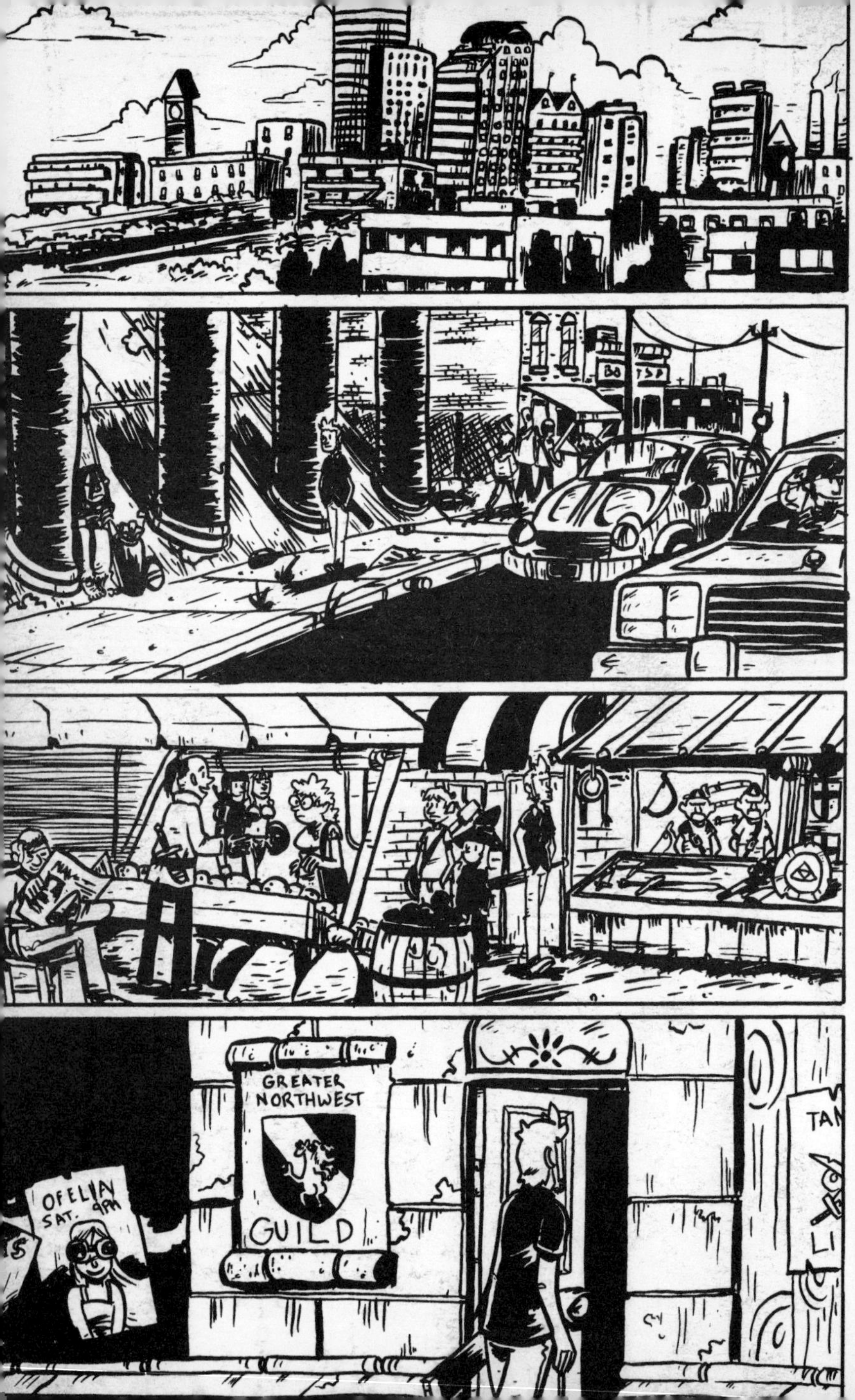
GREATER
NORTHWEST
GUILD
OFELIA
SAT. 9PM

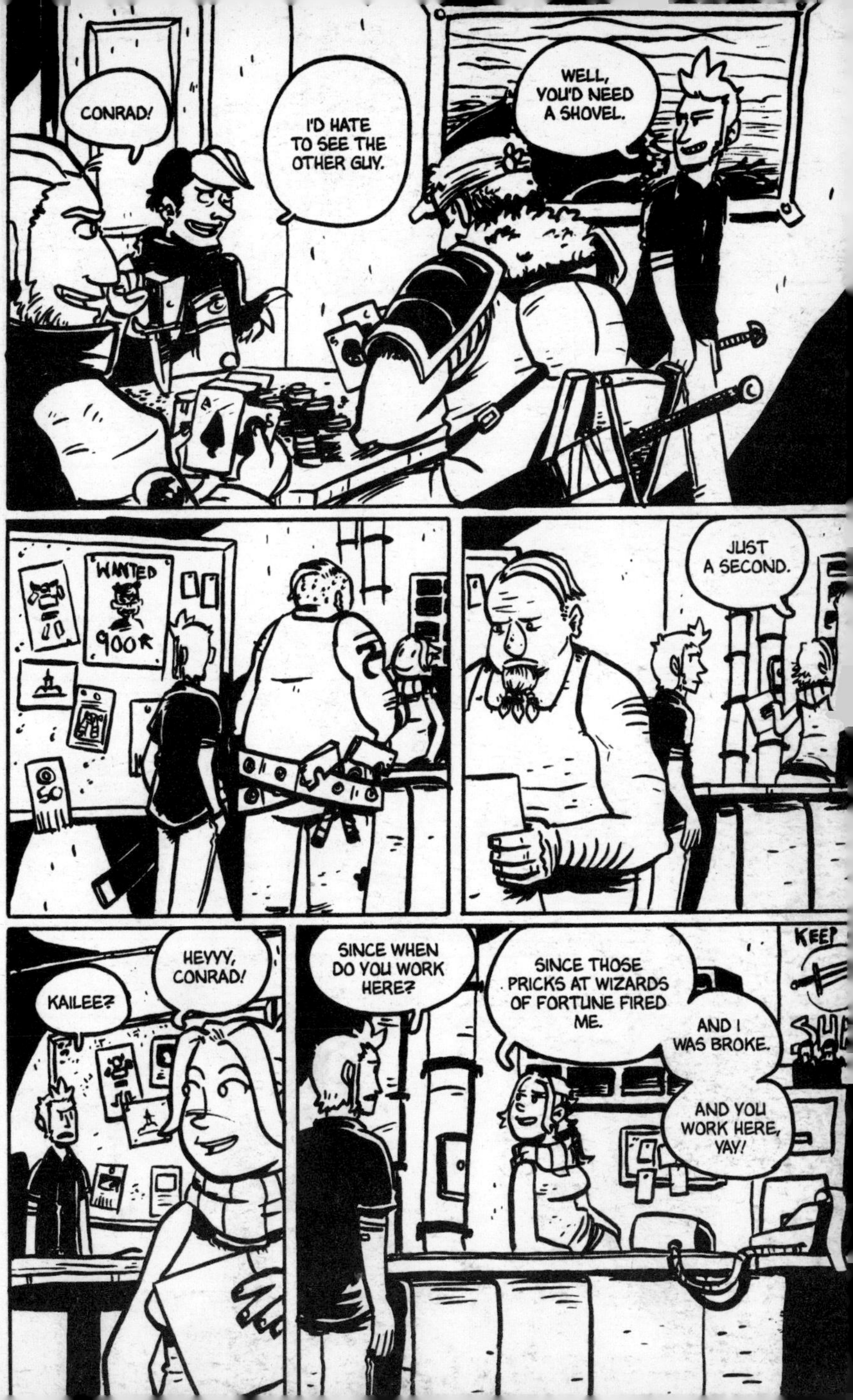
CONRAD!
I'D HATE TO SEE THE OTHER GUY.
WELL, YOU'D NEED A SHOVEL.
WANTED
900
50
JUST A SECOND.
KAILEE?
HEYYY, CONRAD!
SINCE WHEN DO YOU WORK HERE?
SINCE THOSE PRICKS AT WIZARDS OF FORTUNE FIRED ME.
AND I WAS BROKE.
AND YOU WORK HERE, YAY!
KEEP

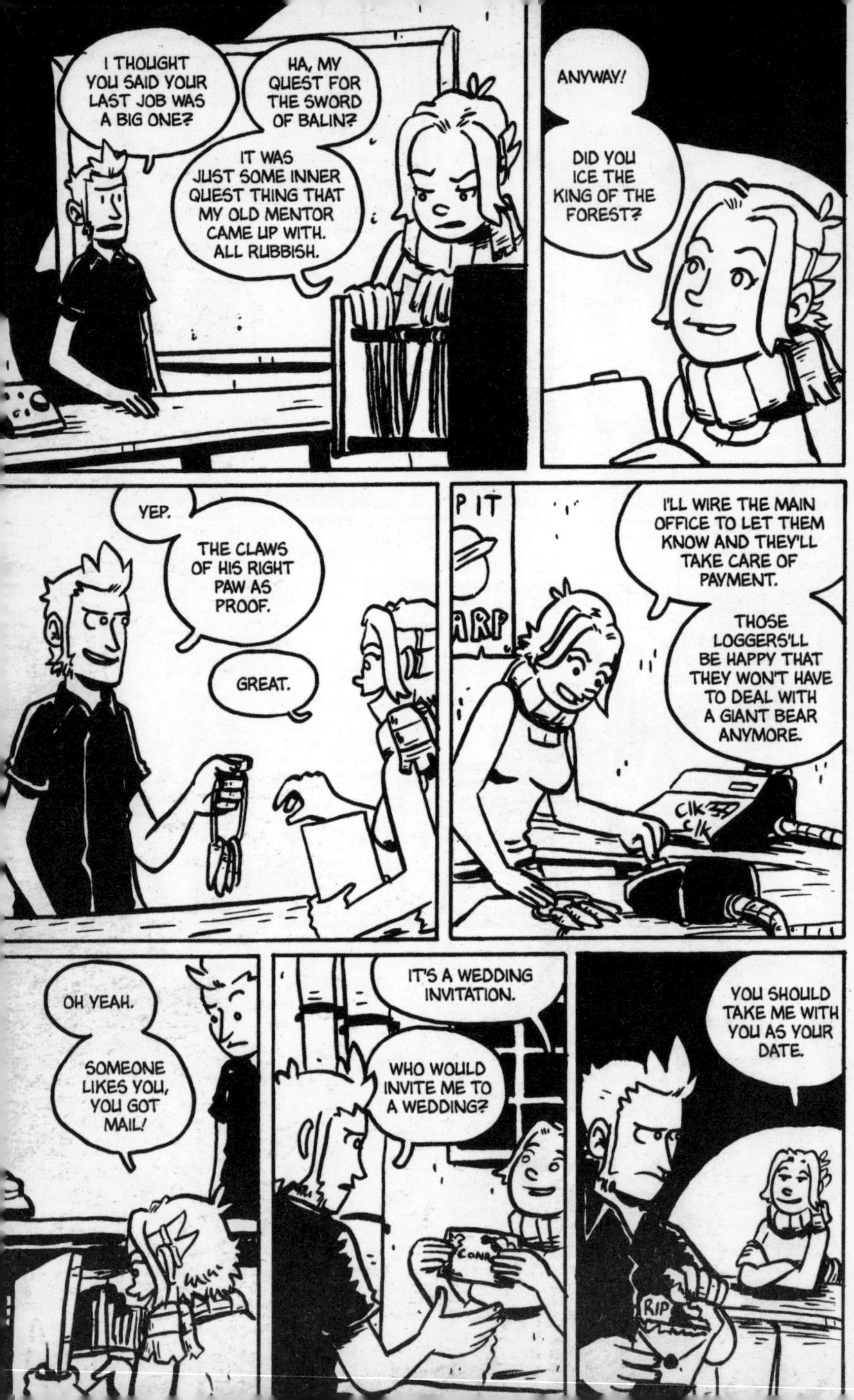
I THOUGHT YOU SAID YOUR LAST JOB WAS A BIG ONE?
HA, MY QUEST FOR THE SWORD OF BALIN?
IT WAS JUST SOME INNER QUEST THING THAT MY OLD MENTOR CAME UP WITH. ALL RUBBISH.
ANYWAY!
DID YOU ICE THE KING OF THE FOREST?
YEP.
THE CLAWS OF HIS RIGHT PAW AS PROOF.
GREAT.
P IT
ARP
I'LL WIRE THE MAIN OFFICE TO LET THEM KNOW AND THEY'LL TAKE CARE OF PAYMENT.
THOSE LOGGERS'LL BE HAPPY THAT THEY WON'T HAVE TO DEAL WITH A GIANT BEAR ANYMORE.
CLK CLK
OH YEAH.
SOMEONE LIKES YOU, YOU GOT MAIL!
IT'S A WEDDING INVITATION.
WHO WOULD INVITE ME TO A WEDDING?
YOU SHOULD TAKE ME WITH YOU AS YOUR DATE.
RIP

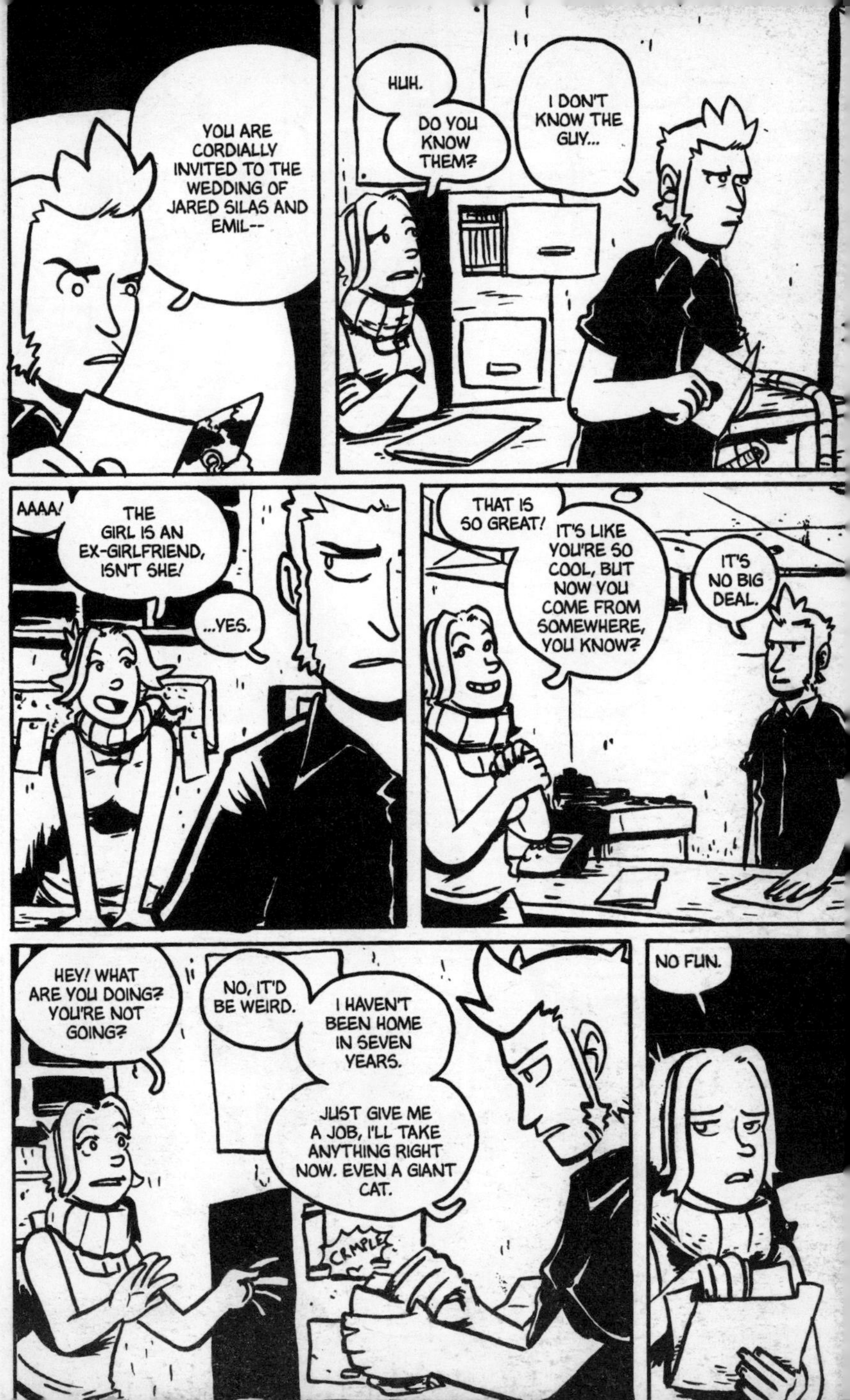
YOU ARE CORDIALLY INVITED TO THE WEDDING OF JARED SILAS AND EMIL--
HUH.
DO YOU KNOW THEM?
I DON'T KNOW THE GUY...
AAAA!
THE GIRL IS AN EX-GIRLFRIEND, ISN'T SHE!
...YES.
THAT IS SO GREAT!
IT'S LIKE YOU'RE SO COOL, BUT NOW YOU COME FROM SOMEWHERE, YOU KNOW?
IT'S NO BIG DEAL.
HEY! WHAT ARE YOU DOING? YOU'RE NOT GOING?
NO, IT'D BE WEIRD.
I HAVEN'T BEEN HOME IN SEVEN YEARS.
JUST GIVE ME A JOB, I'LL TAKE ANYTHING RIGHT NOW. EVEN A GIANT CAT.
CRMPLE
NO FUN.

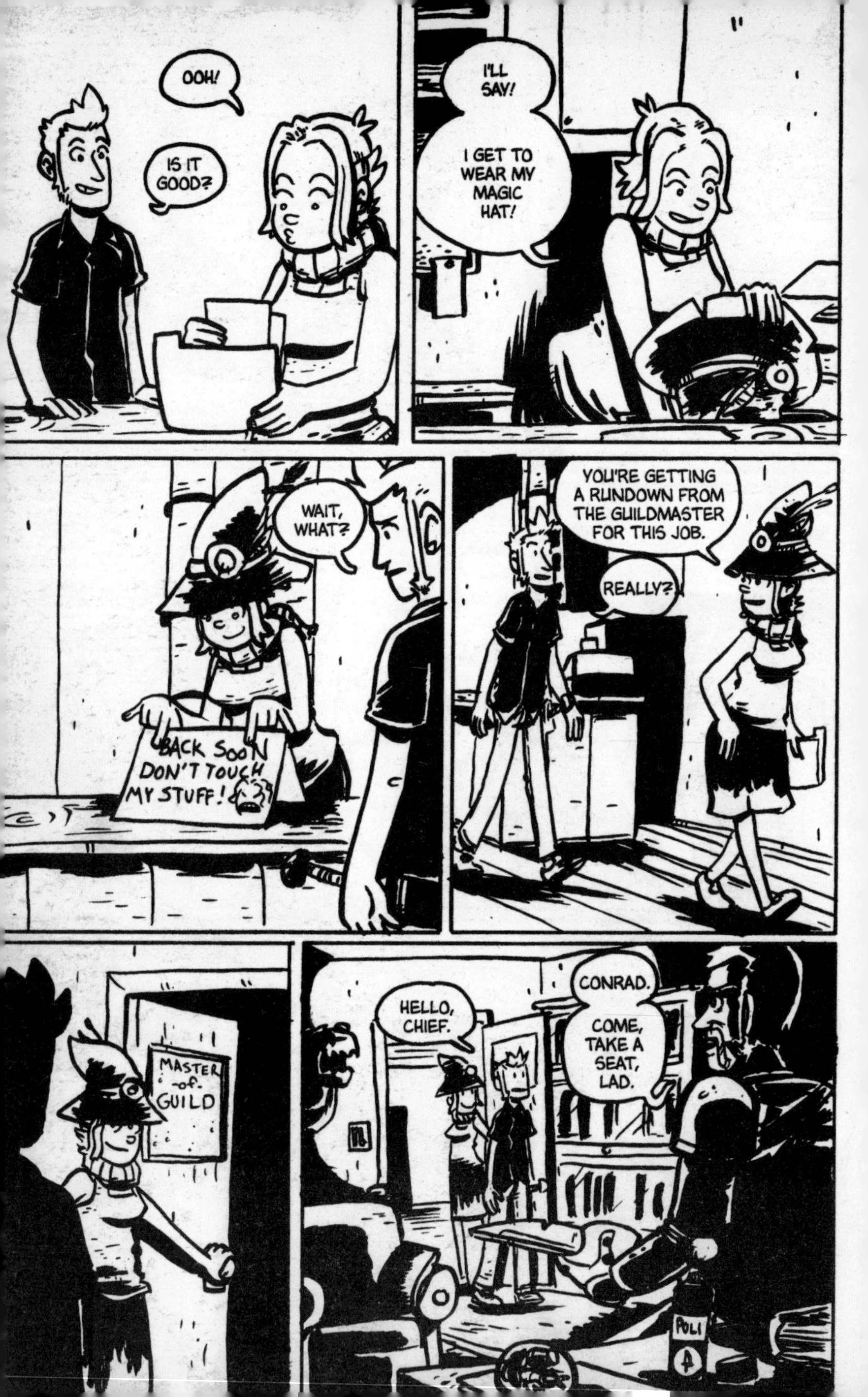
OOH!
IS IT GOOD?
I'LL SAY!
I GET TO WEAR MY MAGIC HAT!
WAIT, WHAT?
BACK SOON DON'T TOUCH MY STUFF!
YOU'RE GETTING A RUNDOWN FROM THE GUILDMASTER FOR THIS JOB.
REALLY?
MASTER -of- GUILD
HELLO, CHIEF.
CONRAD.
COME, TAKE A SEAT, LAD.
POLI

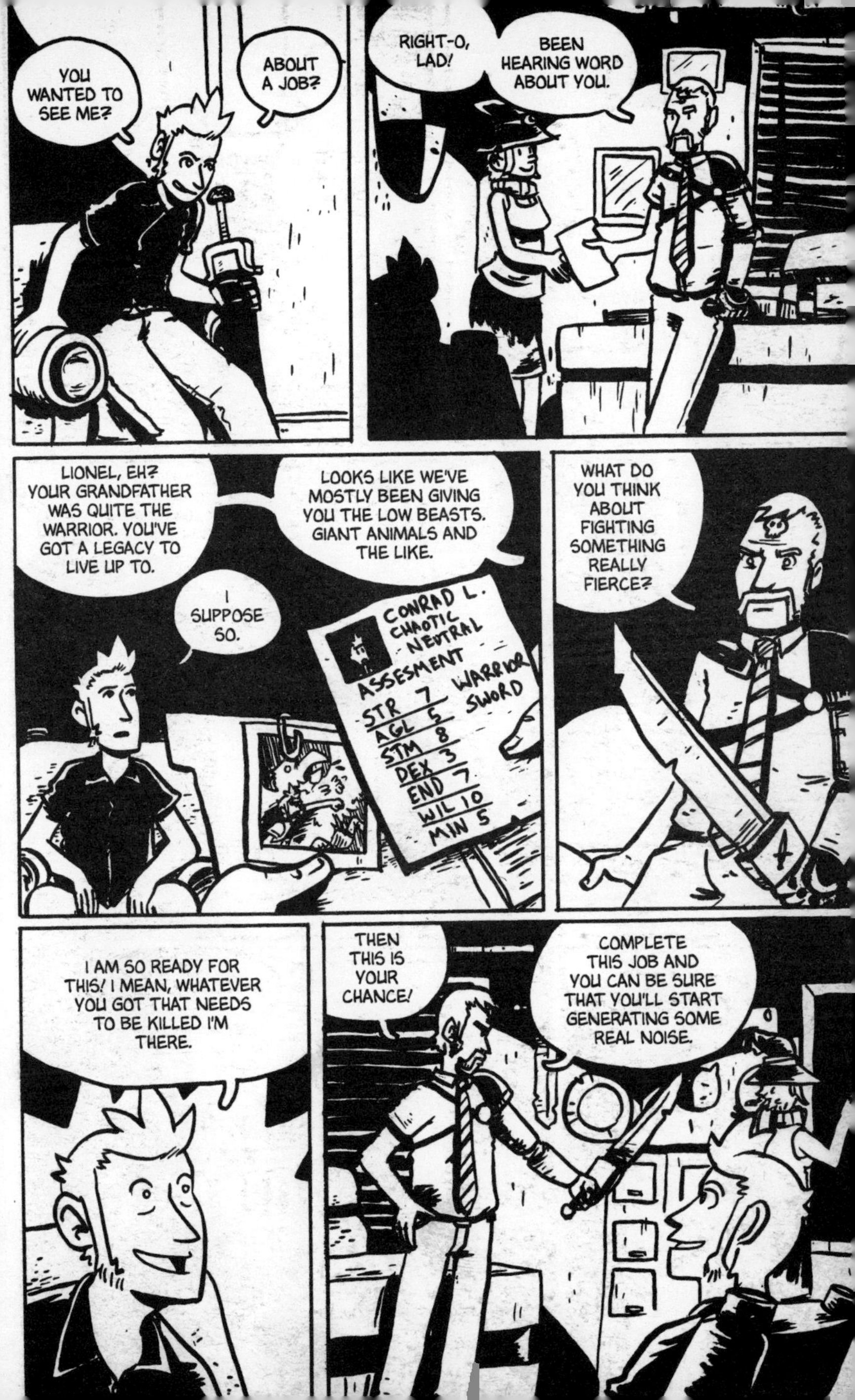
YOU WANTED TO SEE ME?
ABOUT A JOB?
RIGHT-O, LAD!
BEEN HEARING WORD ABOUT YOU.
LIONEL, EH? YOUR GRANDFATHER WAS QUITE THE WARRIOR. YOU'VE GOT A LEGACY TO LIVE UP TO.
LOOKS LIKE WE'VE MOSTLY BEEN GIVING YOU THE LOW BEASTS. GIANT ANIMALS AND THE LIKE.
I SUPPOSE SO.
CONRAD L.
CHAOTIC NEUTRAL
ASSESMENT
STR 7
AGL 5
STM 8
DEX 3
END 7
WIL 10
MIN 5
WARRIOR
SWORD
WHAT DO YOU THINK ABOUT FIGHTING SOMETHING REALLY FIERCE?
I AM SO READY FOR THIS! I MEAN, WHATEVER YOU GOT THAT NEEDS TO BE KILLED I'M THERE.
THEN THIS IS YOUR CHANCE!
COMPLETE THIS JOB AND YOU CAN BE SURE THAT YOU'LL START GENERATING SOME REAL NOISE.

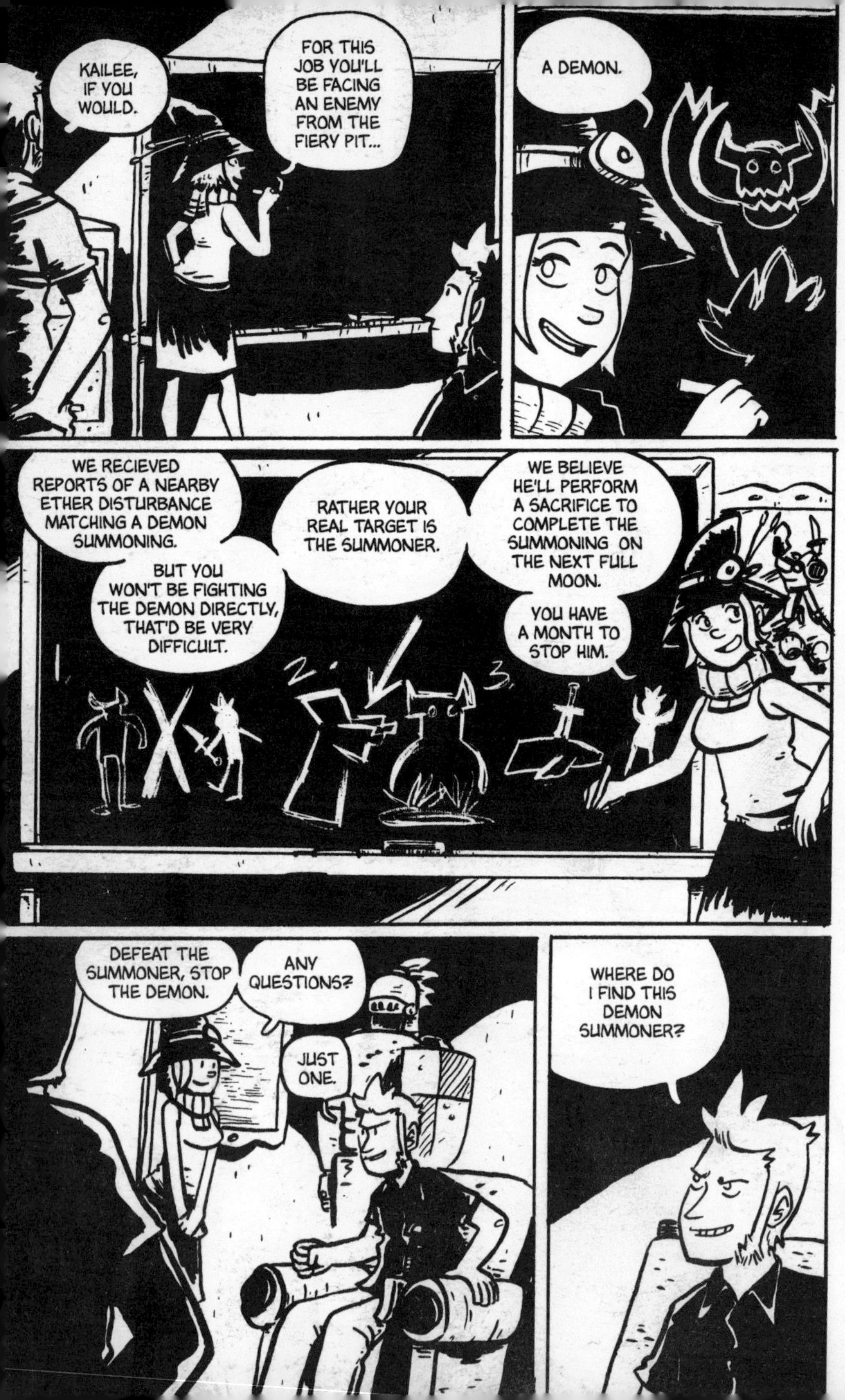
KAILEE, IF YOU WOULD.
FOR THIS JOB YOU'LL BE FACING AN ENEMY FROM THE FIERY PIT...
A DEMON.
WE RECIEVED REPORTS OF A NEARBY ETHER DISTURBANCE MATCHING A DEMON SUMMONING.
BUT YOU WON'T BE FIGHTING THE DEMON DIRECTLY, THAT'D BE VERY DIFFICULT.
RATHER YOUR REAL TARGET IS THE SUMMONER.
WE BELIEVE HE'LL PERFORM A SACRIFICE TO COMPLETE THE SUMMONING ON THE NEXT FULL MOON.
YOU HAVE A MONTH TO STOP HIM.
1.
2.
3.
DEFEAT THE SUMMONER, STOP THE DEMON.
ANY QUESTIONS?
JUST ONE.
WHERE DO I FIND THIS DEMON SUMMONER?

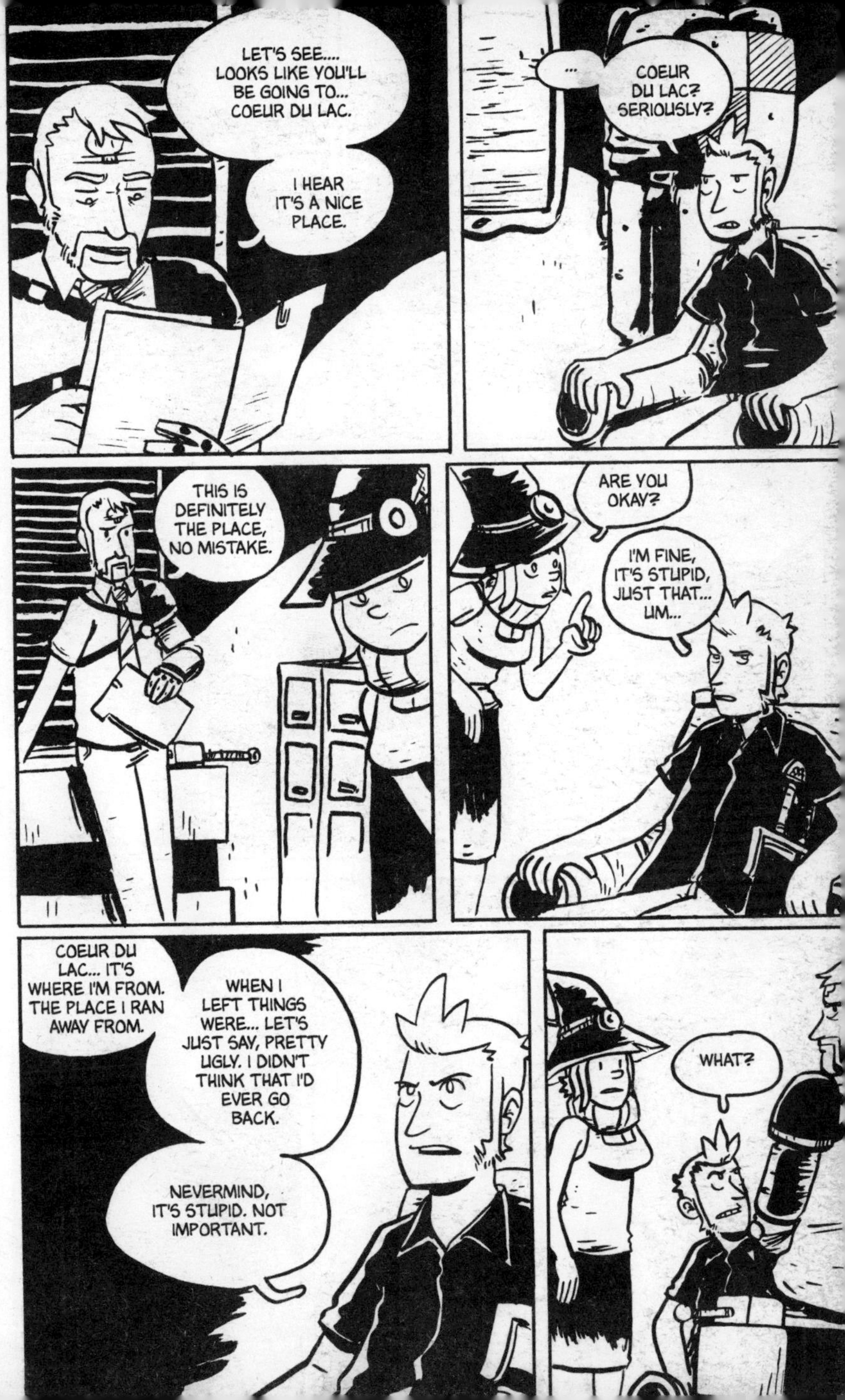
LET'S SEE.... LOOKS LIKE YOU'LL BE GOING TO... COEUR DU LAC.
I HEAR IT'S A NICE PLACE.
...
COEUR DU LAC? SERIOUSLY?
THIS IS DEFINITELY THE PLACE, NO MISTAKE.
ARE YOU OKAY?
I'M FINE, IT'S STUPID, JUST THAT... UM...
COEUR DU LAC... IT'S WHERE I'M FROM. THE PLACE I RAN AWAY FROM.
WHEN I LEFT THINGS WERE... LET'S JUST SAY, PRETTY UGLY. I DIDN'T THINK THAT I'D EVER GO BACK.
NEVERMIND, IT'S STUPID. NOT IMPORTANT.
WHAT?

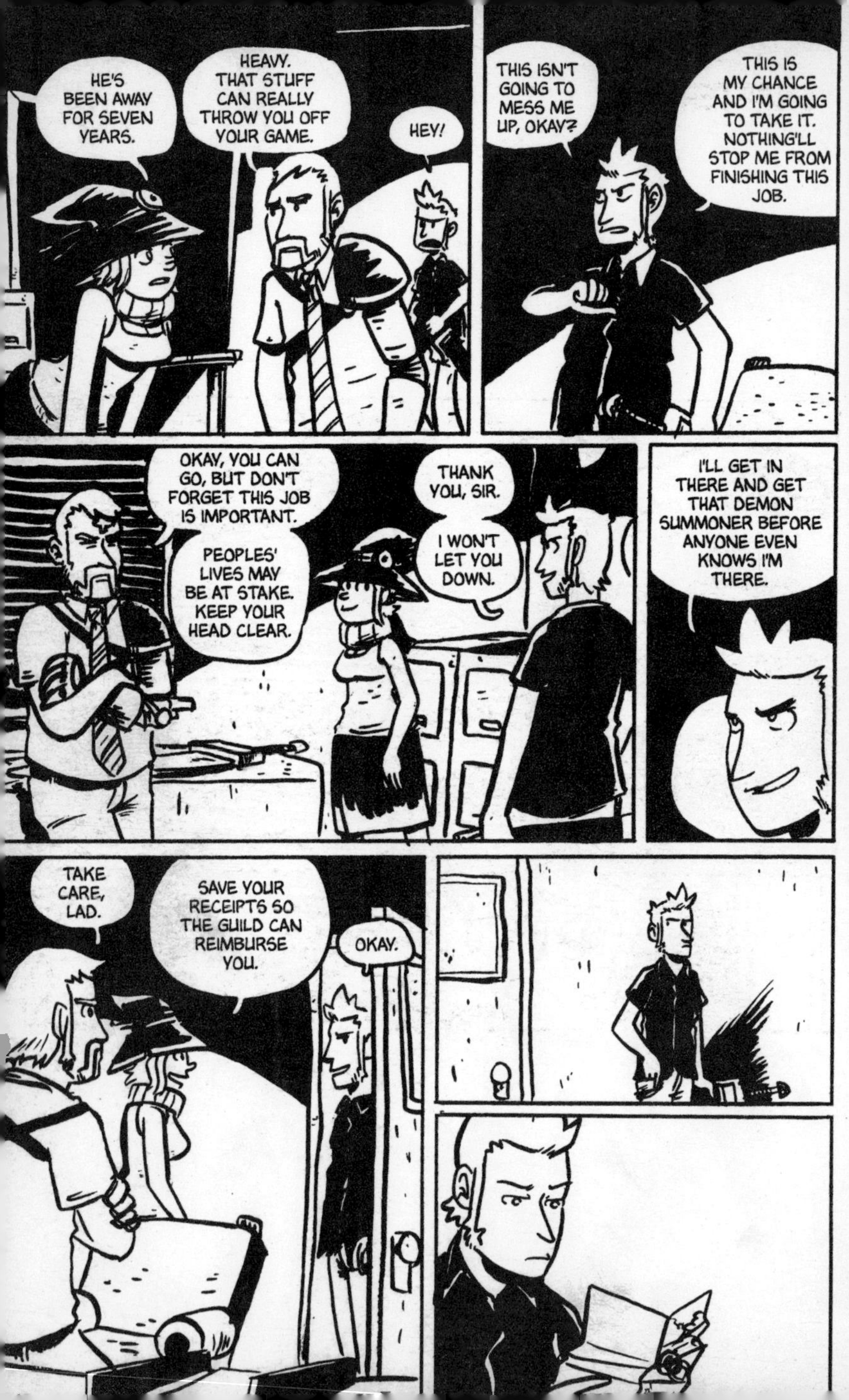
HE'S BEEN AWAY FOR SEVEN YEARS.
HEAVY. THAT STUFF CAN REALLY THROW YOU OFF YOUR GAME.
HEY!
THIS ISN'T GOING TO MESS ME UP, OKAY?
THIS IS MY CHANCE AND I'M GOING TO TAKE IT. NOTHING'LL STOP ME FROM FINISHING THIS JOB.
OKAY, YOU CAN GO, BUT DON'T FORGET THIS JOB IS IMPORTANT.
PEOPLES' LIVES MAY BE AT STAKE. KEEP YOUR HEAD CLEAR.
THANK YOU, SIR.
I WON'T LET YOU DOWN.
I'LL GET IN THERE AND GET THAT DEMON SUMMONER BEFORE ANYONE EVEN KNOWS I'M THERE.
TAKE CARE, LAD.
SAVE YOUR RECEIPTS SO THE GUILD CAN REIMBURSE YOU.
OKAY.

CHAPTER 2

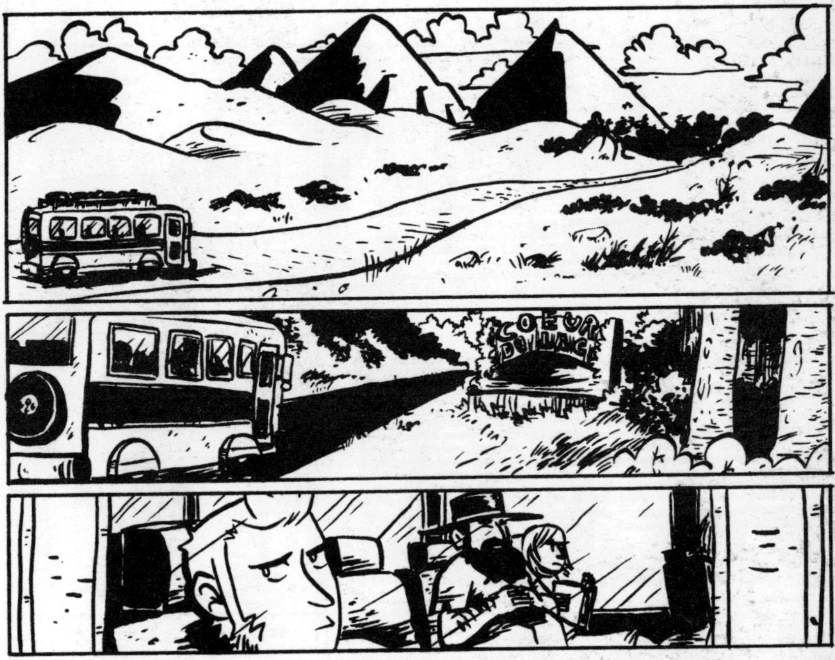
COEUR

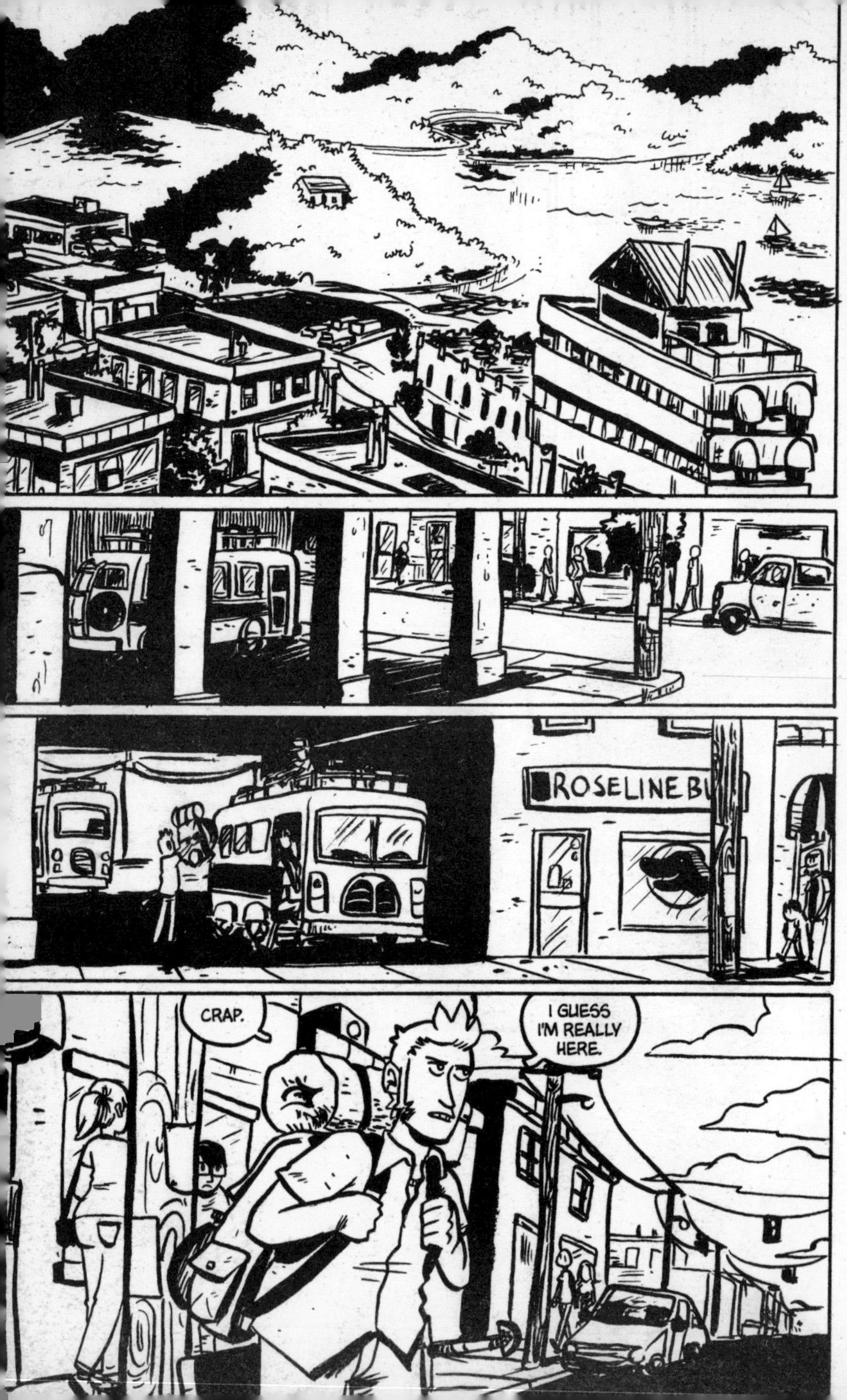
ROSELINE BU
CRAP.
I GUESS I'M REALLY HERE.

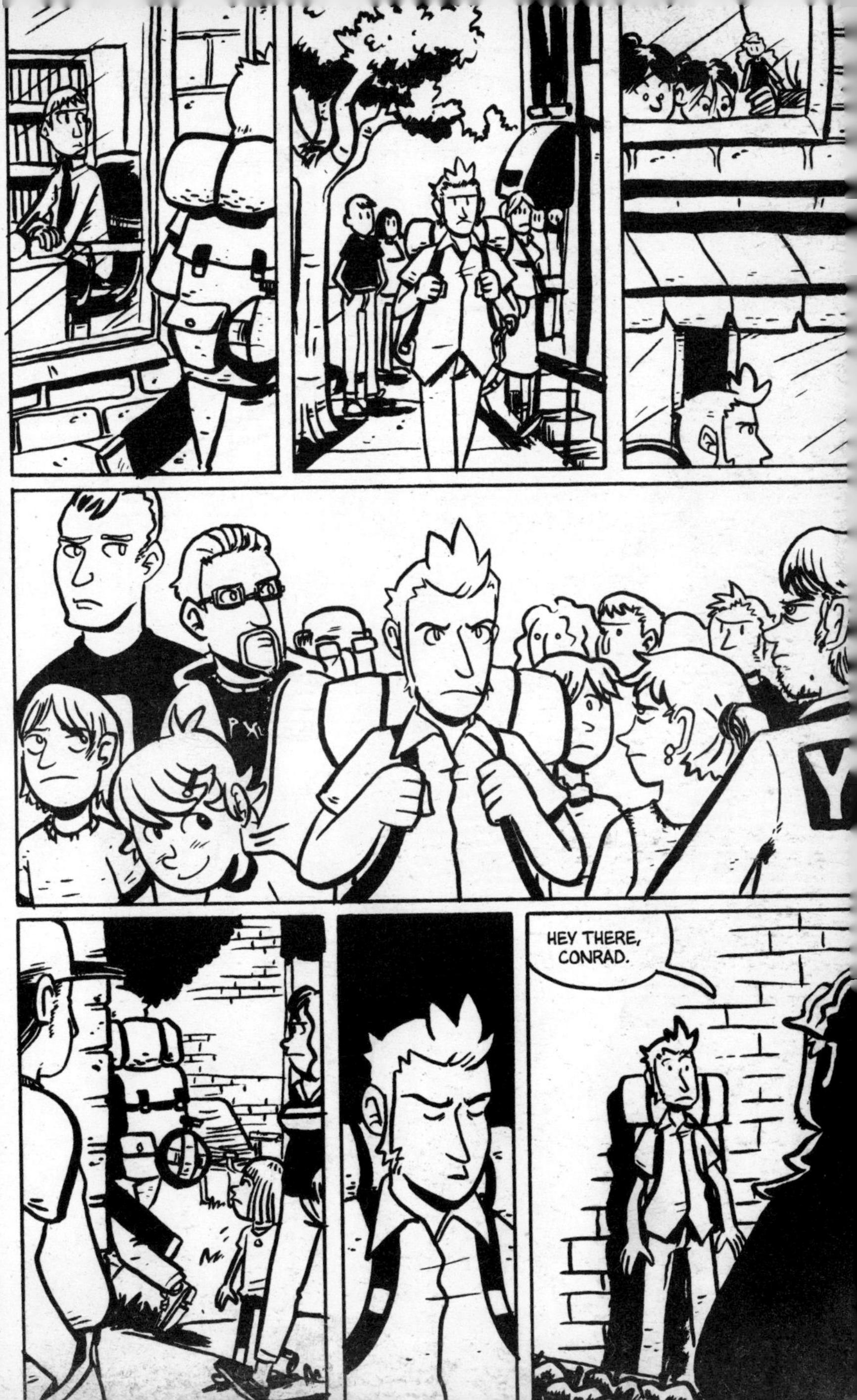
HEY THERE, CONRAD.

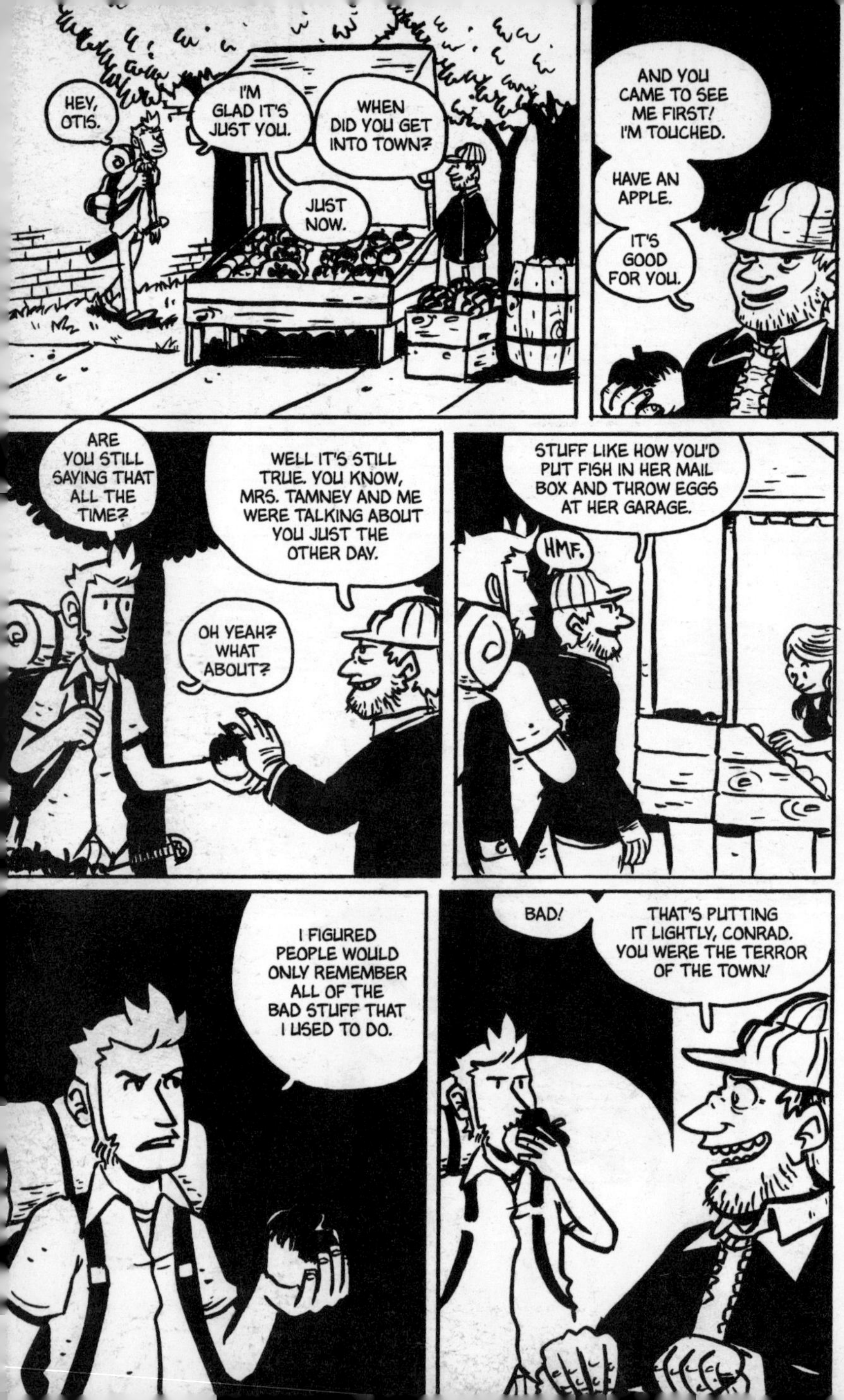
HEY, OTIS.
I'M GLAD IT'S JUST YOU.
WHEN DID YOU GET INTO TOWN?
JUST NOW.
AND YOU CAME TO SEE ME FIRST! I'M TOUCHED.
HAVE AN APPLE.
IT'S GOOD FOR YOU.
ARE YOU STILL SAYING THAT ALL THE TIME?
WELL IT'S STILL TRUE. YOU KNOW, MRS. TAMNEY AND ME WERE TALKING ABOUT YOU JUST THE OTHER DAY.
OH YEAH? WHAT ABOUT?
STUFF LIKE HOW YOU'D PUT FISH IN HER MAIL BOX AND THROW EGGS AT HER GARAGE.
HMF.
I FIGURED PEOPLE WOULD ONLY REMEMBER ALL OF THE BAD STUFF THAT I USED TO DO.
BAD!
THAT'S PUTTING IT LIGHTLY, CONRAD. YOU WERE THE TERROR OF THE TOWN!

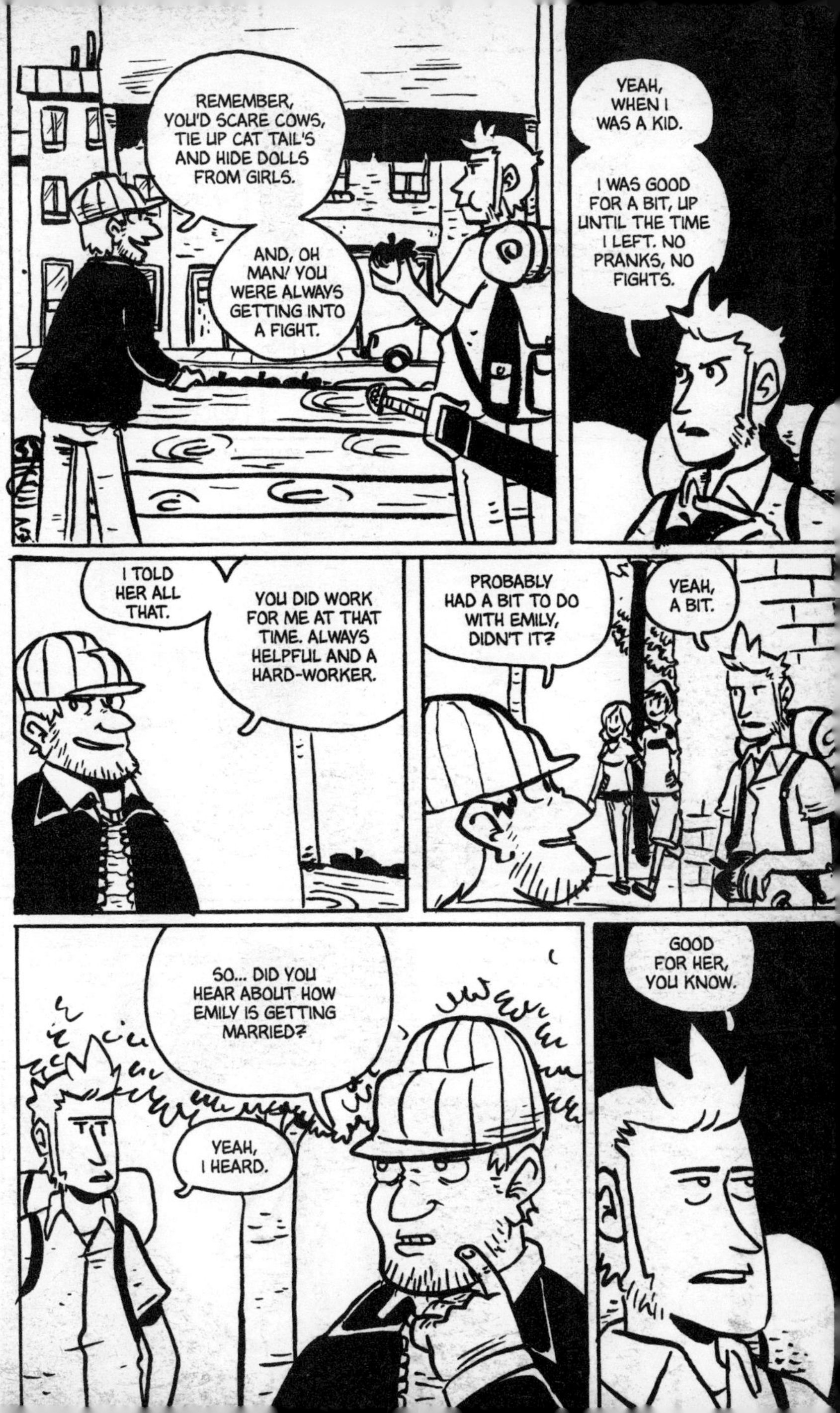
REMEMBER, YOU'D SCARE COWS, TIE UP CAT TAIL'S AND HIDE DOLLS FROM GIRLS.
AND, OH MAN! YOU WERE ALWAYS GETTING INTO A FIGHT.
YEAH, WHEN I WAS A KID.
I WAS GOOD FOR A BIT, UP UNTIL THE TIME I LEFT. NO PRANKS, NO FIGHTS.
I TOLD HER ALL THAT.
YOU DID WORK FOR ME AT THAT TIME. ALWAYS HELPFUL AND A HARD-WORKER.
PROBABLY HAD A BIT TO DO WITH EMILY, DIDN'T IT?
YEAH, A BIT.
SO... DID YOU HEAR ABOUT HOW EMILY IS GETTING MARRIED?
YEAH, I HEARD.
GOOD FOR HER, YOU KNOW.

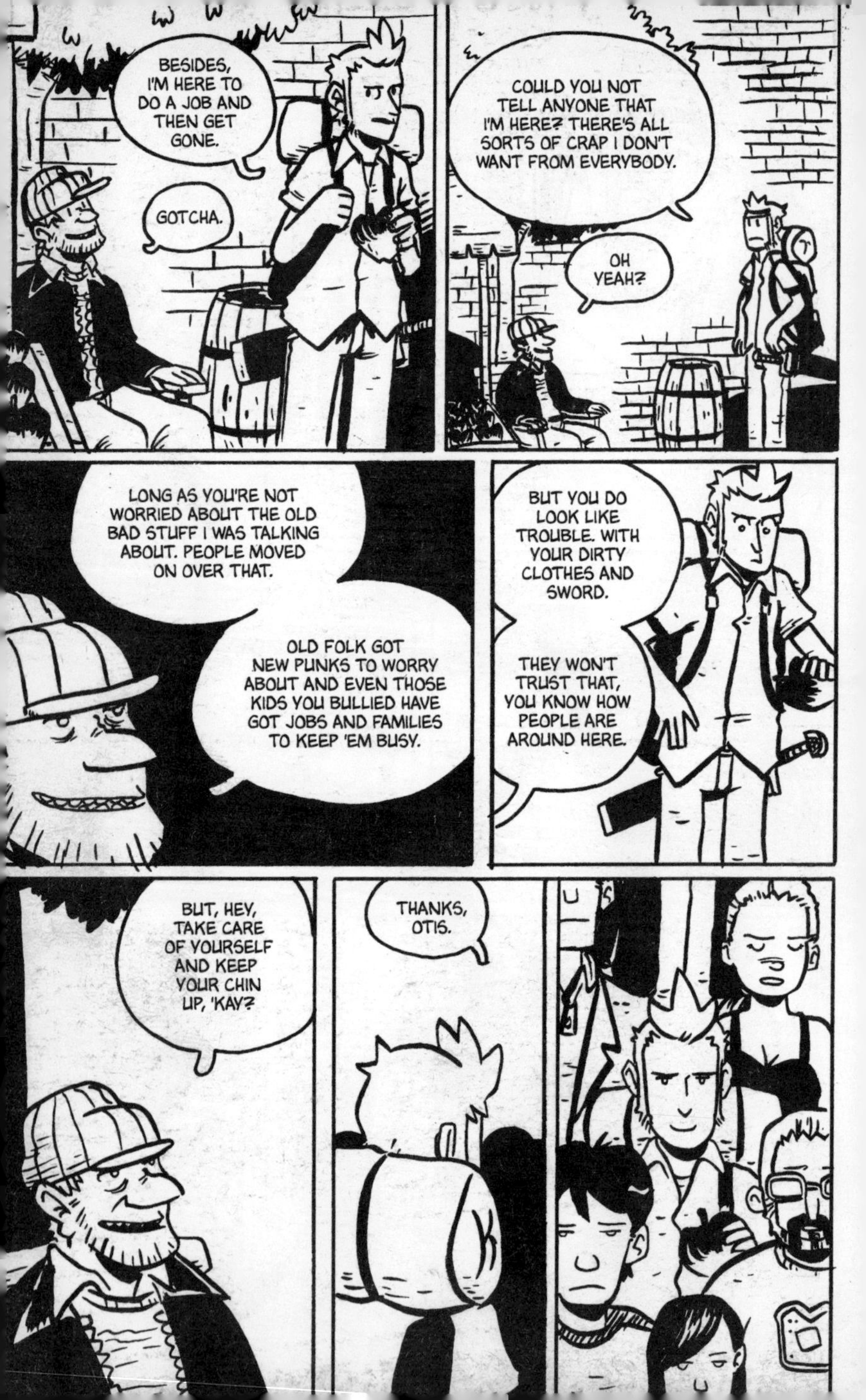
BESIDES, I'M HERE TO DO A JOB AND THEN GET GONE.
GOTCHA.
COULD YOU NOT TELL ANYONE THAT I'M HERE? THERE'S ALL SORTS OF CRAP I DON'T WANT FROM EVERYBODY.
OH YEAH?
LONG AS YOU'RE NOT WORRIED ABOUT THE OLD BAD STUFF I WAS TALKING ABOUT. PEOPLE MOVED ON OVER THAT.
OLD FOLK GOT NEW PUNKS TO WORRY ABOUT AND EVEN THOSE KIDS YOU BULLIED HAVE GOT JOBS AND FAMILIES TO KEEP 'EM BUSY.
BUT YOU DO LOOK LIKE TROUBLE. WITH YOUR DIRTY CLOTHES AND SWORD.
THEY WON'T TRUST THAT, YOU KNOW HOW PEOPLE ARE AROUND HERE.
BUT, HEY, TAKE CARE OF YOURSELF AND KEEP YOUR CHIN UP, 'KAY?
THANKS, OTIS.

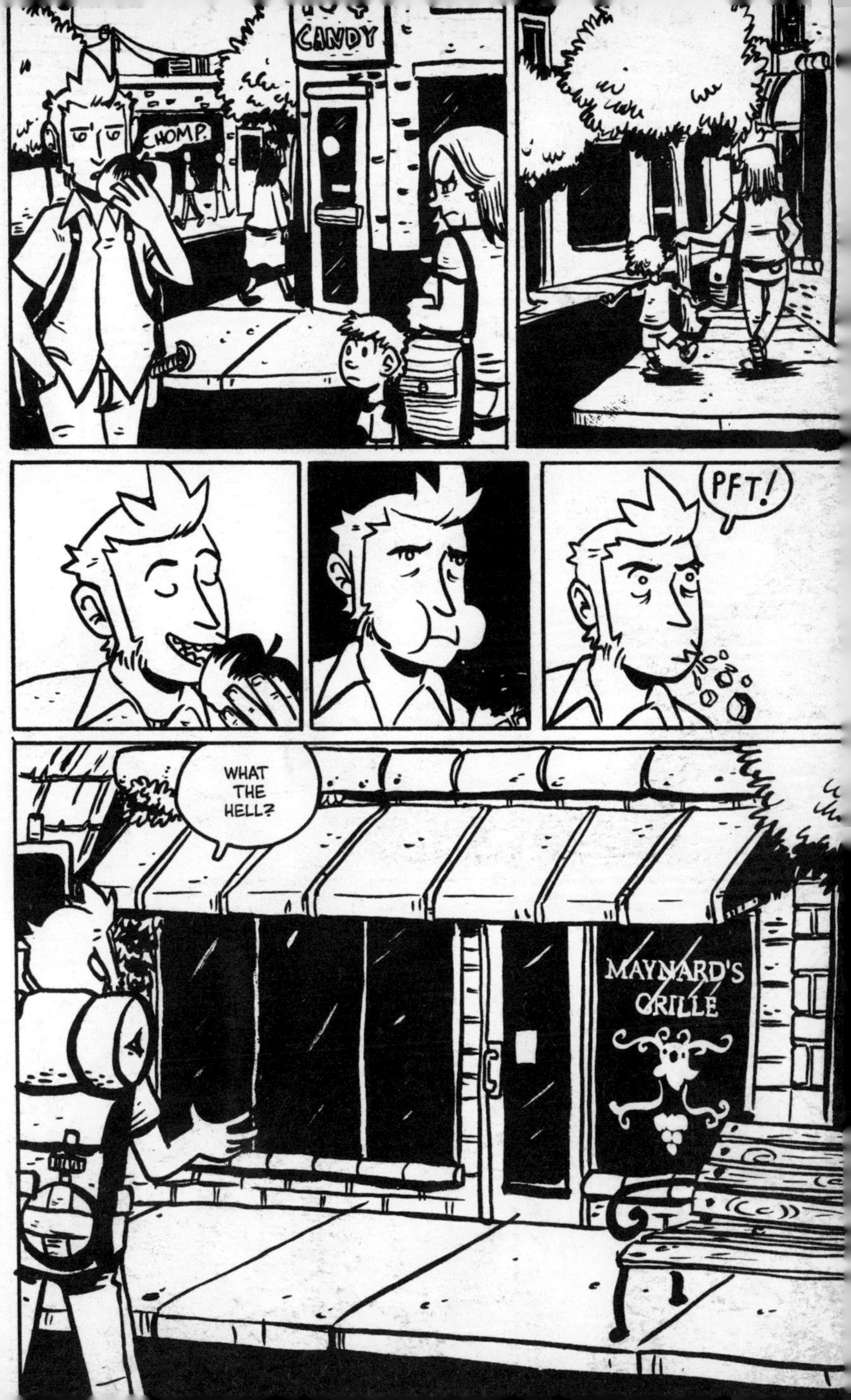

CANDY
CHOMP.
PFT!
WHAT THE HELL?
MAYNARD'S GRILLE

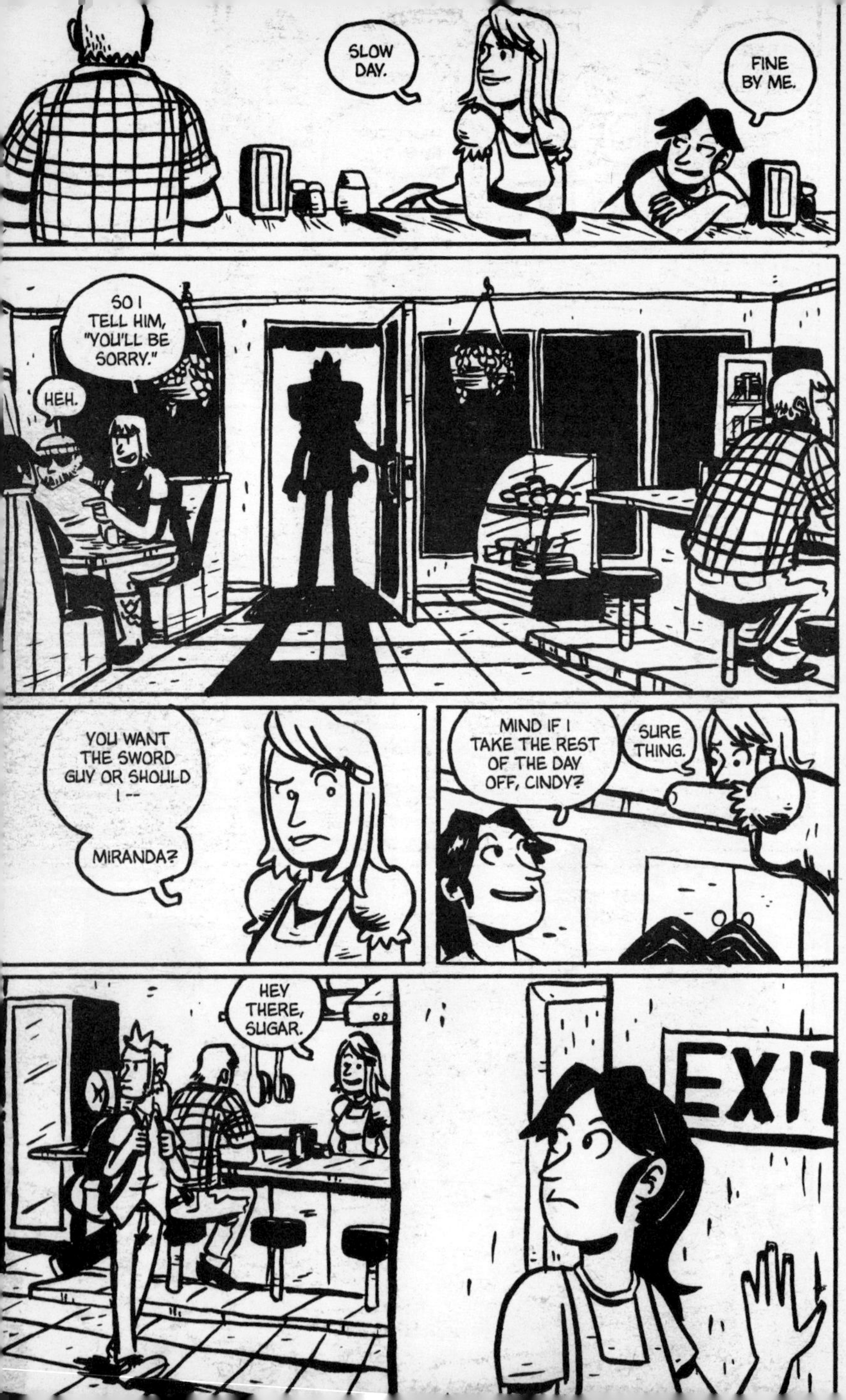
SLOW DAY.
FINE BY ME.
SO I TELL HIM, "YOU'LL BE SORRY."
HEH.
YOU WANT THE SWORD GUY OR SHOULD I --
MIRANDA?
MIND IF I TAKE THE REST OF THE DAY OFF, CINDY?
SURE THING.
HEY THERE, SUGAR.
EXIT

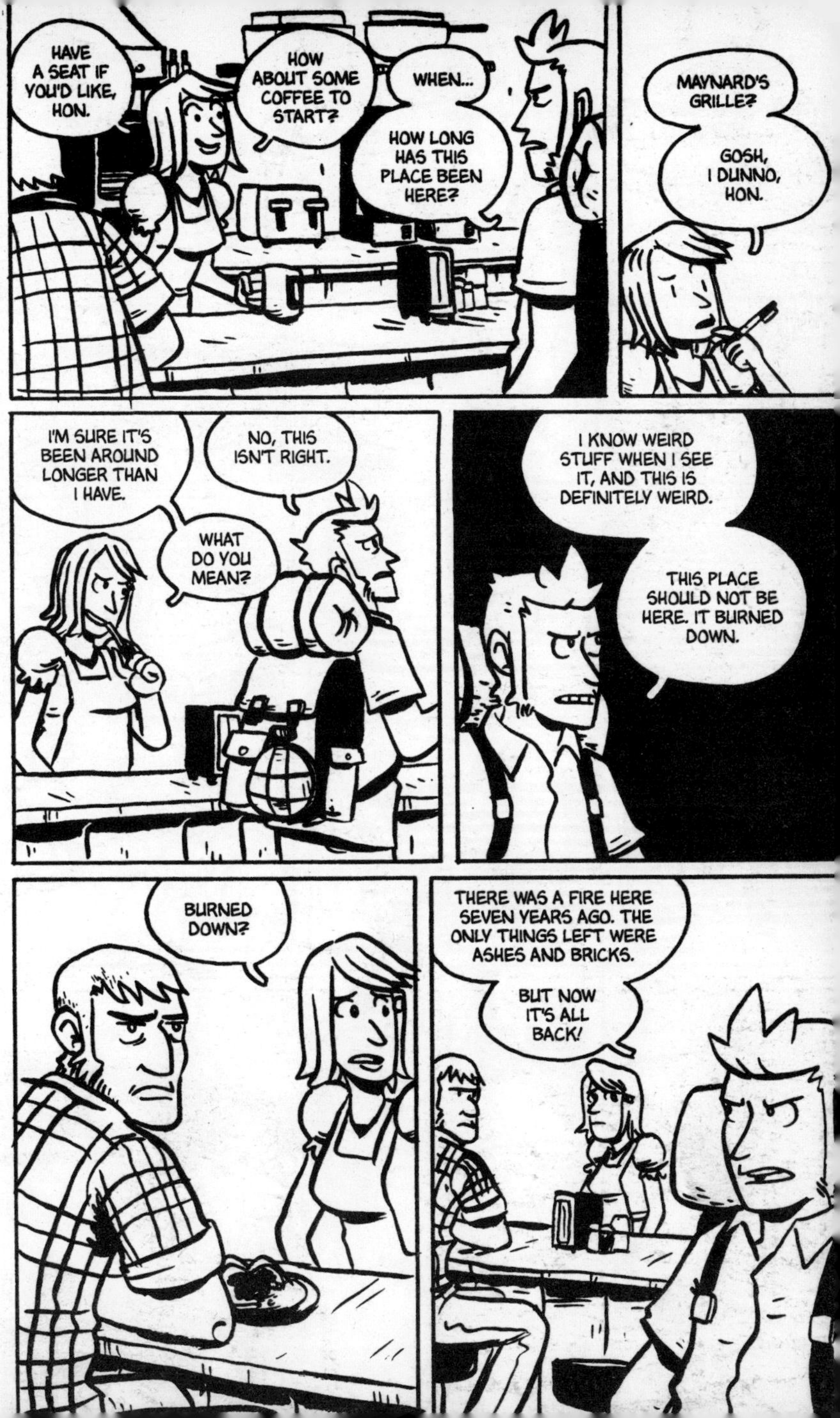
HAVE A SEAT IF YOU'D LIKE, HON.
HOW ABOUT SOME COFFEE TO START?
WHEN...
HOW LONG HAS THIS PLACE BEEN HERE?
MAYNARD'S GRILLE?
GOSH, I DUNNO, HON.
I'M SURE IT'S BEEN AROUND LONGER THAN I HAVE.
NO, THIS ISN'T RIGHT.
WHAT DO YOU MEAN?
I KNOW WEIRD STUFF WHEN I SEE IT, AND THIS IS DEFINITELY WEIRD.
THIS PLACE SHOULD NOT BE HERE. IT BURNED DOWN.
BURNED DOWN?
THERE WAS A FIRE HERE SEVEN YEARS AGO. THE ONLY THINGS LEFT WERE ASHES AND BRICKS.
BUT NOW IT'S ALL BACK!

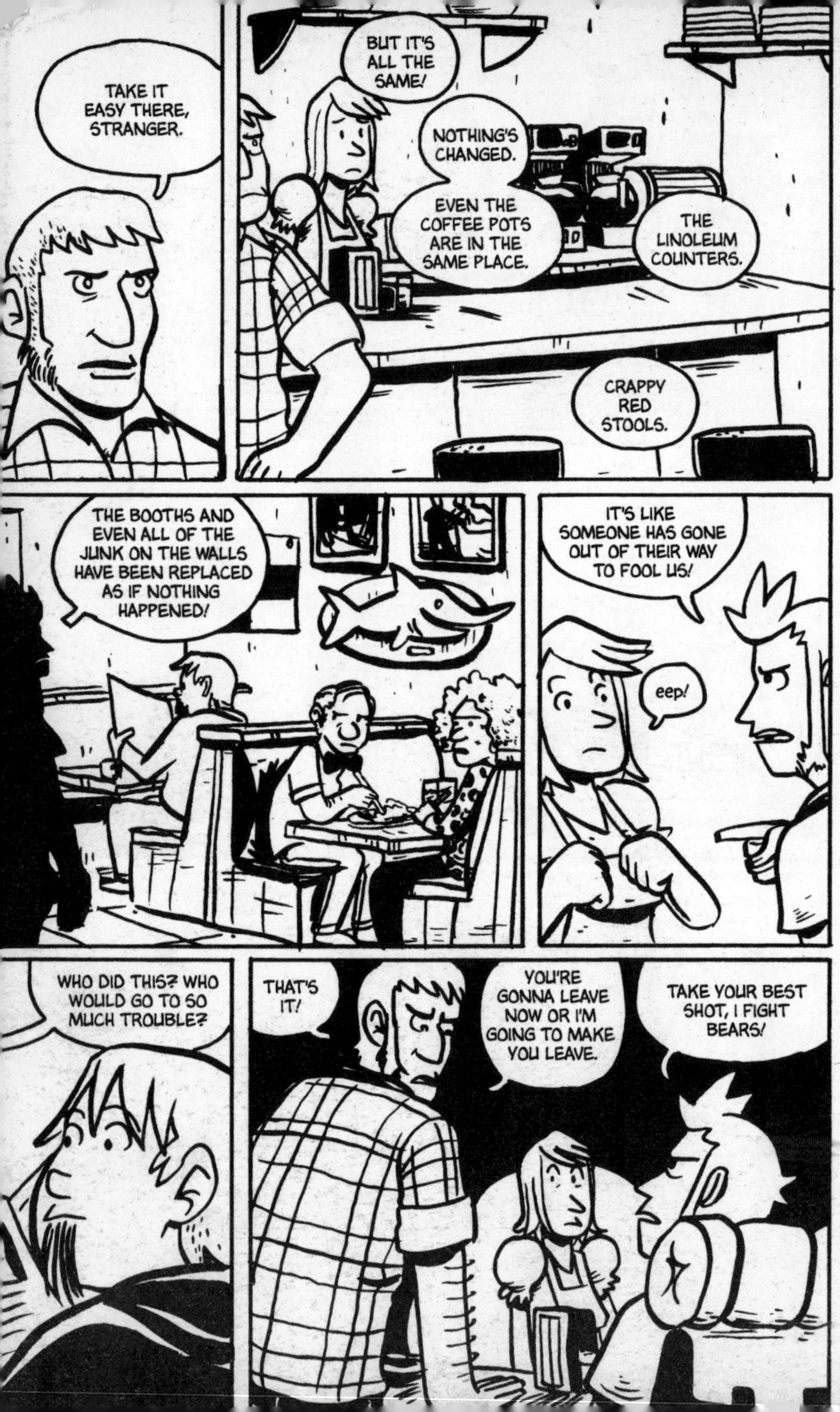
TAKE IT EASY THERE, STRANGER.
BUT IT'S ALL THE SAME!
NOTHING'S CHANGED.
EVEN THE COFFEE POTS ARE IN THE SAME PLACE.
THE LINOLEUM COUNTERS.
CRAPPY RED STOOLS.
THE BOOTHS AND EVEN ALL OF THE JUNK ON THE WALLS HAVE BEEN REPLACED AS IF NOTHING HAPPENED!
IT'S LIKE SOMEONE HAS GONE OUT OF THEIR WAY TO FOOL US!
eep!
WHO DID THIS? WHO WOULD GO TO SO MUCH TROUBLE?
THAT'S IT!
YOU'RE GONNA LEAVE NOW OR I'M GOING TO MAKE YOU LEAVE.
TAKE YOUR BEST SHOT, I FIGHT BEARS!

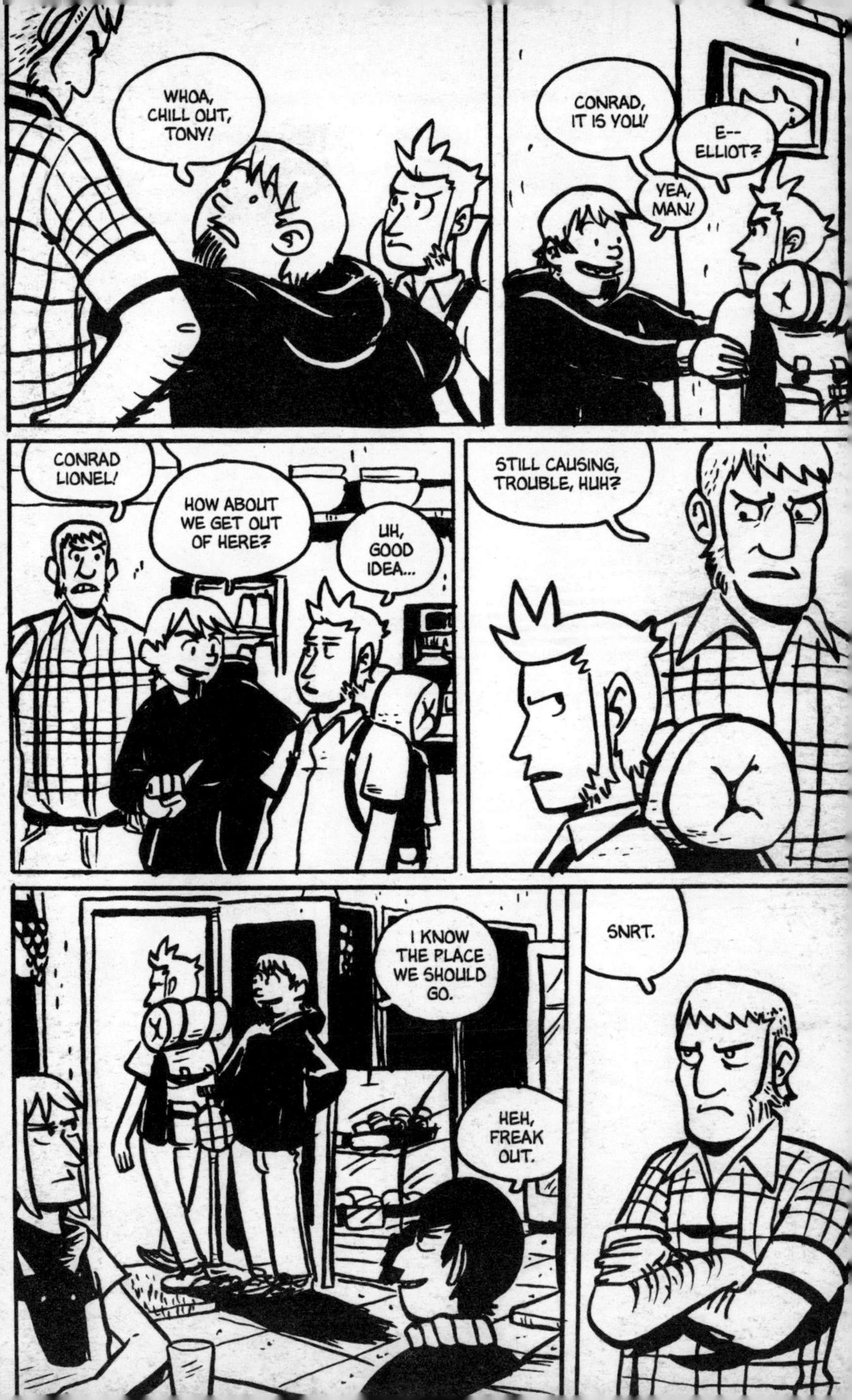
WHOA, CHILL OUT, TONY!
CONRAD, IT IS YOU!
E-- ELLIOT?
YEA, MAN!
CONRAD LIONEL!
HOW ABOUT WE GET OUT OF HERE?
UH, GOOD IDEA...
STILL CAUSING, TROUBLE, HUH?
I KNOW THE PLACE WE SHOULD GO.
HEH, FREAK OUT.
SNRT.

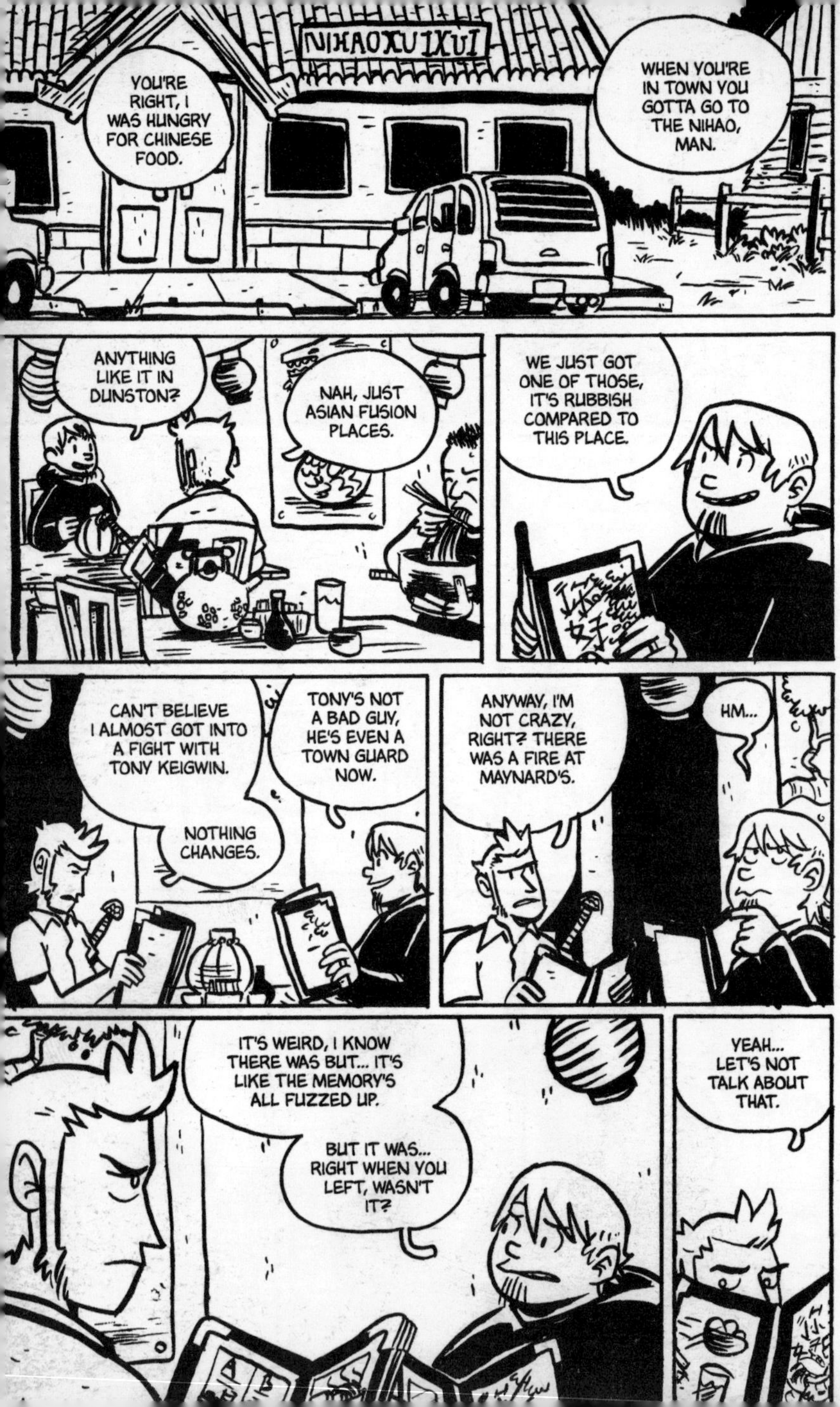
NIHAOXUIXUI
YOU'RE RIGHT, I WAS HUNGRY FOR CHINESE FOOD.
WHEN YOU'RE IN TOWN YOU GOTTA GO TO THE NIHAO, MAN.
ANYTHING LIKE IT IN DUNSTON?
NAH, JUST ASIAN FUSION PLACES.
WE JUST GOT ONE OF THOSE, IT'S RUBBISH COMPARED TO THIS PLACE.
CAN'T BELIEVE I ALMOST GOT INTO A FIGHT WITH TONY KEIGWIN.
NOTHING CHANGES.
TONY'S NOT A BAD GUY, HE'S EVEN A TOWN GUARD NOW.
ANYWAY, I'M NOT CRAZY, RIGHT? THERE WAS A FIRE AT MAYNARD'S.
HM...
IT'S WEIRD, I KNOW THERE WAS BUT... IT'S LIKE THE MEMORY'S ALL FUZZED UP.
BUT IT WAS... RIGHT WHEN YOU LEFT, WASN'T IT?
YEAH... LET'S NOT TALK ABOUT THAT.

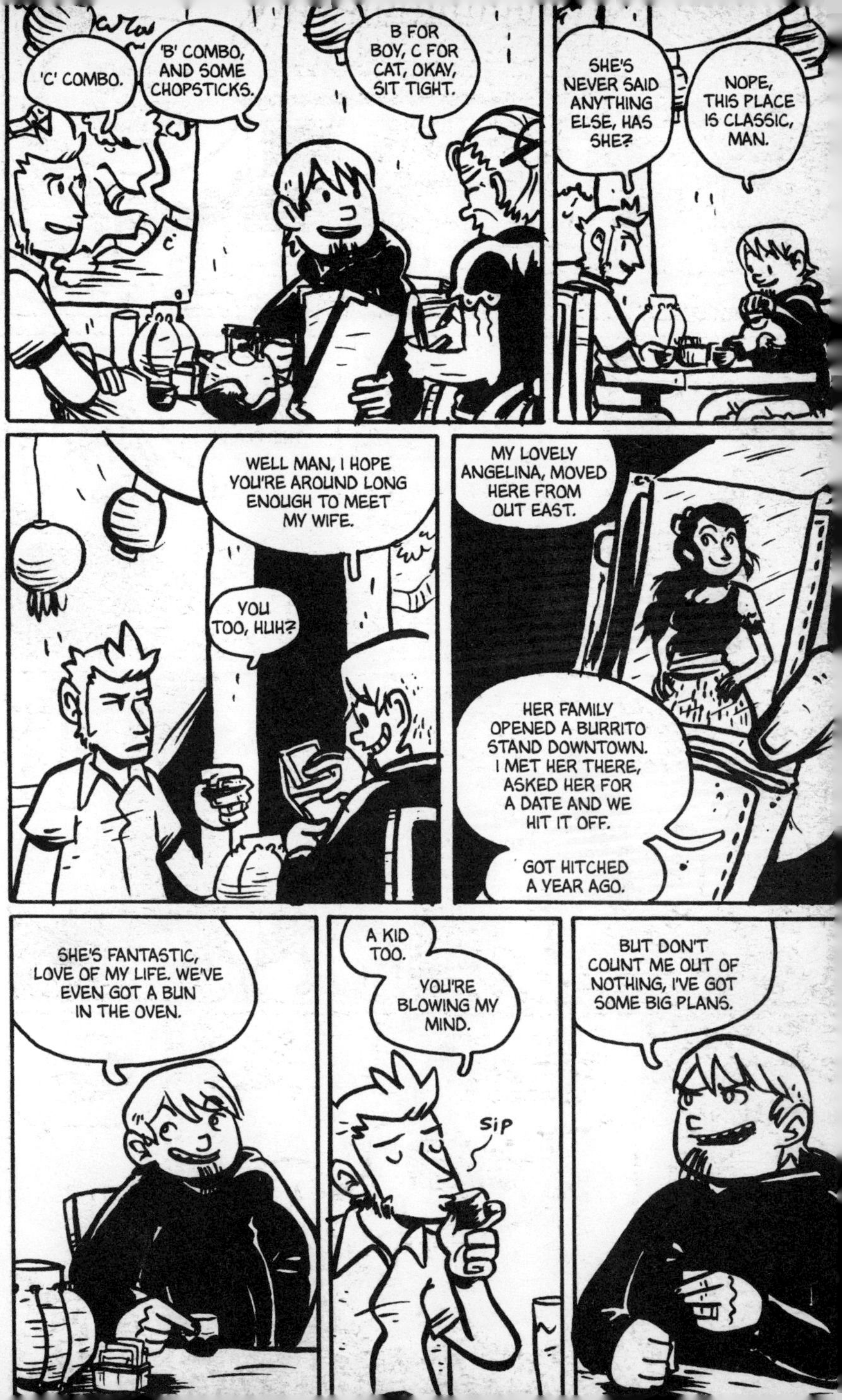
'C' COMBO.
'B' COMBO, AND SOME CHOPSTICKS.
B FOR BOY, C FOR CAT, OKAY, SIT TIGHT.
SHE'S NEVER SAID ANYTHING ELSE, HAS SHE?
NOPE, THIS PLACE IS CLASSIC, MAN.
WELL MAN, I HOPE YOU'RE AROUND LONG ENOUGH TO MEET MY WIFE.
YOU TOO, HUH?
MY LOVELY ANGELINA, MOVED HERE FROM OUT EAST.
HER FAMILY OPENED A BURRITO STAND DOWNTOWN. I MET HER THERE, ASKED HER FOR A DATE AND WE HIT IT OFF.
GOT HITCHED A YEAR AGO.
SHE'S FANTASTIC, LOVE OF MY LIFE. WE'VE EVEN GOT A BUN IN THE OVEN.
A KID TOO.
YOU'RE BLOWING MY MIND.
SIP
BUT DON'T COUNT ME OUT OF NOTHING, I'VE GOT SOME BIG PLANS.

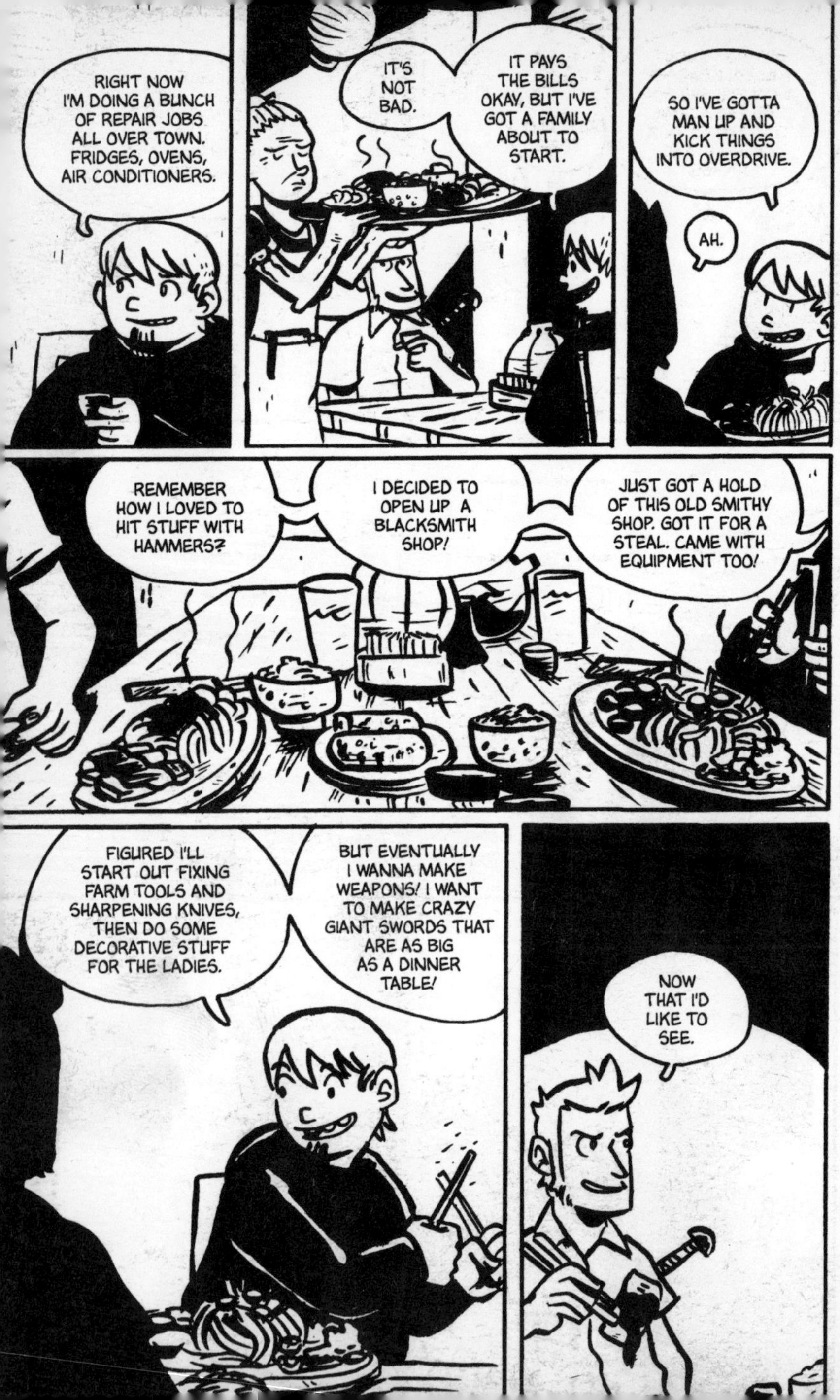
RIGHT NOW I'M DOING A BUNCH OF REPAIR JOBS ALL OVER TOWN. FRIDGES, OVENS, AIR CONDITIONERS.
IT'S NOT BAD.
IT PAYS THE BILLS OKAY, BUT I'VE GOT A FAMILY ABOUT TO START.
SO I'VE GOTTA MAN UP AND KICK THINGS INTO OVERDRIVE.
AH.
REMEMBER HOW I LOVED TO HIT STUFF WITH HAMMERS?
I DECIDED TO OPEN UP A BLACKSMITH SHOP!
JUST GOT A HOLD OF THIS OLD SMITHY SHOP. GOT IT FOR A STEAL. CAME WITH EQUIPMENT TOO!
FIGURED I'LL START OUT FIXING FARM TOOLS AND SHARPENING KNIVES, THEN DO SOME DECORATIVE STUFF FOR THE LADIES.
BUT EVENTUALLY I WANNA MAKE WEAPONS! I WANT TO MAKE CRAZY GIANT SWORDS THAT ARE AS BIG AS A DINNER TABLE!
NOW THAT I'D LIKE TO SEE.

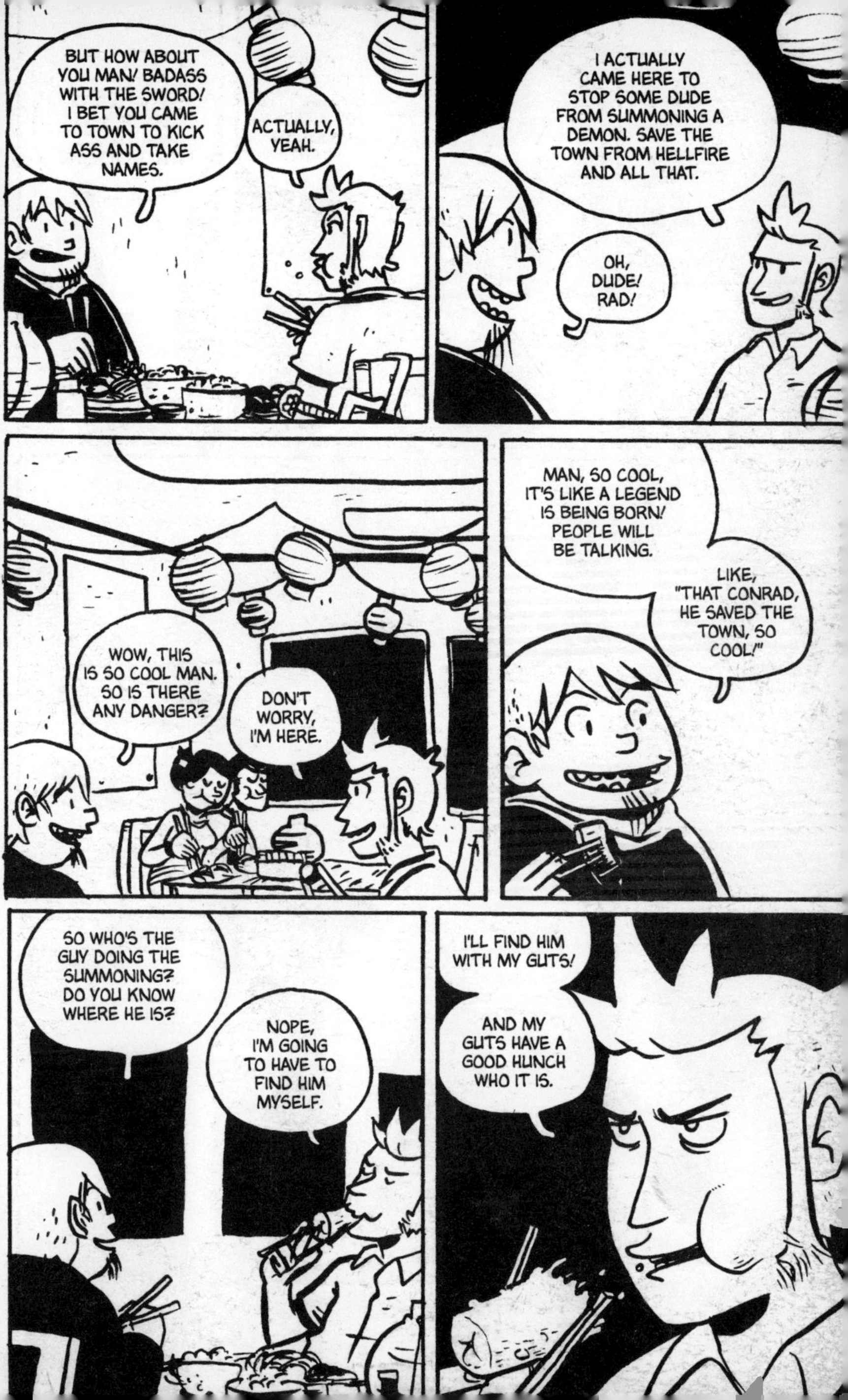
BUT HOW ABOUT YOU MAN! BADASS WITH THE SWORD! I BET YOU CAME TO TOWN TO KICK ASS AND TAKE NAMES.
ACTUALLY, YEAH.
I ACTUALLY CAME HERE TO STOP SOME DUDE FROM SUMMONING A DEMON. SAVE THE TOWN FROM HELLFIRE AND ALL THAT.
OH, DUDE! RAD!
WOW, THIS IS SO COOL MAN. SO IS THERE ANY DANGER?
DON'T WORRY, I'M HERE.
MAN, SO COOL, IT'S LIKE A LEGEND IS BEING BORN! PEOPLE WILL BE TALKING.
LIKE, "THAT CONRAD, HE SAVED THE TOWN, SO COOL!"
SO WHO'S THE GUY DOING THE SUMMONING? DO YOU KNOW WHERE HE IS?
NOPE, I'M GOING TO HAVE TO FIND HIM MYSELF.
I'LL FIND HIM WITH MY GUTS!
AND MY GUTS HAVE A GOOD HUNCH WHO IT IS.

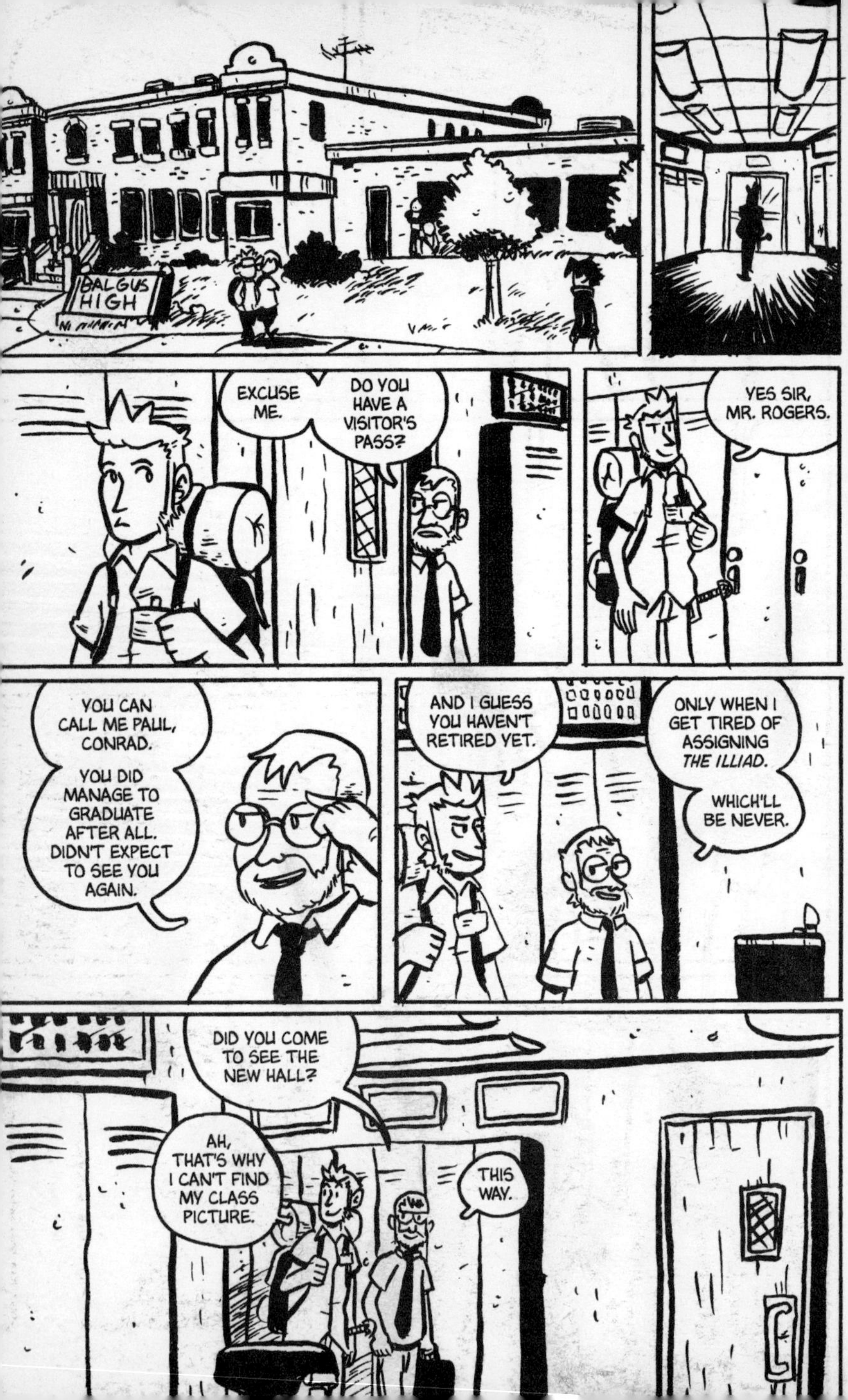
BALGUS HIGH
EXCUSE ME.
DO YOU HAVE A VISITOR'S PASS?
YES SIR, MR. ROGERS.
YOU CAN CALL ME PAUL, CONRAD.
YOU DID MANAGE TO GRADUATE AFTER ALL. DIDN'T EXPECT TO SEE YOU AGAIN.
AND I GUESS YOU HAVEN'T RETIRED YET.
ONLY WHEN I GET TIRED OF ASSIGNING *THE ILLIAD*.
WHICH'LL BE NEVER.
DID YOU COME TO SEE THE NEW HALL?
AH, THAT'S WHY I CAN'T FIND MY CLASS PICTURE.
THIS WAY.

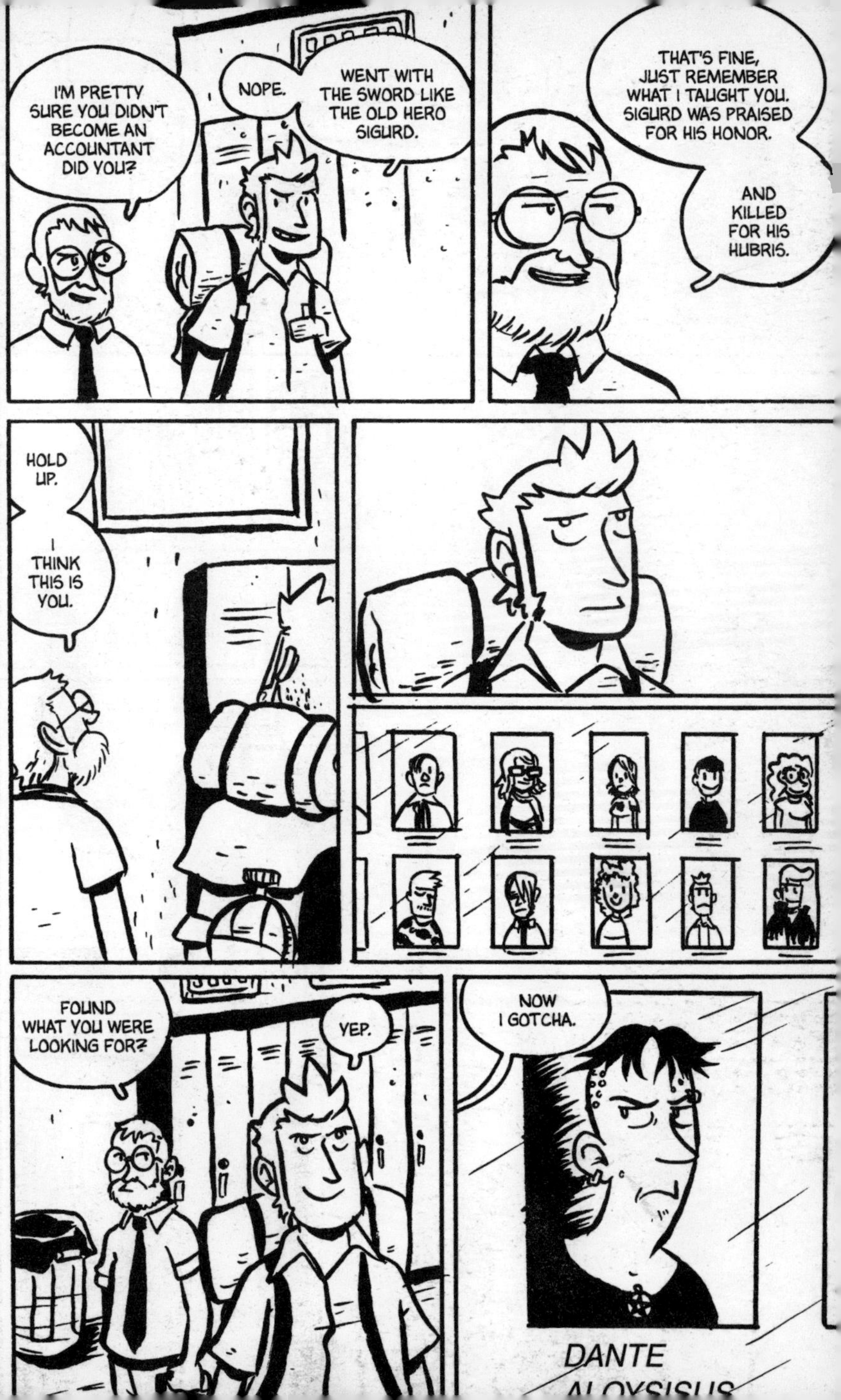

I'M PRETTY SURE YOU DIDN'T BECOME AN ACCOUNTANT DID YOU?
NOPE.
WENT WITH THE SWORD LIKE THE OLD HERO SIGURD.
THAT'S FINE, JUST REMEMBER WHAT I TAUGHT YOU. SIGURD WAS PRAISED FOR HIS HONOR.
AND KILLED FOR HIS HUBRIS.
HOLD UP.
I THINK THIS IS YOU.
FOUND WHAT YOU WERE LOOKING FOR?
YEP.
NOW I GOTCHA.
DANTE

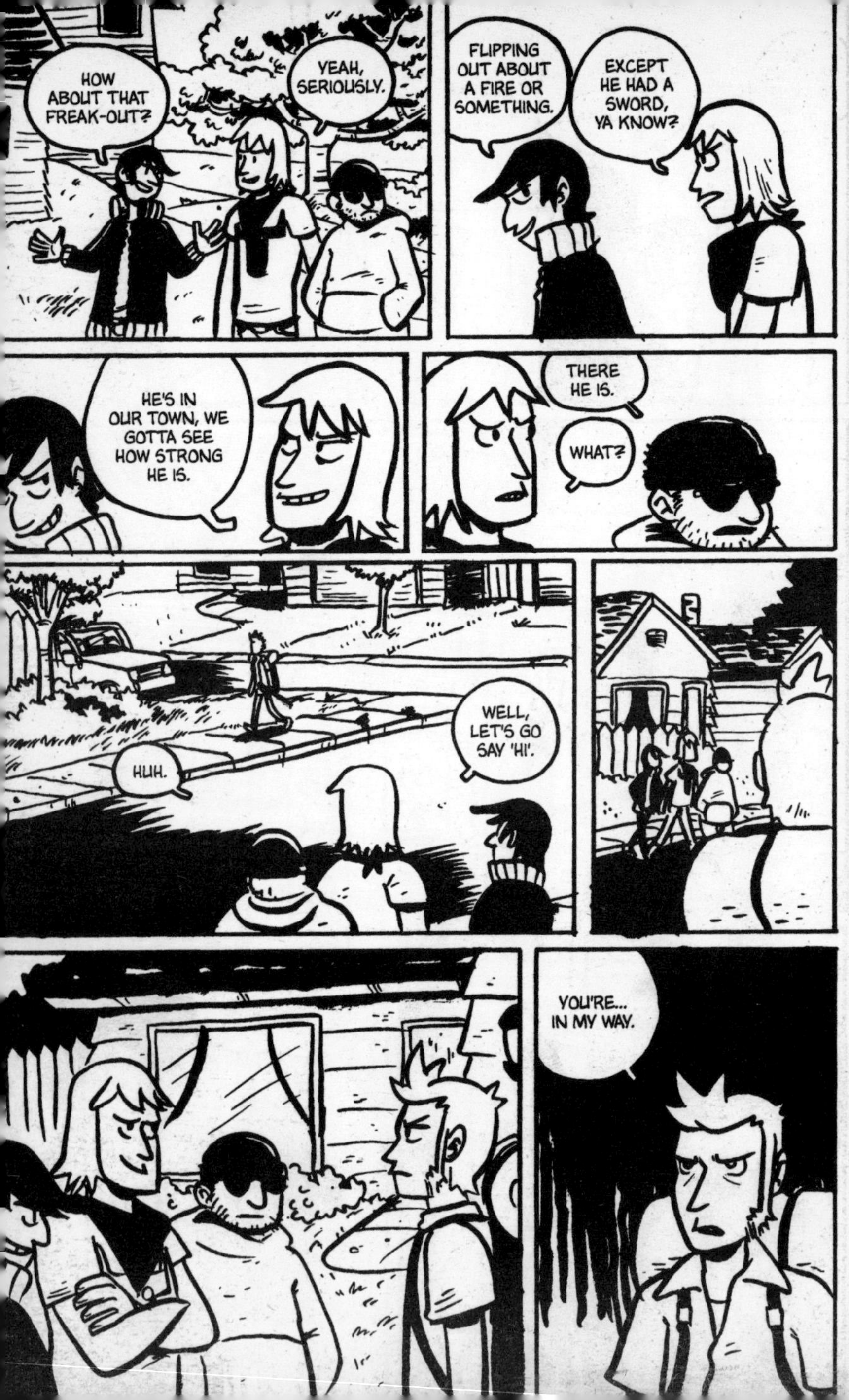
HOW ABOUT THAT FREAK-OUT?
YEAH, SERIOUSLY.
FLIPPING OUT ABOUT A FIRE OR SOMETHING.
EXCEPT HE HAD A SWORD, YA KNOW?
HE'S IN OUR TOWN, WE GOTTA SEE HOW STRONG HE IS.
THERE HE IS.
WHAT?
HUH.
WELL, LET'S GO SAY 'HI'.
YOU'RE... IN MY WAY.

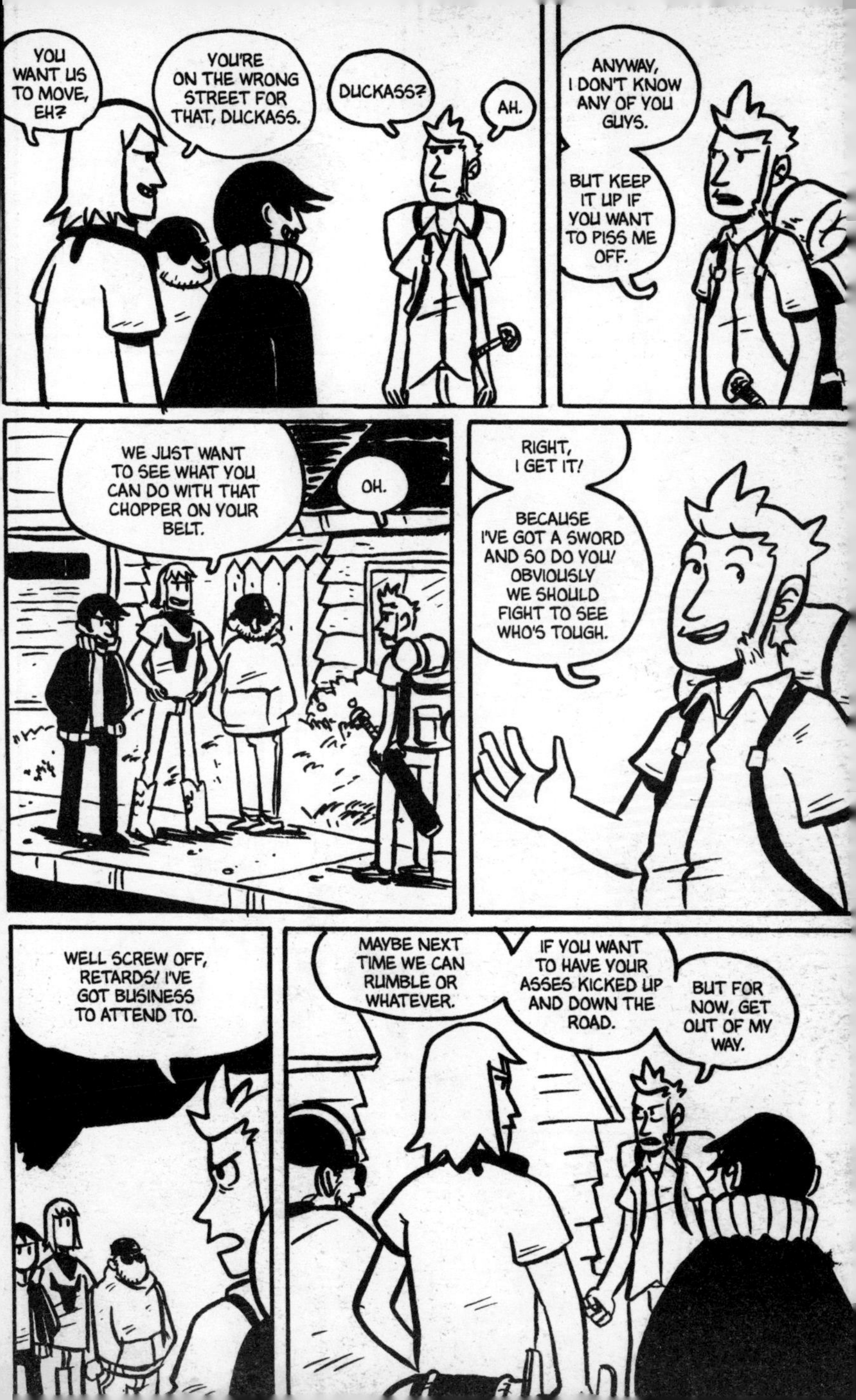
YOU WANT US TO MOVE, EH?
YOU'RE ON THE WRONG STREET FOR THAT, DUCKASS.
DUCKASS?
AH.
ANYWAY, I DON'T KNOW ANY OF YOU GUYS.
BUT KEEP IT UP IF YOU WANT TO PISS ME OFF.
WE JUST WANT TO SEE WHAT YOU CAN DO WITH THAT CHOPPER ON YOUR BELT.
OH.
RIGHT, I GET IT!
BECAUSE I'VE GOT A SWORD AND SO DO YOU! OBVIOUSLY WE SHOULD FIGHT TO SEE WHO'S TOUGH.
WELL SCREW OFF, RETARDS! I'VE GOT BUSINESS TO ATTEND TO.
MAYBE NEXT TIME WE CAN RUMBLE OR WHATEVER.
IF YOU WANT TO HAVE YOUR ASSES KICKED UP AND DOWN THE ROAD.
BUT FOR NOW, GET OUT OF MY WAY.

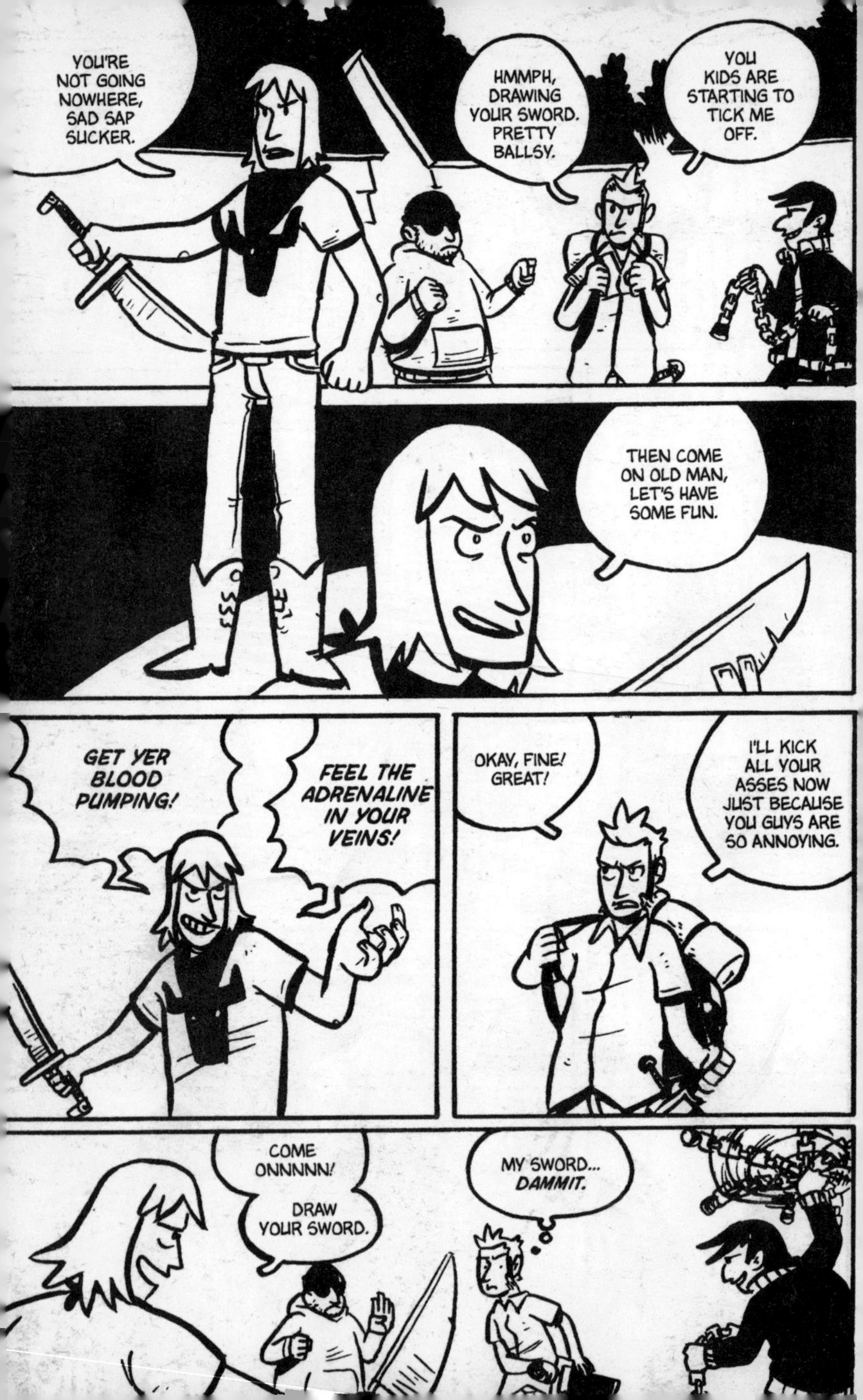
YOU'RE NOT GOING NOWHERE, SAD SAP SUCKER.
HMMPH, DRAWING YOUR SWORD. PRETTY BALLSY.
YOU KIDS ARE STARTING TO TICK ME OFF.
THEN COME ON OLD MAN, LET'S HAVE SOME FUN.
GET YER BLOOD PUMPING!
FEEL THE ADRENALINE IN YOUR VEINS!
OKAY, FINE! GREAT!
I'LL KICK ALL YOUR ASSES NOW JUST BECAUSE YOU GUYS ARE SO ANNOYING.
COME ONNNNN!
DRAW YOUR SWORD.
MY SWORD... DAMMIT.

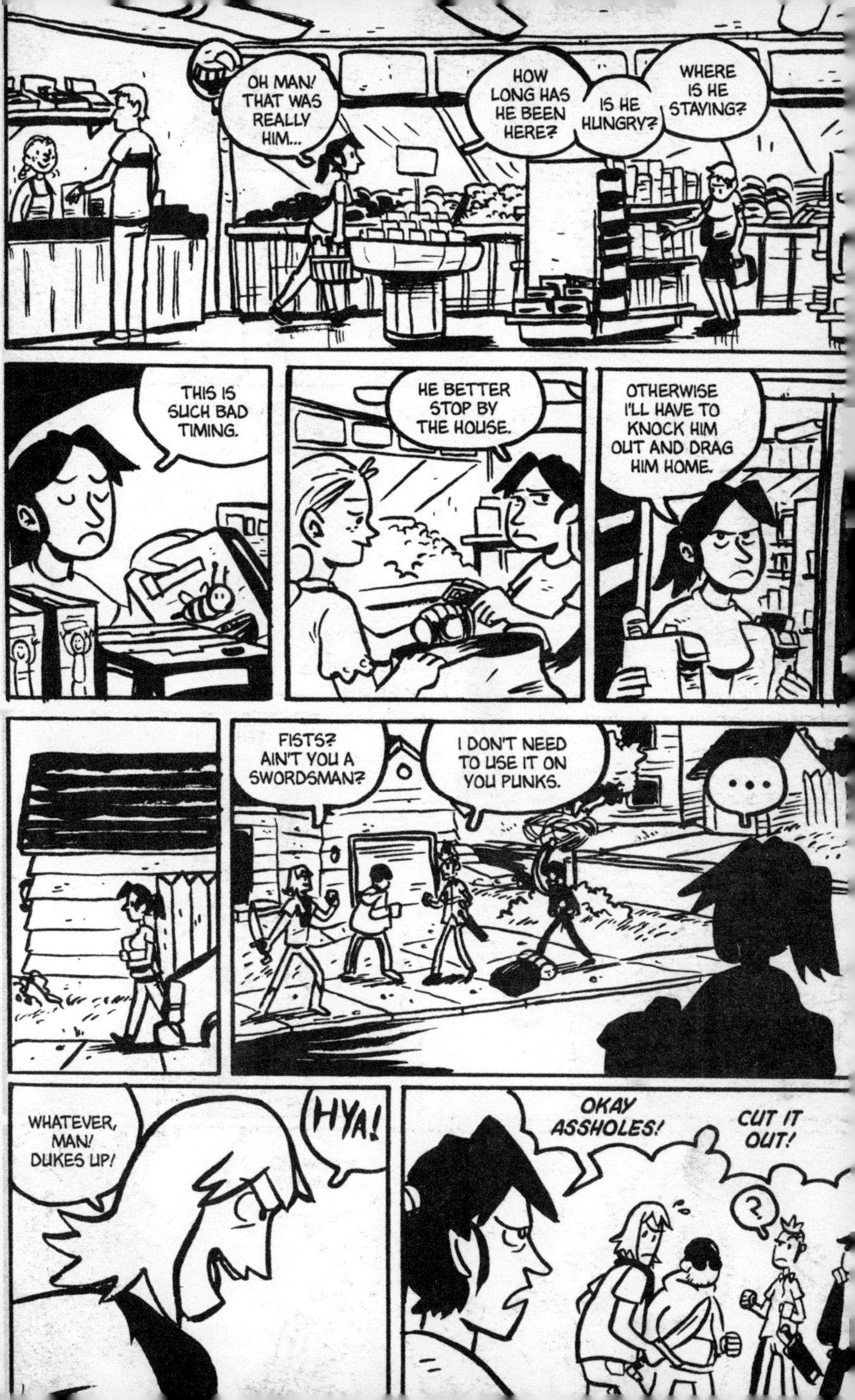
OH MAN! THAT WAS REALLY HIM...
HOW LONG HAS HE BEEN HERE?
IS HE HUNGRY?
WHERE IS HE STAYING?
THIS IS SUCH BAD TIMING.
HE BETTER STOP BY THE HOUSE.
OTHERWISE I'LL HAVE TO KNOCK HIM OUT AND DRAG HIM HOME.
FISTS? AIN'T YOU A SWORDSMAN?
I DON'T NEED TO USE IT ON YOU PUNKS.
...
WHATEVER, MAN! DUKES UP!
HYA!
OKAY ASSHOLES!
CUT IT OUT!
?

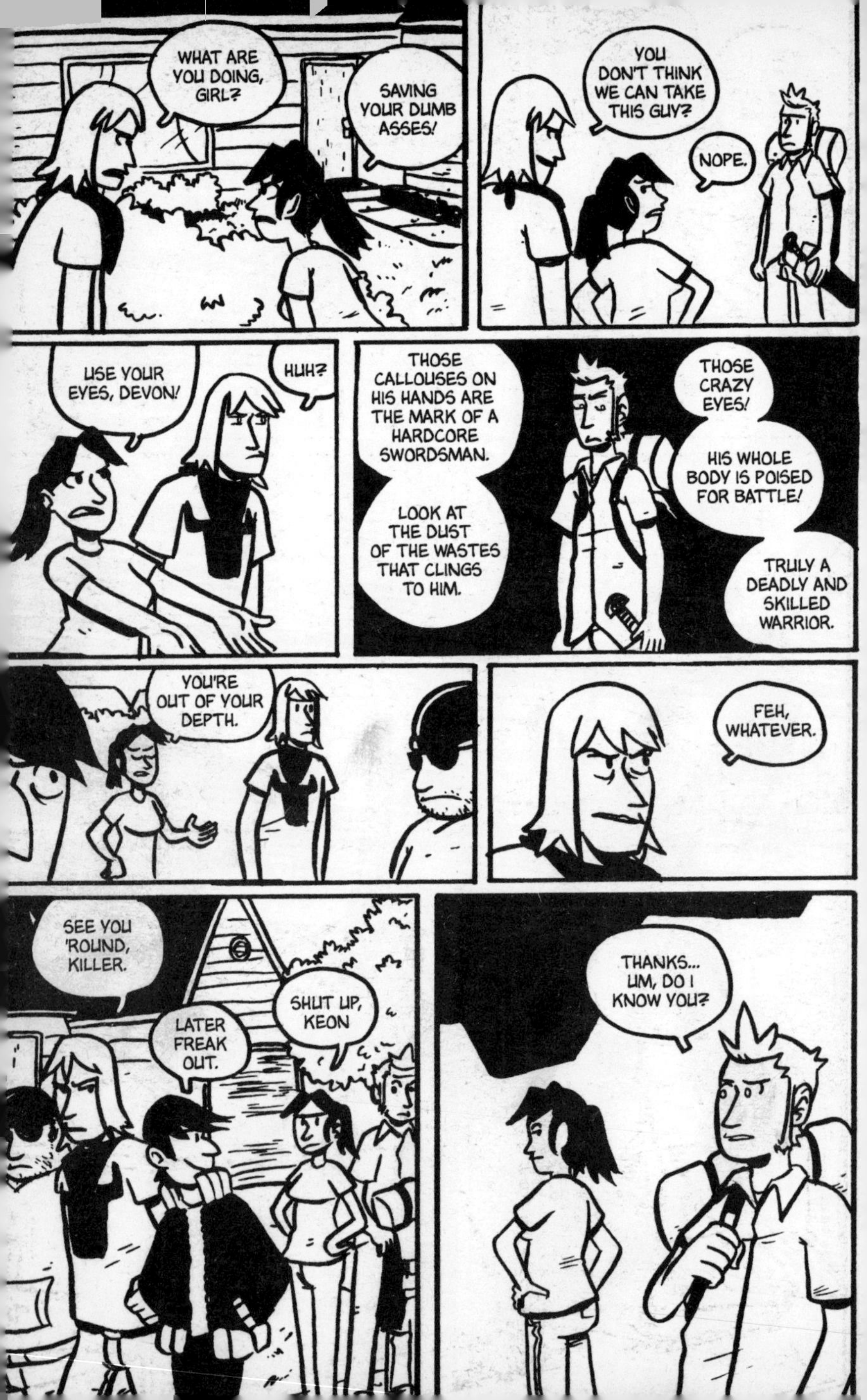
WHAT ARE YOU DOING, GIRL?
SAVING YOUR DUMB ASSES!
YOU DON'T THINK WE CAN TAKE THIS GUY?
NOPE.
USE YOUR EYES, DEVON!
HUH?
THOSE CALLOUSES ON HIS HANDS ARE THE MARK OF A HARDCORE SWORDSMAN.
LOOK AT THE DUST OF THE WASTES THAT CLINGS TO HIM.
THOSE CRAZY EYES!
HIS WHOLE BODY IS POISED FOR BATTLE!
TRULY A DEADLY AND SKILLED WARRIOR.
YOU'RE OUT OF YOUR DEPTH.
FEH, WHATEVER.
SEE YOU 'ROUND, KILLER.
LATER FREAK OUT.
SHUT UP, KEON
THANKS... UM, DO I KNOW YOU?

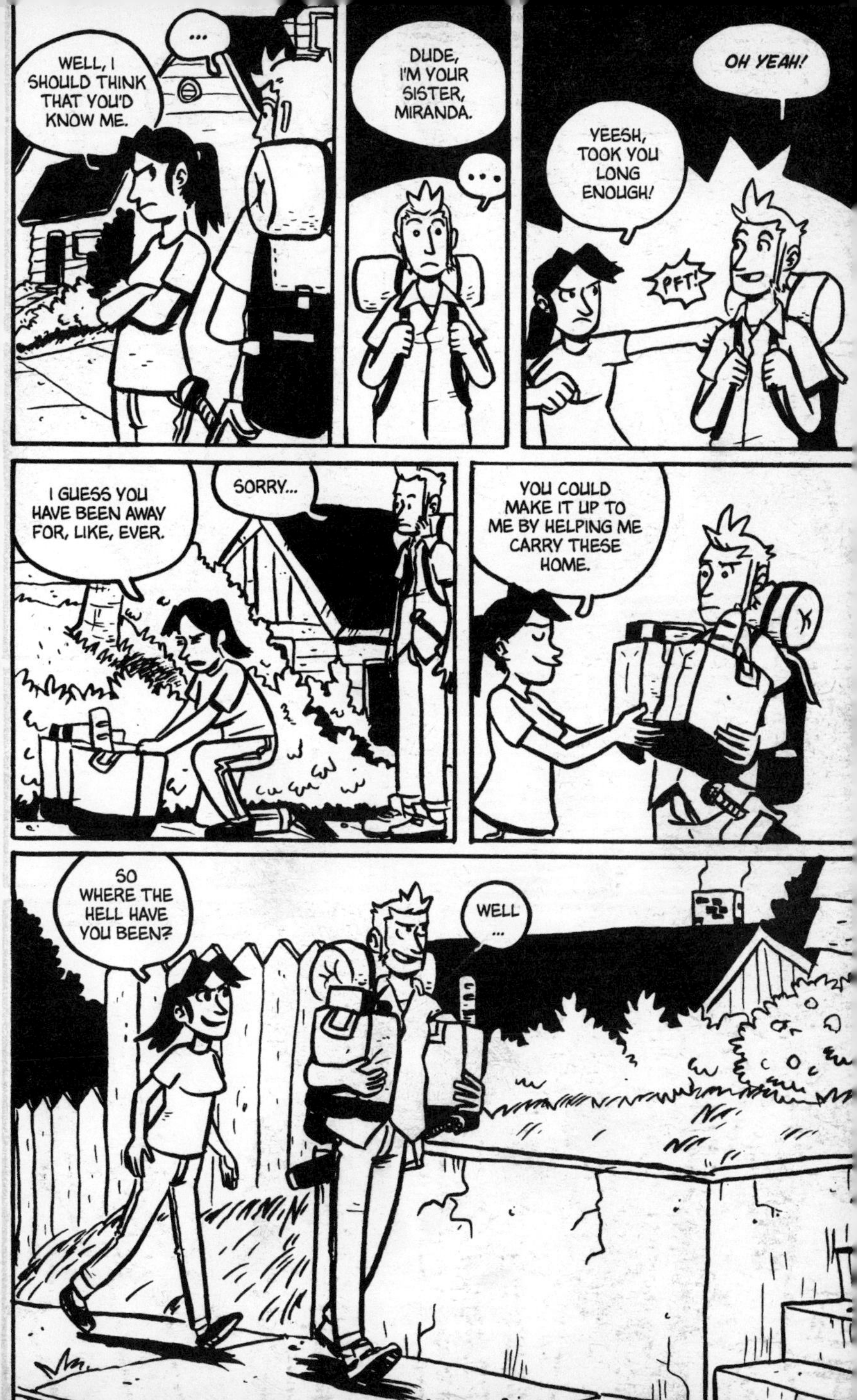
WELL, I SHOULD THINK THAT YOU'D KNOW ME.
...
DUDE, I'M YOUR SISTER, MIRANDA.
...
YEESH, TOOK YOU LONG ENOUGH!
OH YEAH!
PFT!
I GUESS YOU HAVE BEEN AWAY FOR, LIKE, EVER.
SORRY...
YOU COULD MAKE IT UP TO ME BY HELPING ME CARRY THESE HOME.
SO WHERE THE HELL HAVE YOU BEEN?
WELL ...

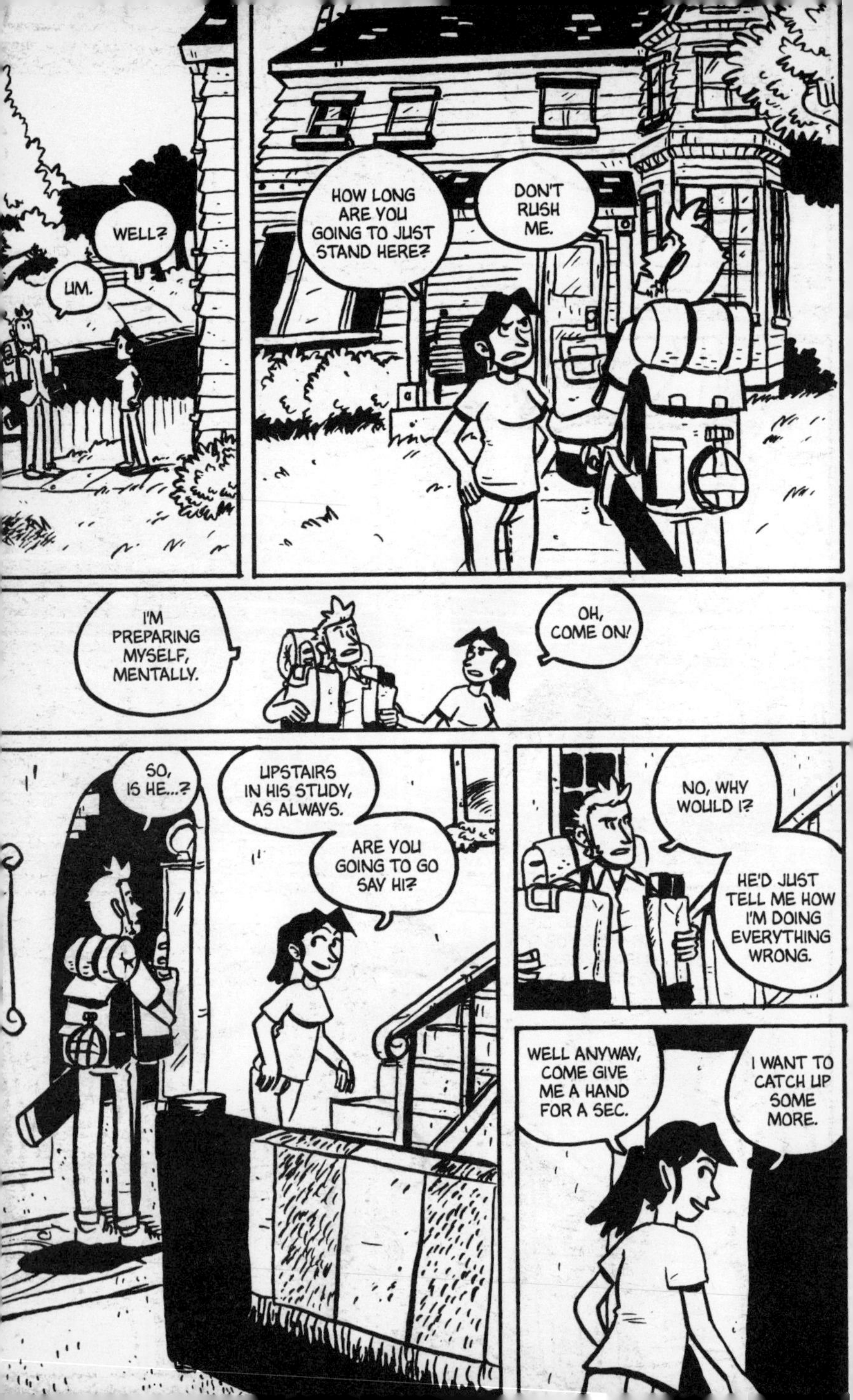
WELL?
UM.
HOW LONG ARE YOU GOING TO JUST STAND HERE?
DON'T RUSH ME.
I'M PREPARING MYSELF, MENTALLY.
OH, COME ON!
SO, IS HE...?
UPSTAIRS IN HIS STUDY, AS ALWAYS.
ARE YOU GOING TO GO SAY HI?
NO, WHY WOULD I?
HE'D JUST TELL ME HOW I'M DOING EVERYTHING WRONG.
WELL ANYWAY, COME GIVE ME A HAND FOR A SEC.
I WANT TO CATCH UP SOME MORE.

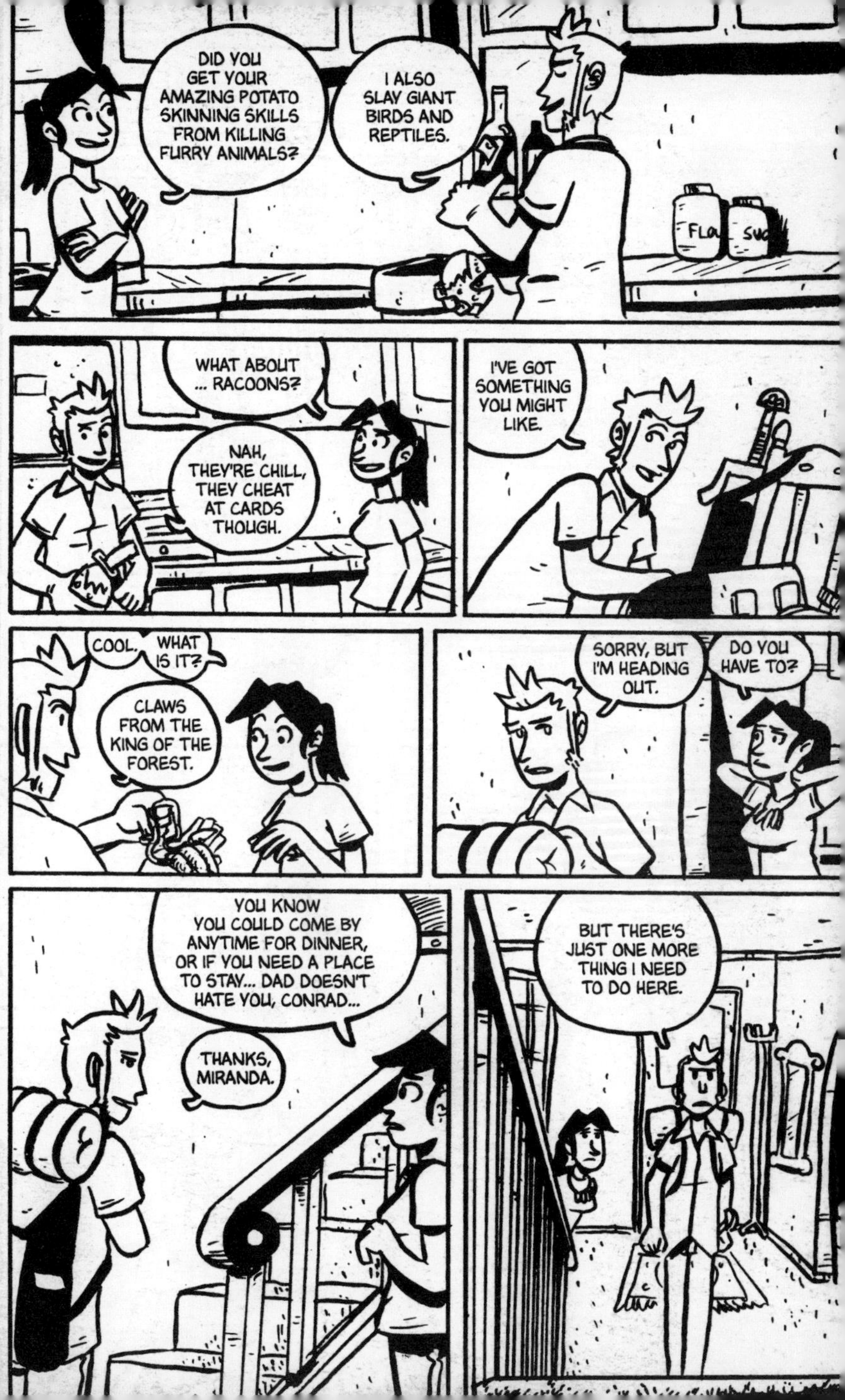
DID YOU GET YOUR AMAZING POTATO SKINNING SKILLS FROM KILLING FURRY ANIMALS?
I ALSO SLAY GIANT BIRDS AND REPTILES.
FLO
SUG
WHAT ABOUT ... RACOONS?
NAH, THEY'RE CHILL, THEY CHEAT AT CARDS THOUGH.
I'VE GOT SOMETHING YOU MIGHT LIKE.
COOL.
WHAT IS IT?
CLAWS FROM THE KING OF THE FOREST.
SORRY, BUT I'M HEADING OUT.
DO YOU HAVE TO?
YOU KNOW YOU COULD COME BY ANYTIME FOR DINNER, OR IF YOU NEED A PLACE TO STAY... DAD DOESN'T HATE YOU, CONRAD...
THANKS, MIRANDA.
BUT THERE'S JUST ONE MORE THING I NEED TO DO HERE.

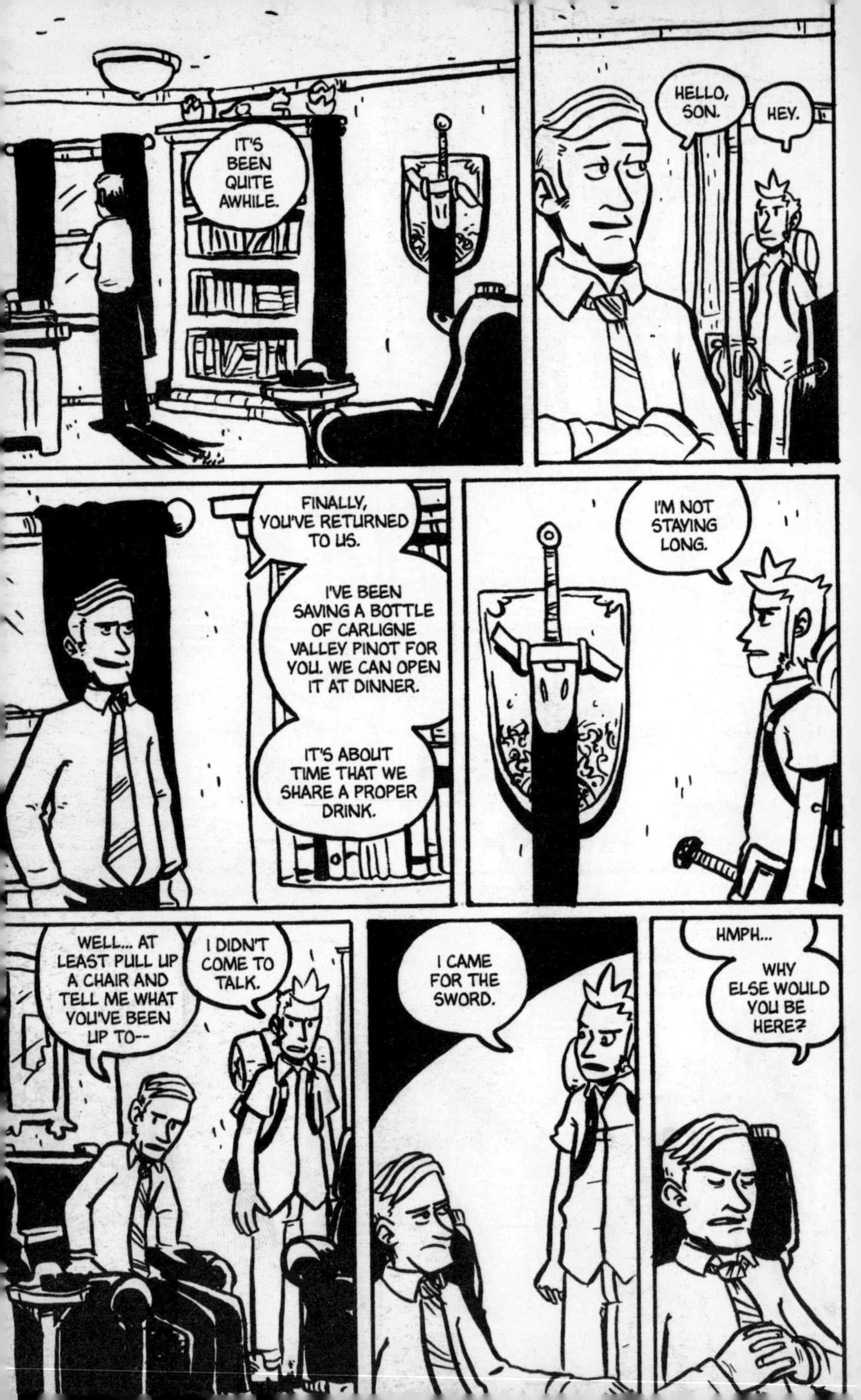
IT'S BEEN QUITE AWHILE.
HELLO, SON.
HEY.
FINALLY, YOU'VE RETURNED TO US.
I'VE BEEN SAVING A BOTTLE OF CARLIGNE VALLEY PINOT FOR YOU. WE CAN OPEN IT AT DINNER.
IT'S ABOUT TIME THAT WE SHARE A PROPER DRINK.
I'M NOT STAYING LONG.
WELL... AT LEAST PULL UP A CHAIR AND TELL ME WHAT YOU'VE BEEN UP TO--
I DIDN'T COME TO TALK.
I CAME FOR THE SWORD.
HMPH...
WHY ELSE WOULD YOU BE HERE?

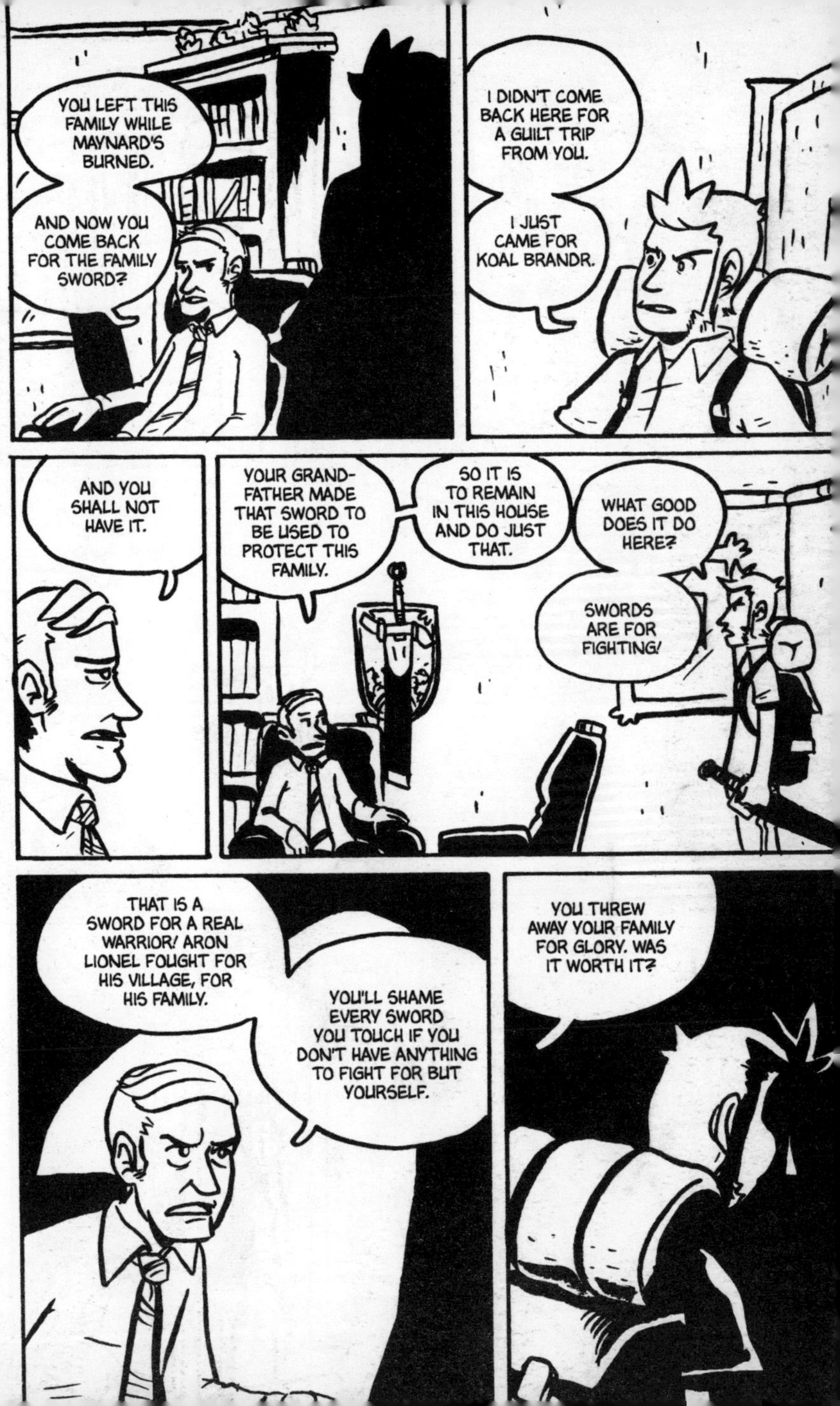
YOU LEFT THIS FAMILY WHILE MAYNARD'S BURNED.
AND NOW YOU COME BACK FOR THE FAMILY SWORD?
I DIDN'T COME BACK HERE FOR A GUILT TRIP FROM YOU.
I JUST CAME FOR KOAL BRANDR.
AND YOU SHALL NOT HAVE IT.
YOUR GRAND-FATHER MADE THAT SWORD TO BE USED TO PROTECT THIS FAMILY.
SO IT IS TO REMAIN IN THIS HOUSE AND DO JUST THAT.
WHAT GOOD DOES IT DO HERE?
SWORDS ARE FOR FIGHTING!
THAT IS A SWORD FOR A REAL WARRIOR! ARON LIONEL FOUGHT FOR HIS VILLAGE, FOR HIS FAMILY.
YOU'LL SHAME EVERY SWORD YOU TOUCH IF YOU DON'T HAVE ANYTHING TO FIGHT FOR BUT YOURSELF.
YOU THREW AWAY YOUR FAMILY FOR GLORY. WAS IT WORTH IT?

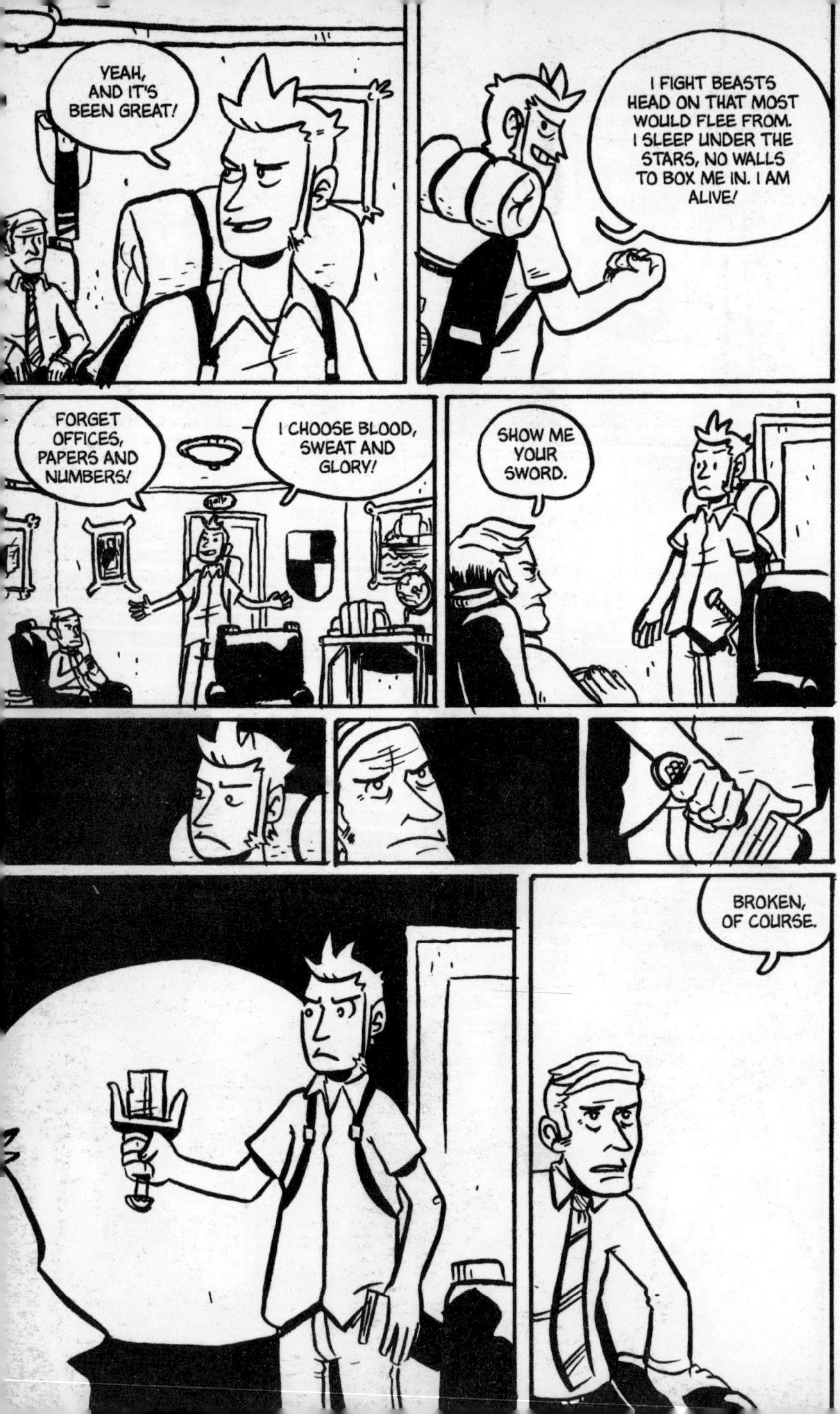
YEAH, AND IT'S BEEN GREAT!
I FIGHT BEASTS HEAD ON THAT MOST WOULD FLEE FROM. I SLEEP UNDER THE STARS, NO WALLS TO BOX ME IN. I AM ALIVE!
FORGET OFFICES, PAPERS AND NUMBERS!
I CHOOSE BLOOD, SWEAT AND GLORY!
SHOW ME YOUR SWORD.
BROKEN, OF COURSE.

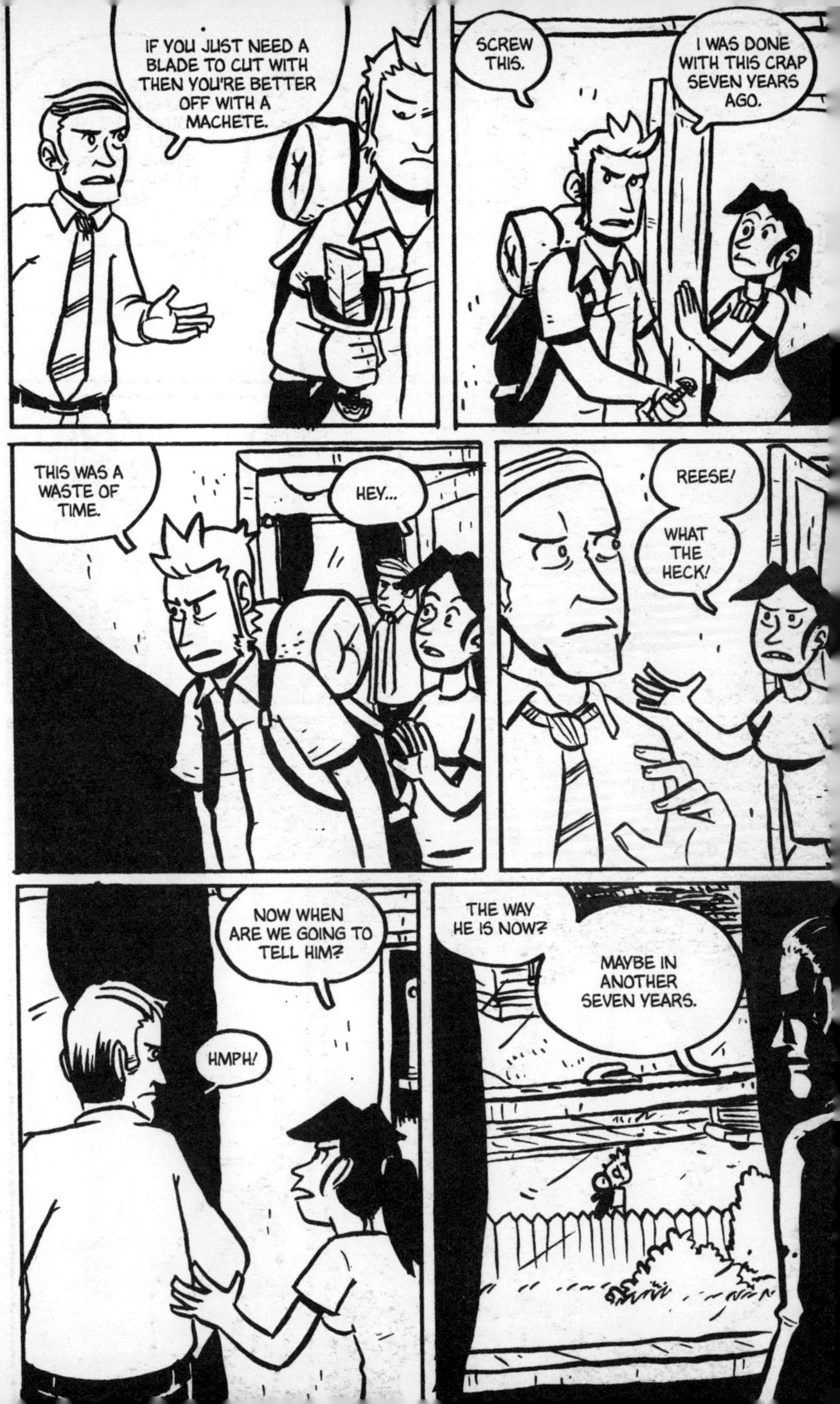
IF YOU JUST NEED A BLADE TO CUT WITH THEN YOU'RE BETTER OFF WITH A MACHETE.
SCREW THIS.
I WAS DONE WITH THIS CRAP SEVEN YEARS AGO.
THIS WAS A WASTE OF TIME.
HEY...
REESE!
WHAT THE HECK!
NOW WHEN ARE WE GOING TO TELL HIM?
HMPH!
THE WAY HE IS NOW?
MAYBE IN ANOTHER SEVEN YEARS.

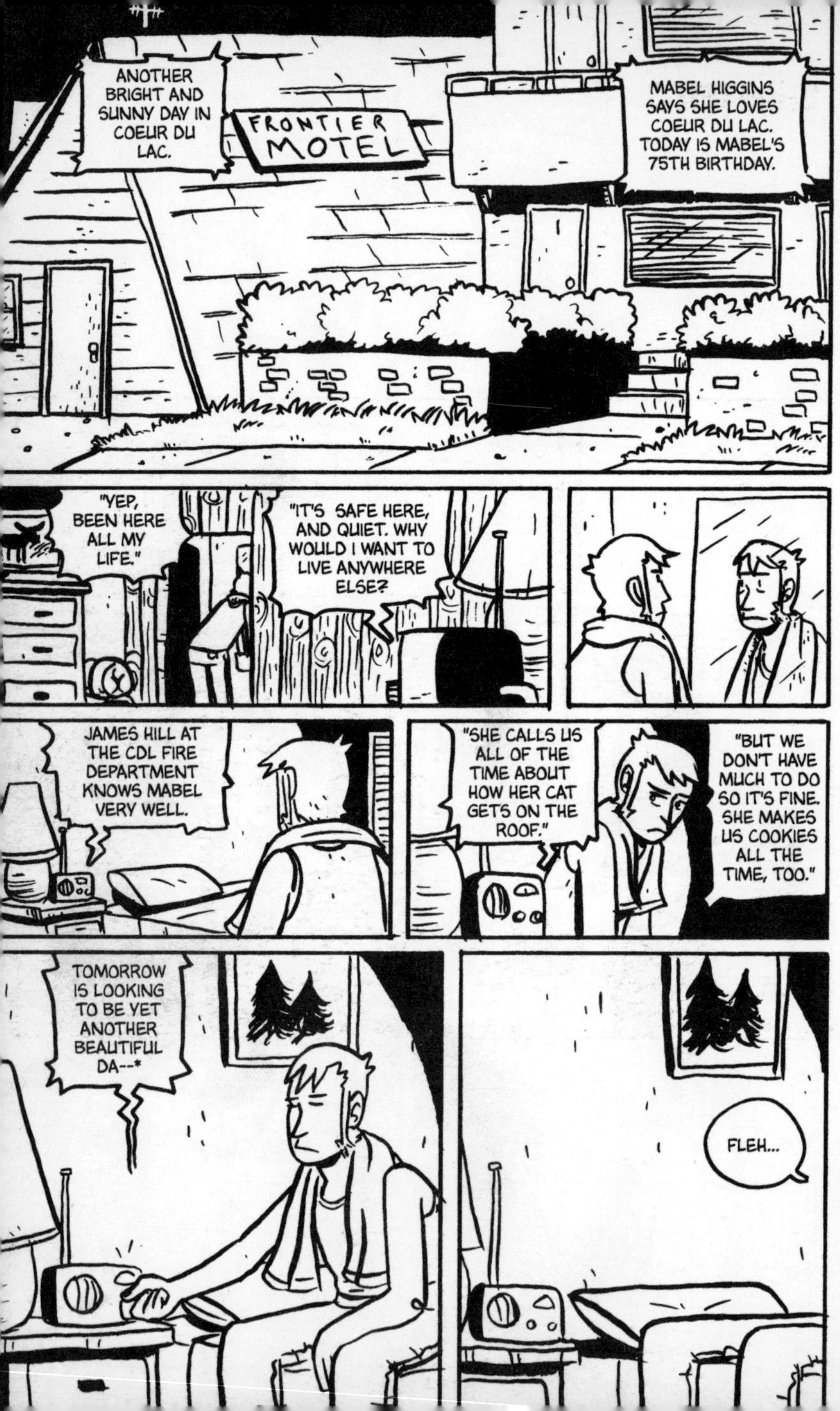
ANOTHER BRIGHT AND SUNNY DAY IN COEUR DU LAC.
FRONTIER MOTEL
MABEL HIGGINS SAYS SHE LOVES COEUR DU LAC. TODAY IS MABEL'S 75TH BIRTHDAY.
"YEP, BEEN HERE ALL MY LIFE."
"IT'S SAFE HERE, AND QUIET. WHY WOULD I WANT TO LIVE ANYWHERE ELSE?"
JAMES HILL AT THE CDL FIRE DEPARTMENT KNOWS MABEL VERY WELL.
"SHE CALLS US ALL OF THE TIME ABOUT HOW HER CAT GETS ON THE ROOF."
"BUT WE DON'T HAVE MUCH TO DO SO IT'S FINE. SHE MAKES US COOKIES ALL THE TIME, TOO."
TOMORROW IS LOOKING TO BE YET ANOTHER BEAUTIFUL DA--*
FLEH...

CHAPTER 3

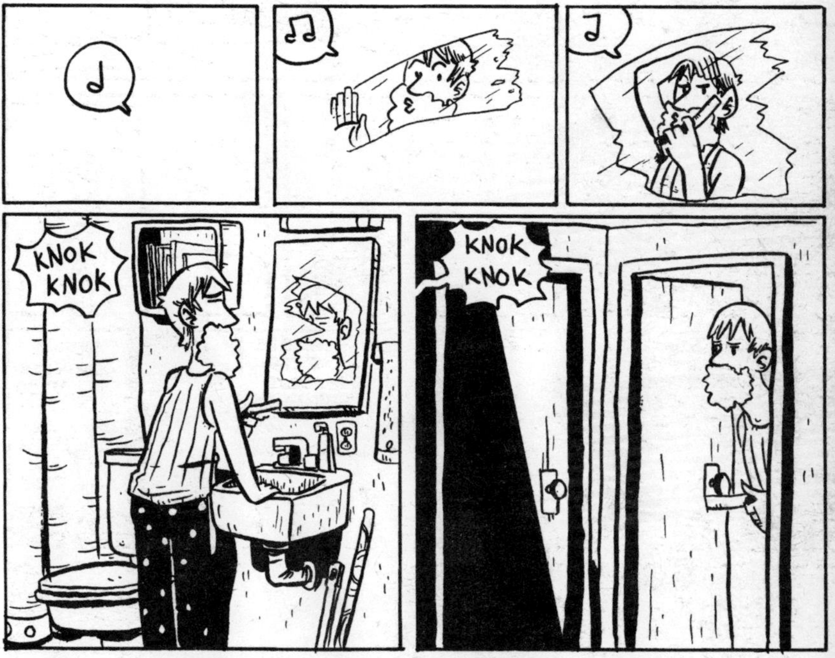
KNOK KNOK
KNOK KNOK

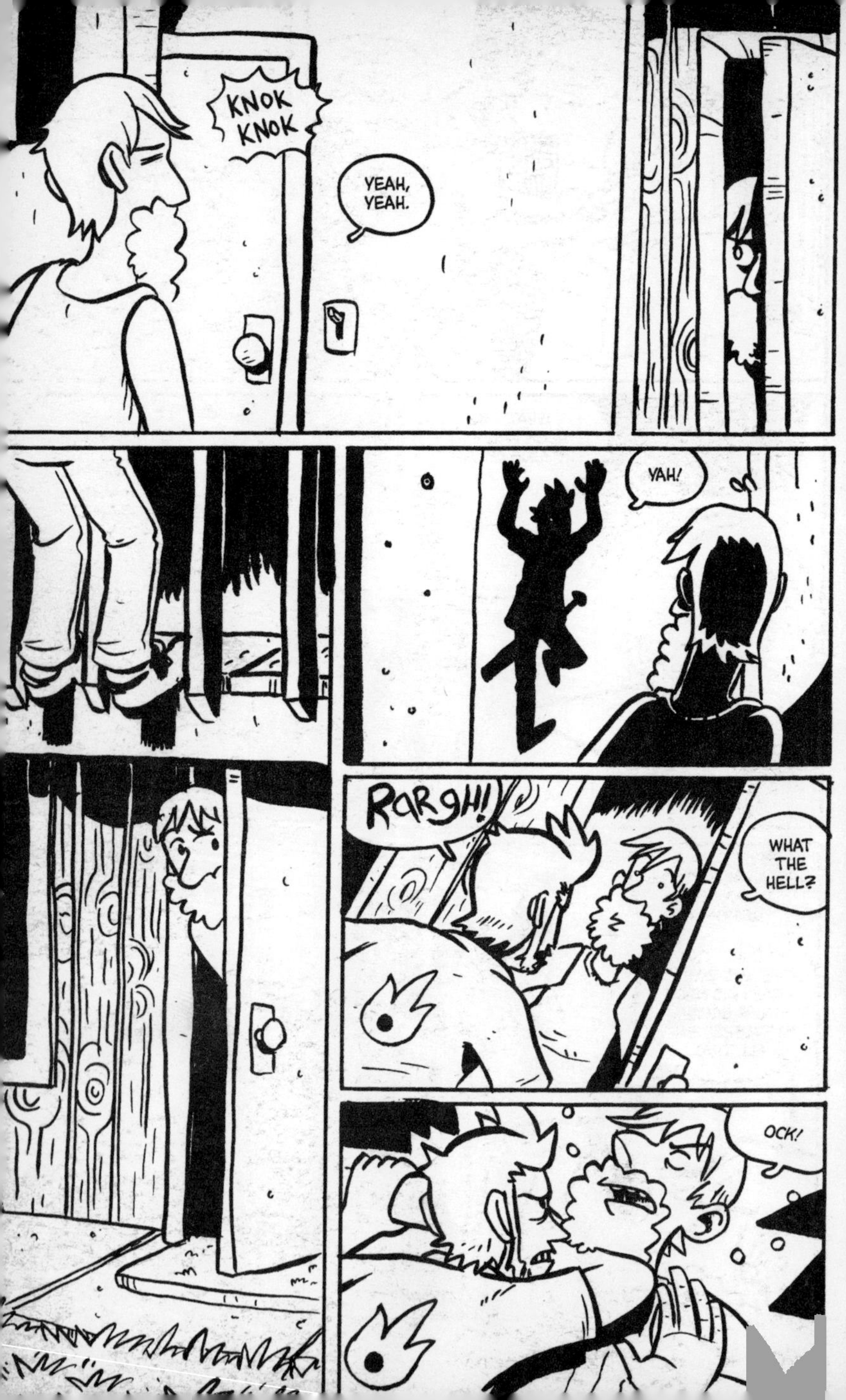
KNOK KNOK
YEAH, YEAH.
YAH!
RARGH!
WHAT THE HELL?
OCK!

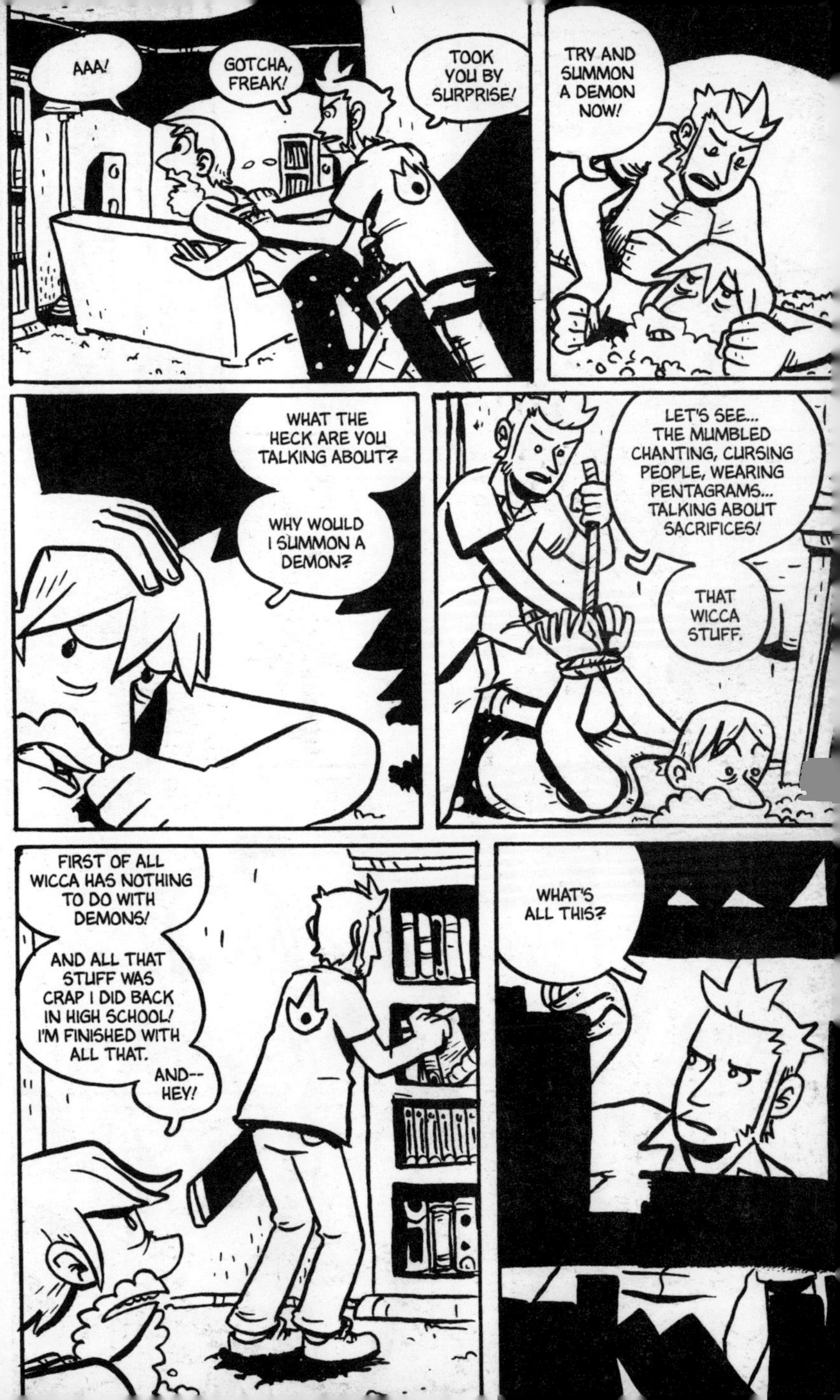
AAA!
GOTCHA, FREAK!
TOOK YOU BY SURPRISE!
TRY AND SUMMON A DEMON NOW!
WHAT THE HECK ARE YOU TALKING ABOUT?
WHY WOULD I SUMMON A DEMON?
LET'S SEE... THE MUMBLED CHANTING, CURSING PEOPLE, WEARING PENTAGRAMS... TALKING ABOUT SACRIFICES!
THAT WICCA STUFF.
FIRST OF ALL WICCA HAS NOTHING TO DO WITH DEMONS!
AND ALL THAT STUFF WAS CRAP I DID BACK IN HIGH SCHOOL! I'M FINISHED WITH ALL THAT.
AND-- HEY!
WHAT'S ALL THIS?

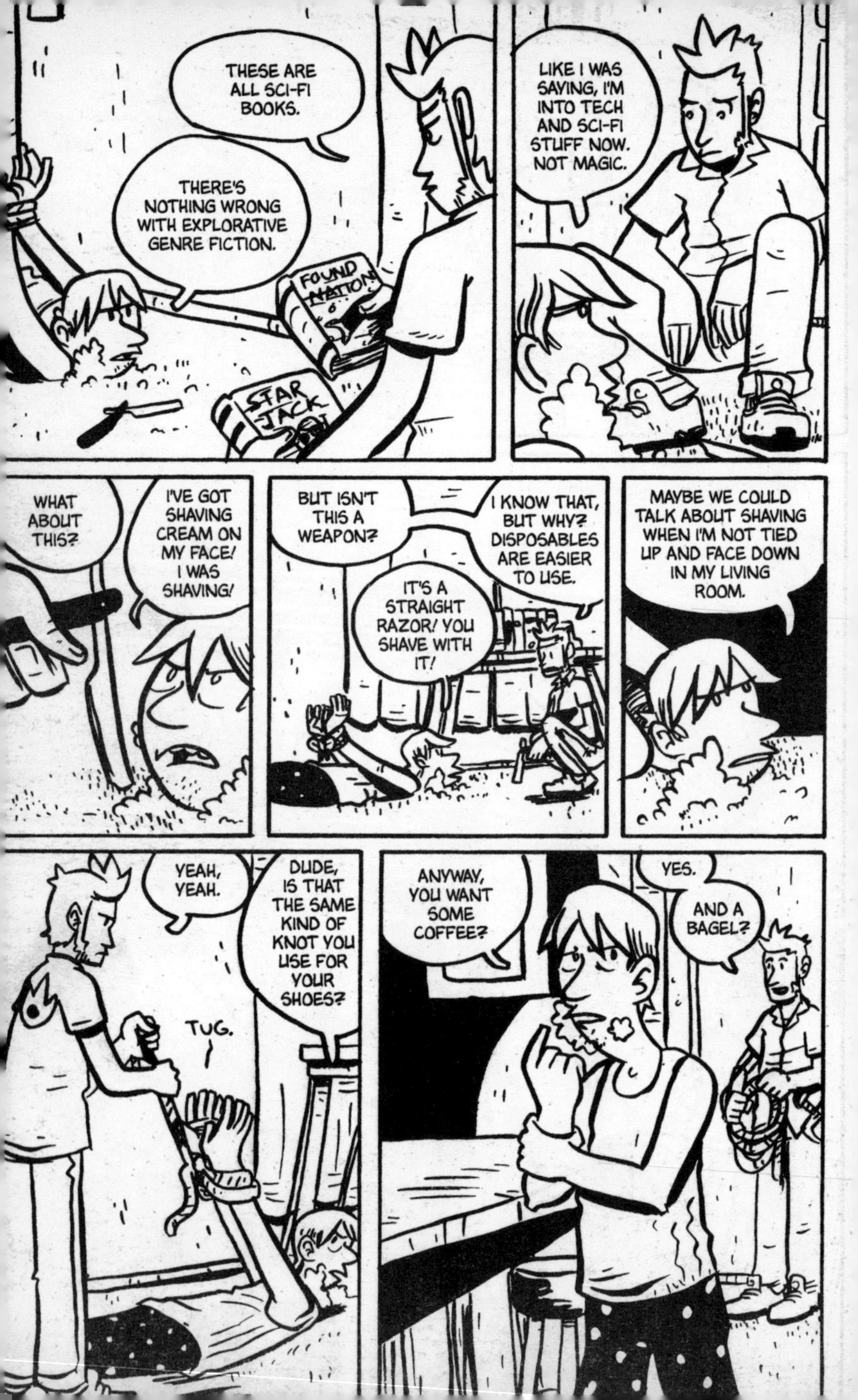
THESE ARE ALL SCI-FI BOOKS.
THERE'S NOTHING WRONG WITH EXPLORATIVE GENRE FICTION.
FOUND NATION
STAR JACK
LIKE I WAS SAYING, I'M INTO TECH AND SCI-FI STUFF NOW. NOT MAGIC.
WHAT ABOUT THIS?
I'VE GOT SHAVING CREAM ON MY FACE! I WAS SHAVING!
BUT ISN'T THIS A WEAPON?
IT'S A STRAIGHT RAZOR! YOU SHAVE WITH IT!
I KNOW THAT, BUT WHY? DISPOSABLES ARE EASIER TO USE.
MAYBE WE COULD TALK ABOUT SHAVING WHEN I'M NOT TIED UP AND FACE DOWN IN MY LIVING ROOM.
YEAH, YEAH.
TUG.
DUDE, IS THAT THE SAME KIND OF KNOT YOU USE FOR YOUR SHOES?
ANYWAY, YOU WANT SOME COFFEE?
YES.
AND A BAGEL?

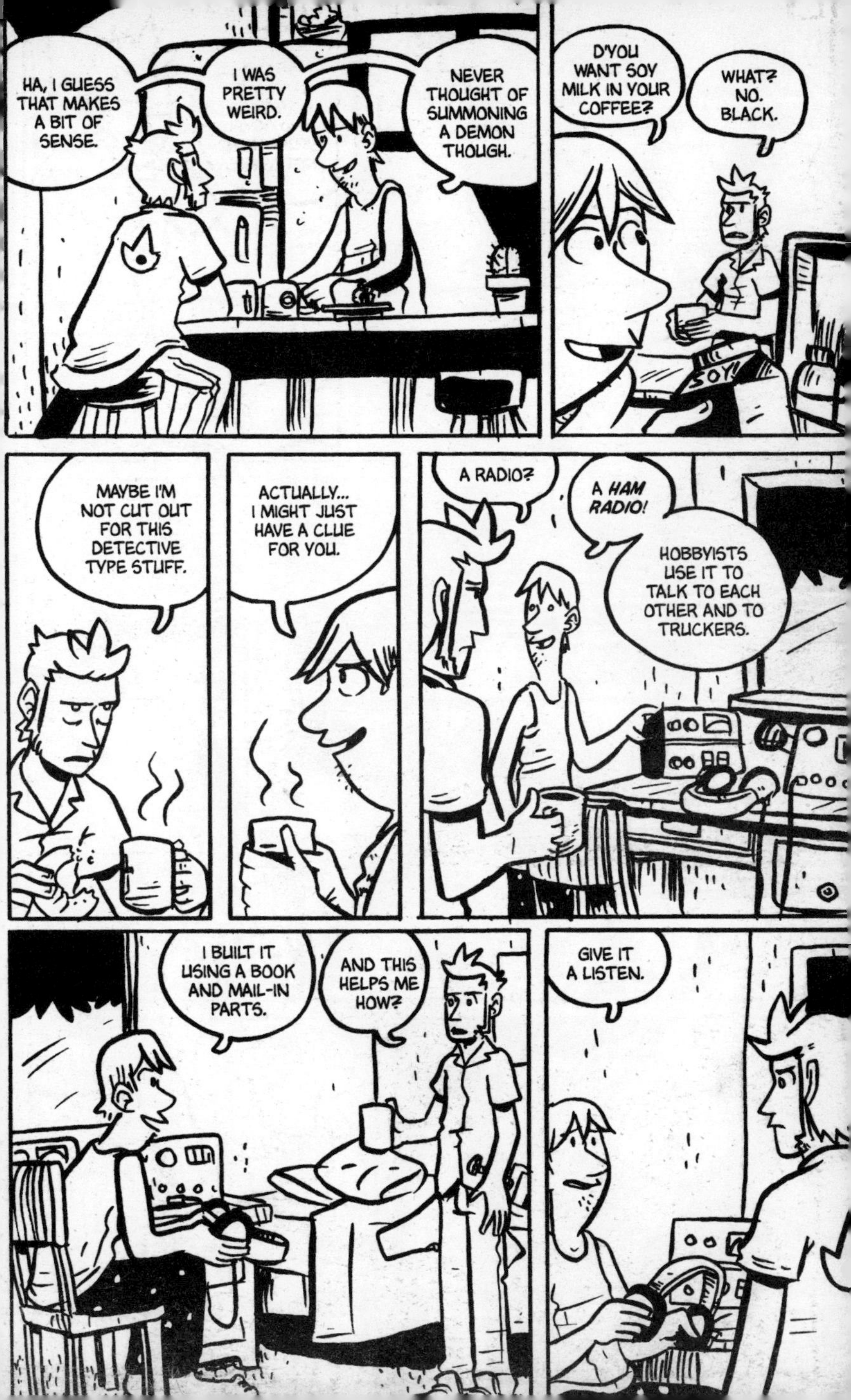
HA, I GUESS THAT MAKES A BIT OF SENSE.
I WAS PRETTY WEIRD.
NEVER THOUGHT OF SUMMONING A DEMON THOUGH.
D'YOU WANT SOY MILK IN YOUR COFFEE?
WHAT? NO. BLACK.
SOY!
MAYBE I'M NOT CUT OUT FOR THIS DETECTIVE TYPE STUFF.
ACTUALLY... I MIGHT JUST HAVE A CLUE FOR YOU.
A RADIO?
A HAM RADIO!
HOBBYISTS USE IT TO TALK TO EACH OTHER AND TO TRUCKERS.
I BUILT IT USING A BOOK AND MAIL-IN PARTS.
AND THIS HELPS ME HOW?
GIVE IT A LISTEN.

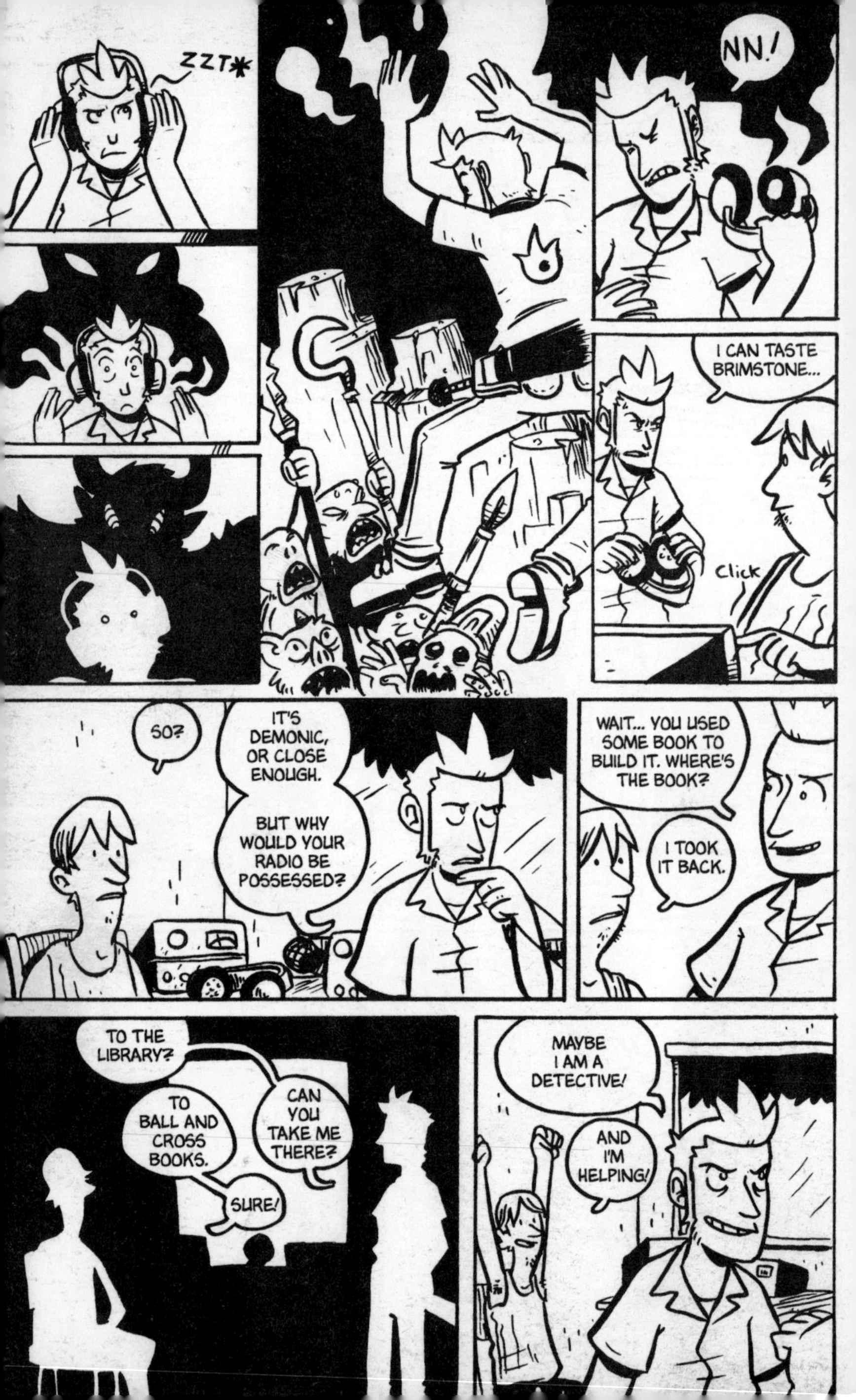
ZZZT
NN!
I CAN TASTE BRIMSTONE...
Click
SO?
IT'S DEMONIC, OR CLOSE ENOUGH.
BUT WHY WOULD YOUR RADIO BE POSSESSED?
WAIT... YOU USED SOME BOOK TO BUILD IT. WHERE'S THE BOOK?
I TOOK IT BACK.
TO THE LIBRARY?
TO BALL AND CROSS BOOKS.
CAN YOU TAKE ME THERE?
SURE!
MAYBE I AM A DETECTIVE!
AND I'M HELPING!

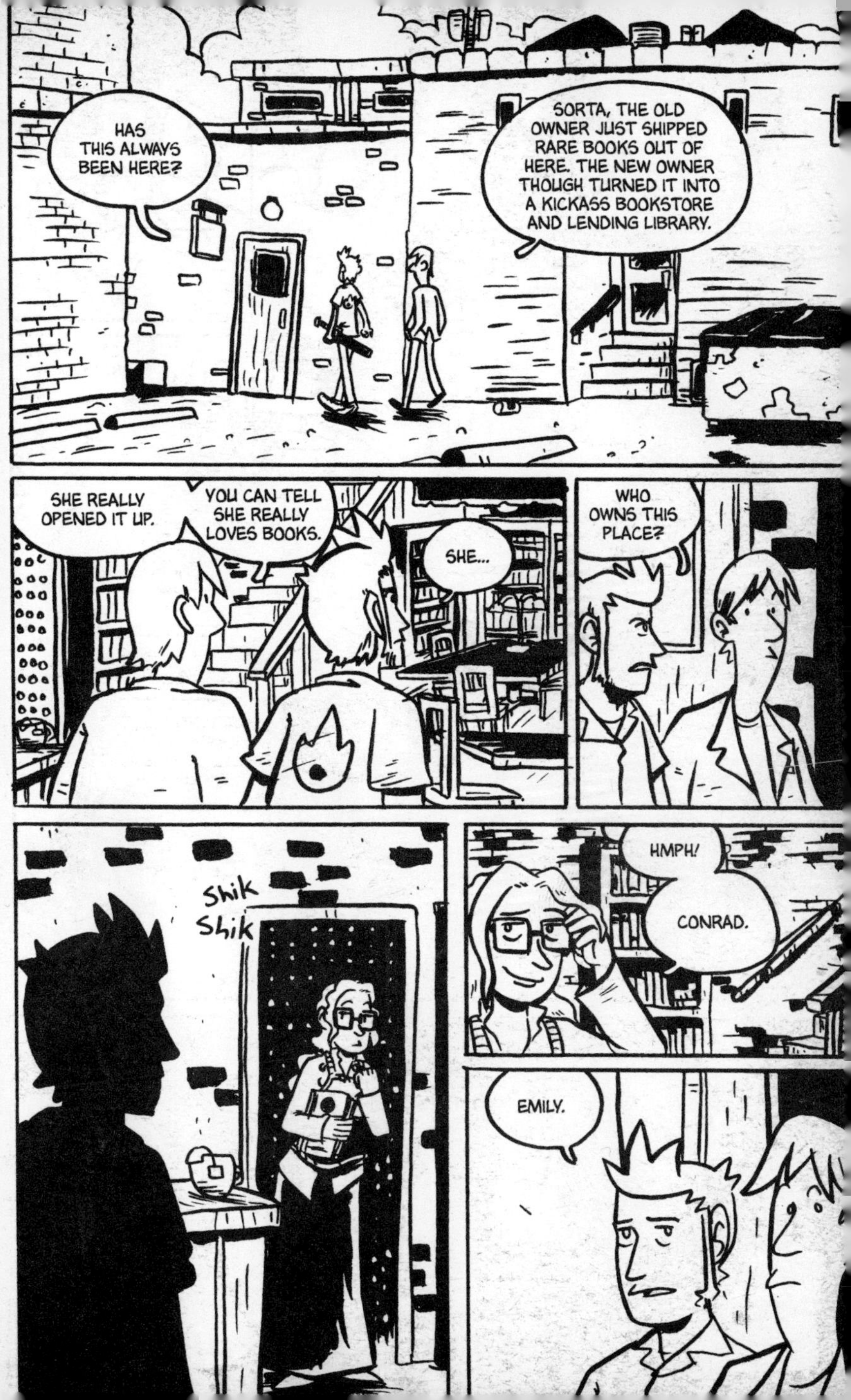
HAS THIS ALWAYS BEEN HERE?
SORTA, THE OLD OWNER JUST SHIPPED RARE BOOKS OUT OF HERE. THE NEW OWNER THOUGH TURNED IT INTO A KICKASS BOOKSTORE AND LENDING LIBRARY.
SHE REALLY OPENED IT UP.
YOU CAN TELL SHE REALLY LOVES BOOKS.
SHE...
WHO OWNS THIS PLACE?
SHIK
SHIK
HMPH!
CONRAD.
EMILY.

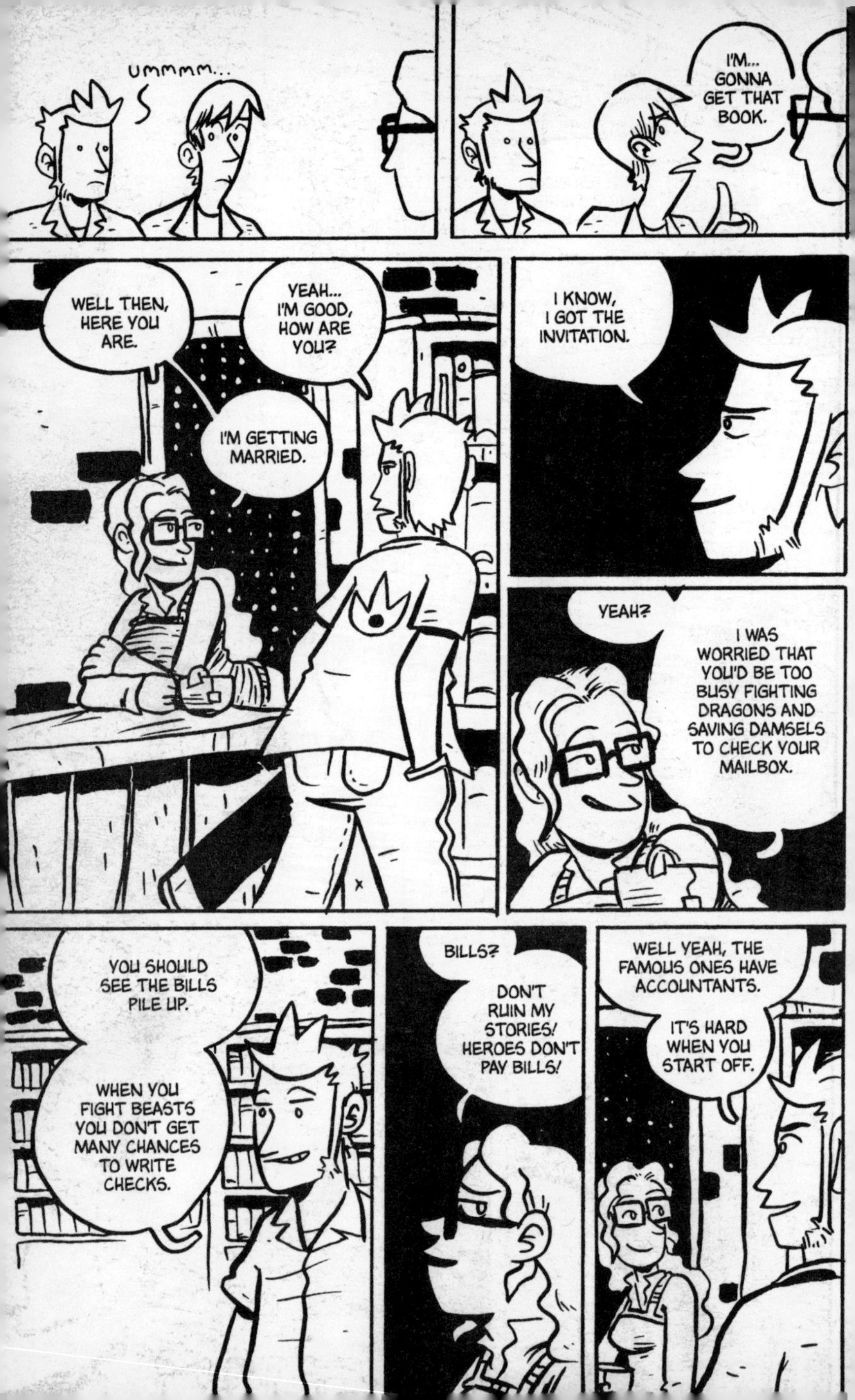
UMMMM...
I'M... GONNA GET THAT BOOK.
WELL THEN, HERE YOU ARE.
YEAH... I'M GOOD, HOW ARE YOU?
I'M GETTING MARRIED.
I KNOW, I GOT THE INVITATION.
YEAH?
I WAS WORRIED THAT YOU'D BE TOO BUSY FIGHTING DRAGONS AND SAVING DAMSELS TO CHECK YOUR MAILBOX.
YOU SHOULD SEE THE BILLS PILE UP.
WHEN YOU FIGHT BEASTS YOU DON'T GET MANY CHANCES TO WRITE CHECKS.
BILLS?
DON'T RUIN MY STORIES! HEROES DON'T PAY BILLS!
WELL YEAH, THE FAMOUS ONES HAVE ACCOUNTANTS.
IT'S HARD WHEN YOU START OFF.

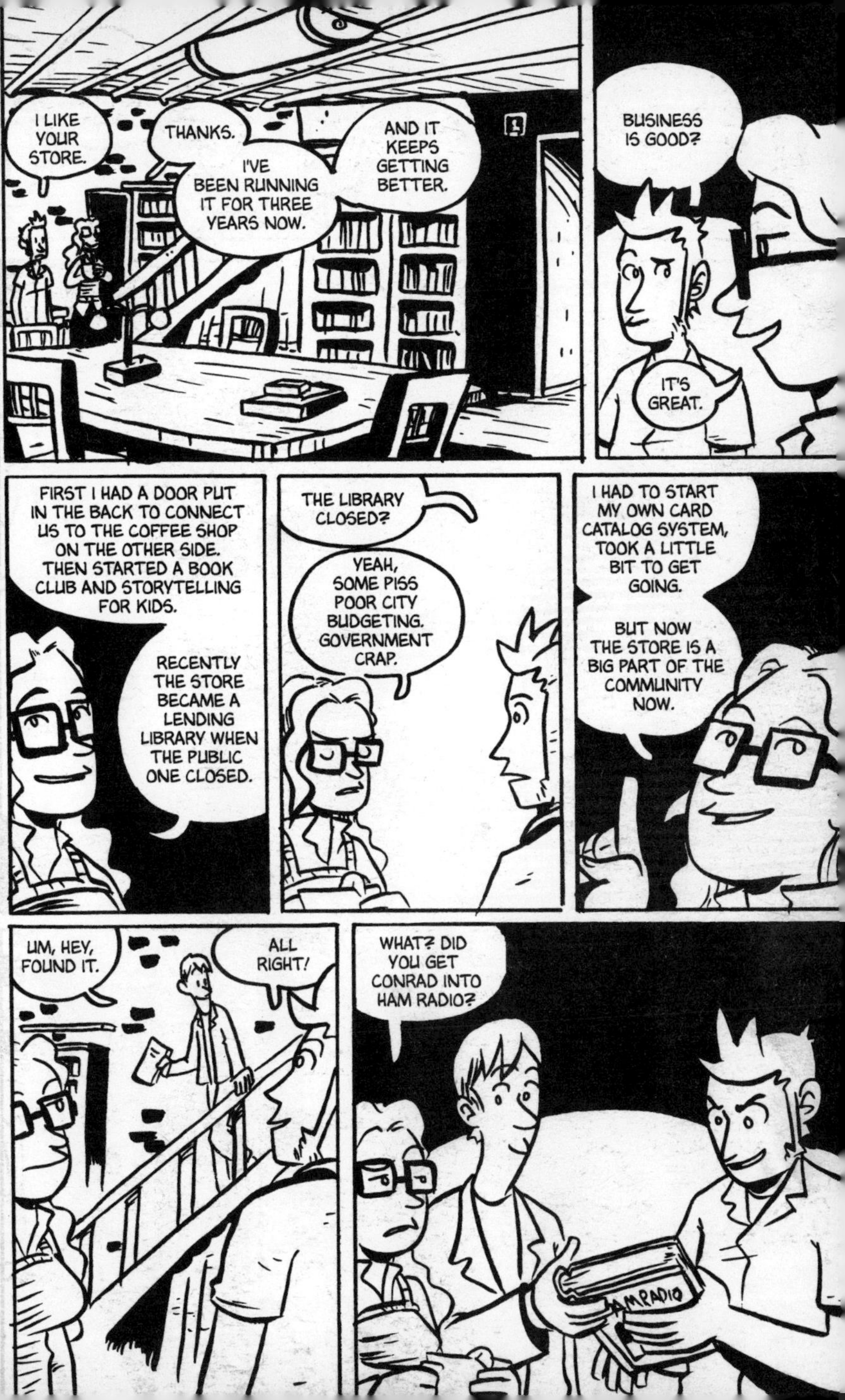
I LIKE YOUR STORE.
THANKS.
I'VE BEEN RUNNING IT FOR THREE YEARS NOW.
AND IT KEEPS GETTING BETTER.
BUSINESS IS GOOD?
IT'S GREAT.
FIRST I HAD A DOOR PUT IN THE BACK TO CONNECT US TO THE COFFEE SHOP ON THE OTHER SIDE. THEN STARTED A BOOK CLUB AND STORYTELLING FOR KIDS.
RECENTLY THE STORE BECAME A LENDING LIBRARY WHEN THE PUBLIC ONE CLOSED.
THE LIBRARY CLOSED?
YEAH, SOME PISS POOR CITY BUDGETING. GOVERNMENT CRAP.
I HAD TO START MY OWN CARD CATALOG SYSTEM, TOOK A LITTLE BIT TO GET GOING.
BUT NOW THE STORE IS A BIG PART OF THE COMMUNITY NOW.
UM, HEY, FOUND IT.
ALL RIGHT!
WHAT? DID YOU GET CONRAD INTO HAM RADIO?

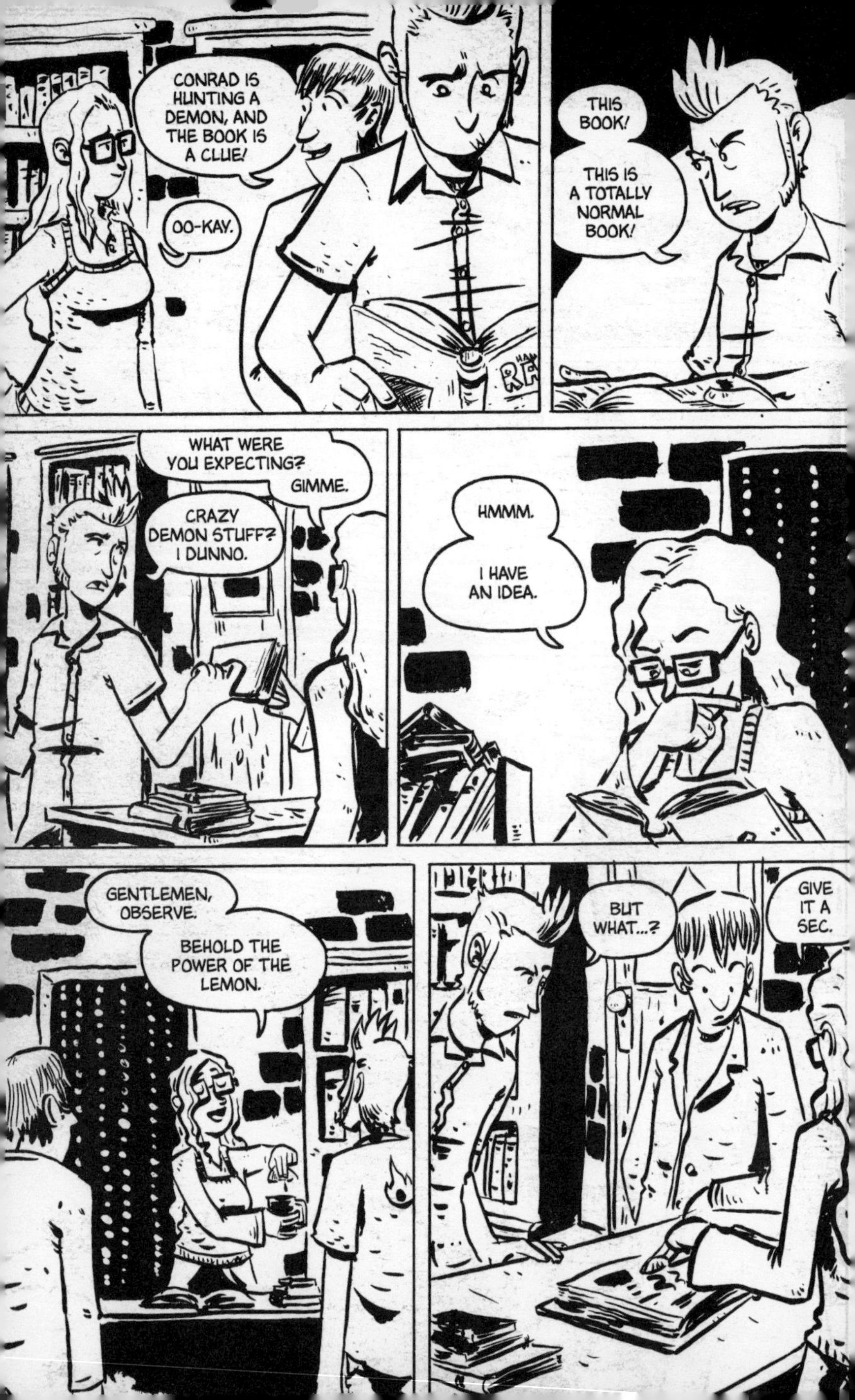
CONRAD IS HUNTING A DEMON, AND THE BOOK IS A CLUE!
OO-KAY.
THIS BOOK!
THIS IS A TOTALLY NORMAL BOOK!
WHAT WERE YOU EXPECTING?
CRAZY DEMON STUFF? I DUNNO.
GIMME.
HMMM.
I HAVE AN IDEA.
GENTLEMEN, OBSERVE.
BEHOLD THE POWER OF THE LEMON.
BUT WHAT...?
GIVE IT A SEC.

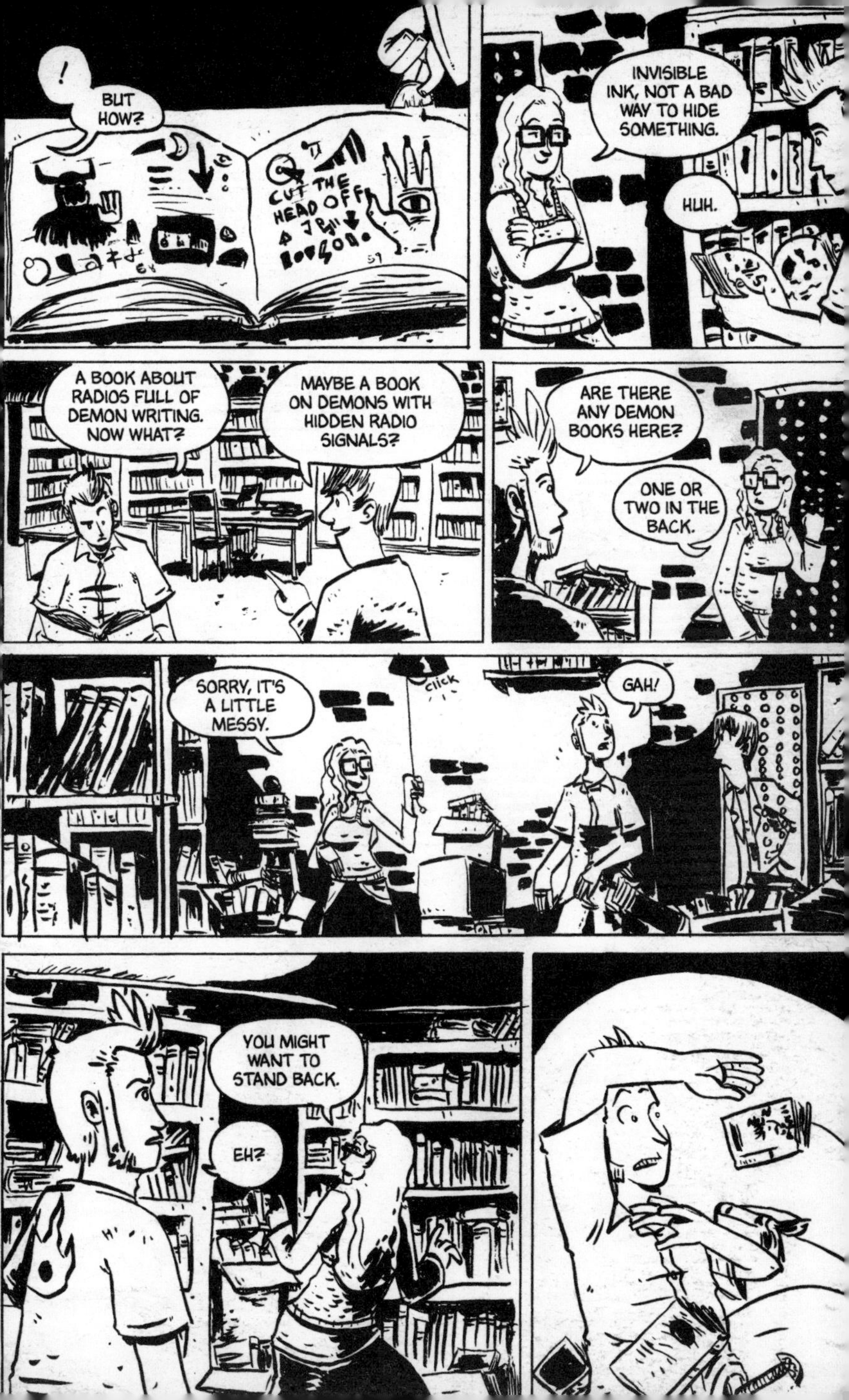
!
BUT HOW?
CUT THE HEAD OFF
INVISIBLE INK, NOT A BAD WAY TO HIDE SOMETHING.
HUH.
A BOOK ABOUT RADIOS FULL OF DEMON WRITING. NOW WHAT?
MAYBE A BOOK ON DEMONS WITH HIDDEN RADIO SIGNALS?
ARE THERE ANY DEMON BOOKS HERE?
ONE OR TWO IN THE BACK.
SORRY, IT'S A LITTLE MESSY.
click
GAH!
YOU MIGHT WANT TO STAND BACK.
EH?

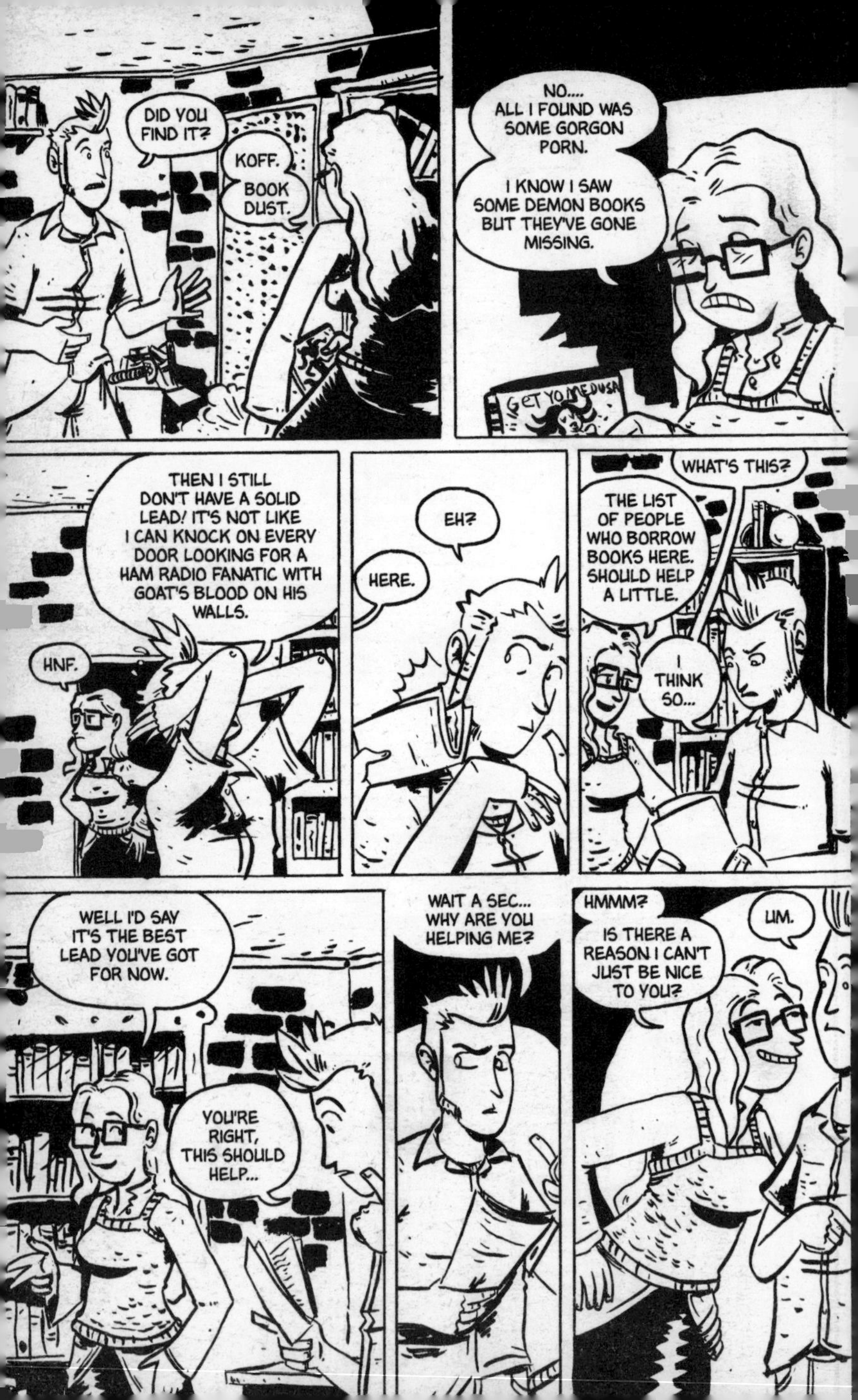
DID YOU FIND IT?
KOFF.
BOOK DUST.
NO.... ALL I FOUND WAS SOME GORGON PORN.
I KNOW I SAW SOME DEMON BOOKS BUT THEY'VE GONE MISSING.
GET YO MEDUSA
THEN I STILL DON'T HAVE A SOLID LEAD! IT'S NOT LIKE I CAN KNOCK ON EVERY DOOR LOOKING FOR A HAM RADIO FANATIC WITH GOAT'S BLOOD ON HIS WALLS.
HNF.
HERE.
EH?
WHAT'S THIS?
THE LIST OF PEOPLE WHO BORROW BOOKS HERE. SHOULD HELP A LITTLE.
I THINK SO...
WELL I'D SAY IT'S THE BEST LEAD YOU'VE GOT FOR NOW.
YOU'RE RIGHT, THIS SHOULD HELP...
WAIT A SEC... WHY ARE YOU HELPING ME?
HMMM?
IS THERE A REASON I CAN'T JUST BE NICE TO YOU?
UM.

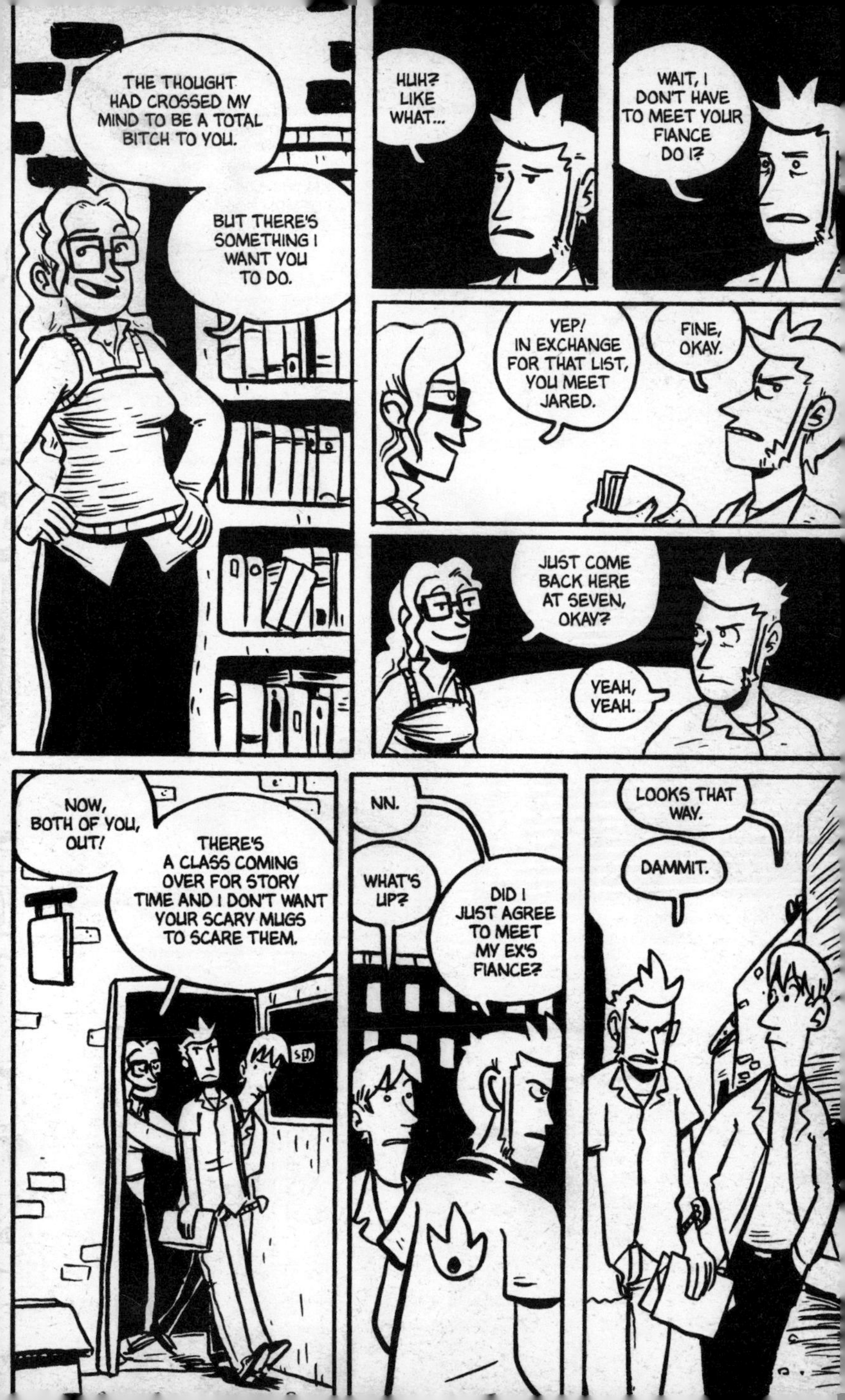
THE THOUGHT HAD CROSSED MY MIND TO BE A TOTAL BITCH TO YOU.
BUT THERE'S SOMETHING I WANT YOU TO DO.
HUH? LIKE WHAT...
WAIT, I DON'T HAVE TO MEET YOUR FIANCE DO I?
YEP! IN EXCHANGE FOR THAT LIST, YOU MEET JARED.
FINE, OKAY.
JUST COME BACK HERE AT SEVEN, OKAY?
YEAH, YEAH.
NOW, BOTH OF YOU, OUT!
THERE'S A CLASS COMING OVER FOR STORY TIME AND I DON'T WANT YOUR SCARY MUGS TO SCARE THEM.
NN.
WHAT'S UP?
DID I JUST AGREE TO MEET MY EX'S FIANCE?
LOOKS THAT WAY.
DAMMIT.

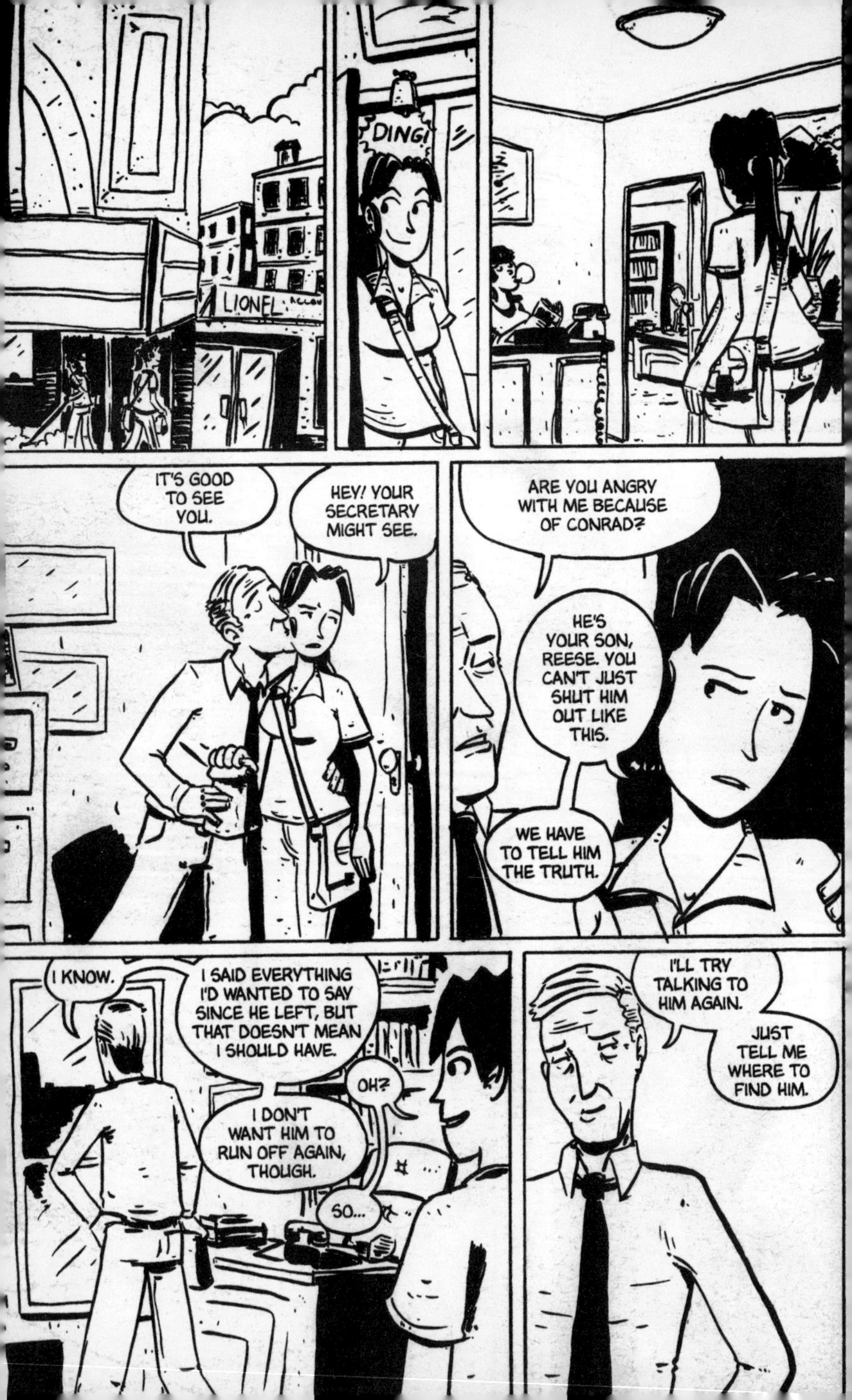
DING!
LIONEL
IT'S GOOD TO SEE YOU.
HEY! YOUR SECRETARY MIGHT SEE.
ARE YOU ANGRY WITH ME BECAUSE OF CONRAD?
HE'S YOUR SON, REESE. YOU CAN'T JUST SHUT HIM OUT LIKE THIS.
WE HAVE TO TELL HIM THE TRUTH.
I KNOW.
I SAID EVERYTHING I'D WANTED TO SAY SINCE HE LEFT, BUT THAT DOESN'T MEAN I SHOULD HAVE.
I DON'T WANT HIM TO RUN OFF AGAIN, THOUGH.
OH?
SO...
I'LL TRY TALKING TO HIM AGAIN.
JUST TELL ME WHERE TO FIND HIM.

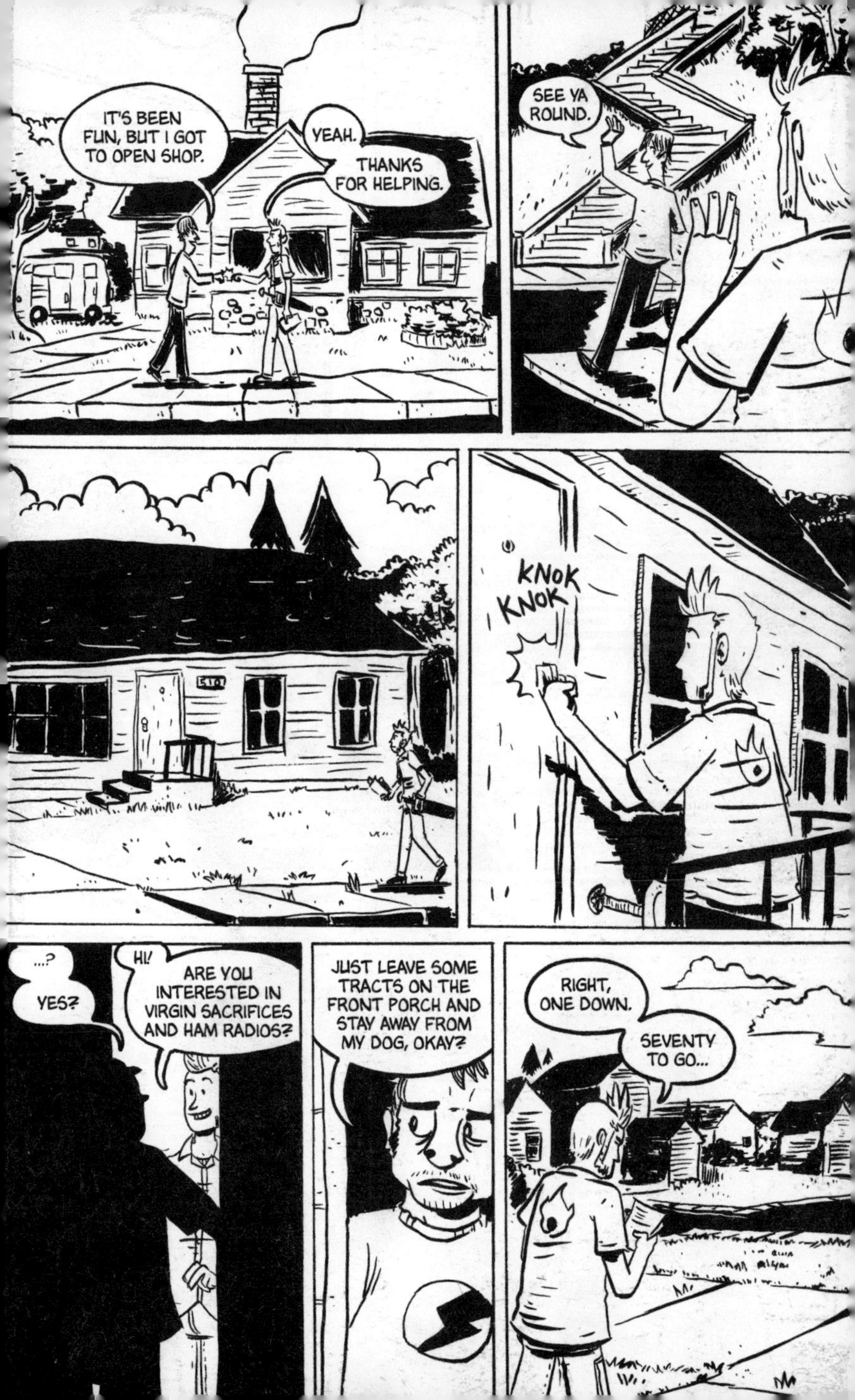
IT'S BEEN FUN, BUT I GOT TO OPEN SHOP.
YEAH.
THANKS FOR HELPING.
SEE YA ROUND.
KNOK KNOK
...?
YES?
HI!
ARE YOU INTERESTED IN VIRGIN SACRIFICES AND HAM RADIOS?
JUST LEAVE SOME TRACTS ON THE FRONT PORCH AND STAY AWAY FROM MY DOG, OKAY?
RIGHT, ONE DOWN.
SEVENTY TO GO...

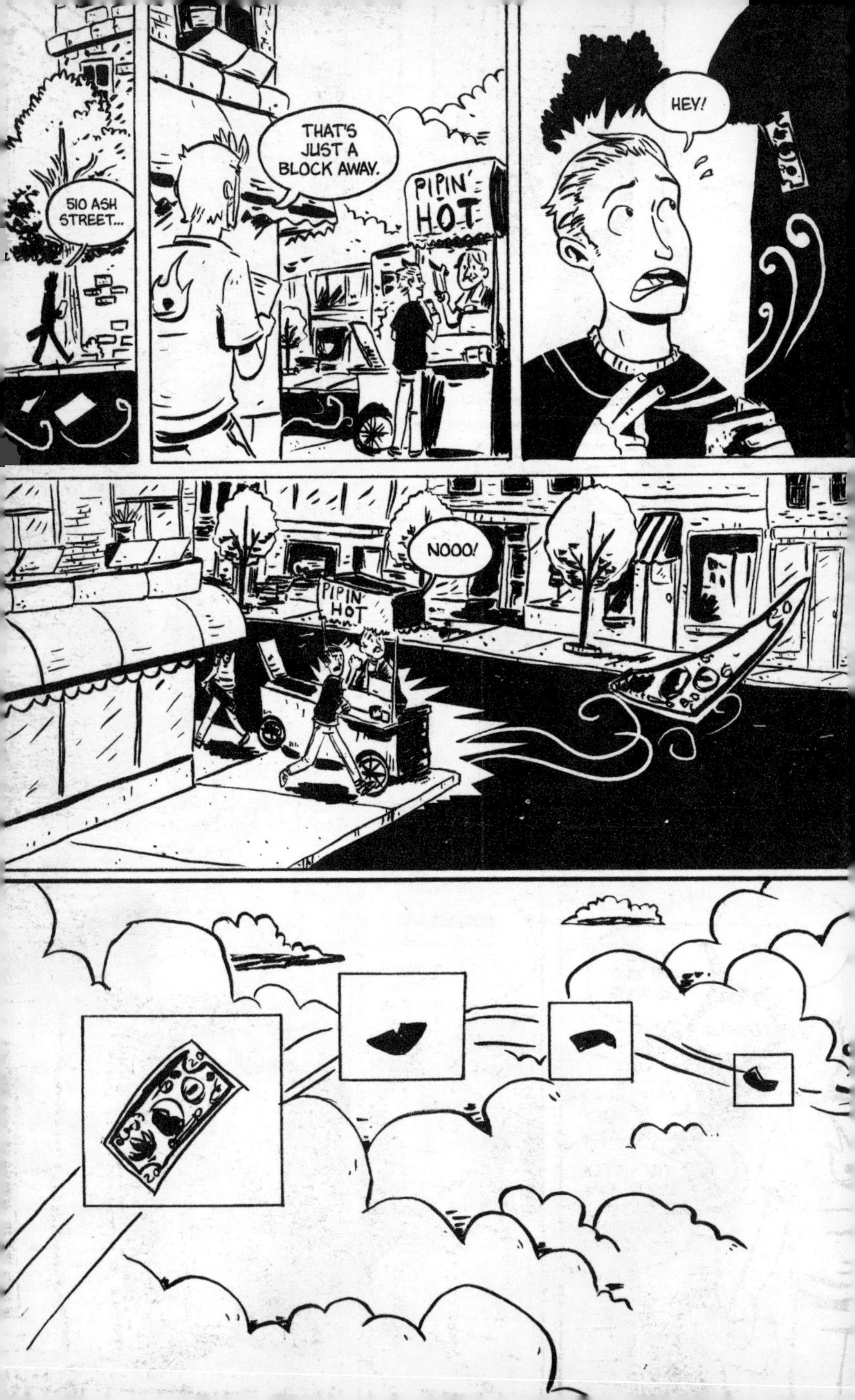
510 ASH STREET...
THAT'S JUST A BLOCK AWAY.
PIPIN' HOT
HEY!
PIPIN' HOT
NOOO!

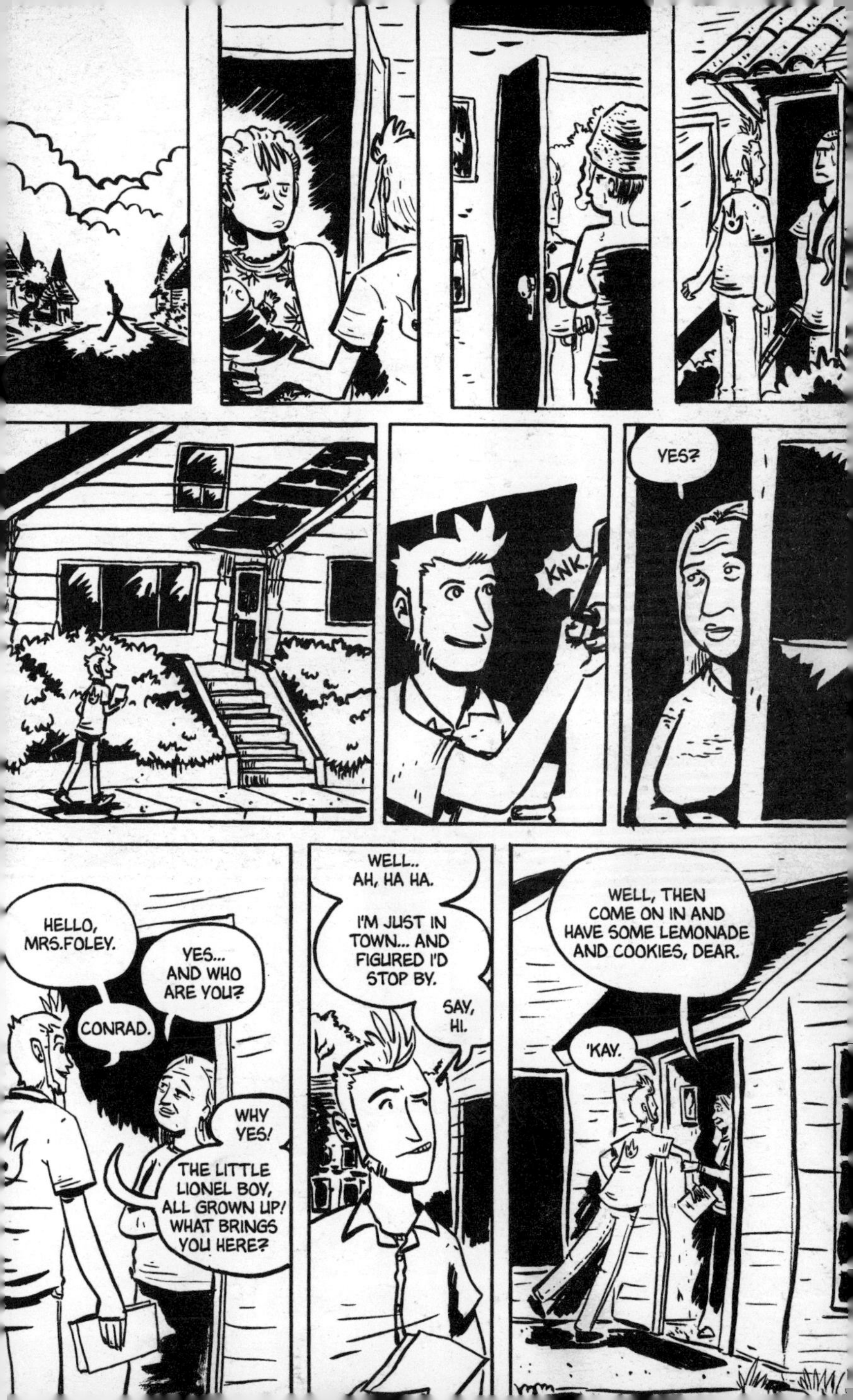
YES?
KNK.
HELLO, MRS.FOLEY.
YES... AND WHO ARE YOU?
CONRAD.
WHY YES!
THE LITTLE LIONEL BOY, ALL GROWN UP! WHAT BRINGS YOU HERE?
WELL.. AH, HA HA.
I'M JUST IN TOWN... AND FIGURED I'D STOP BY.
SAY, HI.
WELL, THEN COME ON IN AND HAVE SOME LEMONADE AND COOKIES, DEAR.
'KAY.

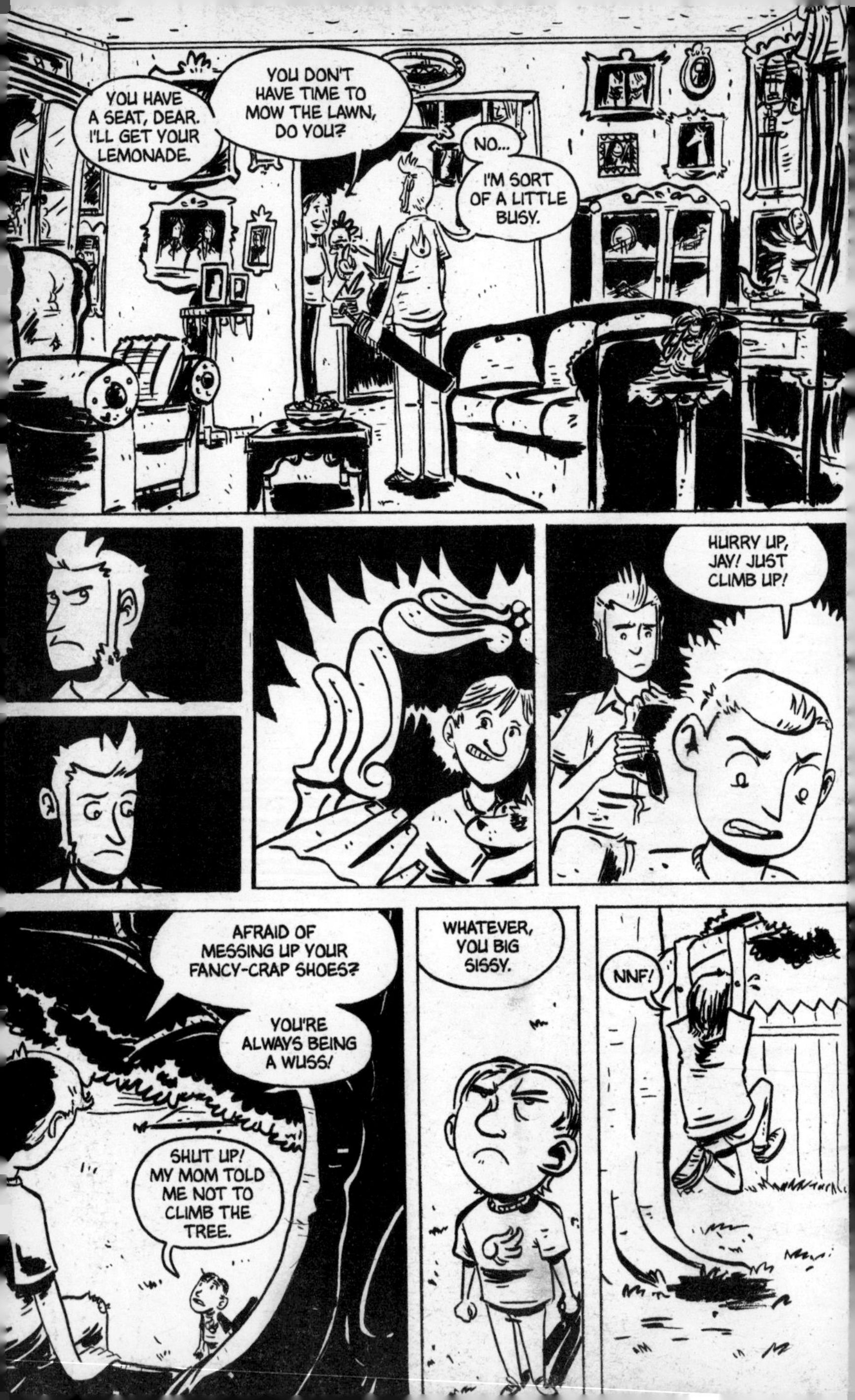
YOU HAVE A SEAT, DEAR. I'LL GET YOUR LEMONADE.
YOU DON'T HAVE TIME TO MOW THE LAWN, DO YOU?
NO...
I'M SORT OF A LITTLE BUSY.
HURRY UP, JAY! JUST CLIMB UP!
AFRAID OF MESSING UP YOUR FANCY-CRAP SHOES?
YOU'RE ALWAYS BEING A WUSS!
SHUT UP! MY MOM TOLD ME NOT TO CLIMB THE TREE.
WHATEVER, YOU BIG SISSY.
NNF!

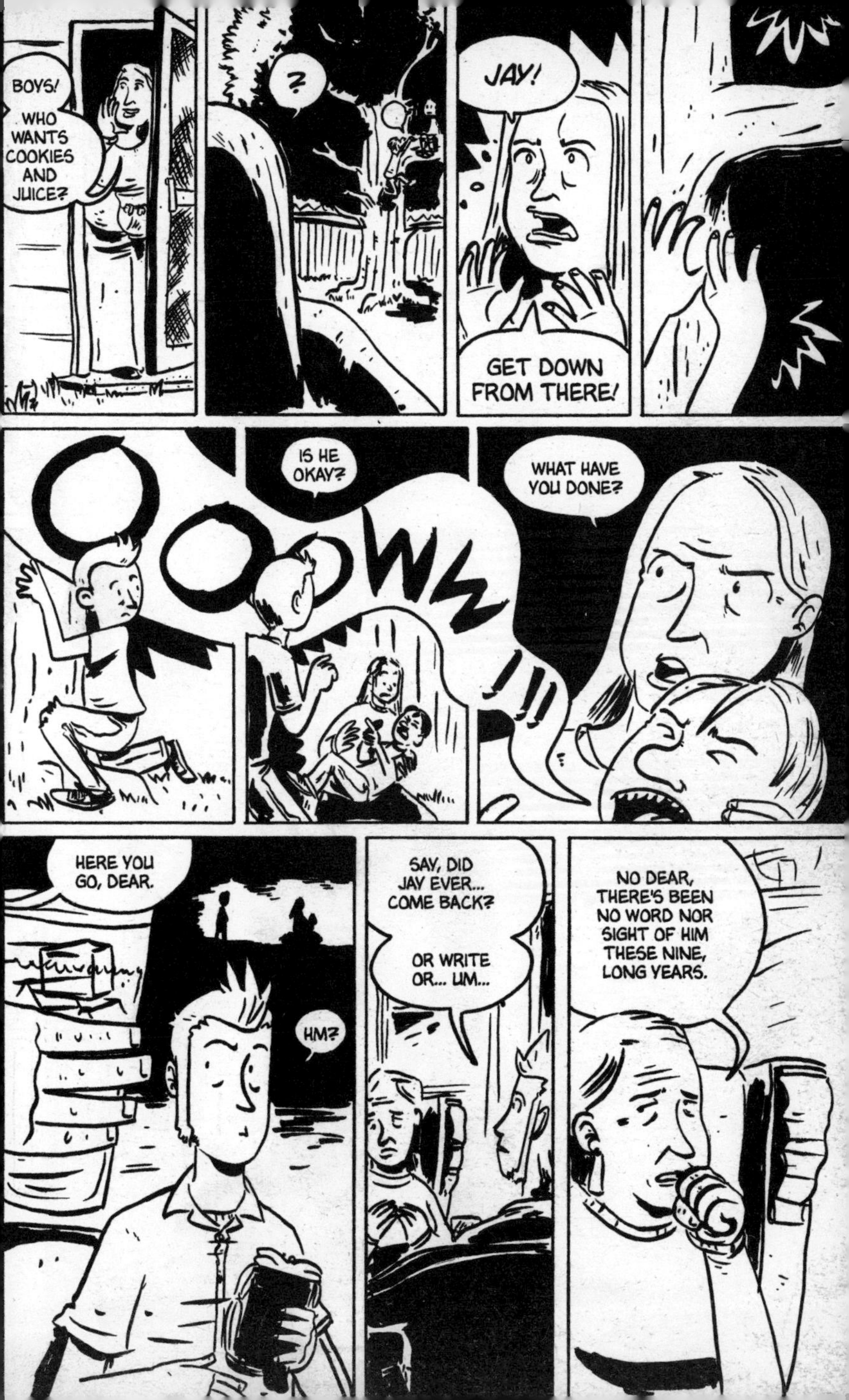
BOYS!
WHO WANTS COOKIES AND JUICE?
?
JAY!
GET DOWN FROM THERE!
OOOWW!!!
IS HE OKAY?
WHAT HAVE YOU DONE?
HERE YOU GO, DEAR.
HM?
SAY, DID JAY EVER... COME BACK?
OR WRITE OR... UM...
NO DEAR, THERE'S BEEN NO WORD NOR SIGHT OF HIM THESE NINE, LONG YEARS.

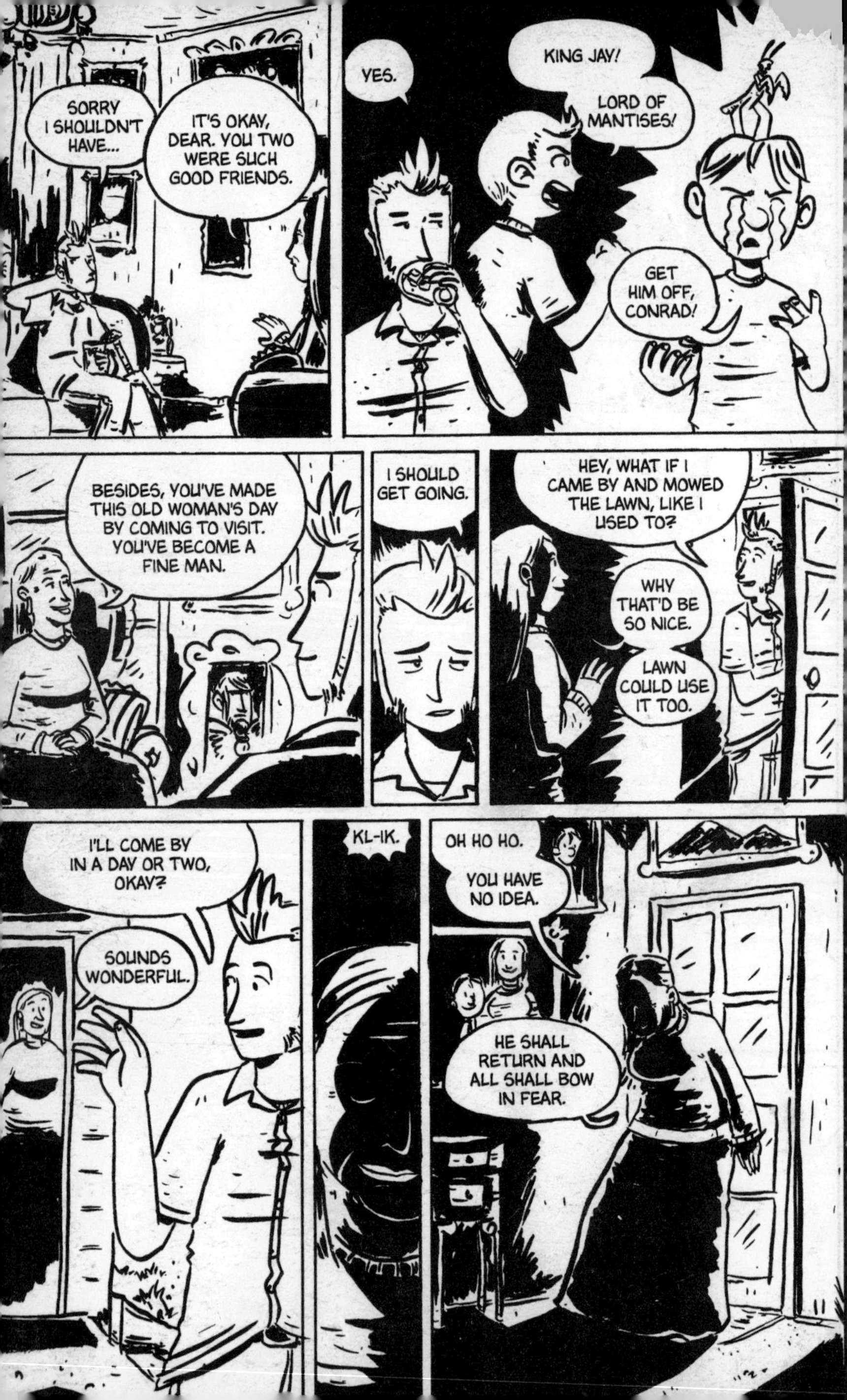
SORRY I SHOULDN'T HAVE...
IT'S OKAY, DEAR. YOU TWO WERE SUCH GOOD FRIENDS.
YES.
KING JAY!
LORD OF MANTISES!
GET HIM OFF, CONRAD!
BESIDES, YOU'VE MADE THIS OLD WOMAN'S DAY BY COMING TO VISIT. YOU'VE BECOME A FINE MAN.
I SHOULD GET GOING.
HEY, WHAT IF I CAME BY AND MOWED THE LAWN, LIKE I USED TO?
WHY THAT'D BE SO NICE.
LAWN COULD USE IT TOO.
I'LL COME BY IN A DAY OR TWO, OKAY?
SOUNDS WONDERFUL.
KL-IK.
OH HO HO.
YOU HAVE NO IDEA.
HE SHALL RETURN AND ALL SHALL BOW IN FEAR.

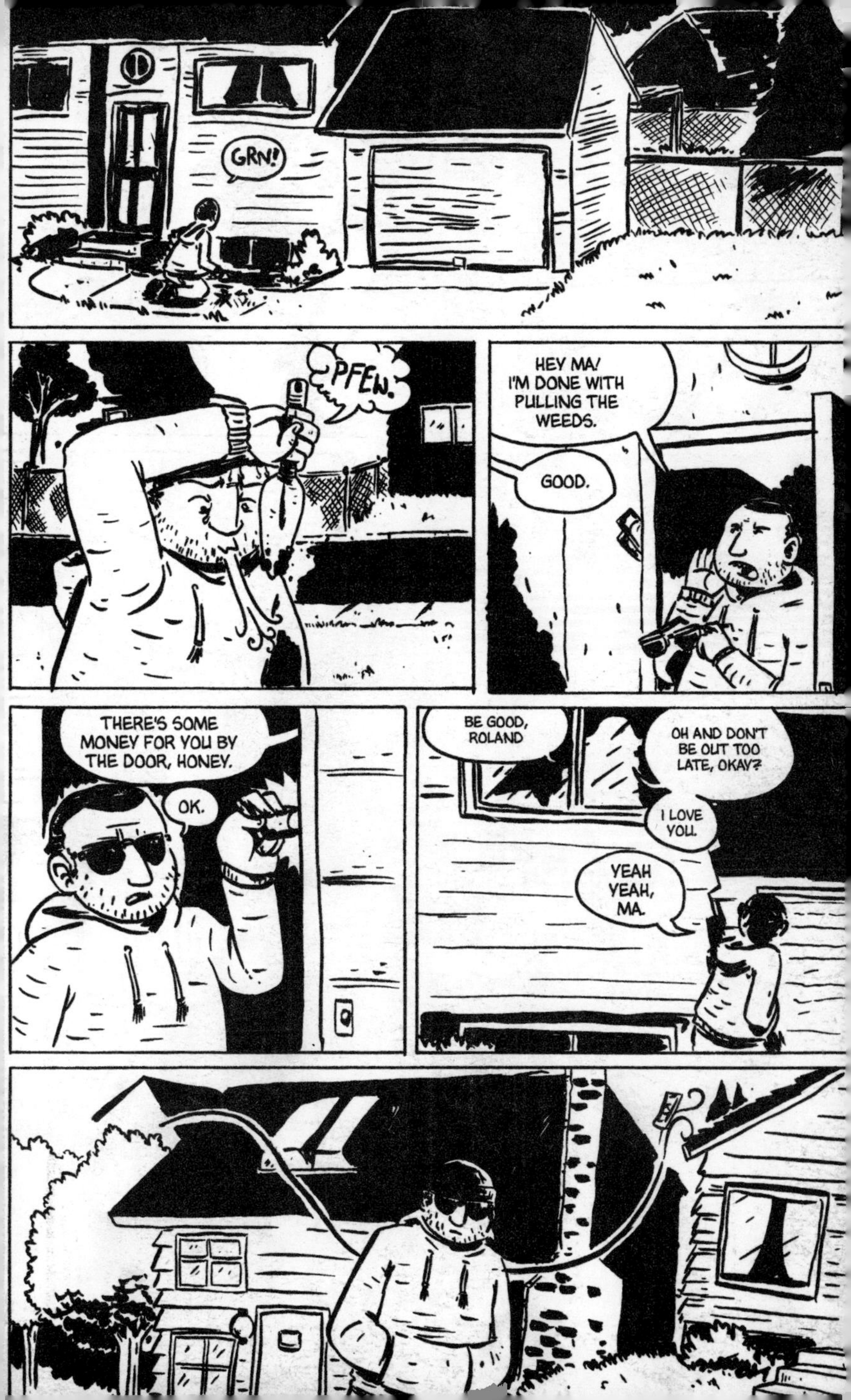
GRN!
PFEW.
HEY MA! I'M DONE WITH PULLING THE WEEDS.
GOOD.
THERE'S SOME MONEY FOR YOU BY THE DOOR, HONEY.
OK.
BE GOOD, ROLAND
OH AND DON'T BE OUT TOO LATE, OKAY?
I LOVE YOU.
YEAH YEAH, MA.

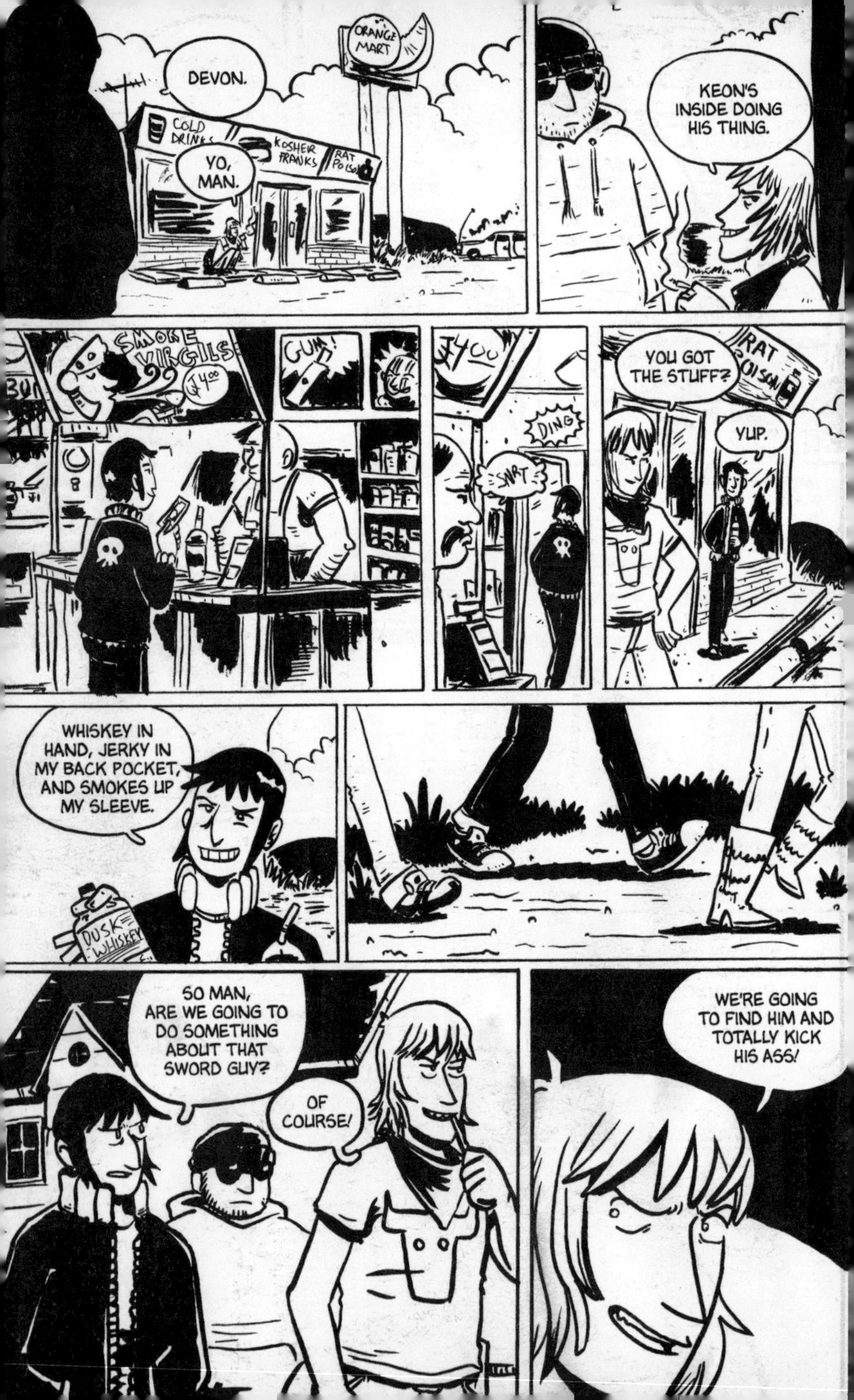
ORANGE MART
DEVON.
COLD DRINKS
KOSHEIR FRANKS
YO, MAN.
KEON'S INSIDE DOING HIS THING.
SMOKE VIRGILS
$4.00
GUM!
DING
SNRT
YOU GOT THE STUFF?
RAT POISON
YUP.
WHISKEY IN HAND, JERKY IN MY BACK POCKET, AND SMOKES UP MY SLEEVE.
DUSK WHISKEY
SO MAN, ARE WE GOING TO DO SOMETHING ABOUT THAT SWORD GUY?
OF COURSE!
WE'RE GOING TO FIND HIM AND TOTALLY KICK HIS ASS!

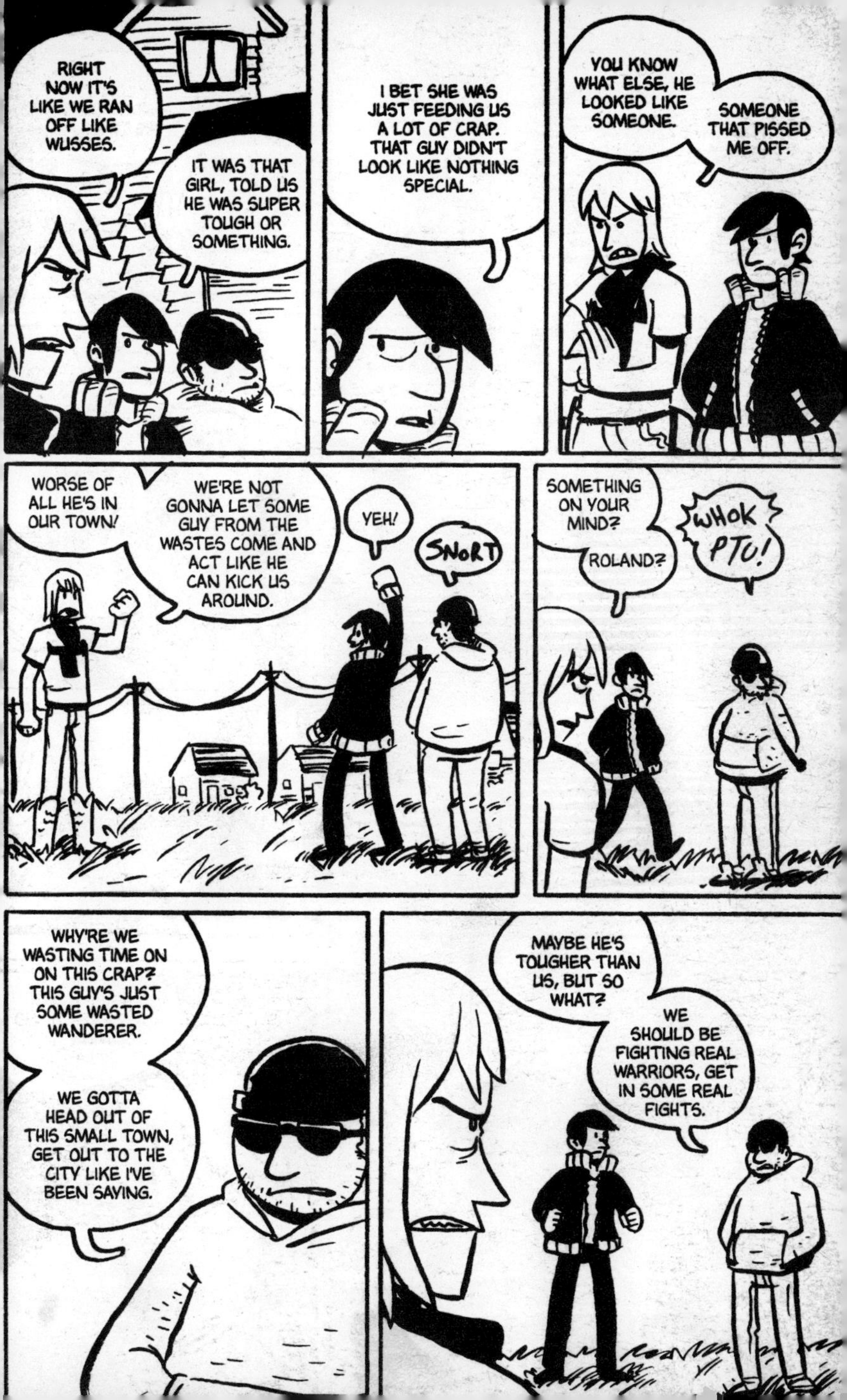
RIGHT NOW IT'S LIKE WE RAN OFF LIKE WUSSES.
IT WAS THAT GIRL, TOLD US HE WAS SUPER TOUGH OR SOMETHING.
I BET SHE WAS JUST FEEDING US A LOT OF CRAP. THAT GUY DIDN'T LOOK LIKE NOTHING SPECIAL.
YOU KNOW WHAT ELSE, HE LOOKED LIKE SOMEONE.
SOMEONE THAT PISSED ME OFF.
WORSE OF ALL HE'S IN OUR TOWN!
WE'RE NOT GONNA LET SOME GUY FROM THE WASTES COME AND ACT LIKE HE CAN KICK US AROUND.
YEH!
SNORT
SOMETHING ON YOUR MIND?
ROLAND?
WHOK PTU!
WHY'RE WE WASTING TIME ON ON THIS CRAP? THIS GUY'S JUST SOME WASTED WANDERER.
WE GOTTA HEAD OUT OF THIS SMALL TOWN, GET OUT TO THE CITY LIKE I'VE BEEN SAYING.
MAYBE HE'S TOUGHER THAN US, BUT SO WHAT?
WE SHOULD BE FIGHTING REAL WARRIORS, GET IN SOME REAL FIGHTS.

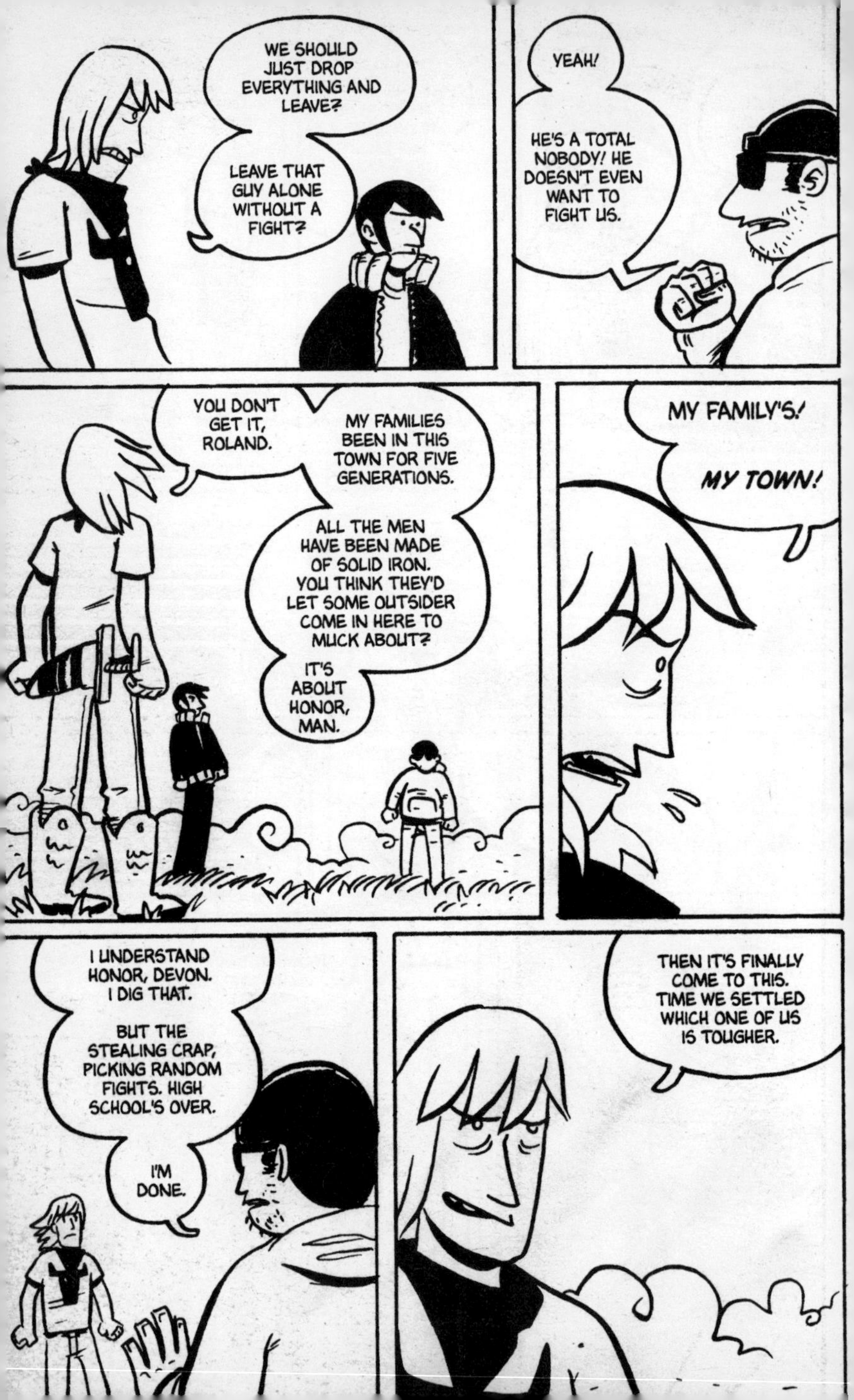
WE SHOULD JUST DROP EVERYTHING AND LEAVE?
LEAVE THAT GUY ALONE WITHOUT A FIGHT?
YEAH!
HE'S A TOTAL NOBODY! HE DOESN'T EVEN WANT TO FIGHT US.
YOU DON'T GET IT, ROLAND.
MY FAMILIES BEEN IN THIS TOWN FOR FIVE GENERATIONS.
ALL THE MEN HAVE BEEN MADE OF SOLID IRON. YOU THINK THEY'D LET SOME OUTSIDER COME IN HERE TO MUCK ABOUT?
IT'S ABOUT HONOR, MAN.
MY FAMILY'S!
MY TOWN!
I UNDERSTAND HONOR, DEVON. I DIG THAT.
BUT THE STEALING CRAP, PICKING RANDOM FIGHTS. HIGH SCHOOL'S OVER.
I'M DONE.
THEN IT'S FINALLY COME TO THIS. TIME WE SETTLED WHICH ONE OF US IS TOUGHER.

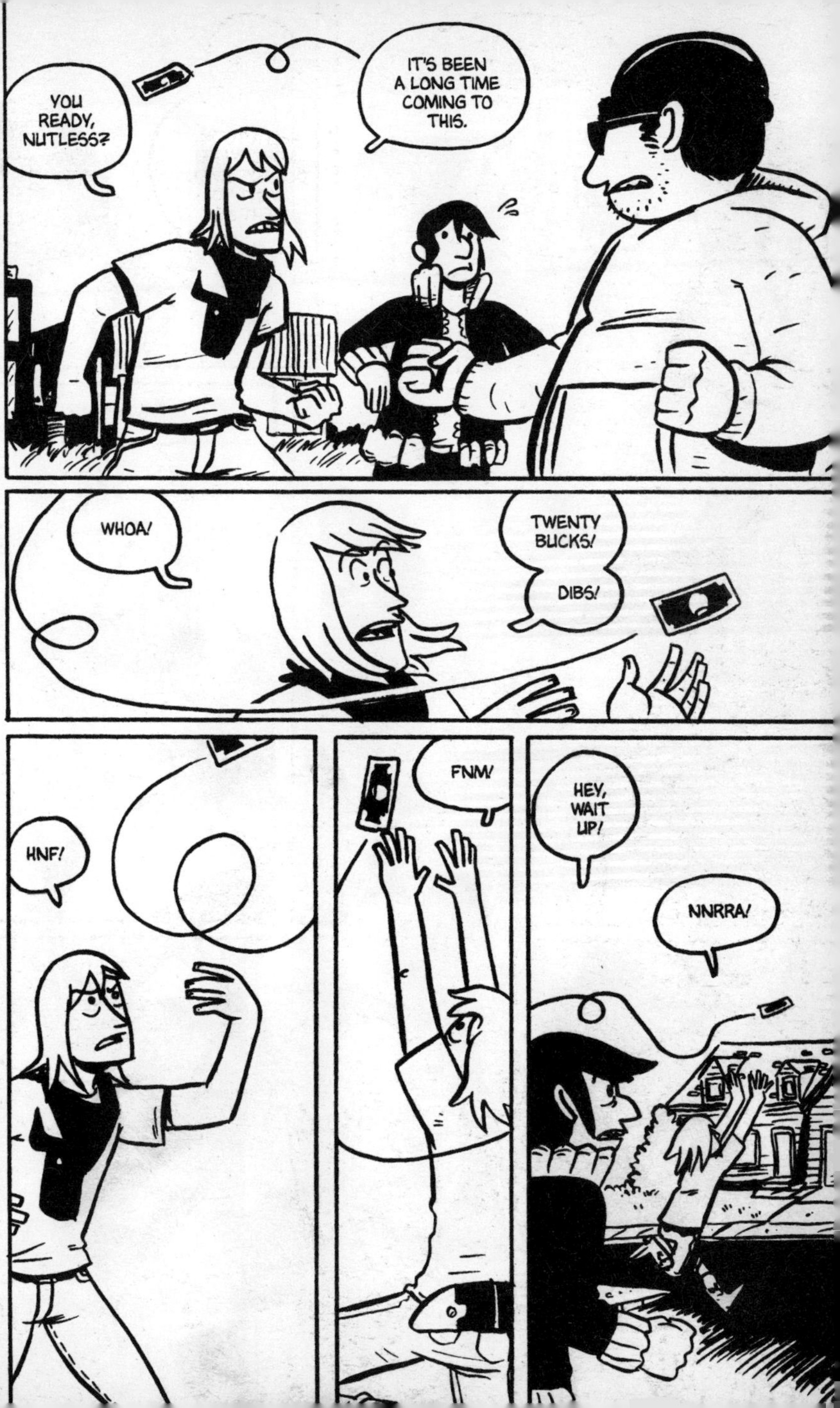
YOU READY, NUTLESS?
IT'S BEEN A LONG TIME COMING TO THIS.
WHOA!
TWENTY BUCKS!
DIBS!
HNF!
FNM!
HEY, WAIT UP!
NNRRA!

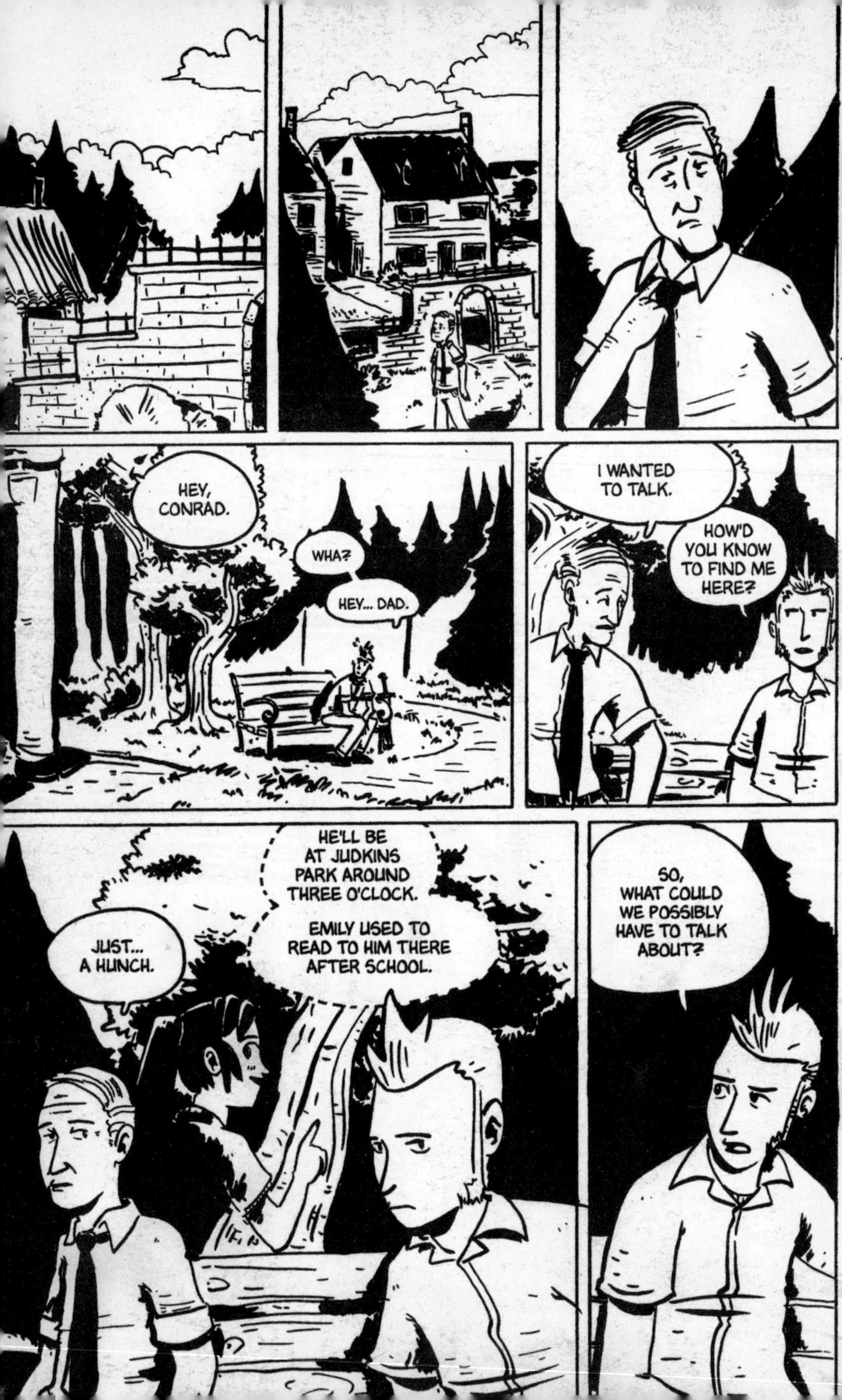
HEY,
CONRAD.
WHA?
HEY... DAD.
I WANTED
TO TALK.
HOW'D
YOU KNOW
TO FIND ME
HERE?
JUST...
A HUNCH.
HE'LL BE
AT JUDKINS
PARK AROUND
THREE O'CLOCK.
EMILY USED TO
READ TO HIM THERE
AFTER SCHOOL.
SO,
WHAT COULD
WE POSSIBLY
HAVE TO TALK
ABOUT?

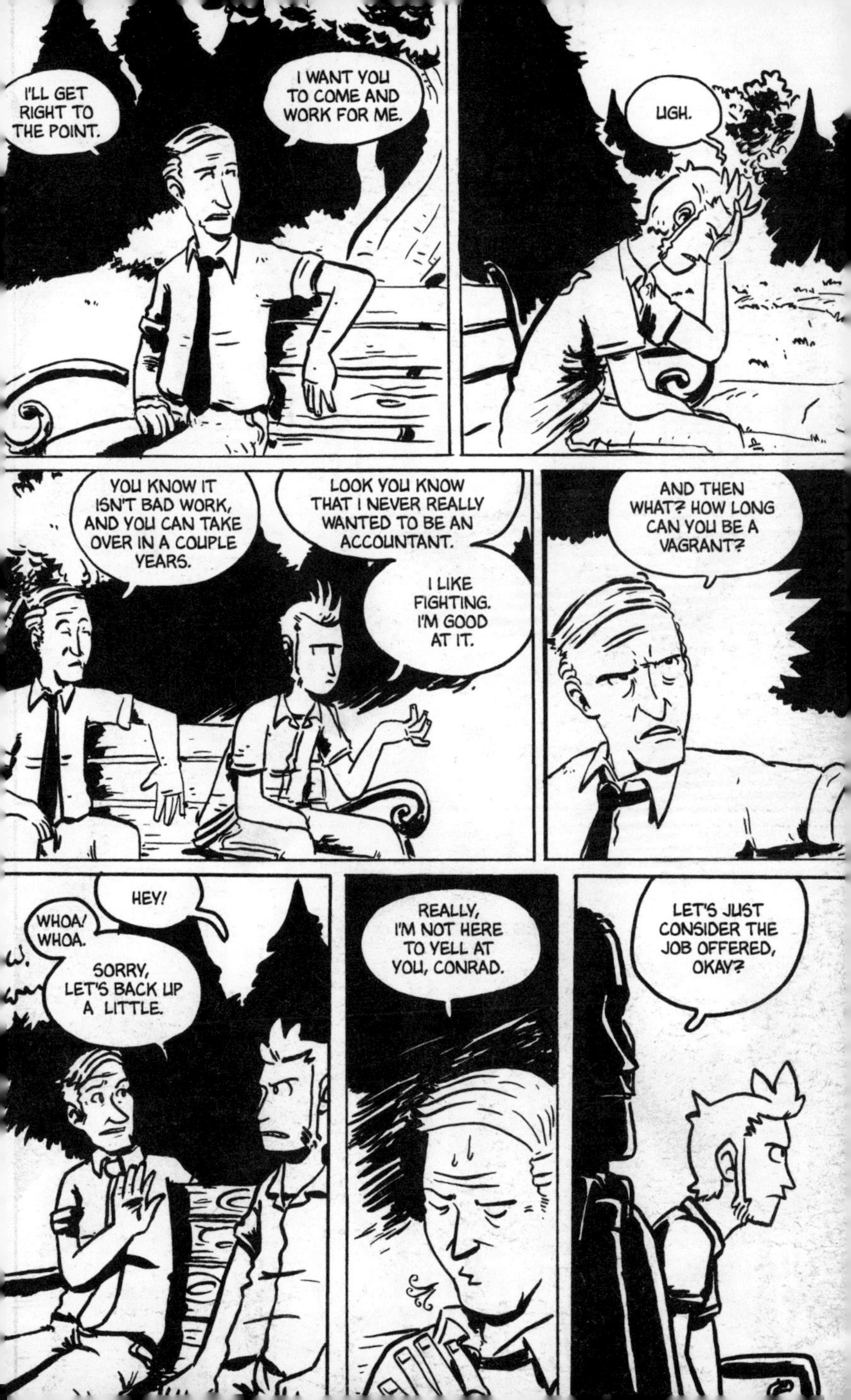
I'LL GET RIGHT TO THE POINT.
I WANT YOU TO COME AND WORK FOR ME.
UGH.
YOU KNOW IT ISN'T BAD WORK, AND YOU CAN TAKE OVER IN A COUPLE YEARS.
LOOK YOU KNOW THAT I NEVER REALLY WANTED TO BE AN ACCOUNTANT.
I LIKE FIGHTING. I'M GOOD AT IT.
AND THEN WHAT? HOW LONG CAN YOU BE A VAGRANT?
HEY!
WHOA! WHOA.
SORRY, LET'S BACK UP A LITTLE.
REALLY, I'M NOT HERE TO YELL AT YOU, CONRAD.
LET'S JUST CONSIDER THE JOB OFFERED, OKAY?

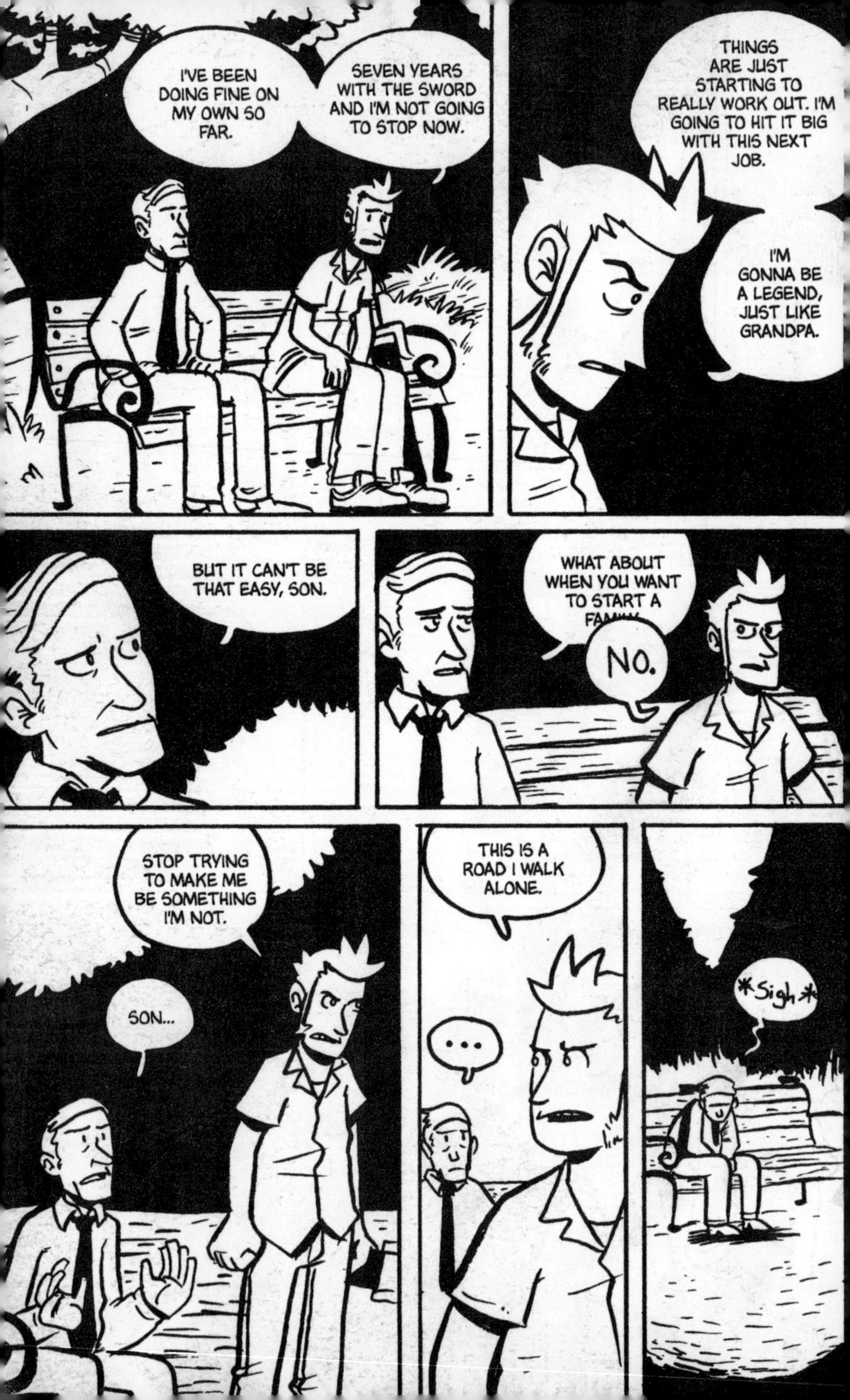
I'VE BEEN DOING FINE ON MY OWN SO FAR.
SEVEN YEARS WITH THE SWORD AND I'M NOT GOING TO STOP NOW.
THINGS ARE JUST STARTING TO REALLY WORK OUT. I'M GOING TO HIT IT BIG WITH THIS NEXT JOB.
I'M GONNA BE A LEGEND, JUST LIKE GRANDPA.
BUT IT CAN'T BE THAT EASY, SON.
WHAT ABOUT WHEN YOU WANT TO START A
NO.
STOP TRYING TO MAKE ME BE SOMETHING I'M NOT.
SON...
THIS IS A ROAD I WALK ALONE.
...
Sigh

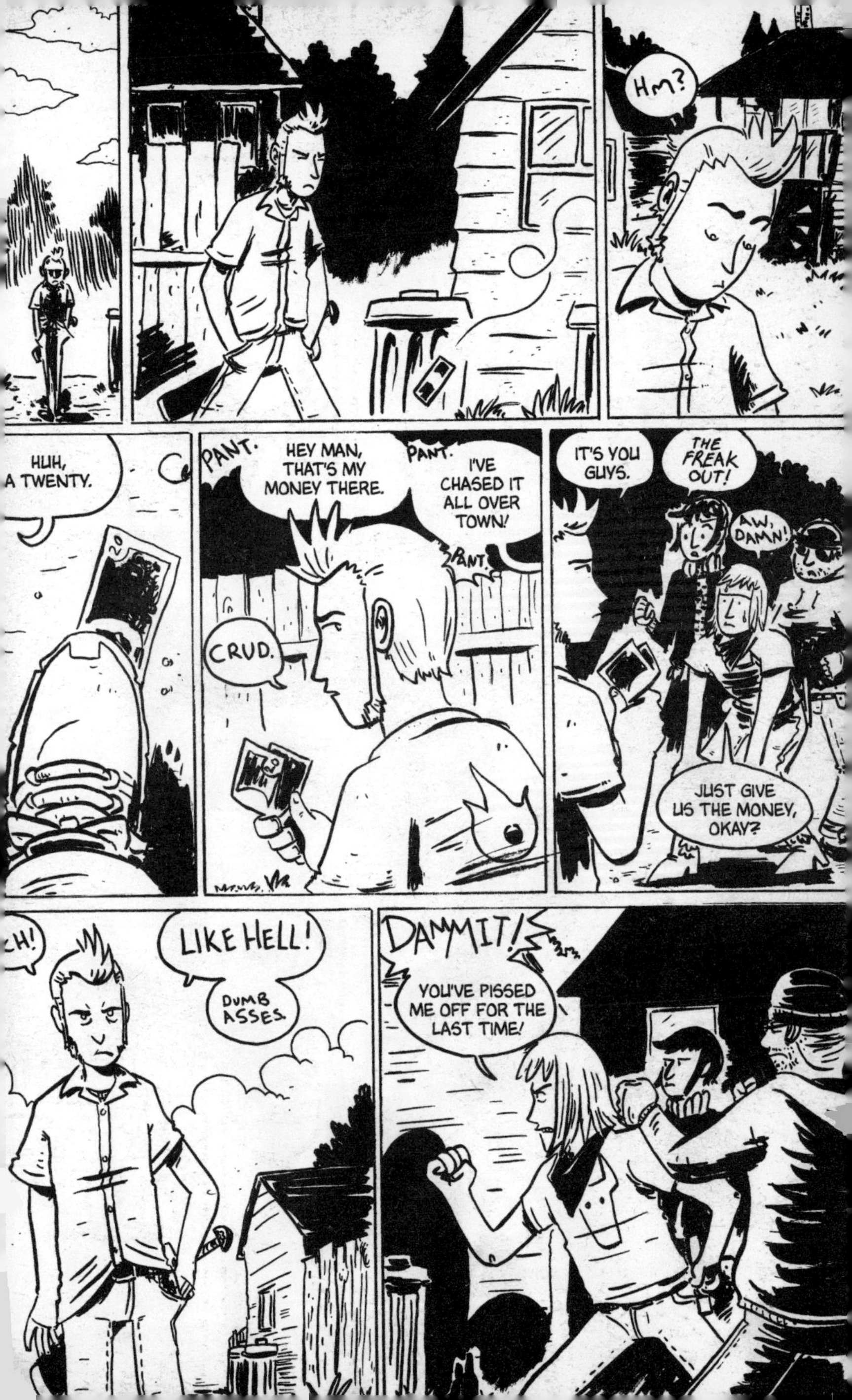
Hm?
HUH, A TWENTY.
PANT.
HEY MAN, THAT'S MY MONEY THERE.
PANT.
I'VE CHASED IT ALL OVER TOWN!
PANT.
CRUD.
IT'S YOU GUYS.
THE FREAK OUT!
AW, DAMN!
JUST GIVE US THE MONEY, OKAY?
LIKE HELL!
DUMB ASSES.
DAMMIT!
YOU'VE PISSED ME OFF FOR THE LAST TIME!

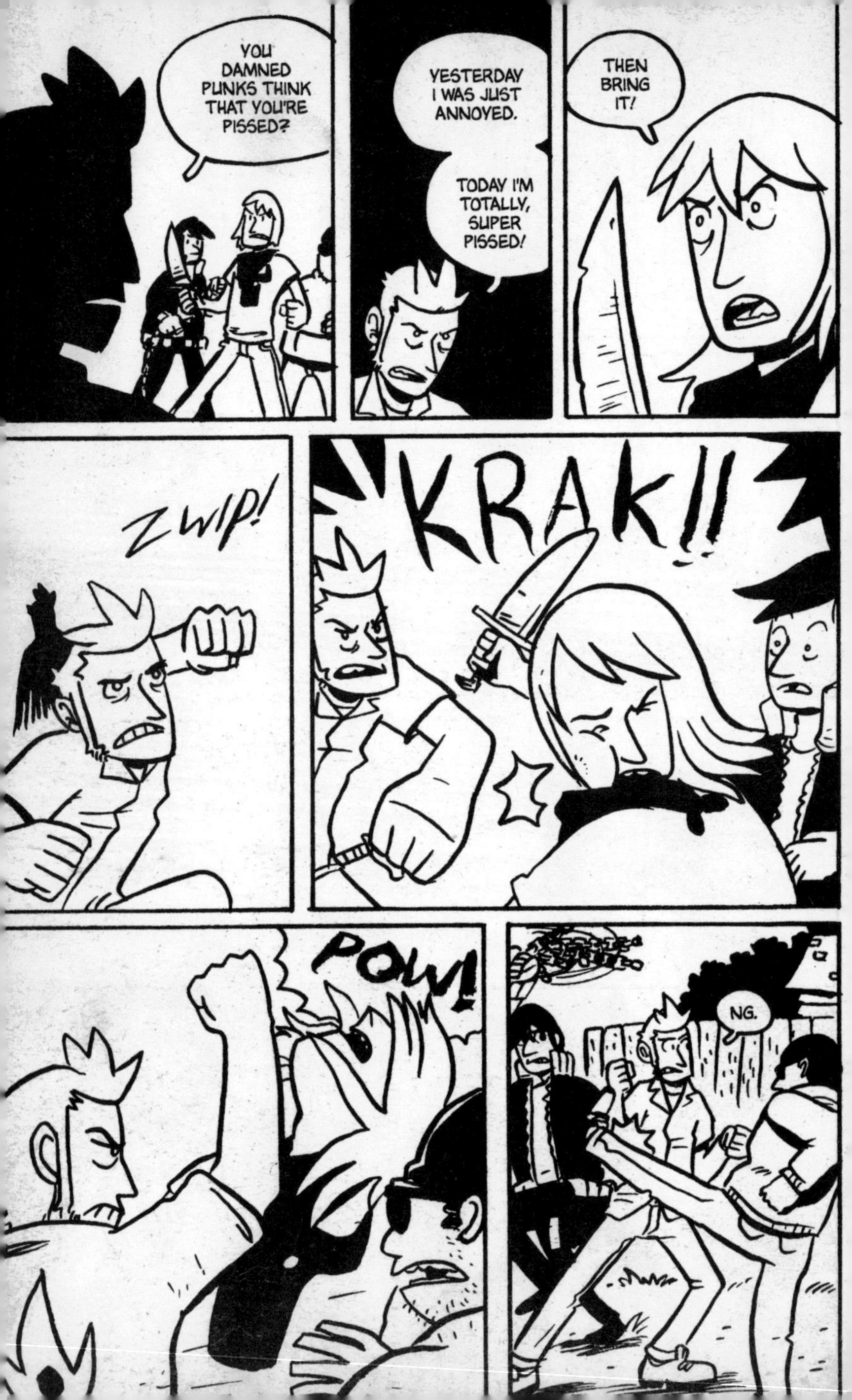
YOU DAMNED PUNKS THINK THAT YOU'RE PISSED?
YESTERDAY I WAS JUST ANNOYED.
TODAY I'M TOTALLY, SUPER PISSED!
THEN BRING IT!
ZWIP!
KRAK!!
POW!
NG.

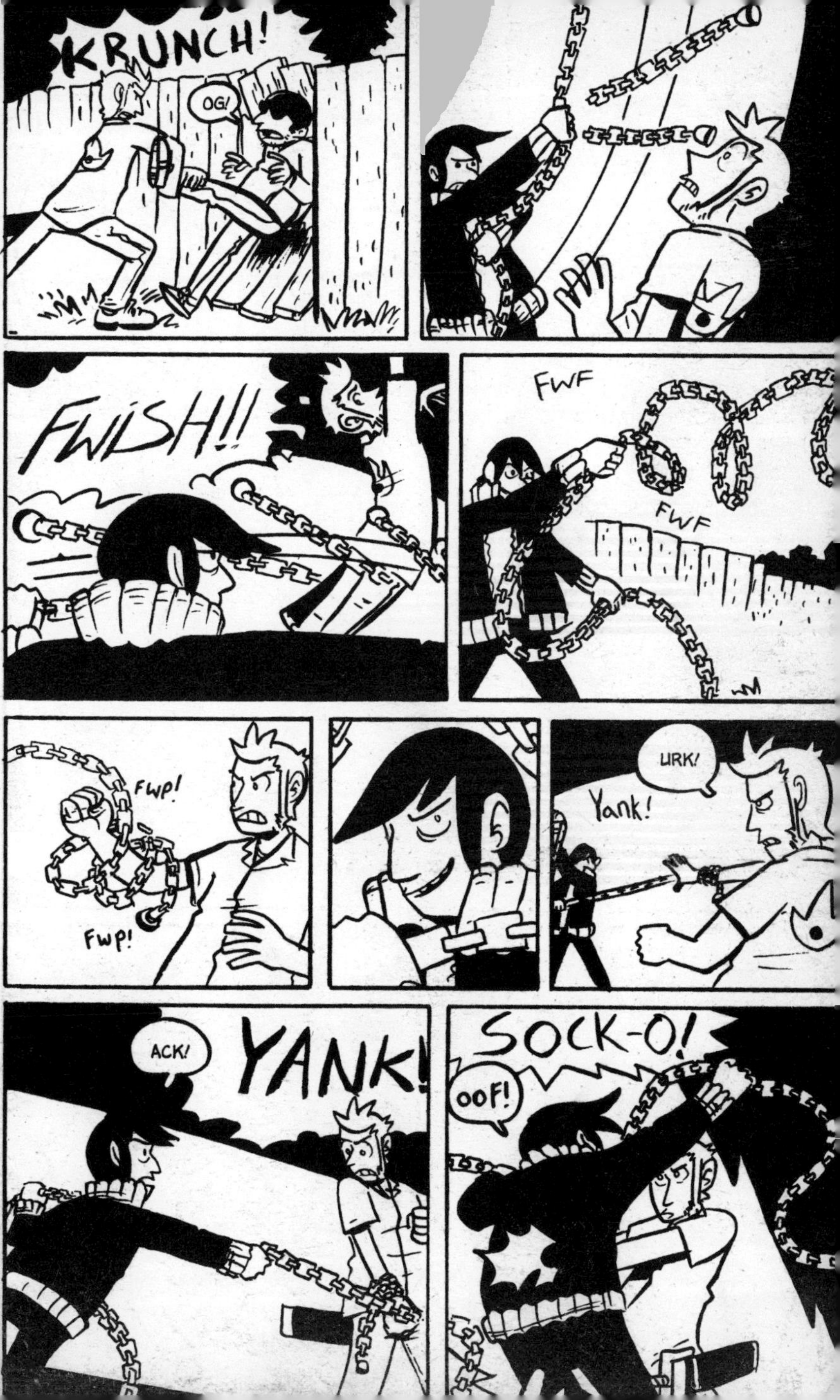
KRUNCH!
OG!
FWISH!!
FWF
FWF
FWP!
FWP!
URK!
Yank!
ACK!
YANK!
SOCK-O!
OOF!

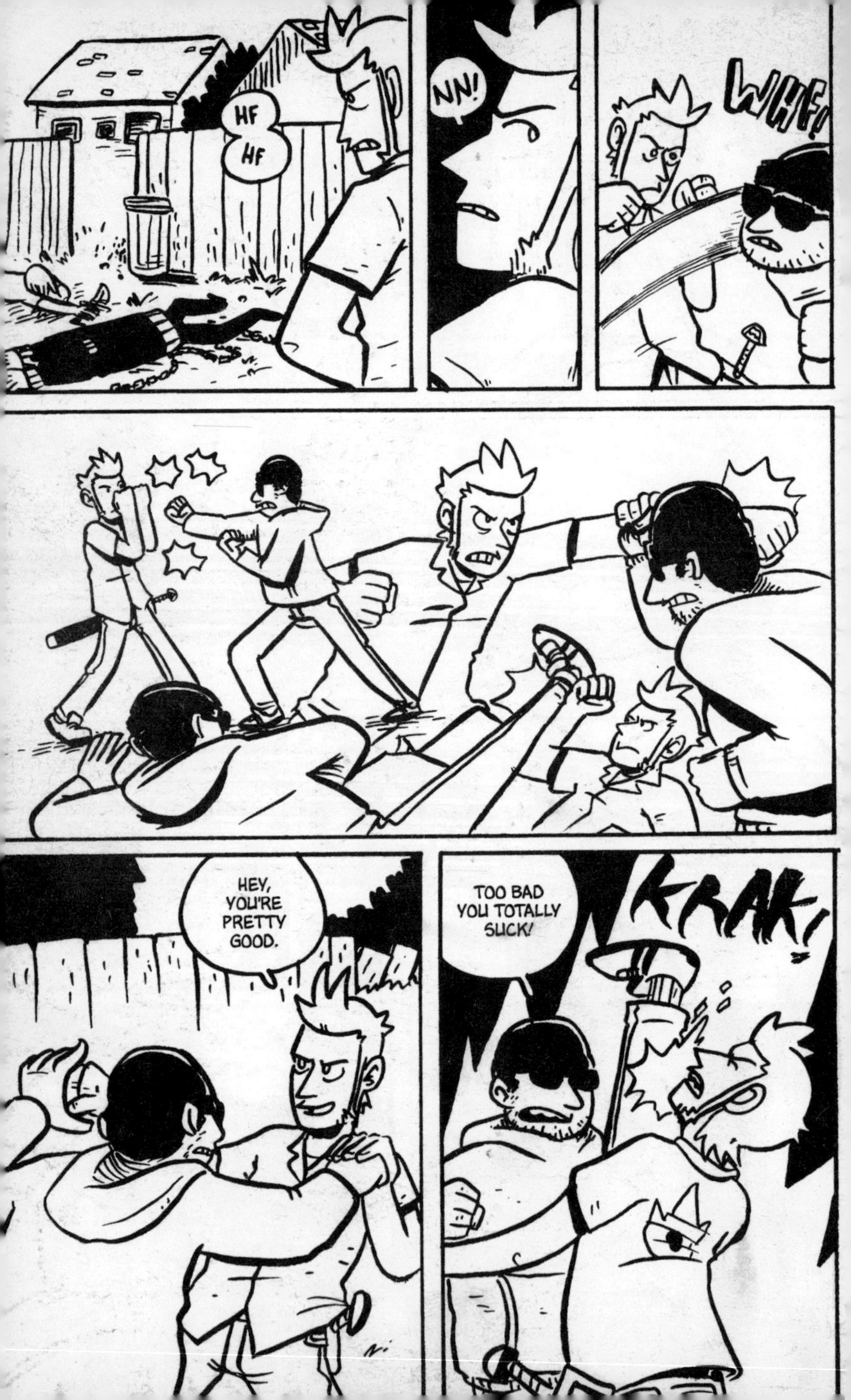
HF
HF
NN!
WHF!
HEY, YOU'RE PRETTY GOOD.
TOO BAD YOU TOTALLY SUCK!
KRAK!

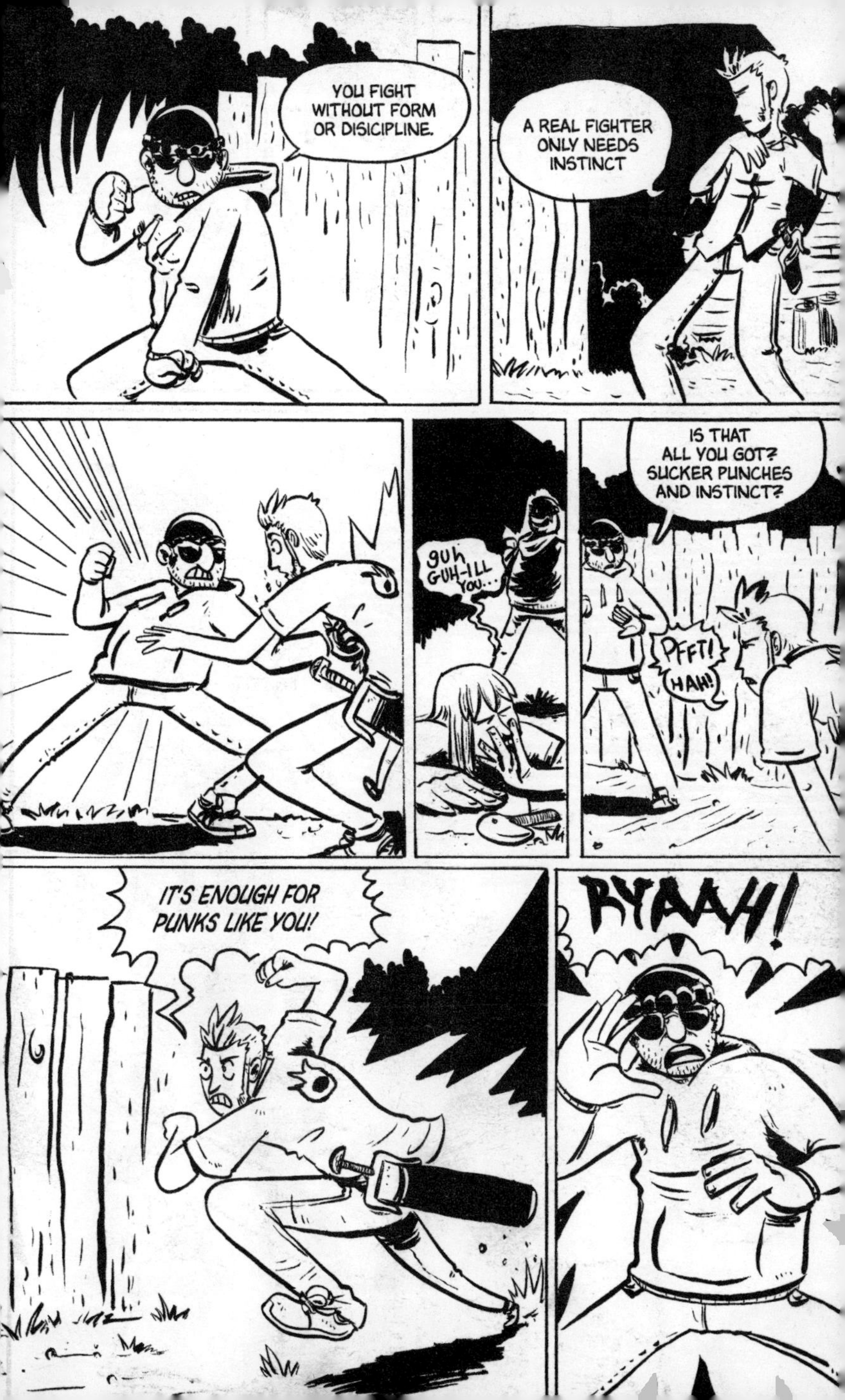
YOU FIGHT WITHOUT FORM OR DISICIPLINE.
A REAL FIGHTER ONLY NEEDS INSTINCT
guh GUH-ILL YOU...
IS THAT ALL YOU GOT? SUCKER PUNCHES AND INSTINCT?
PFFT! HAH!
IT'S ENOUGH FOR PUNKS LIKE YOU!
RYAAH!

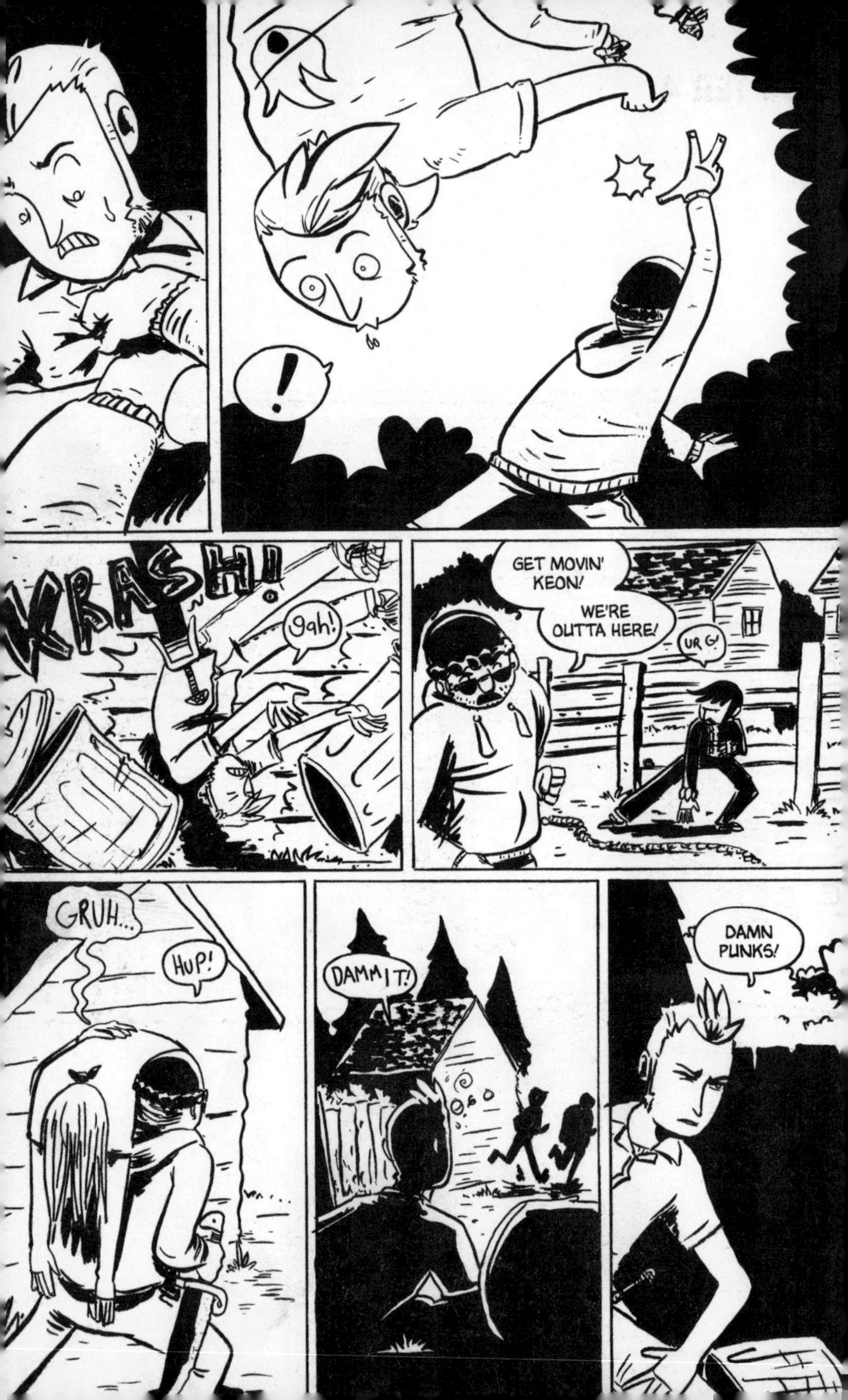
!
KRASH!
gah!
GET MOVIN' KEON!
WE'RE OUTTA HERE!
UR G!
GRUH...
HUP!
DAMMIT!
DAMN PUNKS!

CHAPTER 4

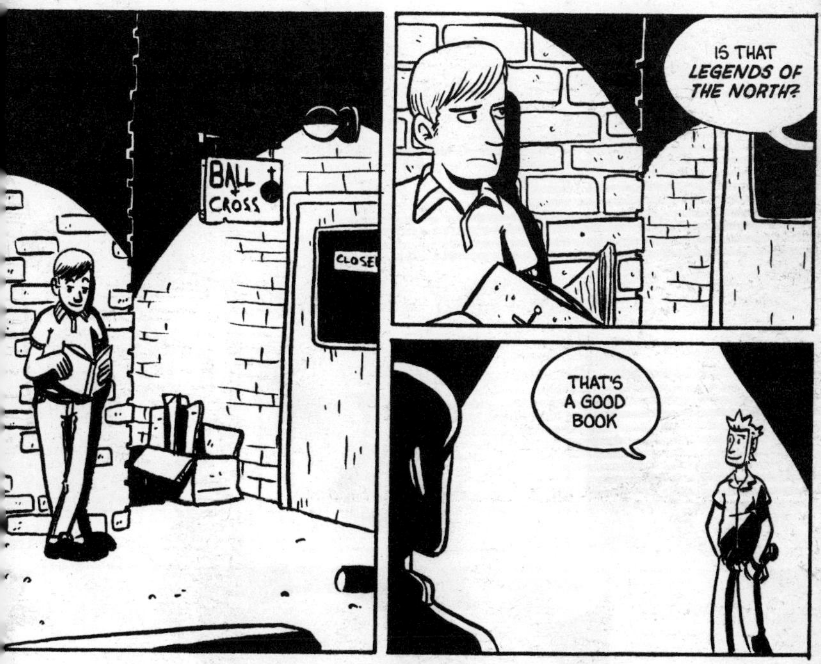
BALL + CROSS
CLOSE
IS THAT *LEGENDS OF THE NORTH*?
THAT'S A GOOD BOOK

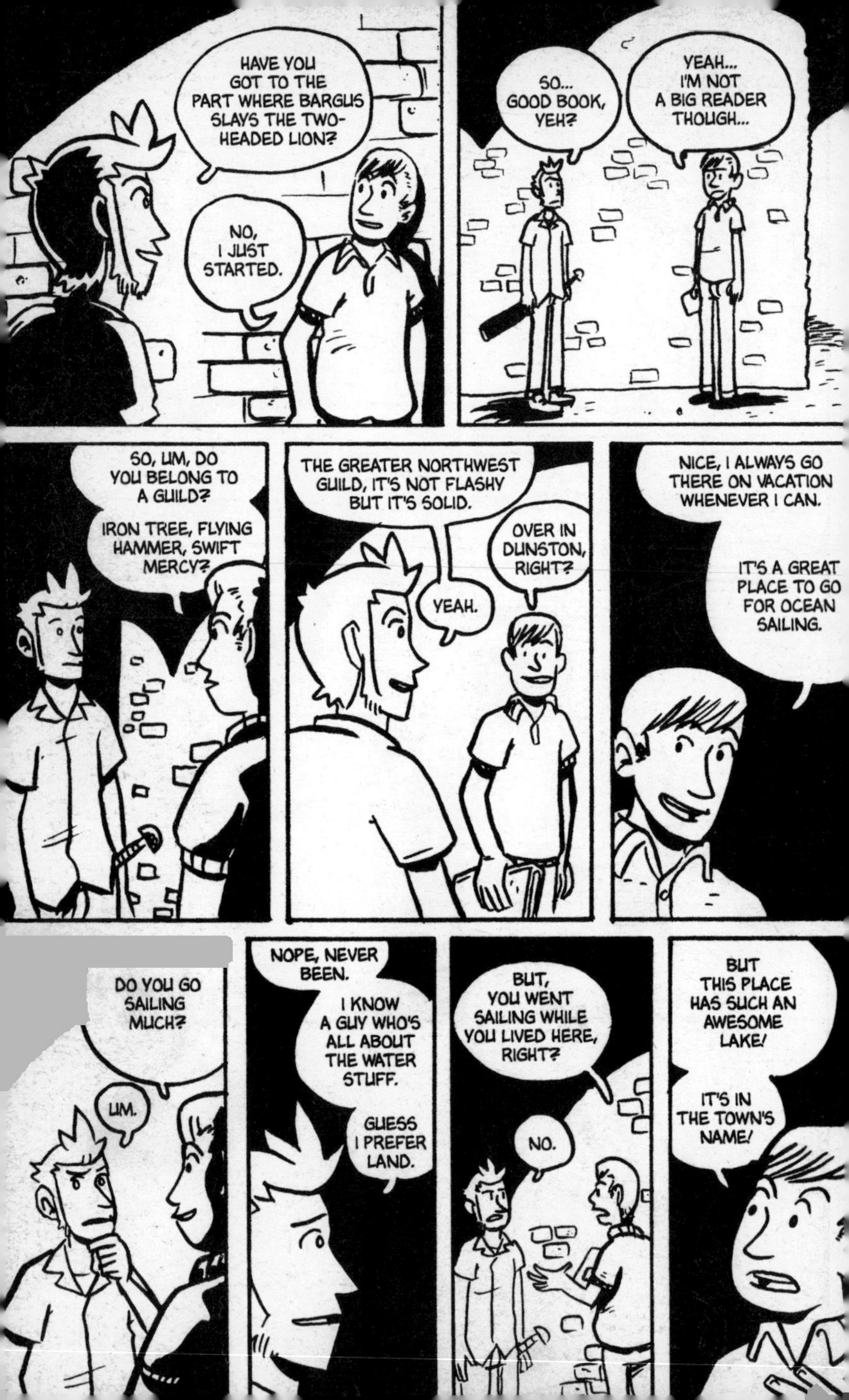
HAVE YOU GOT TO THE PART WHERE BARGUS SLAYS THE TWO-HEADED LION?
NO, I JUST STARTED.
SO... GOOD BOOK, YEH?
YEAH... I'M NOT A BIG READER THOUGH...
SO, UM, DO YOU BELONG TO A GUILD?
IRON TREE, FLYING HAMMER, SWIFT MERCY?
THE GREATER NORTHWEST GUILD, IT'S NOT FLASHY BUT IT'S SOLID.
OVER IN DUNSTON, RIGHT?
YEAH.
NICE, I ALWAYS GO THERE ON VACATION WHENEVER I CAN.
IT'S A GREAT PLACE TO GO FOR OCEAN SAILING.
DO YOU GO SAILING MUCH?
UM.
NOPE, NEVER BEEN.
I KNOW A GUY WHO'S ALL ABOUT THE WATER STUFF.
GUESS I PREFER LAND.
BUT, YOU WENT SAILING WHILE YOU LIVED HERE, RIGHT?
NO.
BUT THIS PLACE HAS SUCH AN AWESOME LAKE!
IT'S IN THE TOWN'S NAME!

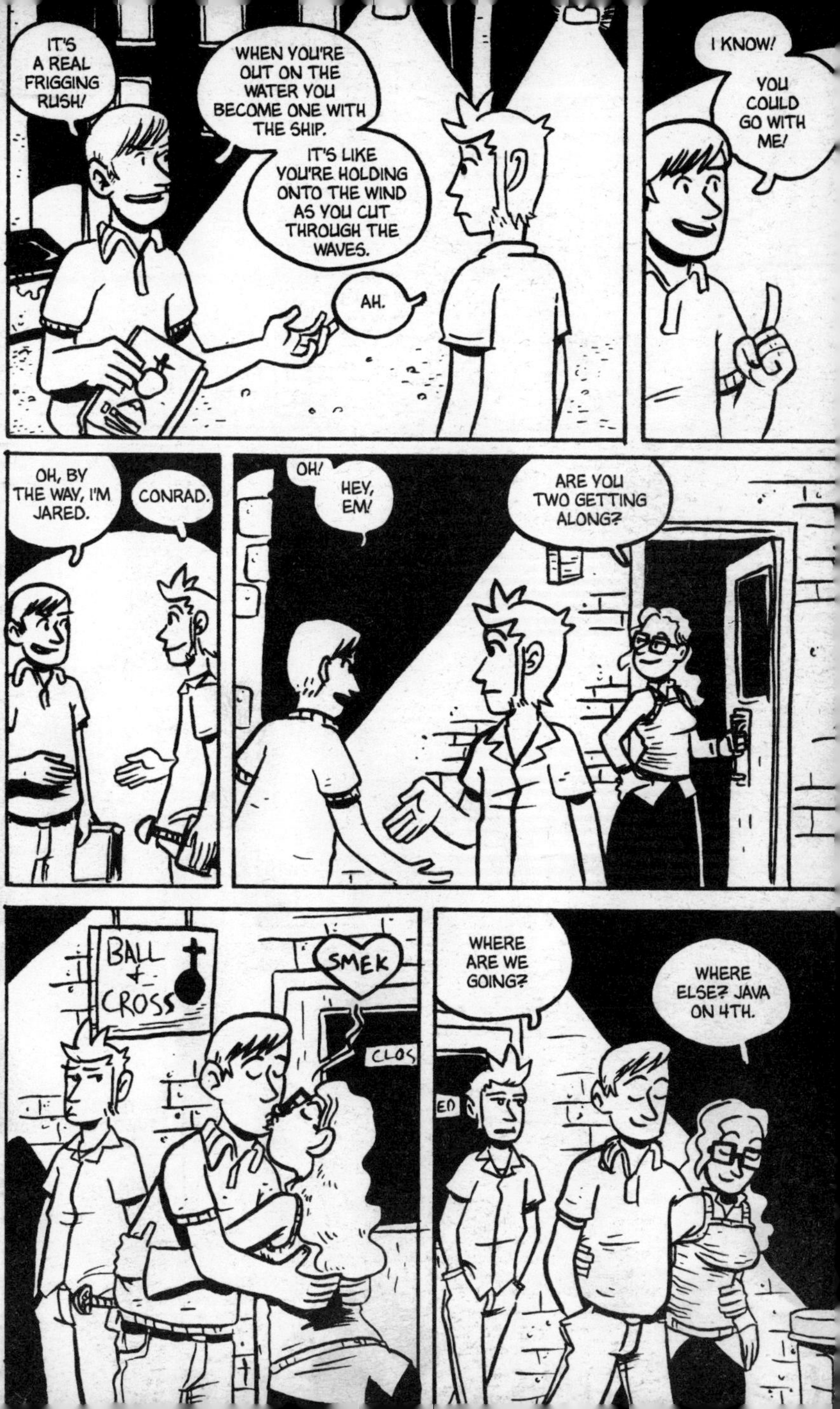
IT'S A REAL FRIGGING RUSH!
WHEN YOU'RE OUT ON THE WATER YOU BECOME ONE WITH THE SHIP.
IT'S LIKE YOU'RE HOLDING ONTO THE WIND AS YOU CUT THROUGH THE WAVES.
AH.
I KNOW!
YOU COULD GO WITH ME!
OH, BY THE WAY, I'M JARED.
CONRAD.
OH!
HEY, EM!
ARE YOU TWO GETTING ALONG?
BALL + CROSS
SMEK
CLOS
WHERE ARE WE GOING?
WHERE ELSE? JAVA ON 4TH.

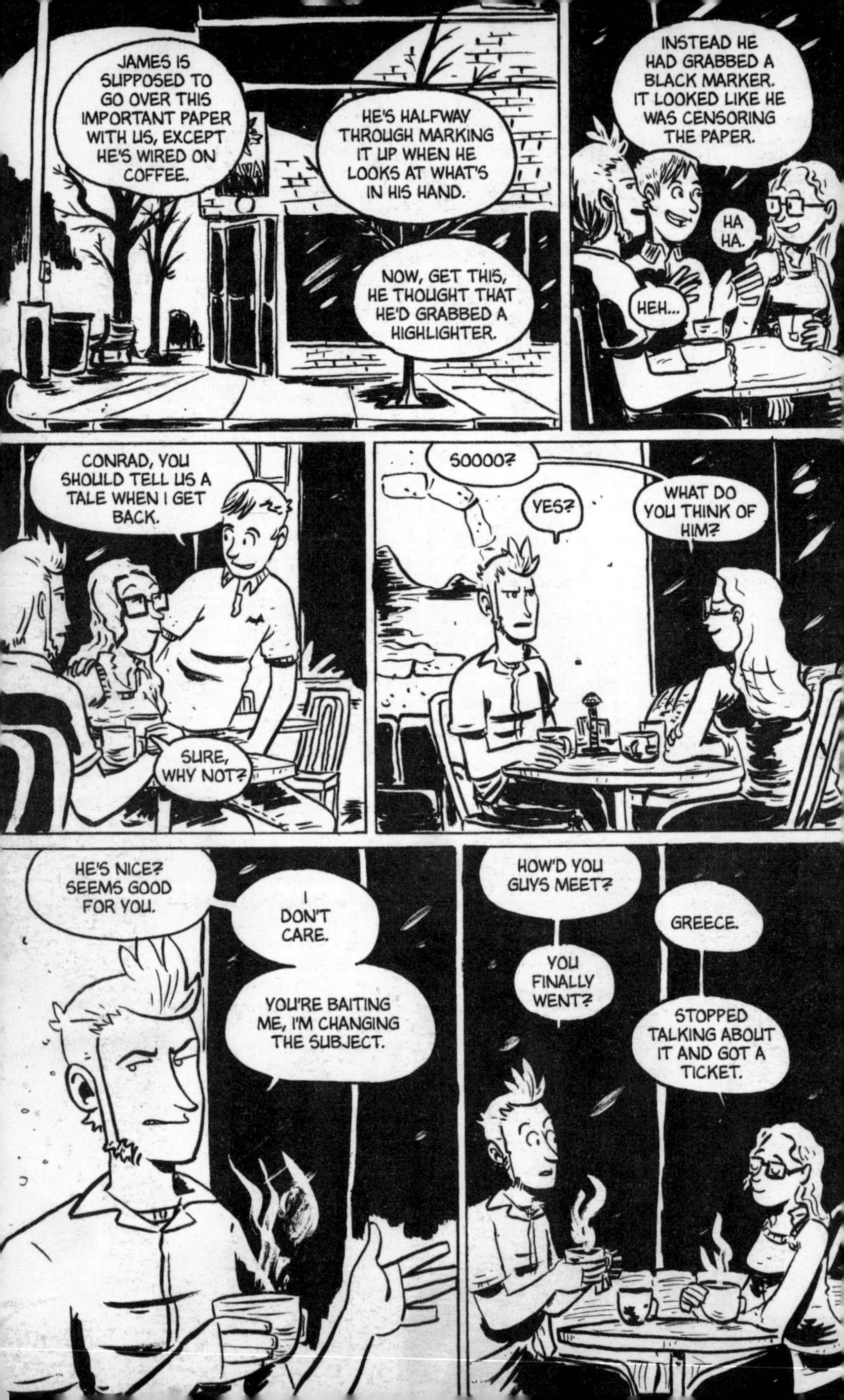
JAMES IS SUPPOSED TO GO OVER THIS IMPORTANT PAPER WITH US, EXCEPT HE'S WIRED ON COFFEE.
HE'S HALFWAY THROUGH MARKING IT UP WHEN HE LOOKS AT WHAT'S IN HIS HAND.
NOW, GET THIS, HE THOUGHT THAT HE'D GRABBED A HIGHLIGHTER.
INSTEAD HE HAD GRABBED A BLACK MARKER. IT LOOKED LIKE HE WAS CENSORING THE PAPER.
HA HA.
HEH...
CONRAD, YOU SHOULD TELL US A TALE WHEN I GET BACK.
SURE, WHY NOT?
SOOOO?
YES?
WHAT DO YOU THINK OF HIM?
HE'S NICE? SEEMS GOOD FOR YOU.
I DON'T CARE.
YOU'RE BAITING ME, I'M CHANGING THE SUBJECT.
HOW'D YOU GUYS MEET?
GREECE.
YOU FINALLY WENT?
STOPPED TALKING ABOUT IT AND GOT A TICKET.

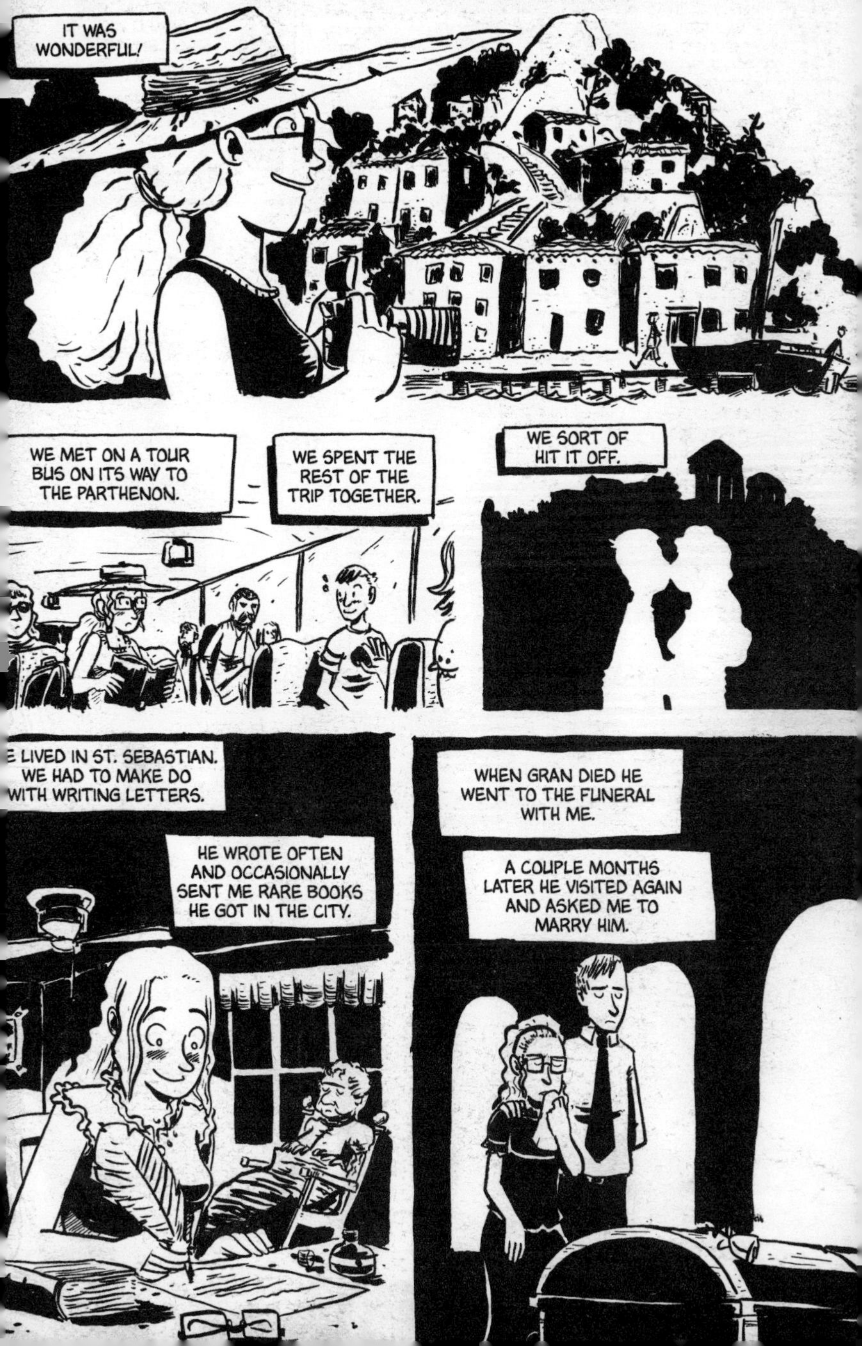
IT WAS WONDERFUL!
WE MET ON A TOUR BUS ON ITS WAY TO THE PARTHENON.
WE SPENT THE REST OF THE TRIP TOGETHER.
WE SORT OF HIT IT OFF.
E LIVED IN ST. SEBASTIAN. WE HAD TO MAKE DO WITH WRITING LETTERS.
HE WROTE OFTEN AND OCCASIONALLY SENT ME RARE BOOKS HE GOT IN THE CITY.
WHEN GRAN DIED HE WENT TO THE FUNERAL WITH ME.
A COUPLE MONTHS LATER HE VISITED AGAIN AND ASKED ME TO MARRY HIM.

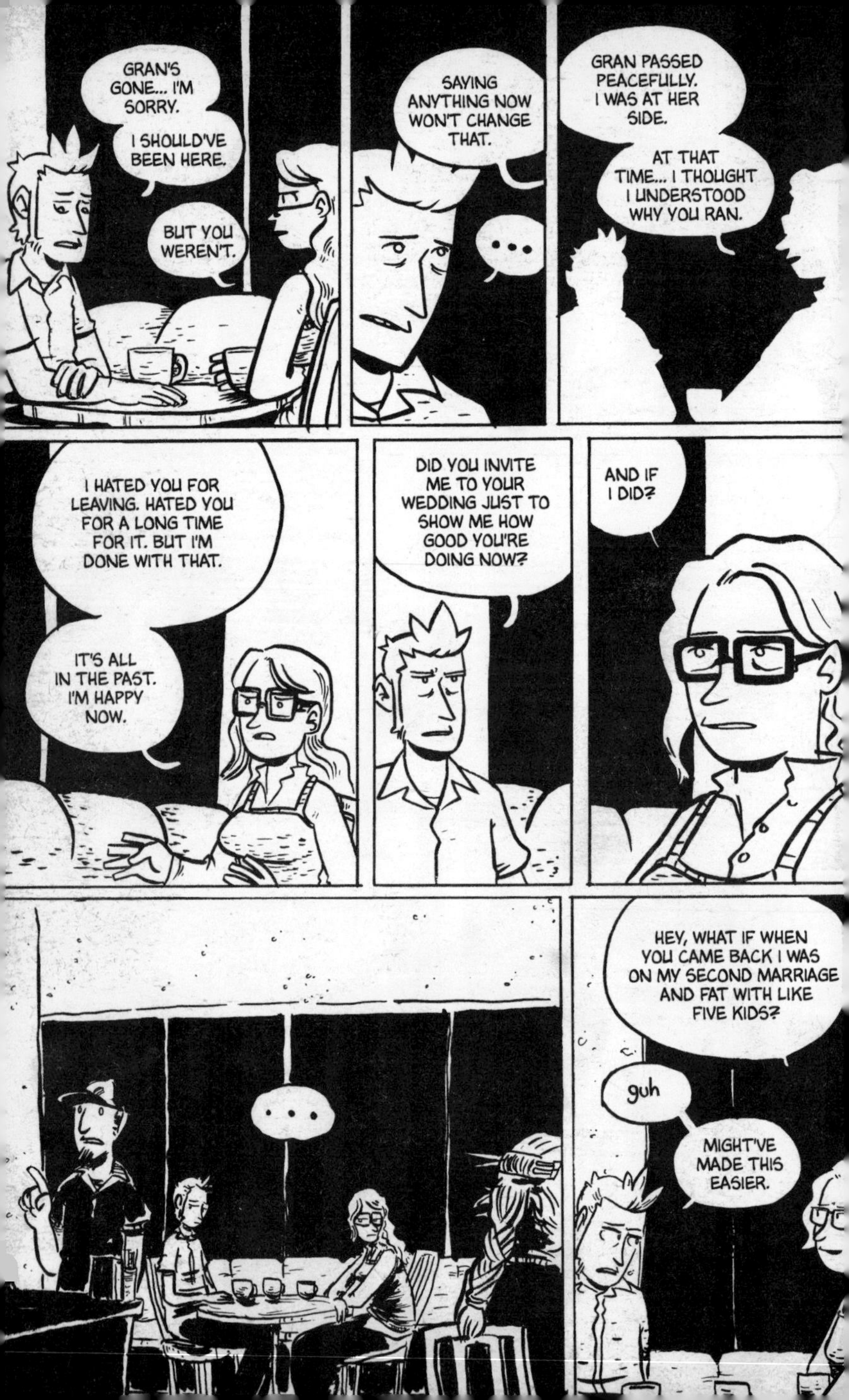
GRAN'S GONE... I'M SORRY.
I SHOULD'VE BEEN HERE.
BUT YOU WEREN'T.
SAYING ANYTHING NOW WON'T CHANGE THAT.
...
GRAN PASSED PEACEFULLY. I WAS AT HER SIDE.
AT THAT TIME... I THOUGHT I UNDERSTOOD WHY YOU RAN.
I HATED YOU FOR LEAVING. HATED YOU FOR A LONG TIME FOR IT. BUT I'M DONE WITH THAT.
IT'S ALL IN THE PAST. I'M HAPPY NOW.
DID YOU INVITE ME TO YOUR WEDDING JUST TO SHOW ME HOW GOOD YOU'RE DOING NOW?
AND IF I DID?
...
HEY, WHAT IF WHEN YOU CAME BACK I WAS ON MY SECOND MARRIAGE AND FAT WITH LIKE FIVE KIDS?
guh
MIGHT'VE MADE THIS EASIER.

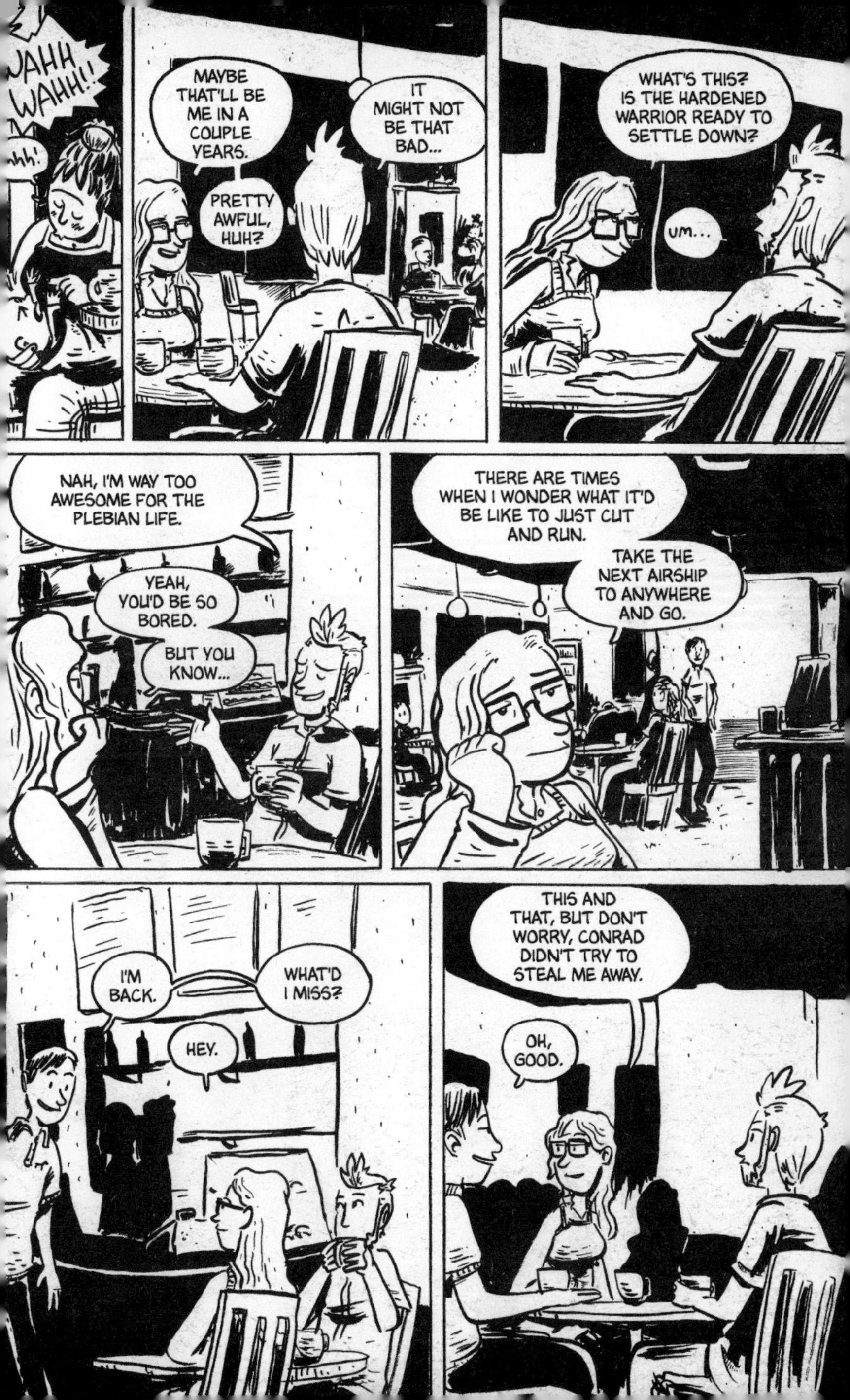
WAHH WAHH!!
MAYBE THAT'LL BE ME IN A COUPLE YEARS.
PRETTY AWFUL, HUH?
IT MIGHT NOT BE THAT BAD...
WHAT'S THIS? IS THE HARDENED WARRIOR READY TO SETTLE DOWN?
UM...
NAH, I'M WAY TOO AWESOME FOR THE PLEBIAN LIFE.
YEAH, YOU'D BE SO BORED.
BUT YOU KNOW...
THERE ARE TIMES WHEN I WONDER WHAT IT'D BE LIKE TO JUST CUT AND RUN.
TAKE THE NEXT AIRSHIP TO ANYWHERE AND GO.
I'M BACK.
WHAT'D I MISS?
HEY.
THIS AND THAT, BUT DON'T WORRY, CONRAD DIDN'T TRY TO STEAL ME AWAY.
OH, GOOD.

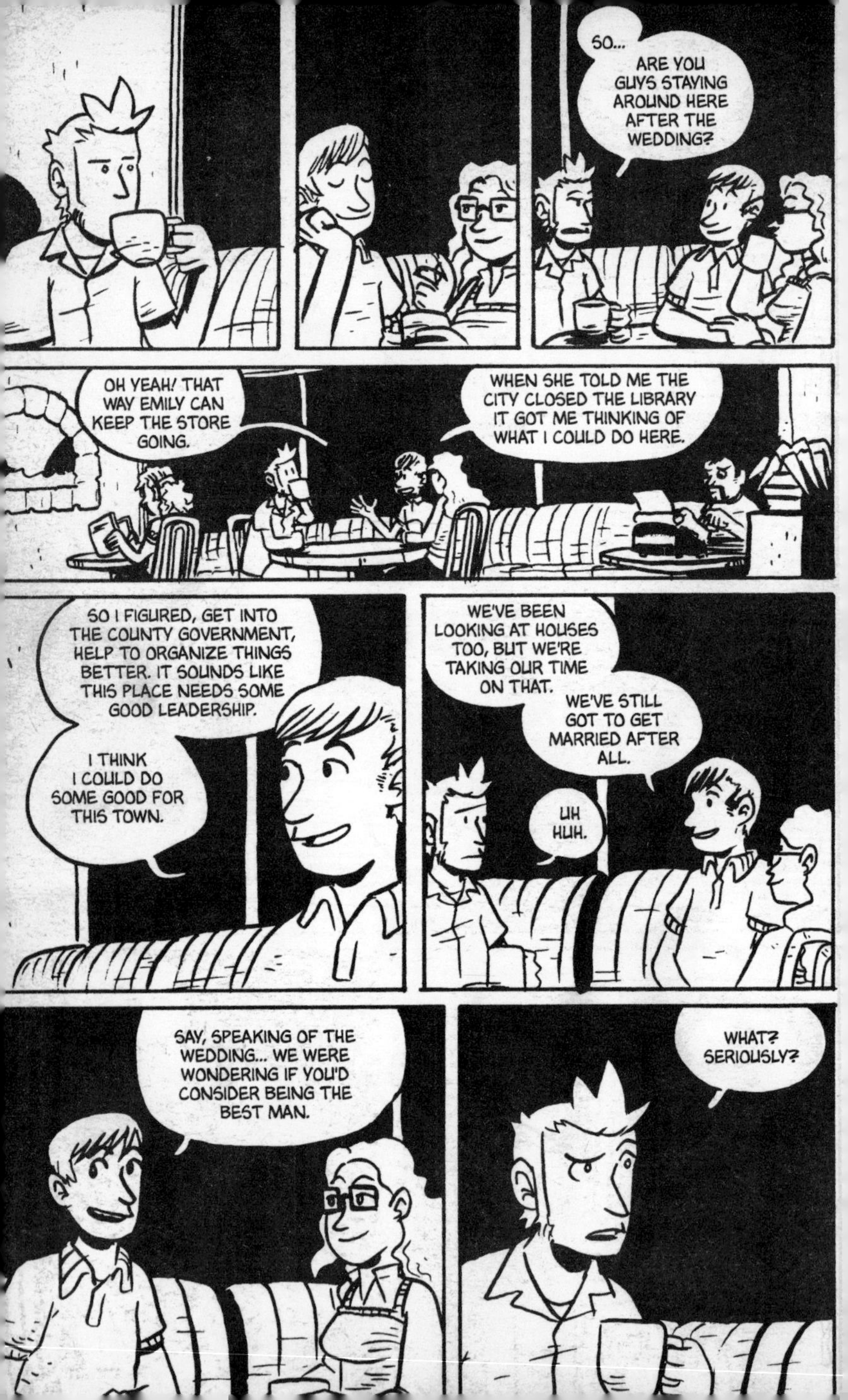
SO...
ARE YOU GUYS STAYING AROUND HERE AFTER THE WEDDING?
OH YEAH! THAT WAY EMILY CAN KEEP THE STORE GOING.
WHEN SHE TOLD ME THE CITY CLOSED THE LIBRARY IT GOT ME THINKING OF WHAT I COULD DO HERE.
SO I FIGURED, GET INTO THE COUNTY GOVERNMENT, HELP TO ORGANIZE THINGS BETTER. IT SOUNDS LIKE THIS PLACE NEEDS SOME GOOD LEADERSHIP.
I THINK I COULD DO SOME GOOD FOR THIS TOWN.
WE'VE BEEN LOOKING AT HOUSES TOO, BUT WE'RE TAKING OUR TIME ON THAT.
WE'VE STILL GOT TO GET MARRIED AFTER ALL.
UH HUH.
SAY, SPEAKING OF THE WEDDING... WE WERE WONDERING IF YOU'D CONSIDER BEING THE BEST MAN.
WHAT? SERIOUSLY?

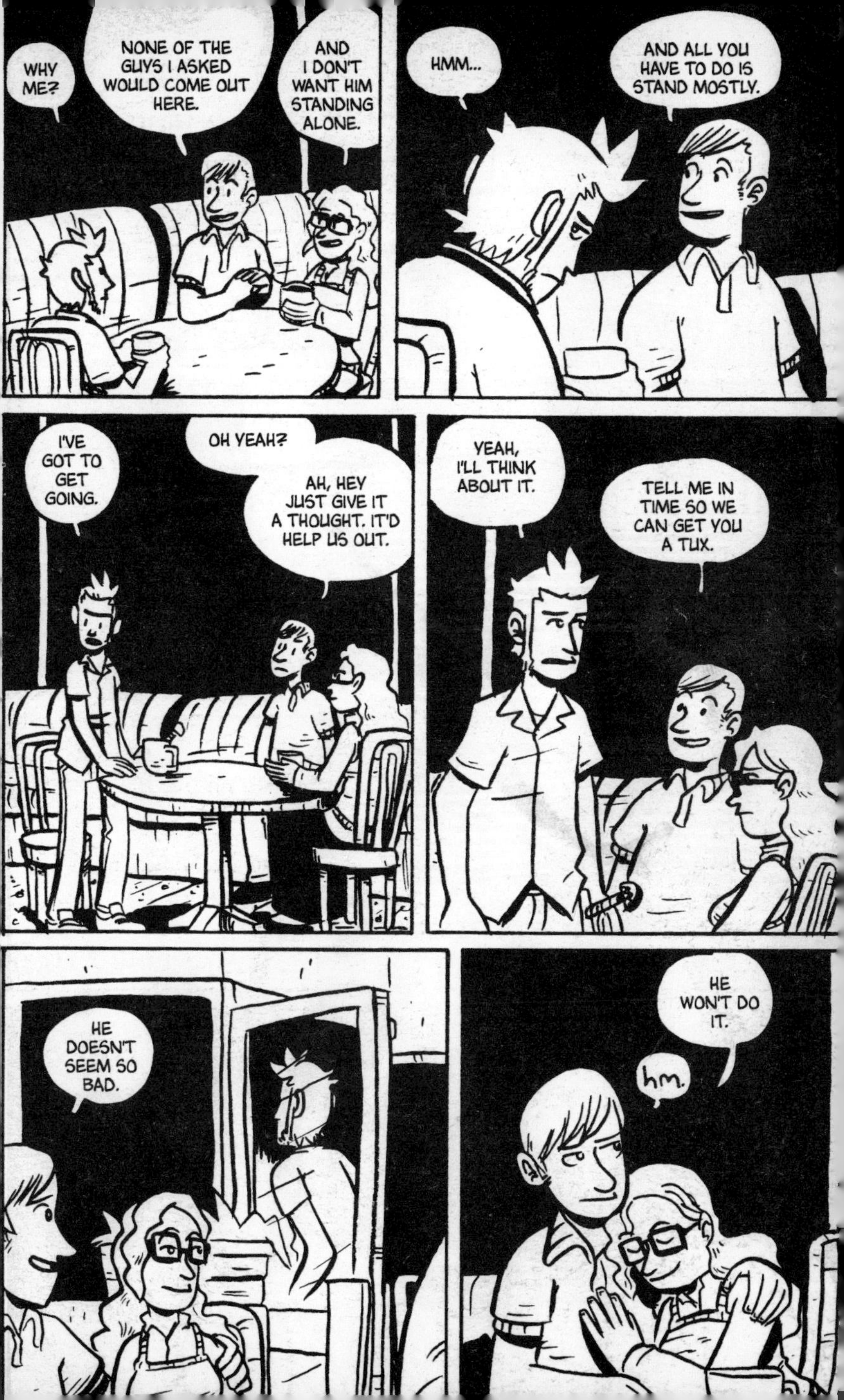
WHY ME?
NONE OF THE GUYS I ASKED WOULD COME OUT HERE.
AND I DON'T WANT HIM STANDING ALONE.
HMM...
AND ALL YOU HAVE TO DO IS STAND MOSTLY.
I'VE GOT TO GET GOING.
OH YEAH?
AH, HEY JUST GIVE IT A THOUGHT. IT'D HELP US OUT.
YEAH, I'LL THINK ABOUT IT.
TELL ME IN TIME SO WE CAN GET YOU A TUX.
HE DOESN'T SEEM SO BAD.
hm.
HE WON'T DO IT.

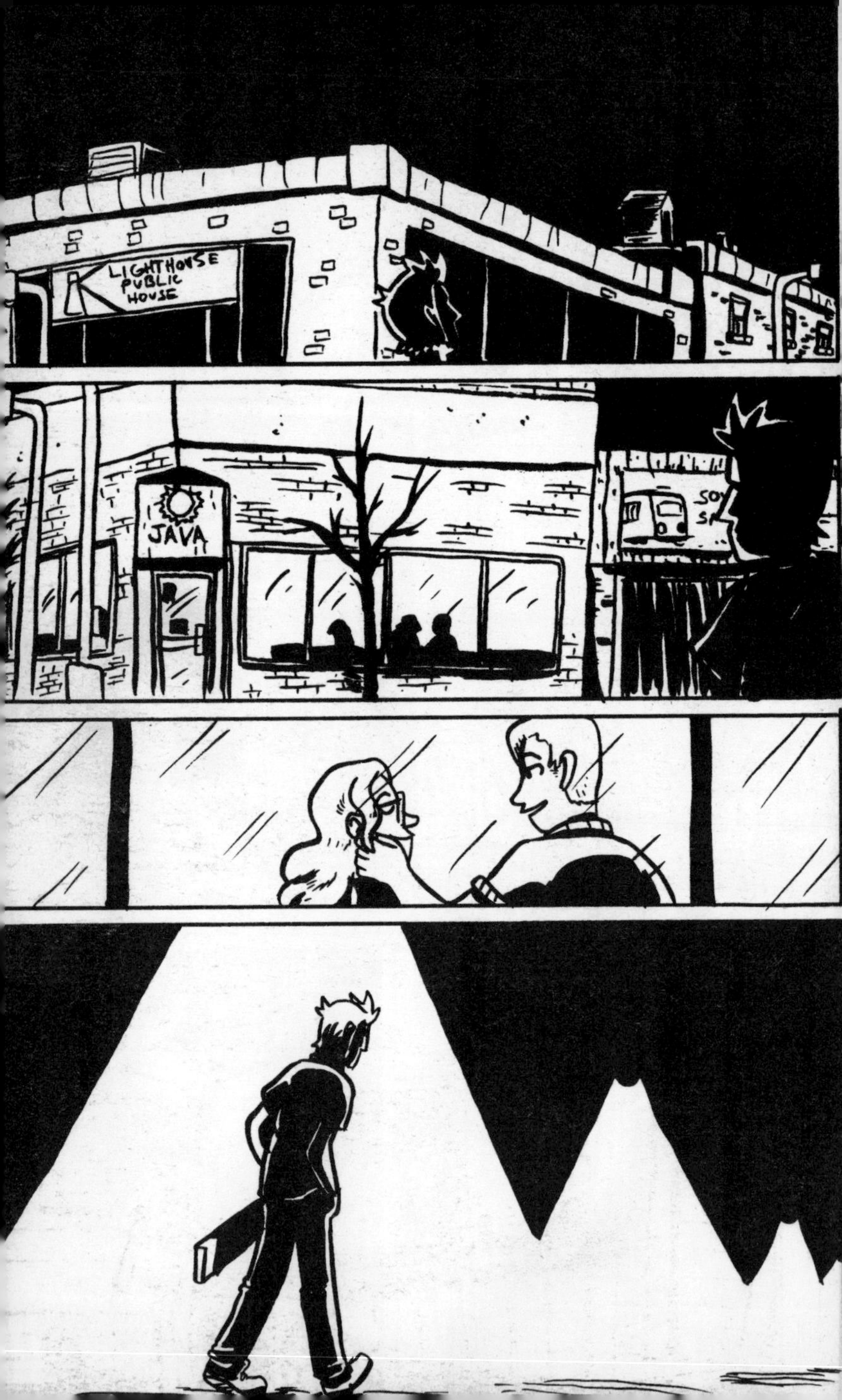
LIGHTHOUSE PUBLIC HOUSE
JAVA

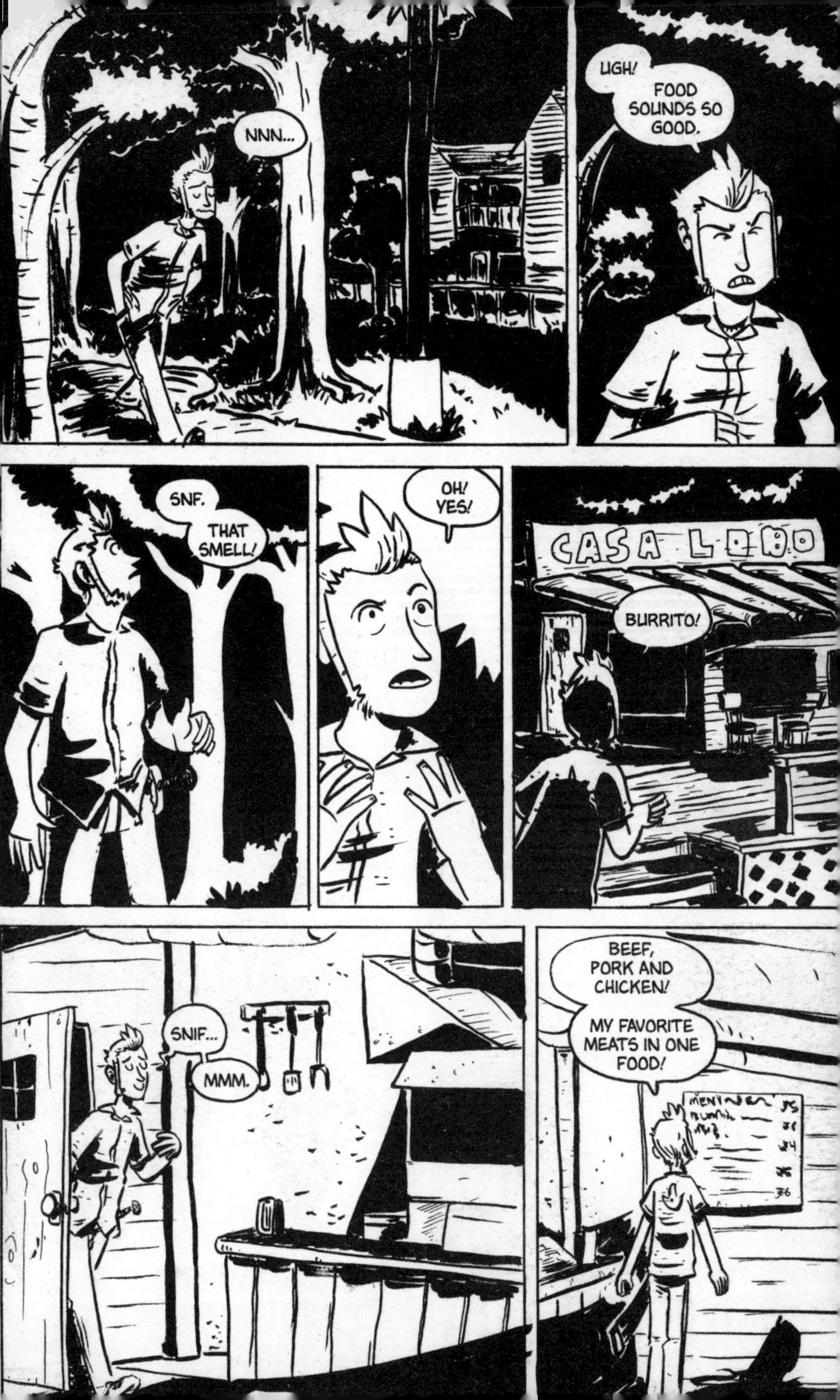
NNN...
UGH!
FOOD SOUNDS SO GOOD.
SNF.
THAT SMELL!
OH! YES!
CASA LOBO
BURRITO!
SNIF...
MMM.
BEEF, PORK AND CHICKEN!
MY FAVORITE MEATS IN ONE FOOD!

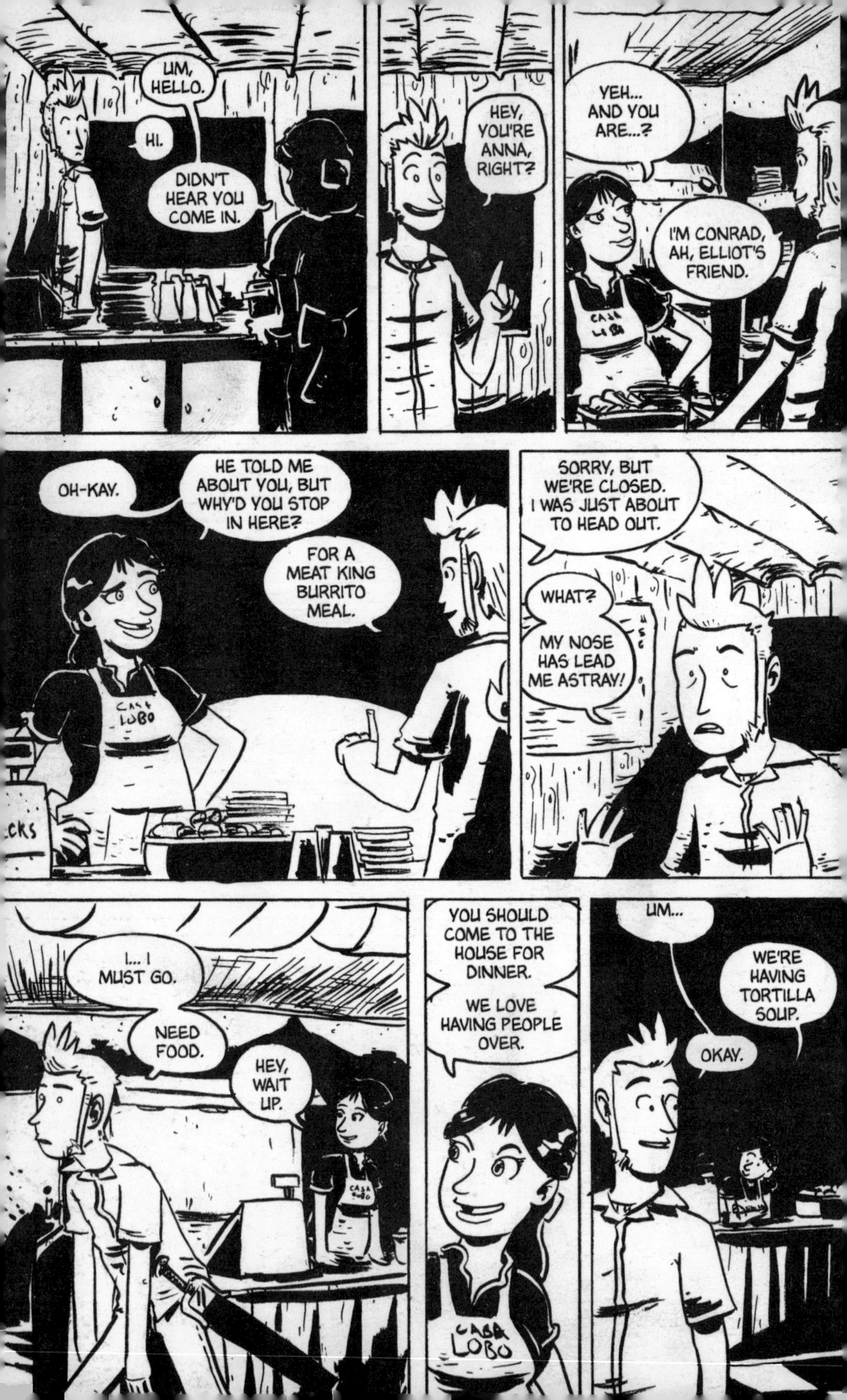
UM, HELLO.
HI.
DIDN'T HEAR YOU COME IN.
HEY, YOU'RE ANNA, RIGHT?
YEH... AND YOU ARE...?
I'M CONRAD, AH, ELLIOT'S FRIEND.
CASA LOBO
OH-KAY.
HE TOLD ME ABOUT YOU, BUT WHY'D YOU STOP IN HERE?
FOR A MEAT KING BURRITO MEAL.
CASA LOBO
SORRY, BUT WE'RE CLOSED. I WAS JUST ABOUT TO HEAD OUT.
WHAT?
MY NOSE HAS LEAD ME ASTRAY!
I... I MUST GO.
NEED FOOD.
HEY, WAIT UP.
YOU SHOULD COME TO THE HOUSE FOR DINNER.
WE LOVE HAVING PEOPLE OVER.
CASA LOBO
UM...
WE'RE HAVING TORTILLA SOUP.
OKAY.

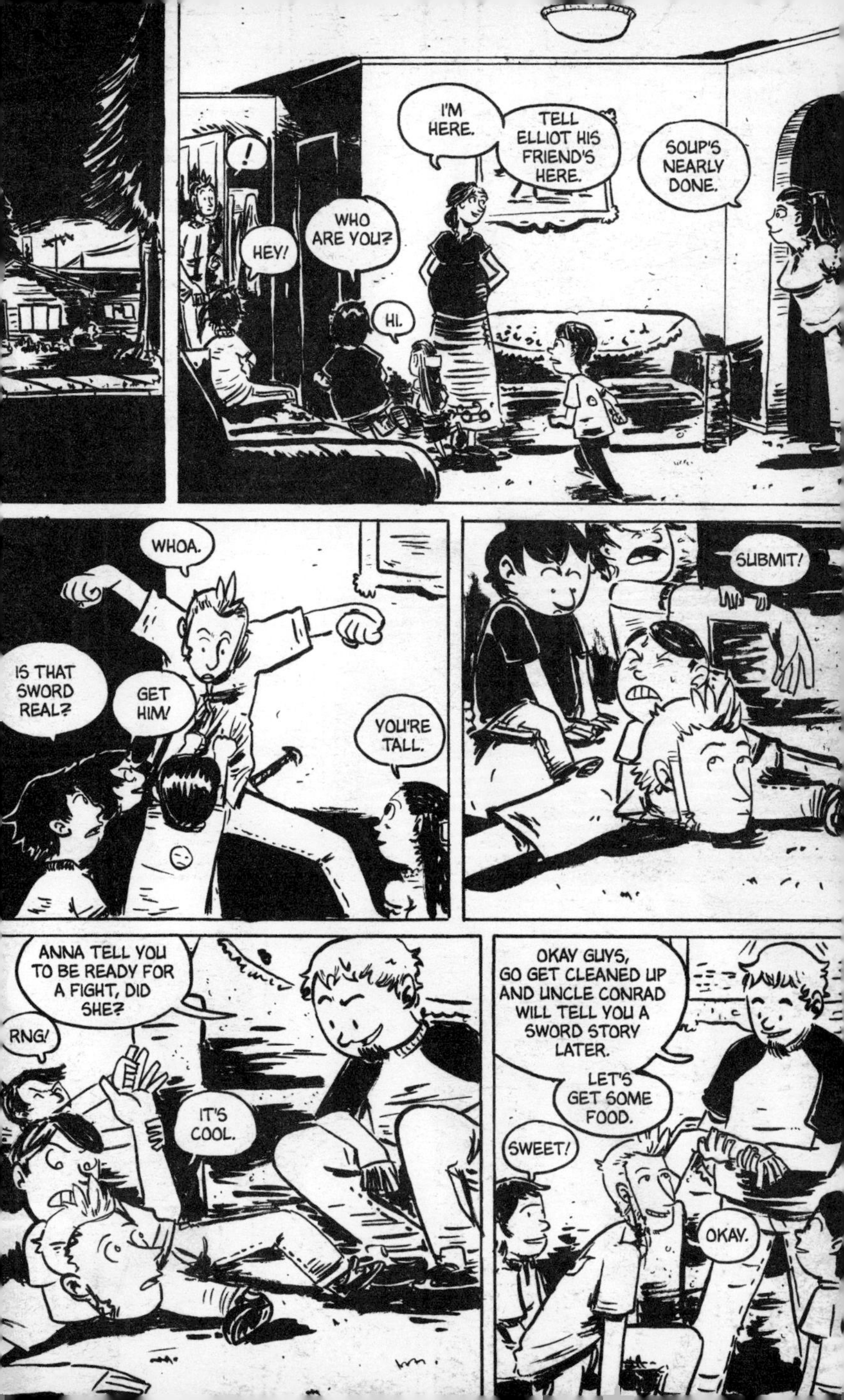
!
HEY!
WHO ARE YOU?
HI.
I'M HERE.
TELL ELLIOT HIS FRIEND'S HERE.
SOUP'S NEARLY DONE.
WHOA.
IS THAT SWORD REAL?
GET HIM!
YOU'RE TALL.
SUBMIT!
ANNA TELL YOU TO BE READY FOR A FIGHT, DID SHE?
RNG!
IT'S COOL.
OKAY GUYS, GO GET CLEANED UP AND UNCLE CONRAD WILL TELL YOU A SWORD STORY LATER.
LET'S GET SOME FOOD.
SWEET!
OKAY.

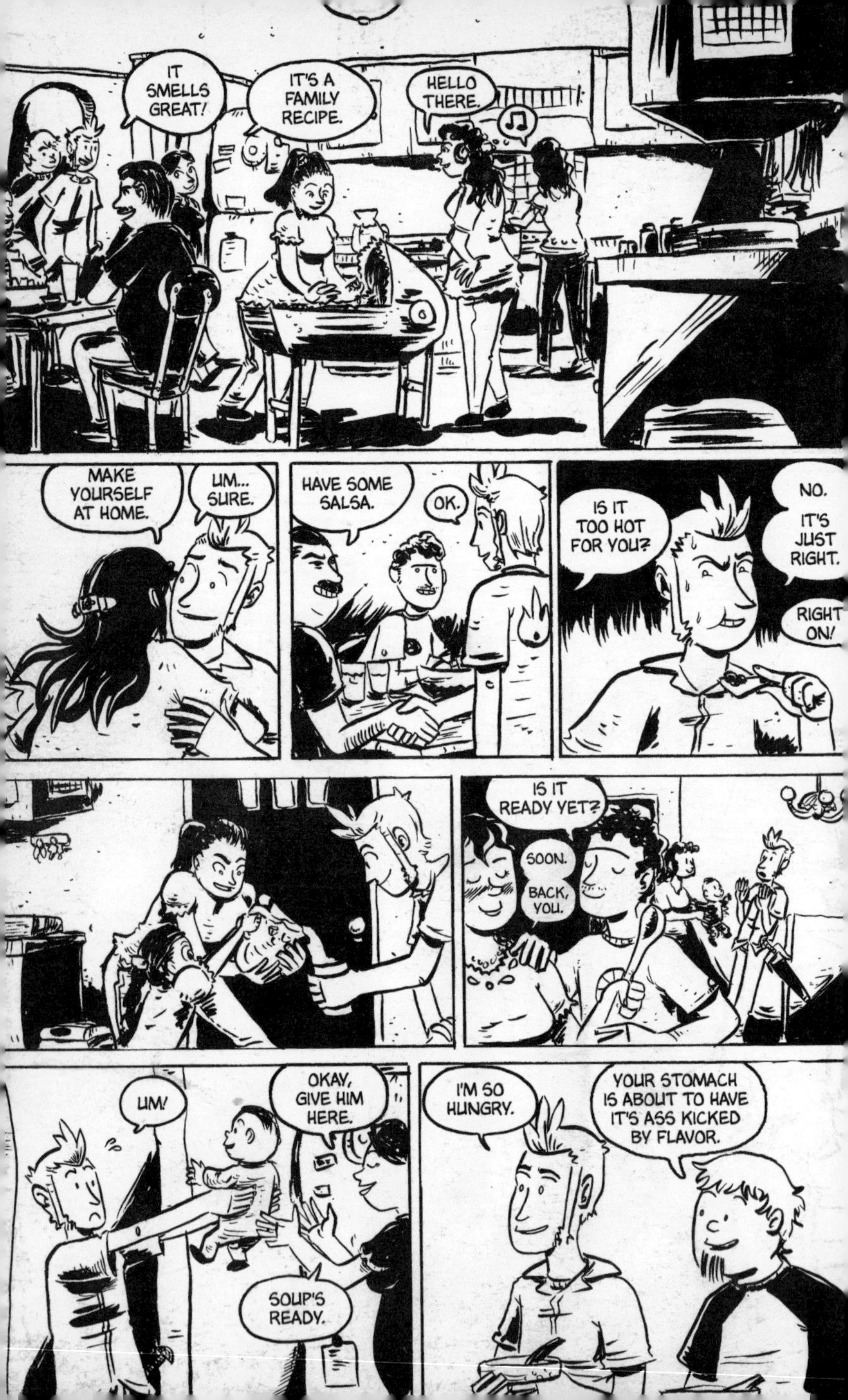
IT SMELLS GREAT!
IT'S A FAMILY RECIPE.
HELLO THERE.
♫
MAKE YOURSELF AT HOME.
UM... SURE.
HAVE SOME SALSA.
OK.
IS IT TOO HOT FOR YOU?
NO.
IT'S JUST RIGHT.
RIGHT ON!
IS IT READY YET?
SOON.
BACK, YOU.
UM!
OKAY, GIVE HIM HERE.
SOUP'S READY.
I'M SO HUNGRY.
YOUR STOMACH IS ABOUT TO HAVE IT'S ASS KICKED BY FLAVOR.

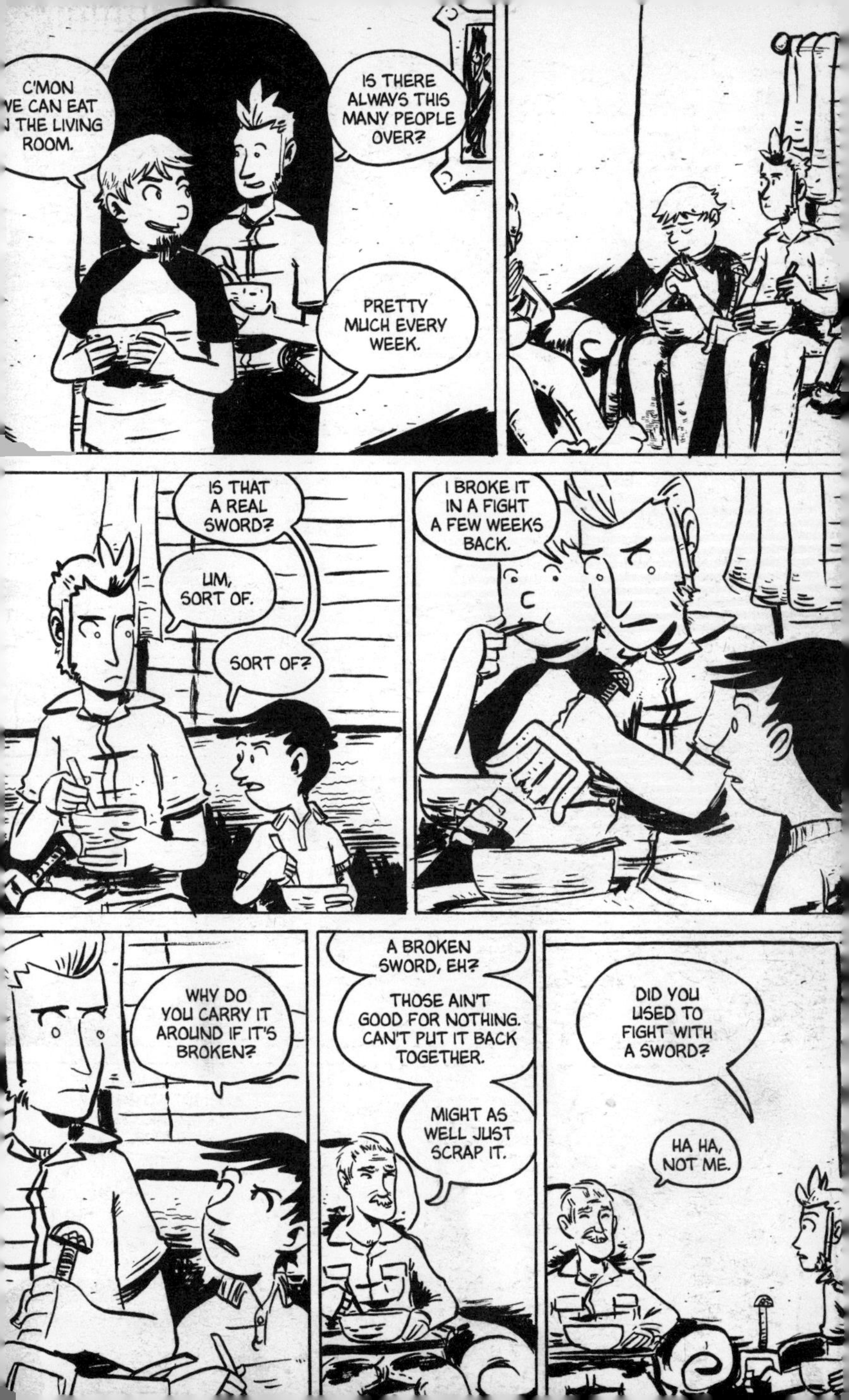
C'MON
WE CAN EAT
IN THE LIVING
ROOM.
IS THERE
ALWAYS THIS
MANY PEOPLE
OVER?
PRETTY
MUCH EVERY
WEEK.
IS THAT
A REAL
SWORD?
UM,
SORT OF.
SORT OF?
I BROKE IT
IN A FIGHT
A FEW WEEKS
BACK.
WHY DO
YOU CARRY IT
AROUND IF IT'S
BROKEN?
A BROKEN
SWORD, EH?
THOSE AIN'T
GOOD FOR NOTHING.
CAN'T PUT IT BACK
TOGETHER.
MIGHT AS
WELL JUST
SCRAP IT.
DID YOU
USED TO
FIGHT WITH
A SWORD?
HA HA,
NOT ME.

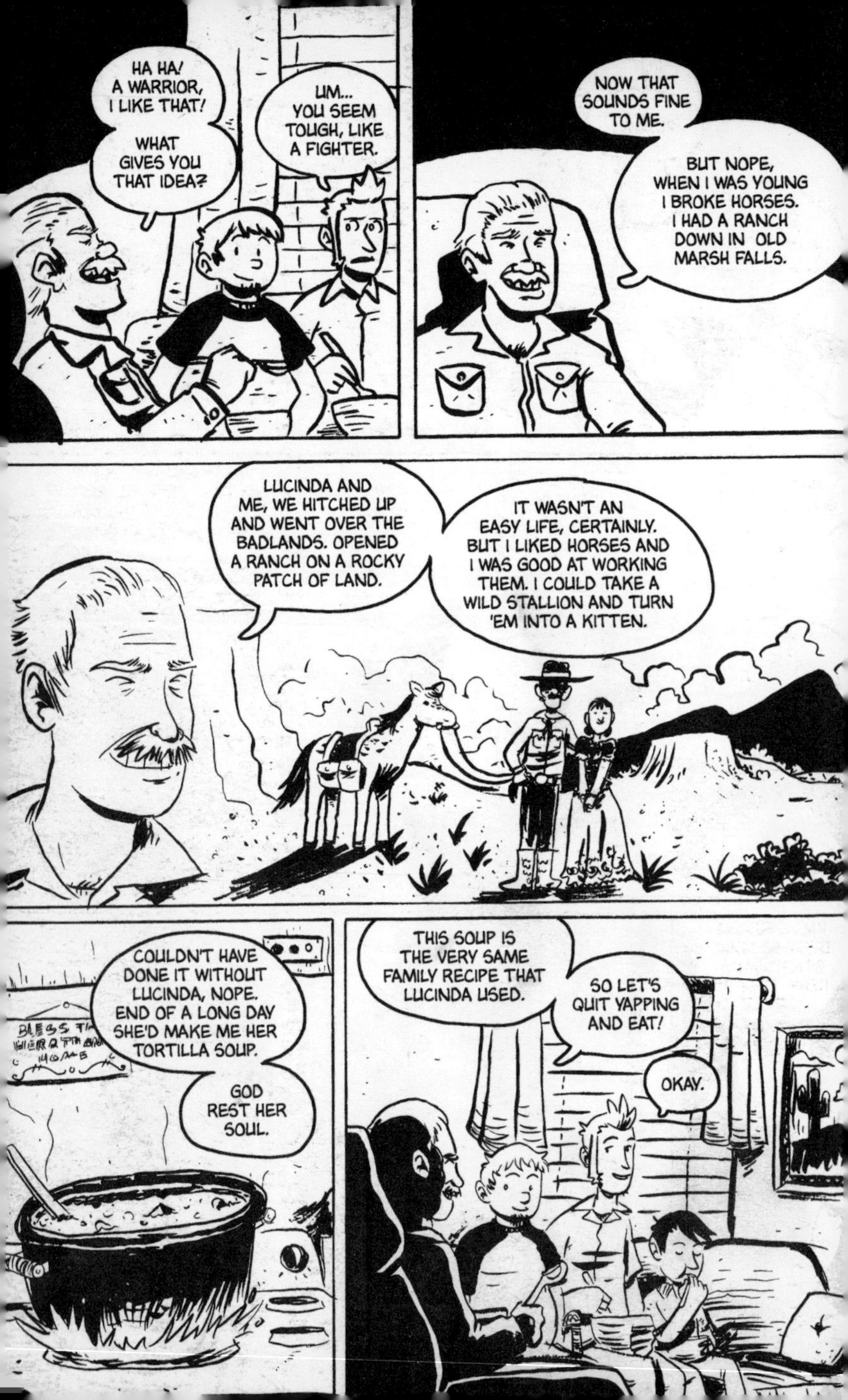
HA HA! A WARRIOR, I LIKE THAT!
WHAT GIVES YOU THAT IDEA?
UM... YOU SEEM TOUGH, LIKE A FIGHTER.
NOW THAT SOUNDS FINE TO ME.
BUT NOPE, WHEN I WAS YOUNG I BROKE HORSES. I HAD A RANCH DOWN IN OLD MARSH FALLS.
LUCINDA AND ME, WE HITCHED UP AND WENT OVER THE BADLANDS. OPENED A RANCH ON A ROCKY PATCH OF LAND.
IT WASN'T AN EASY LIFE, CERTAINLY. BUT I LIKED HORSES AND I WAS GOOD AT WORKING THEM. I COULD TAKE A WILD STALLION AND TURN 'EM INTO A KITTEN.
COULDN'T HAVE DONE IT WITHOUT LUCINDA, NOPE. END OF A LONG DAY SHE'D MAKE ME HER TORTILLA SOUP.
GOD REST HER SOUL.
THIS SOUP IS THE VERY SAME FAMILY RECIPE THAT LUCINDA USED.
SO LET'S QUIT YAPPING AND EAT!
OKAY.

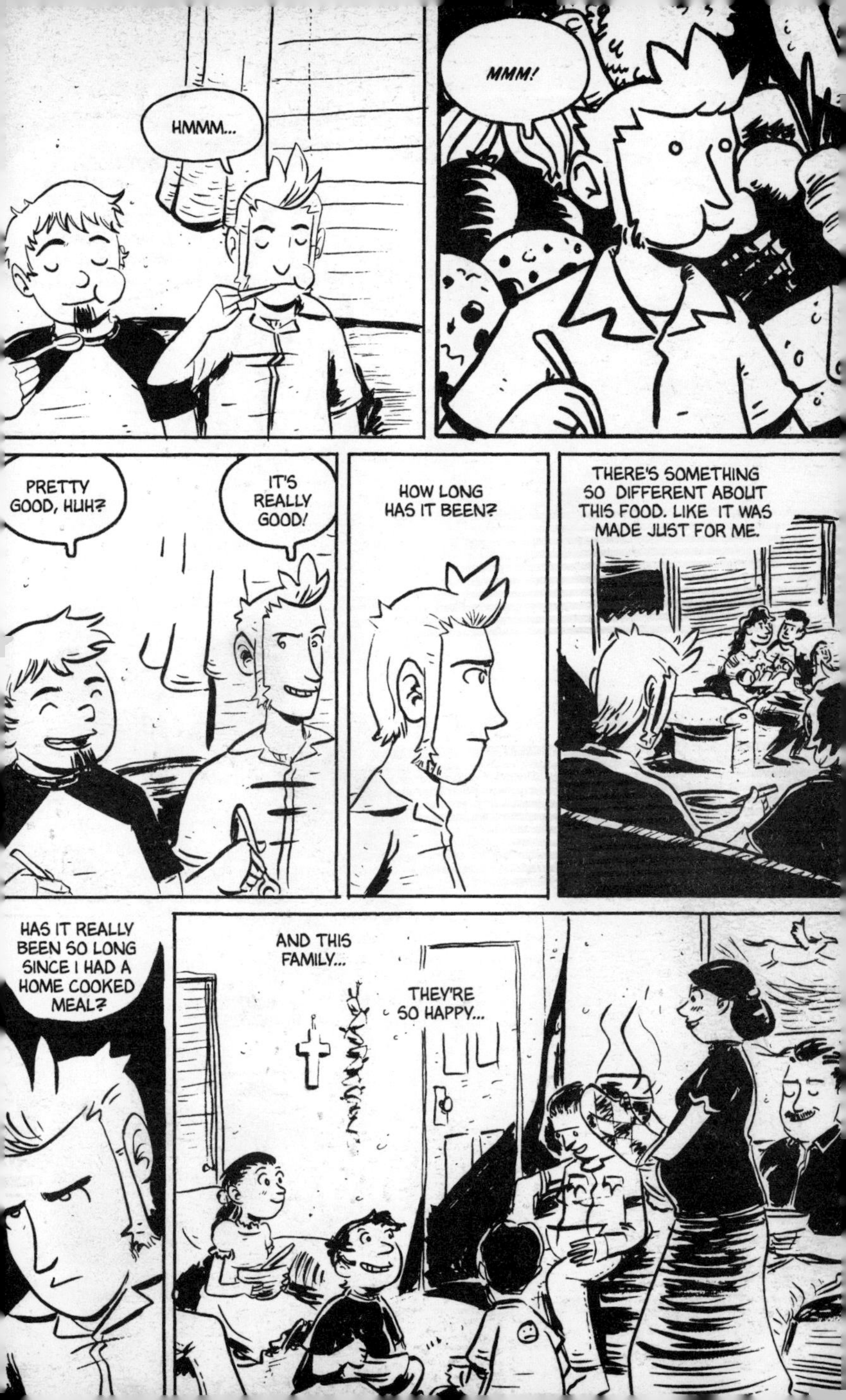
HMMM...
MMM!
PRETTY GOOD, HUH?
IT'S REALLY GOOD!
HOW LONG HAS IT BEEN?
THERE'S SOMETHING SO DIFFERENT ABOUT THIS FOOD. LIKE IT WAS MADE JUST FOR ME.
HAS IT REALLY BEEN SO LONG SINCE I HAD A HOME COOKED MEAL?
AND THIS FAMILY...
THEY'RE SO HAPPY...

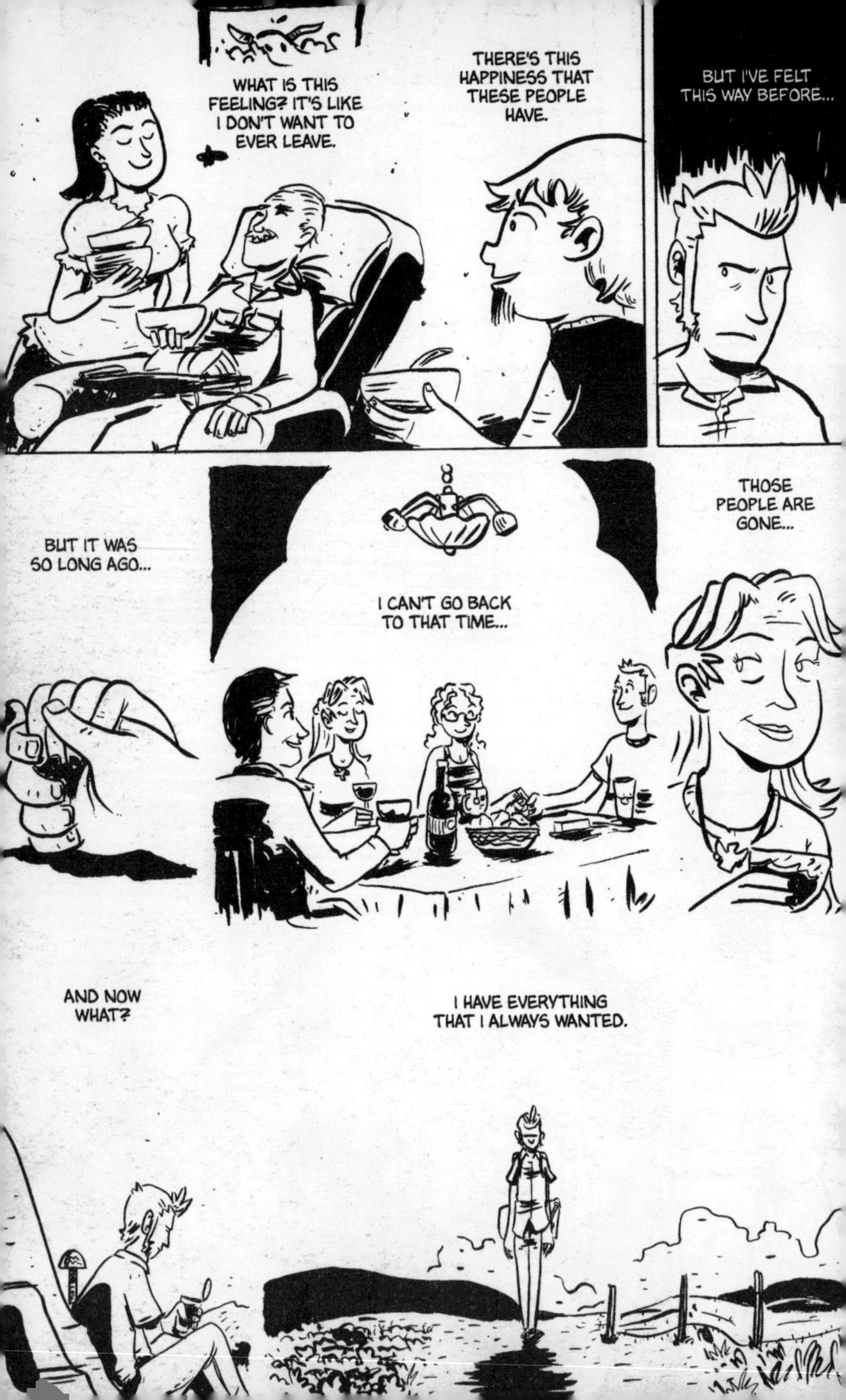
WHAT IS THIS FEELING? IT'S LIKE I DON'T WANT TO EVER LEAVE.
THERE'S THIS HAPPINESS THAT THESE PEOPLE HAVE.
BUT I'VE FELT THIS WAY BEFORE...
BUT IT WAS SO LONG AGO...
I CAN'T GO BACK TO THAT TIME...
THOSE PEOPLE ARE GONE...
AND NOW WHAT?
I HAVE EVERYTHING THAT I ALWAYS WANTED.

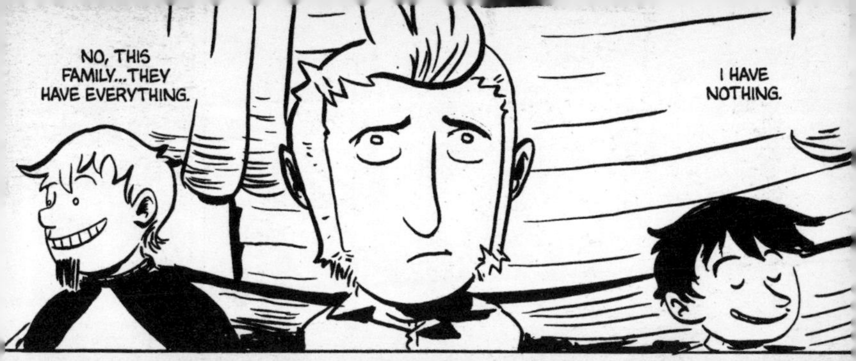
NO, THIS FAMILY...THEY HAVE EVERYTHING.
I HAVE NOTHING.

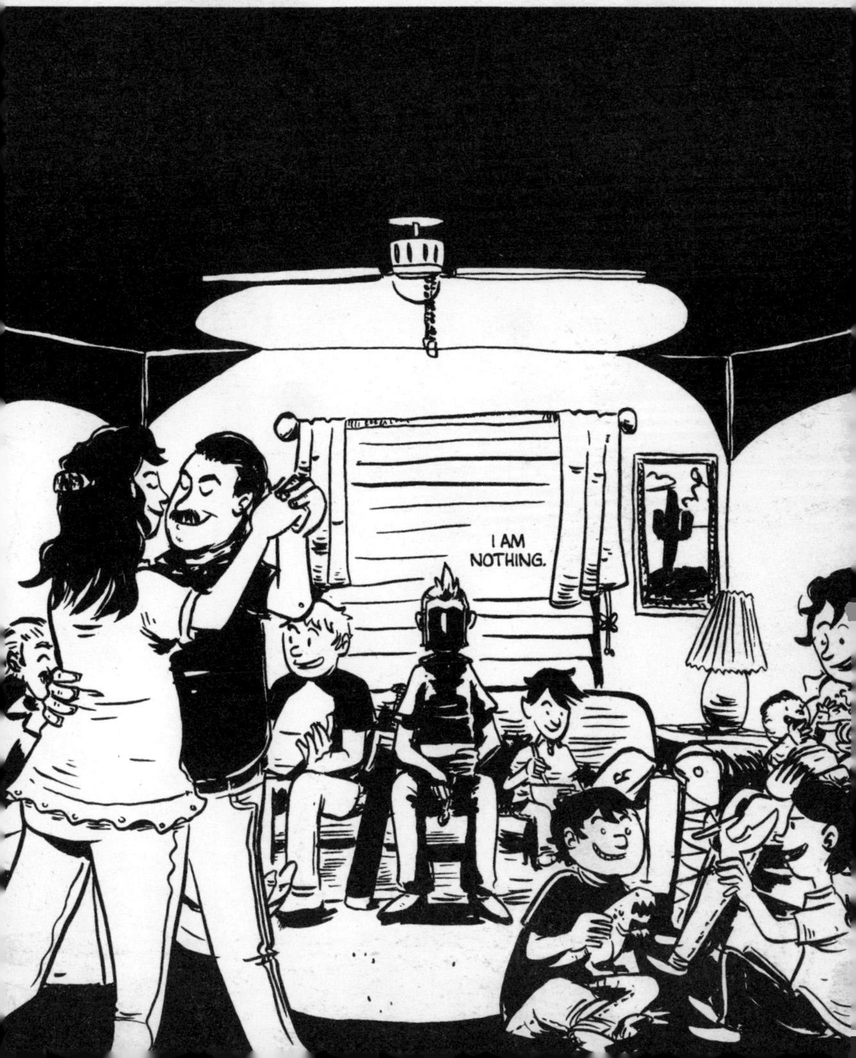
I AM NOTHING.

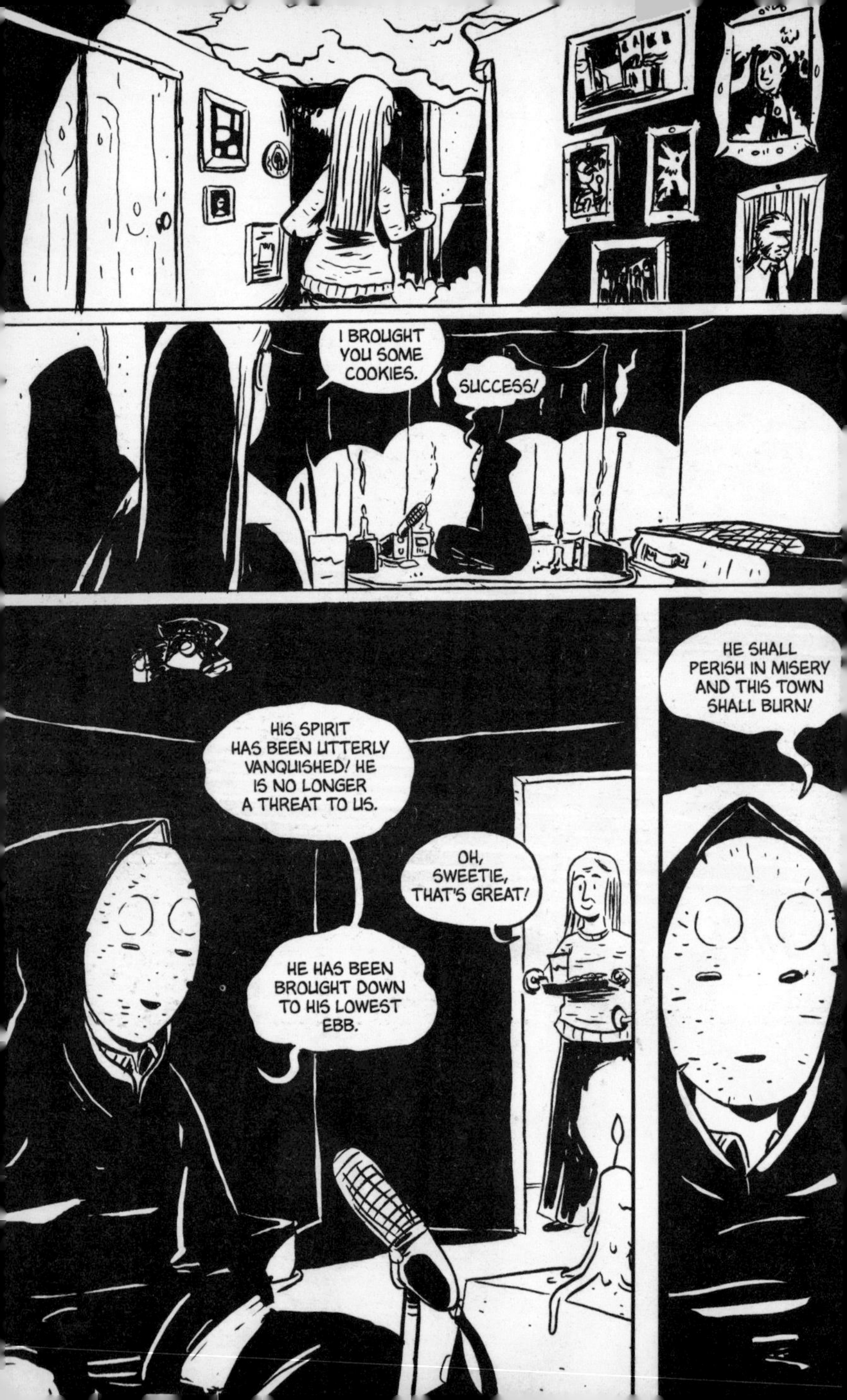
I BROUGHT YOU SOME COOKIES.
SUCCESS!
HIS SPIRIT HAS BEEN UTTERLY VANQUISHED! HE IS NO LONGER A THREAT TO US.
HE HAS BEEN BROUGHT DOWN TO HIS LOWEST EBB.
OH, SWEETIE, THAT'S GREAT!
HE SHALL PERISH IN MISERY AND THIS TOWN SHALL BURN!

CHAPTER 5

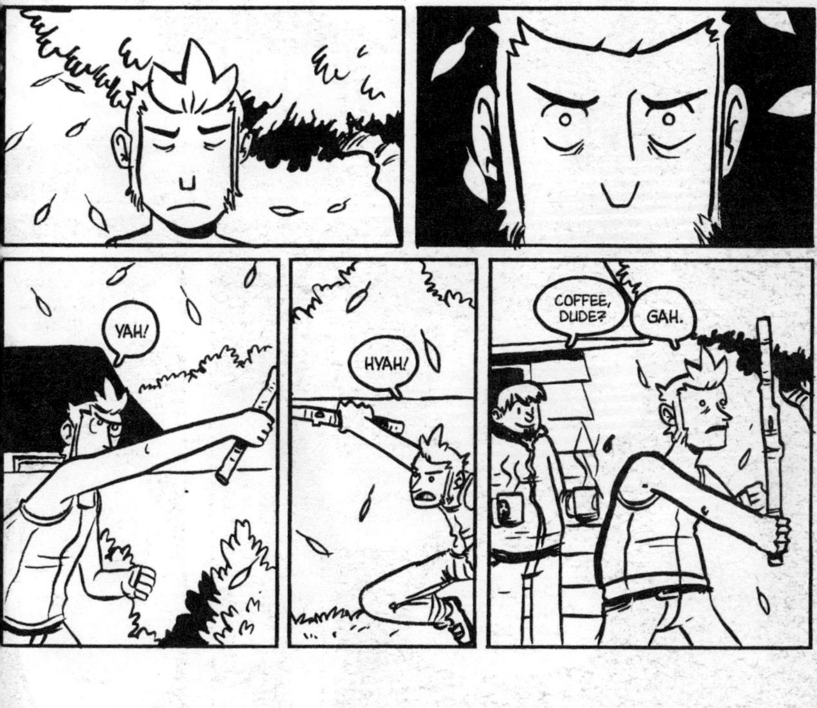
YAH!
HYAH!
COFFEE, DUDE?
GAH.

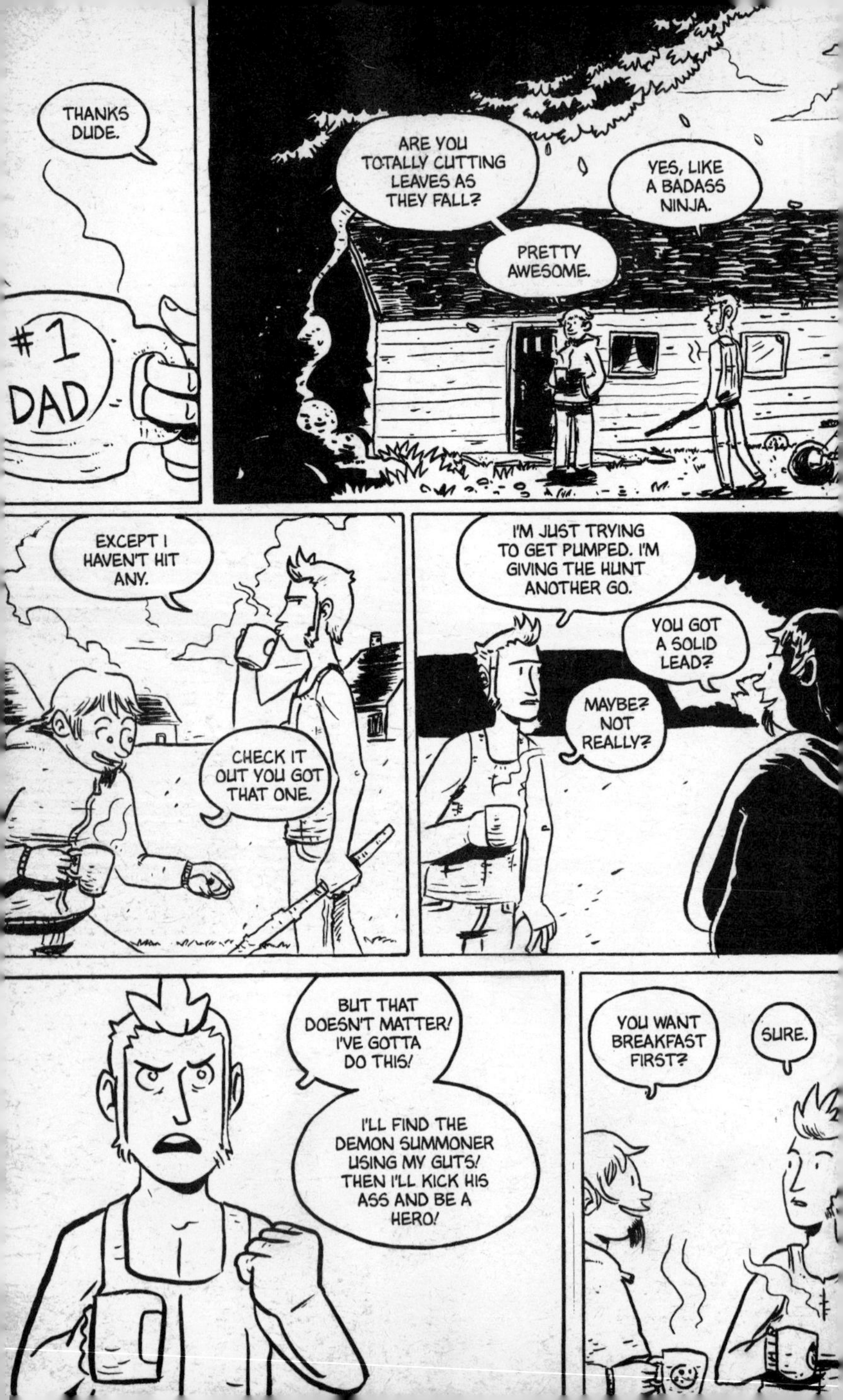
THANKS DUDE.
#1 DAD
ARE YOU TOTALLY CUTTING LEAVES AS THEY FALL?
PRETTY AWESOME.
YES, LIKE A BADASS NINJA.
EXCEPT I HAVEN'T HIT ANY.
CHECK IT OUT YOU GOT THAT ONE.
I'M JUST TRYING TO GET PUMPED. I'M GIVING THE HUNT ANOTHER GO.
YOU GOT A SOLID LEAD?
MAYBE? NOT REALLY?
BUT THAT DOESN'T MATTER! I'VE GOTTA DO THIS!
I'LL FIND THE DEMON SUMMONER USING MY GUTS! THEN I'LL KICK HIS ASS AND BE A HERO!
YOU WANT BREAKFAST FIRST?
SURE.

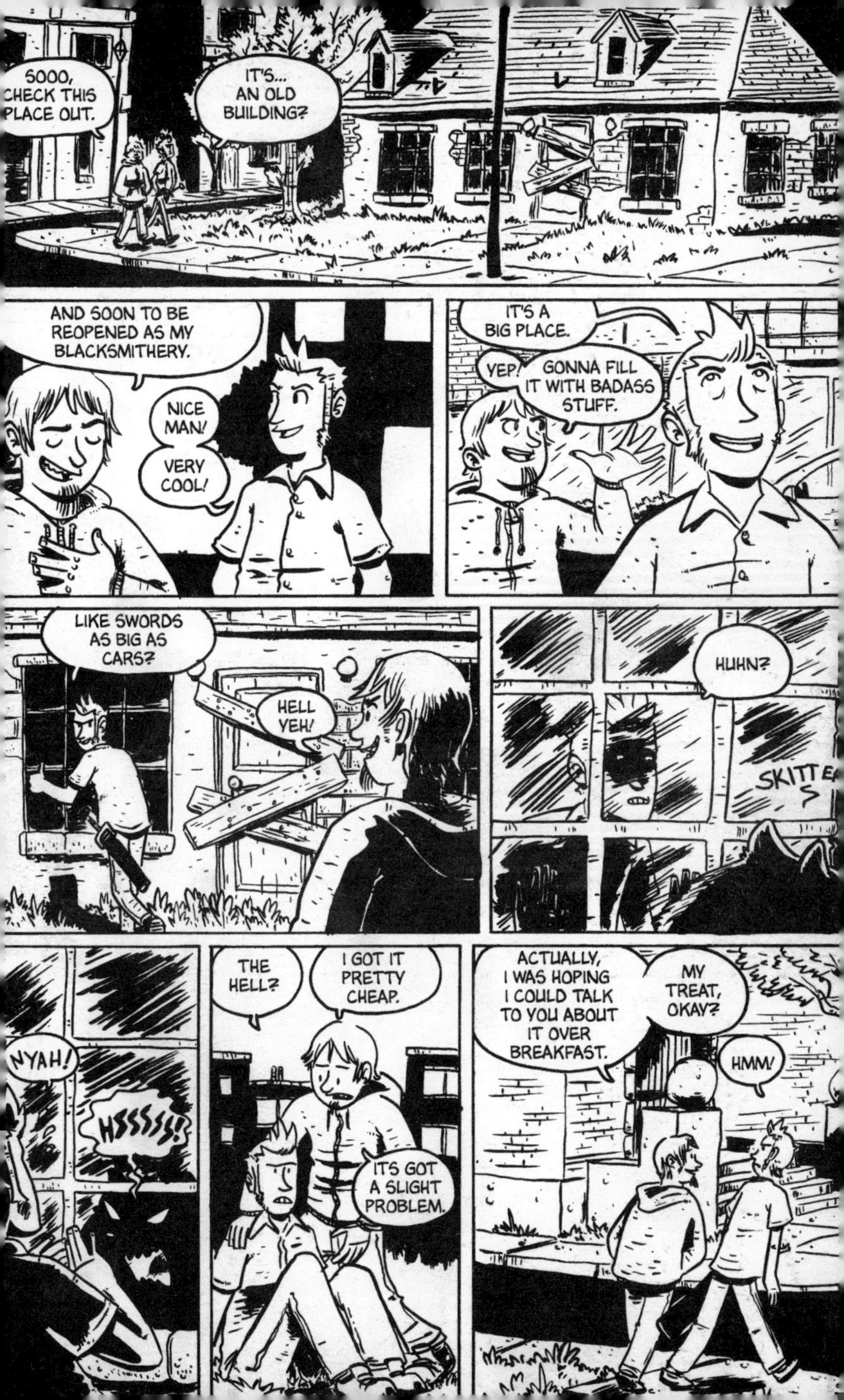
SOOO, CHECK THIS PLACE OUT.
IT'S... AN OLD BUILDING?
AND SOON TO BE REOPENED AS MY BLACKSMITHERY.
NICE MAN!
VERY COOL!
IT'S A BIG PLACE.
YEP!
GONNA FILL IT WITH BADASS STUFF.
LIKE SWORDS AS BIG AS CARS?
HELL YEH!
HUHN?
SKITTE
NYAH!
HSSSSS!
THE HELL?
I GOT IT PRETTY CHEAP.
IT'S GOT A SLIGHT PROBLEM.
ACTUALLY, I WAS HOPING I COULD TALK TO YOU ABOUT IT OVER BREAKFAST.
MY TREAT, OKAY?
HMM!

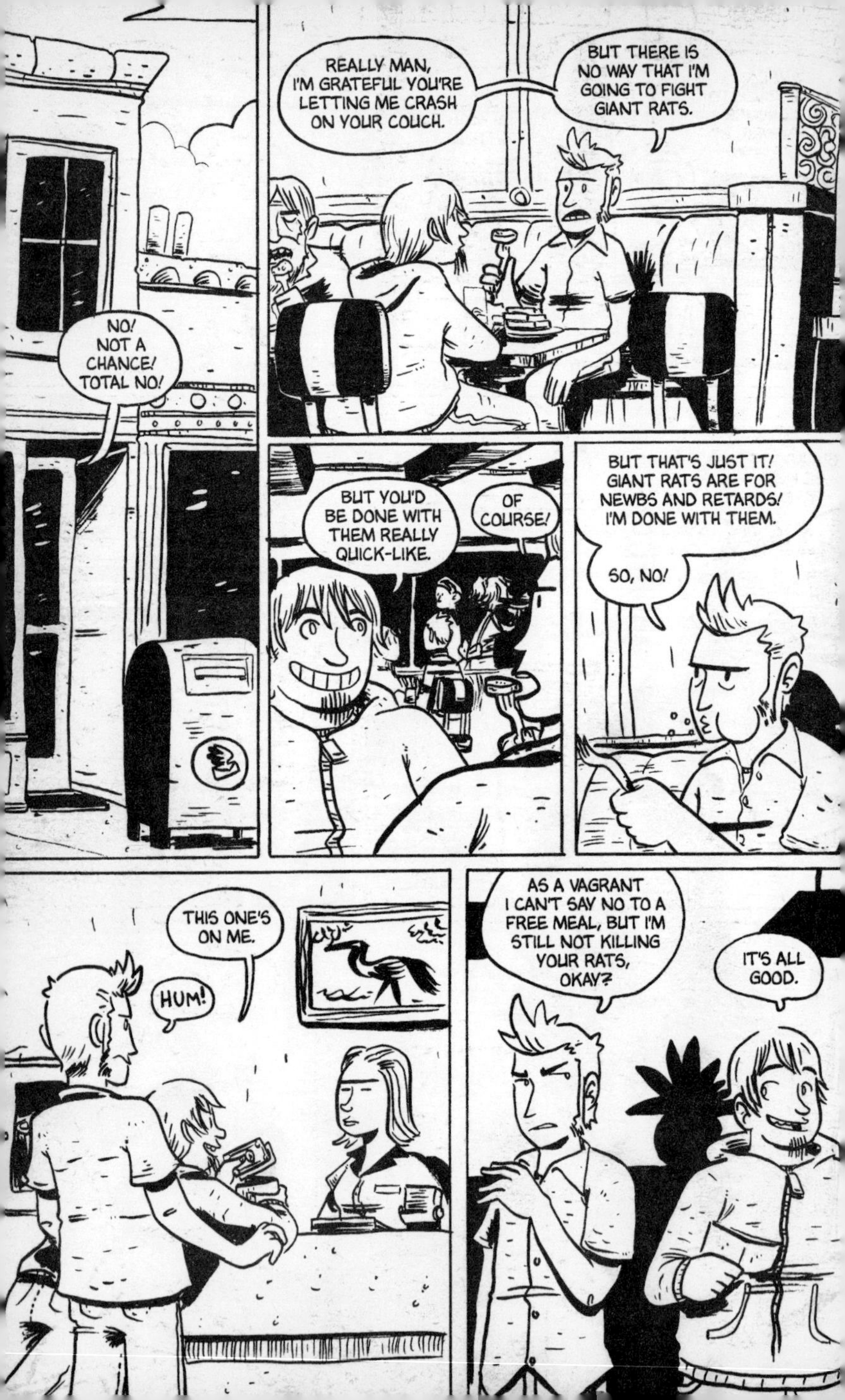
REALLY MAN, I'M GRATEFUL YOU'RE LETTING ME CRASH ON YOUR COUCH.
BUT THERE IS NO WAY THAT I'M GOING TO FIGHT GIANT RATS.
NO! NOT A CHANCE! TOTAL NO!
BUT YOU'D BE DONE WITH THEM REALLY QUICK-LIKE.
OF COURSE!
BUT THAT'S JUST IT! GIANT RATS ARE FOR NEWBS AND RETARDS! I'M DONE WITH THEM.
SO, NO!
HUM!
THIS ONE'S ON ME.
AS A VAGRANT I CAN'T SAY NO TO A FREE MEAL, BUT I'M STILL NOT KILLING YOUR RATS, OKAY?
IT'S ALL GOOD.

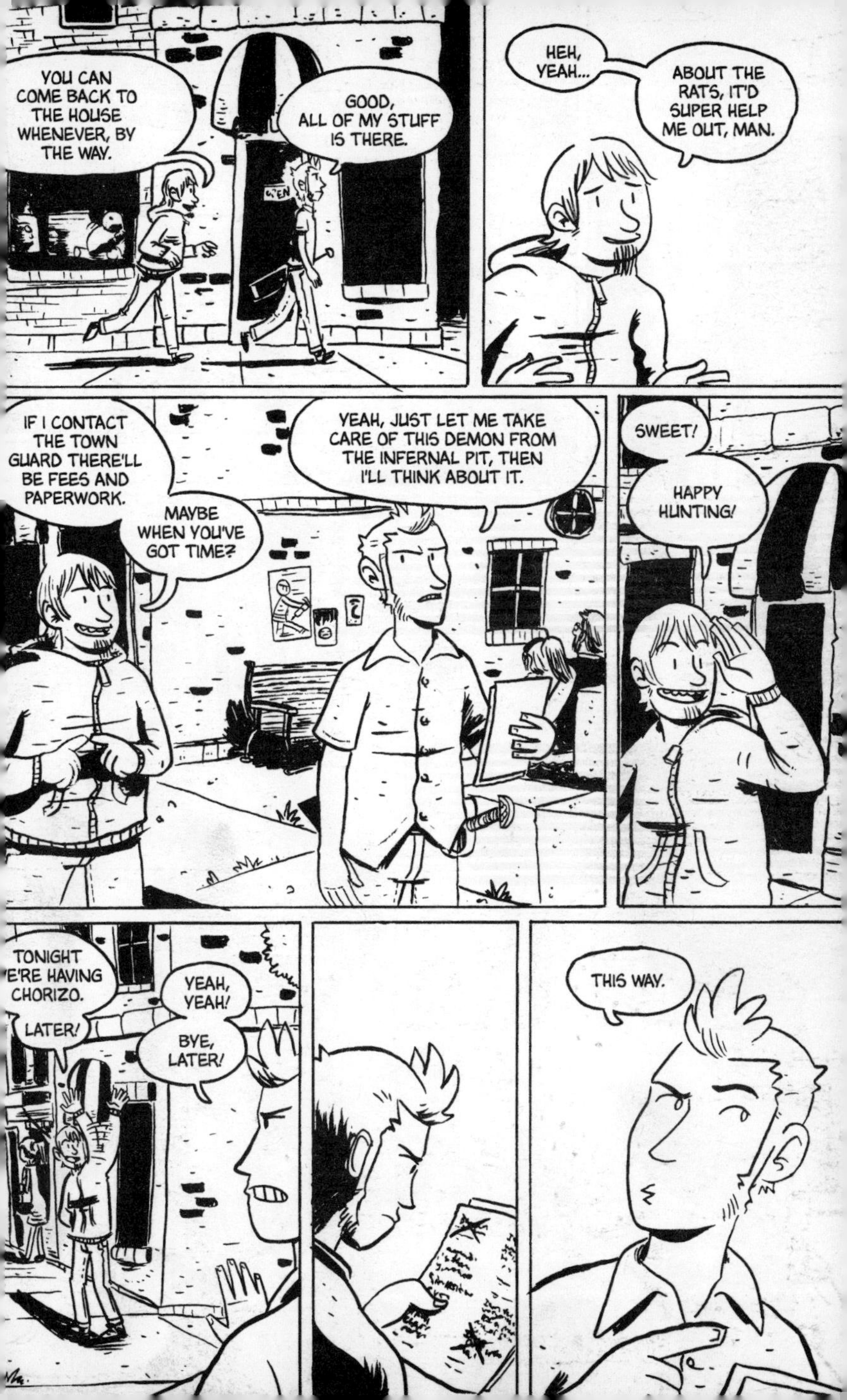
YOU CAN COME BACK TO THE HOUSE WHENEVER, BY THE WAY.
GOOD, ALL OF MY STUFF IS THERE.
HEH, YEAH...
ABOUT THE RATS, IT'D SUPER HELP ME OUT, MAN.
IF I CONTACT THE TOWN GUARD THERE'LL BE FEES AND PAPERWORK.
MAYBE WHEN YOU'VE GOT TIME?
YEAH, JUST LET ME TAKE CARE OF THIS DEMON FROM THE INFERNAL PIT, THEN I'LL THINK ABOUT IT.
SWEET!
HAPPY HUNTING!
TONIGHT E'RE HAVING CHORIZO.
LATER!
YEAH, YEAH!
BYE, LATER!
THIS WAY.

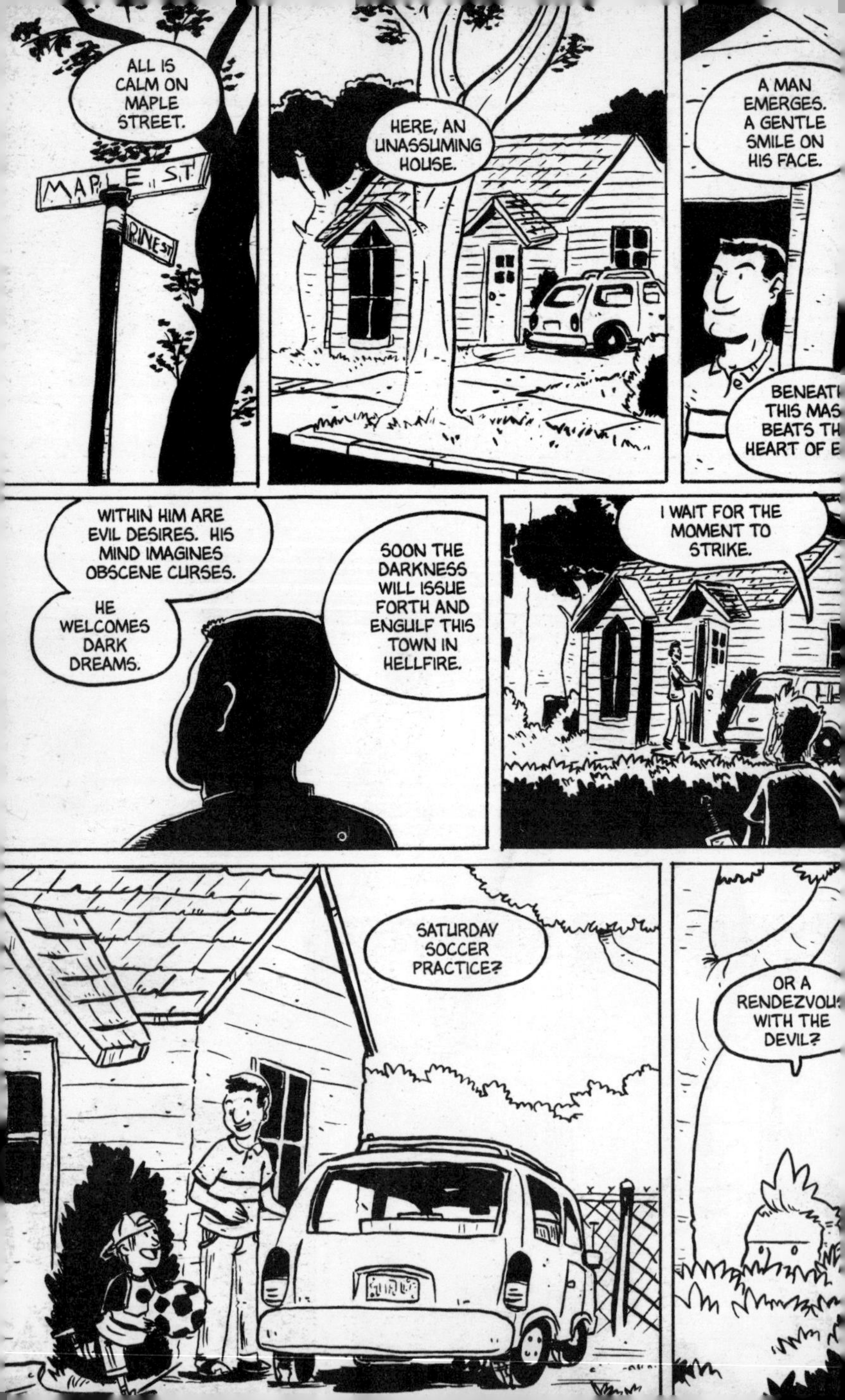
ALL IS CALM ON MAPLE STREET.
MAPLE ST.
PINE ST
HERE, AN UNASSUMING HOUSE.
A MAN EMERGES. A GENTLE SMILE ON HIS FACE.
BENEAT THIS MAS BEATS TH HEART OF E
WITHIN HIM ARE EVIL DESIRES. HIS MIND IMAGINES OBSCENE CURSES.
HE WELCOMES DARK DREAMS.
SOON THE DARKNESS WILL ISSUE FORTH AND ENGULF THIS TOWN IN HELLFIRE.
I WAIT FOR THE MOMENT TO STRIKE.
SATURDAY SOCCER PRACTICE?
OR A RENDEZVOU WITH THE DEVIL?

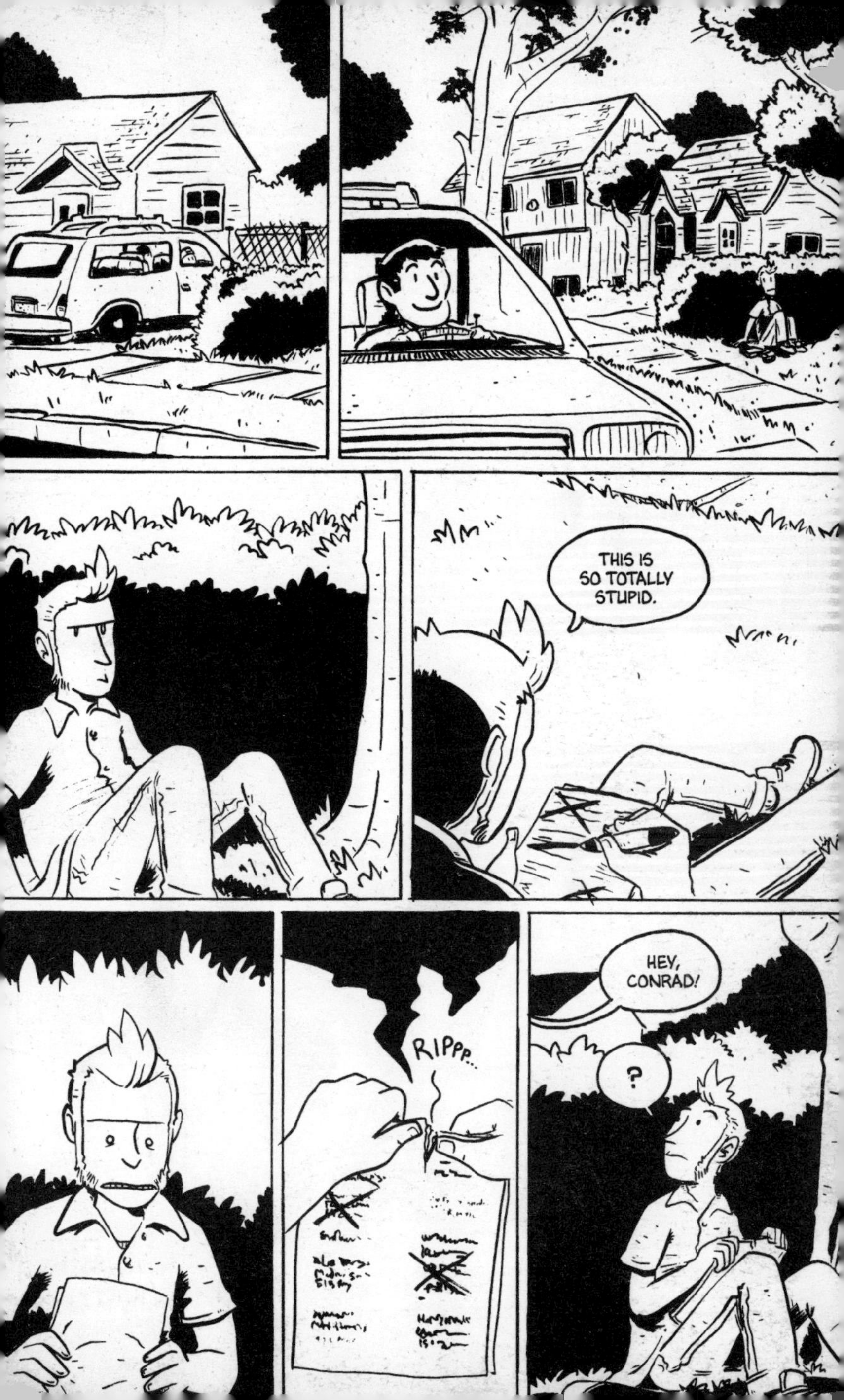
THIS IS SO TOTALLY STUPID.
RIPPP...
HEY, CONRAD!
?

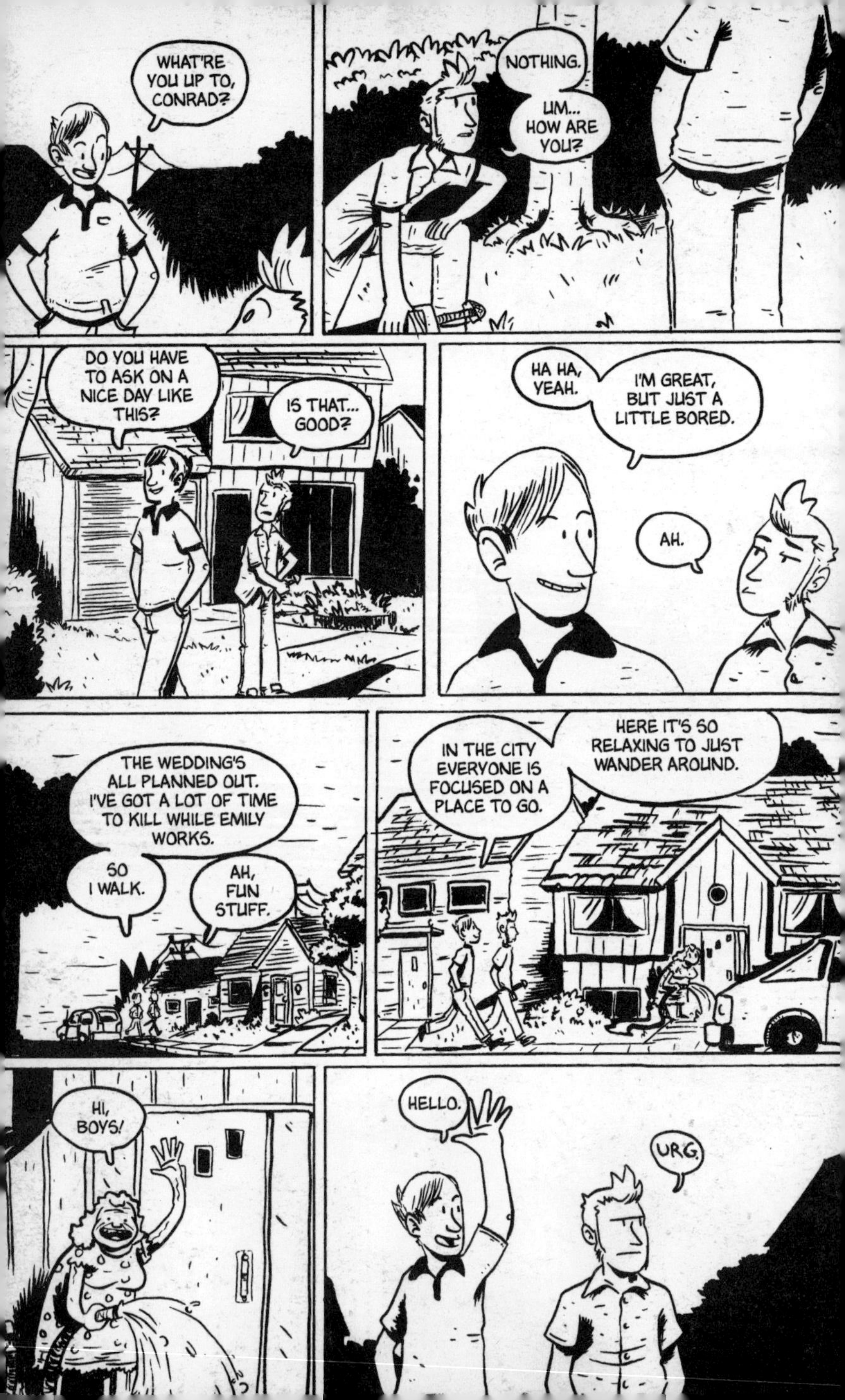
WHAT'RE YOU UP TO, CONRAD?
NOTHING.
UM... HOW ARE YOU?
DO YOU HAVE TO ASK ON A NICE DAY LIKE THIS?
IS THAT... GOOD?
HA HA, YEAH.
I'M GREAT, BUT JUST A LITTLE BORED.
AH.
THE WEDDING'S ALL PLANNED OUT. I'VE GOT A LOT OF TIME TO KILL WHILE EMILY WORKS.
SO I WALK.
AH, FUN STUFF.
IN THE CITY EVERYONE IS FOCUSED ON A PLACE TO GO.
HERE IT'S SO RELAXING TO JUST WANDER AROUND.
HI, BOYS!
HELLO.
URG.

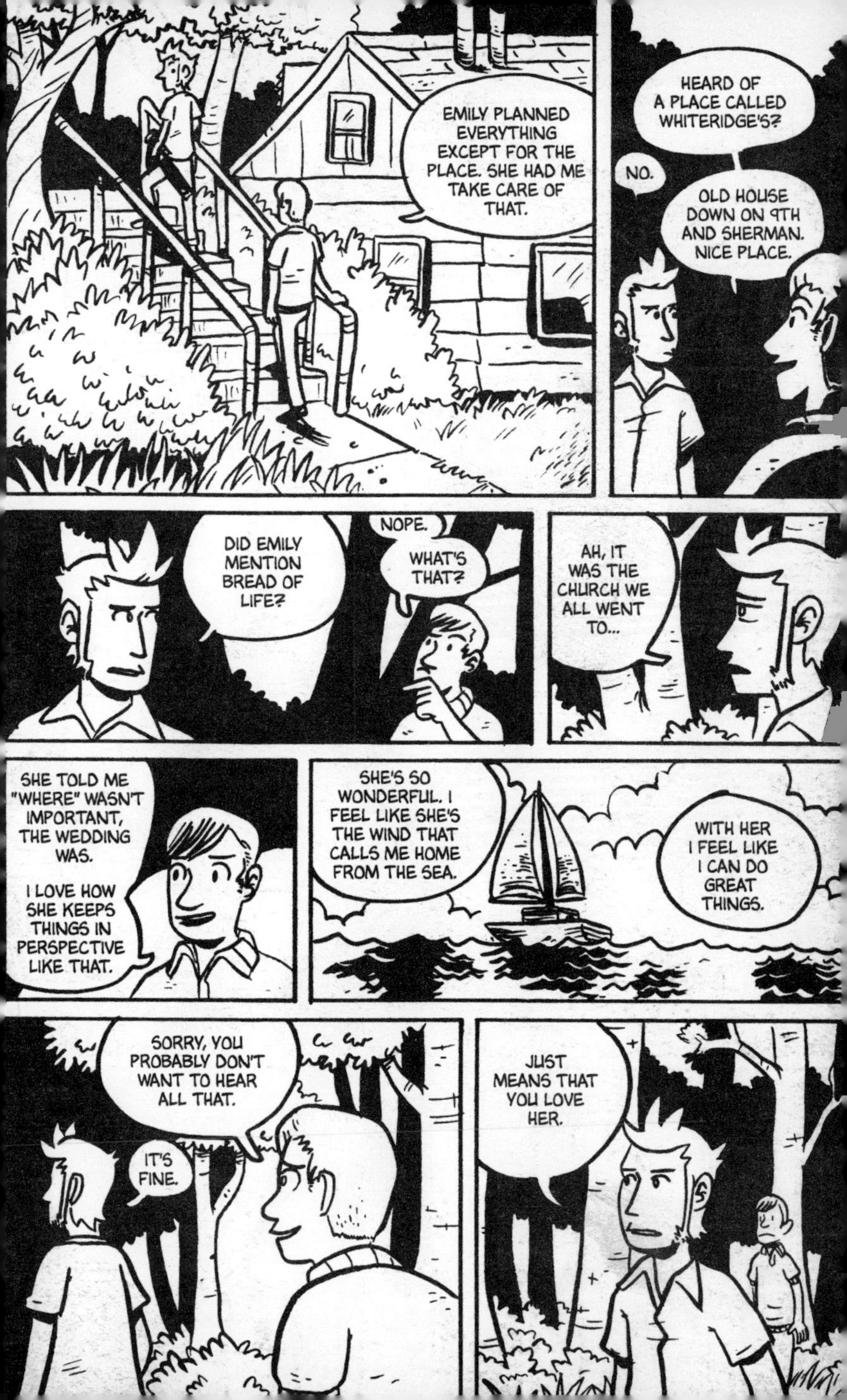
EMILY PLANNED EVERYTHING EXCEPT FOR THE PLACE. SHE HAD ME TAKE CARE OF THAT.
HEARD OF A PLACE CALLED WHITERIDGE'S?
NO.
OLD HOUSE DOWN ON 9TH AND SHERMAN. NICE PLACE.
DID EMILY MENTION BREAD OF LIFE?
NOPE.
WHAT'S THAT?
AH, IT WAS THE CHURCH WE ALL WENT TO...
SHE TOLD ME "WHERE" WASN'T IMPORTANT, THE WEDDING WAS.
I LOVE HOW SHE KEEPS THINGS IN PERSPECTIVE LIKE THAT.
SHE'S SO WONDERFUL. I FEEL LIKE SHE'S THE WIND THAT CALLS ME HOME FROM THE SEA.
WITH HER I FEEL LIKE I CAN DO GREAT THINGS.
SORRY, YOU PROBABLY DON'T WANT TO HEAR ALL THAT.
IT'S FINE.
JUST MEANS THAT YOU LOVE HER.

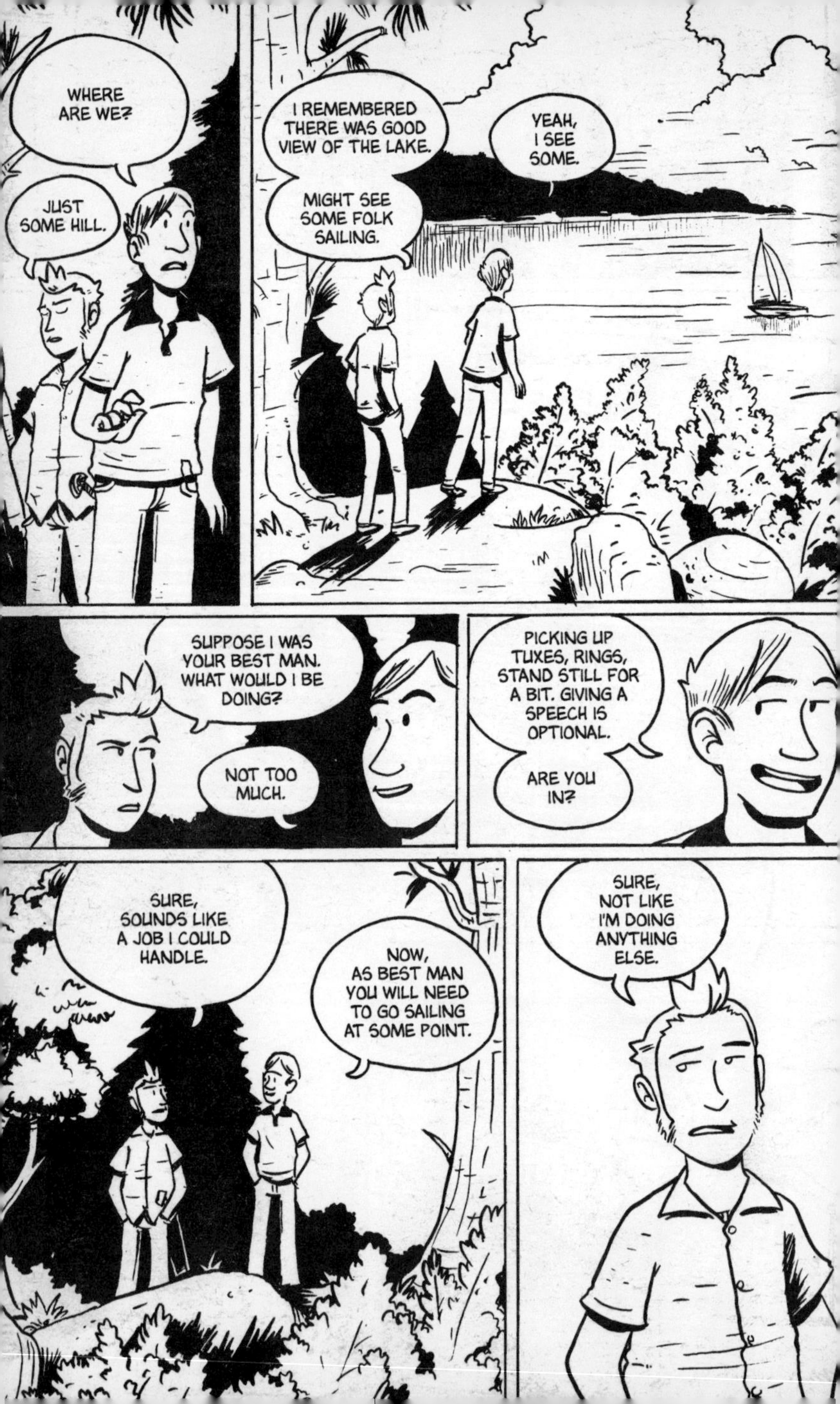
WHERE ARE WE?
JUST SOME HILL.
I REMEMBERED THERE WAS GOOD VIEW OF THE LAKE.
MIGHT SEE SOME FOLK SAILING.
YEAH, I SEE SOME.
SUPPOSE I WAS YOUR BEST MAN. WHAT WOULD I BE DOING?
NOT TOO MUCH.
PICKING UP TUXES, RINGS, STAND STILL FOR A BIT. GIVING A SPEECH IS OPTIONAL.
ARE YOU IN?
SURE, SOUNDS LIKE A JOB I COULD HANDLE.
NOW, AS BEST MAN YOU WILL NEED TO GO SAILING AT SOME POINT.
SURE, NOT LIKE I'M DOING ANYTHING ELSE.

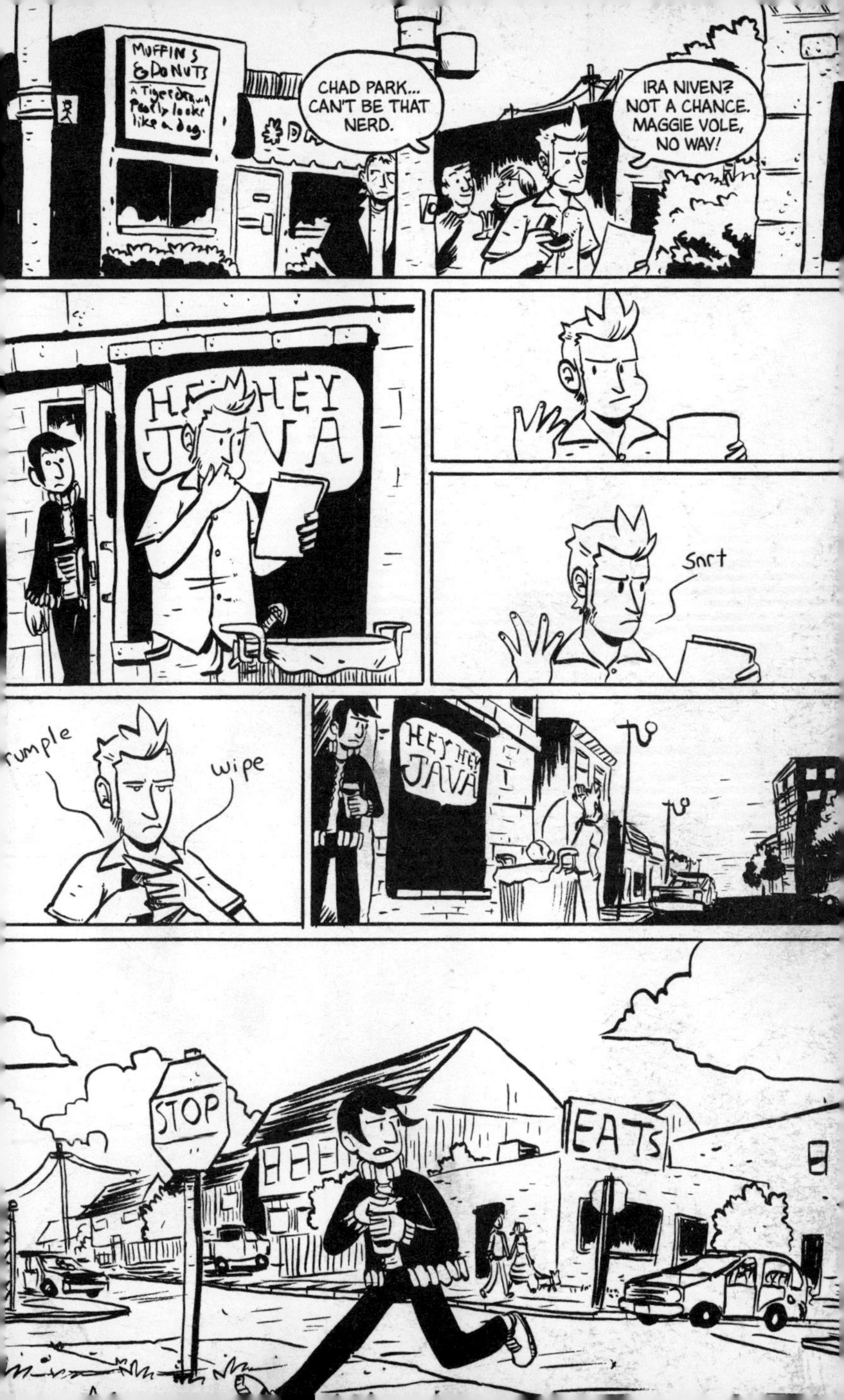
MUFFINS & DONUTS
A Tiger drawn Poorly looks like a dog.
CHAD PARK... CAN'T BE THAT NERD.
IRA NIVEN? NOT A CHANCE. MAGGIE VOLE, NO WAY!
HEY HEY JAVA
snrt
rumple
wipe
HEY HEY JAVA
STOP
EATS

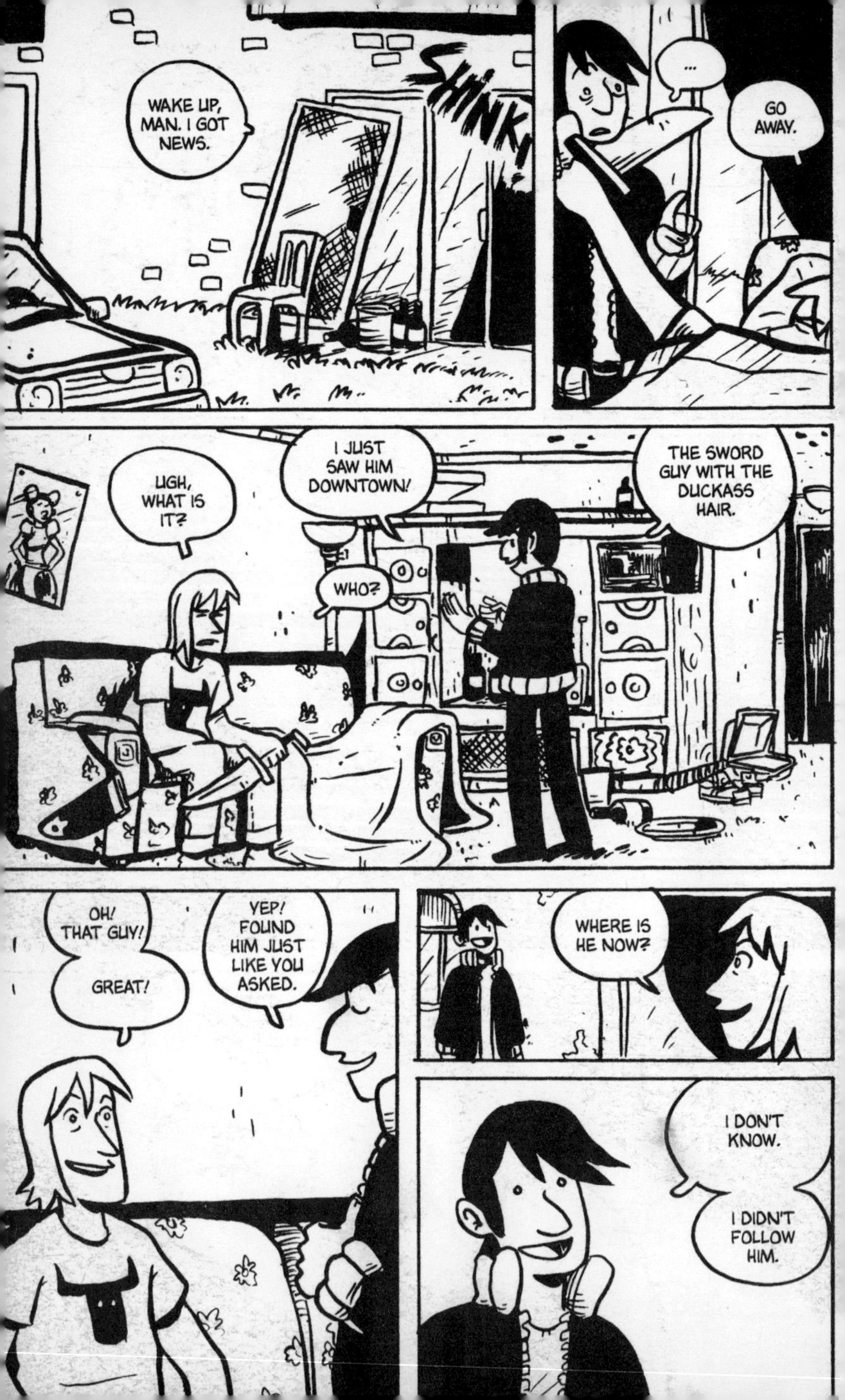
WAKE UP, MAN. I GOT NEWS.
SHINK!
...
GO AWAY.
UGH, WHAT IS IT?
I JUST SAW HIM DOWNTOWN!
THE SWORD GUY WITH THE DUCKASS HAIR.
WHO?
OH! THAT GUY!
GREAT!
YEP! FOUND HIM JUST LIKE YOU ASKED.
WHERE IS HE NOW?
I DON'T KNOW.
I DIDN'T FOLLOW HIM.

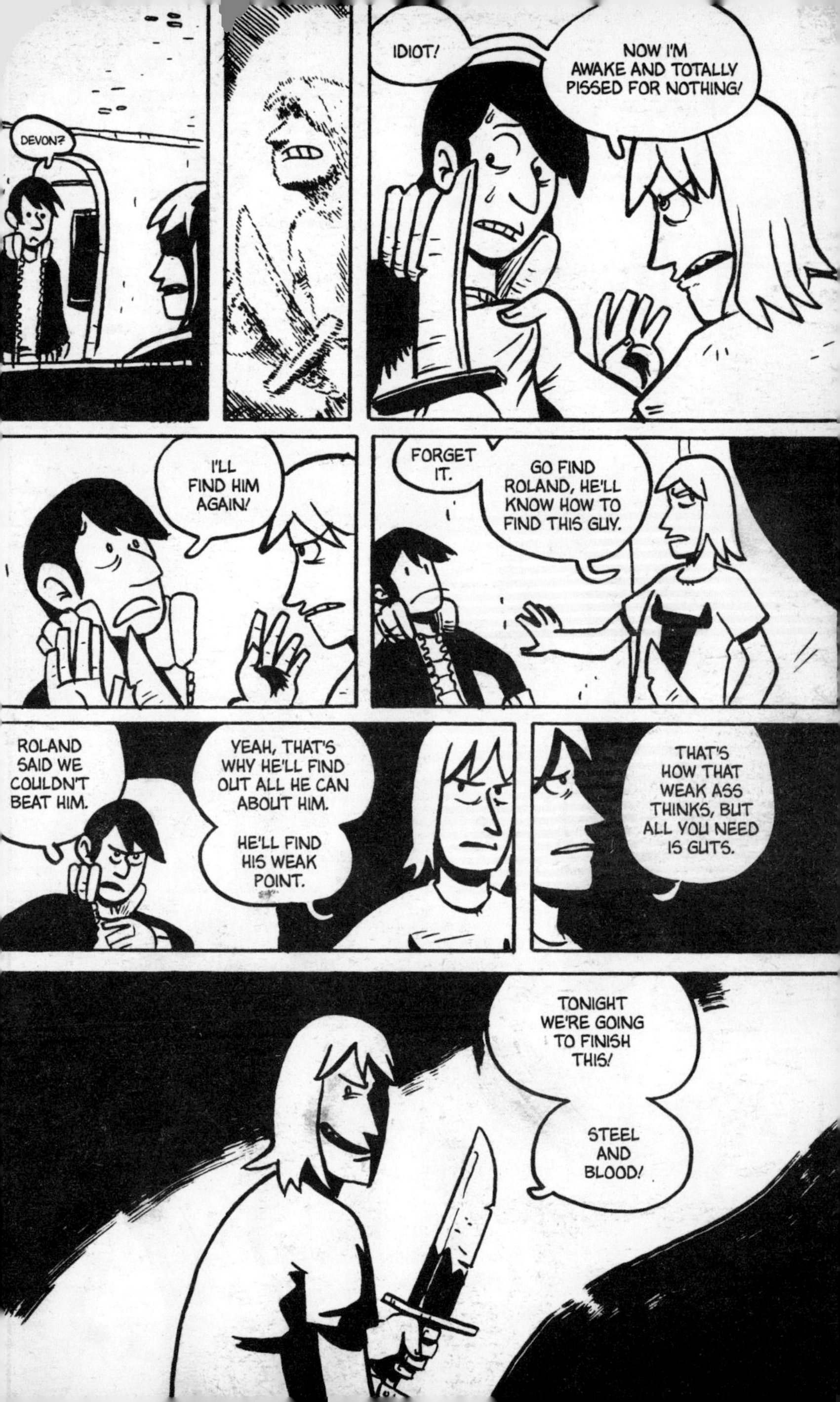
DEVON?
IDIOT!
NOW I'M AWAKE AND TOTALLY PISSED FOR NOTHING!
I'LL FIND HIM AGAIN!
FORGET IT.
GO FIND ROLAND, HE'LL KNOW HOW TO FIND THIS GUY.
ROLAND SAID WE COULDN'T BEAT HIM.
YEAH, THAT'S WHY HE'LL FIND OUT ALL HE CAN ABOUT HIM.
HE'LL FIND HIS WEAK POINT.
THAT'S HOW THAT WEAK ASS THINKS, BUT ALL YOU NEED IS GUTS.
TONIGHT WE'RE GOING TO FINISH THIS!
STEEL AND BLOOD!

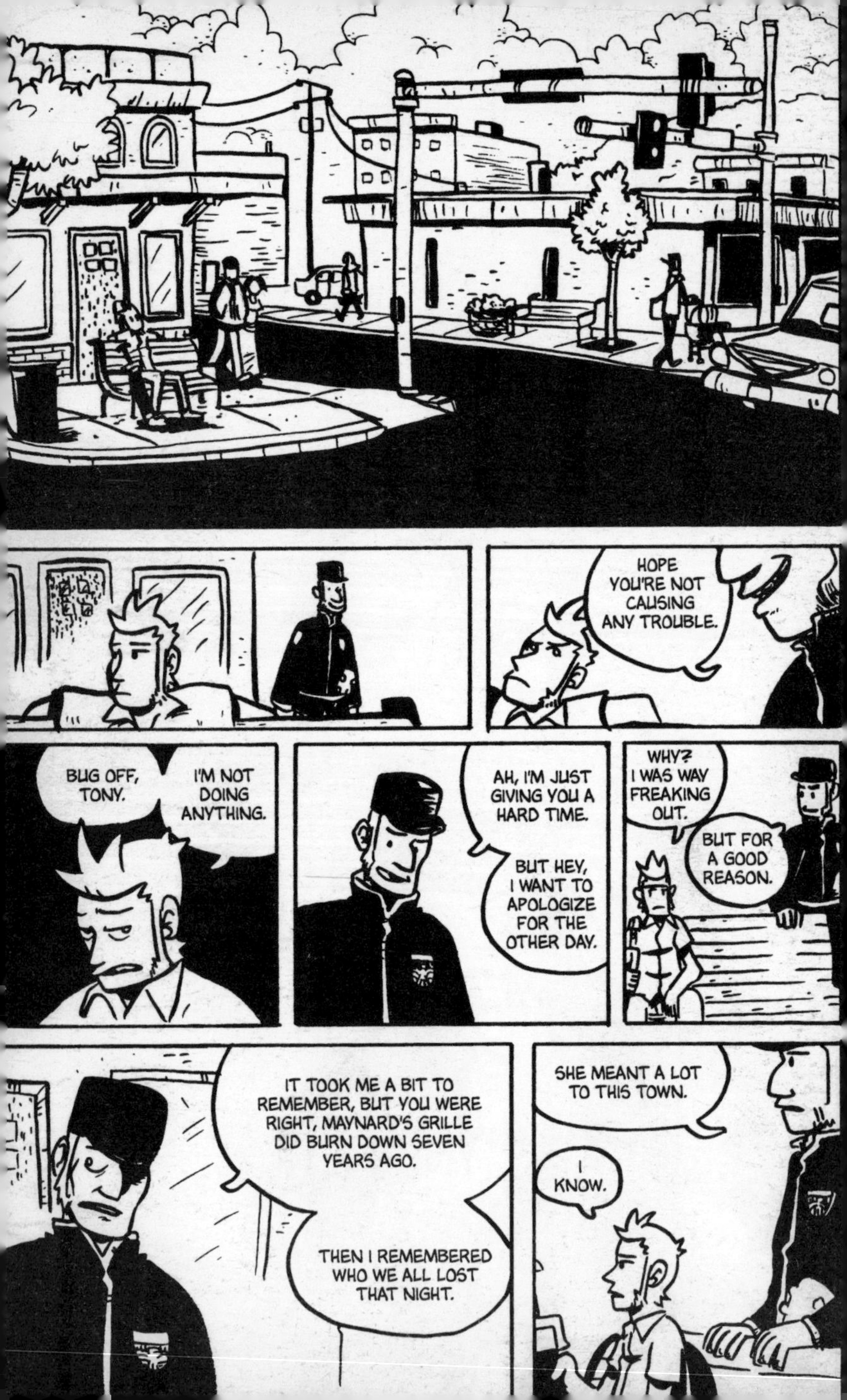
HOPE YOU'RE NOT CAUSING ANY TROUBLE.
BUG OFF, TONY.
I'M NOT DOING ANYTHING.
AH, I'M JUST GIVING YOU A HARD TIME.
BUT HEY, I WANT TO APOLOGIZE FOR THE OTHER DAY.
WHY? I WAS WAY FREAKING OUT.
BUT FOR A GOOD REASON.
IT TOOK ME A BIT TO REMEMBER, BUT YOU WERE RIGHT, MAYNARD'S GRILLE DID BURN DOWN SEVEN YEARS AGO.
THEN I REMEMBERED WHO WE ALL LOST THAT NIGHT.
SHE MEANT A LOT TO THIS TOWN.
I KNOW.

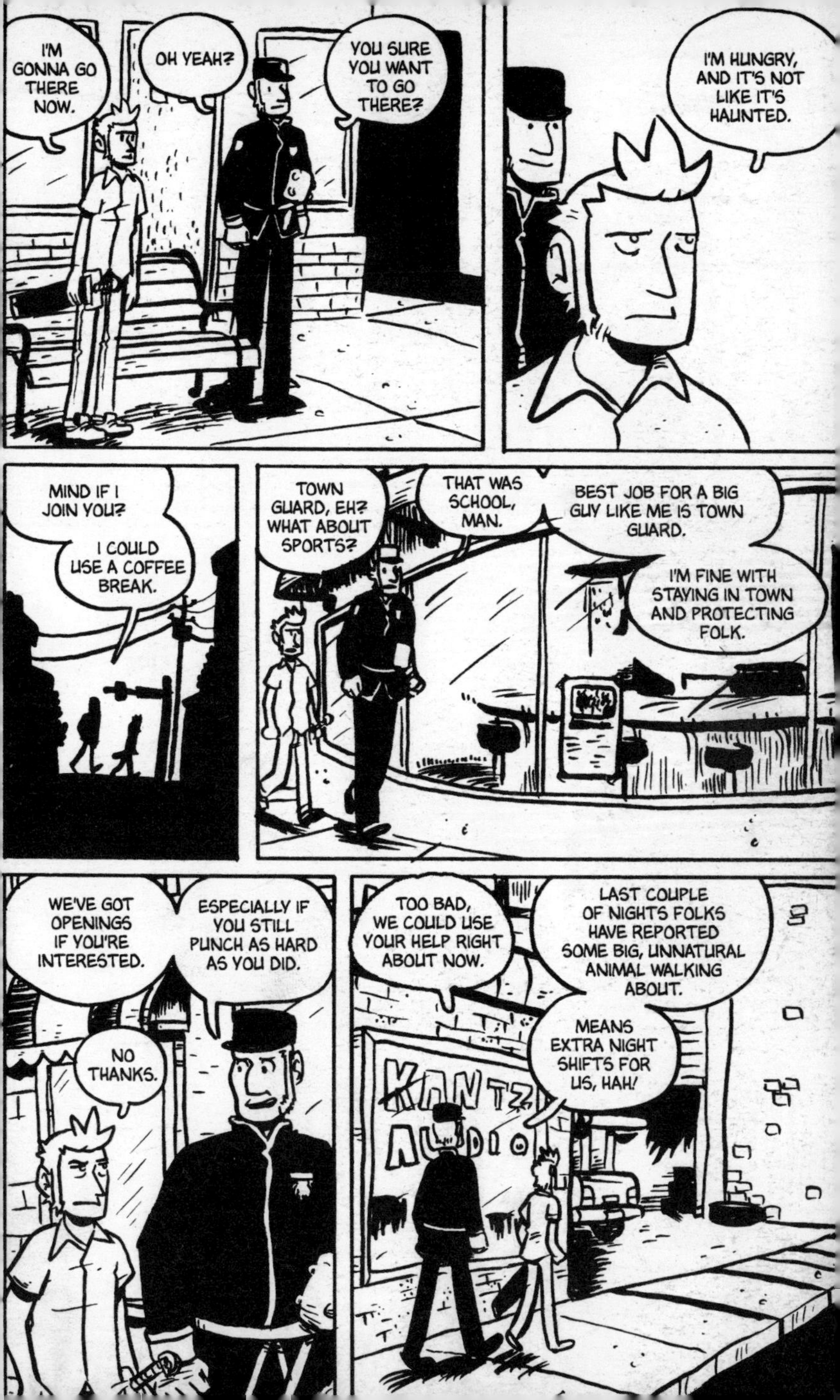
I'M GONNA GO THERE NOW.
OH YEAH?
YOU SURE YOU WANT TO GO THERE?
I'M HUNGRY, AND IT'S NOT LIKE IT'S HAUNTED.
MIND IF I JOIN YOU?
I COULD USE A COFFEE BREAK.
TOWN GUARD, EH? WHAT ABOUT SPORTS?
THAT WAS SCHOOL, MAN.
BEST JOB FOR A BIG GUY LIKE ME IS TOWN GUARD.
I'M FINE WITH STAYING IN TOWN AND PROTECTING FOLK.
WE'VE GOT OPENINGS IF YOU'RE INTERESTED.
ESPECIALLY IF YOU STILL PUNCH AS HARD AS YOU DID.
NO THANKS.
TOO BAD, WE COULD USE YOUR HELP RIGHT ABOUT NOW.
LAST COUPLE OF NIGHTS FOLKS HAVE REPORTED SOME BIG, UNNATURAL ANIMAL WALKING ABOUT.
MEANS EXTRA NIGHT SHIFTS FOR US, HAH!
KANTZ AUDIO

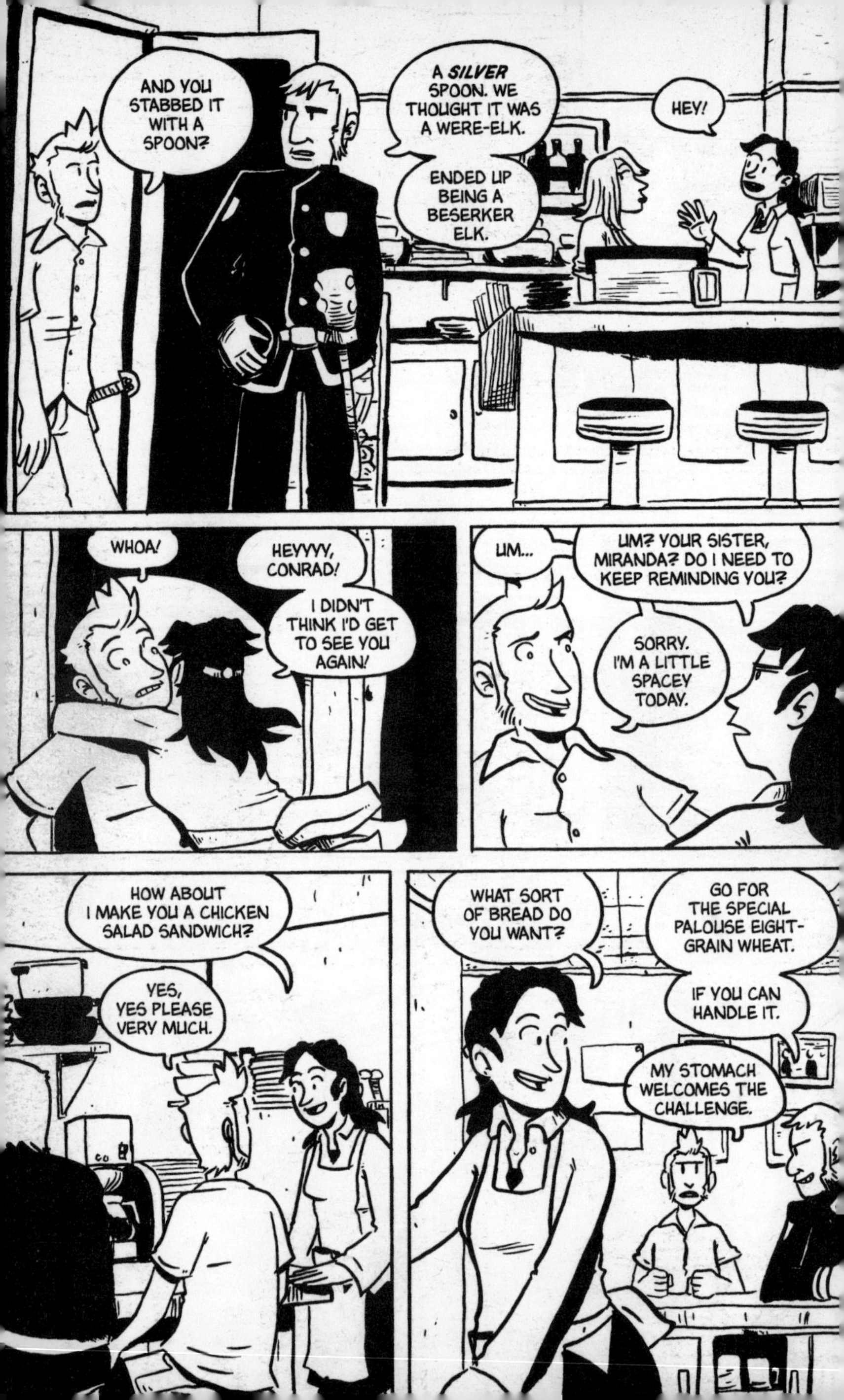
AND YOU STABBED IT WITH A SPOON?
A *SILVER* SPOON. WE THOUGHT IT WAS A WERE-ELK.
ENDED UP BEING A BESERKER ELK.
HEY!
WHOA!
HEYYYY, CONRAD!
I DIDN'T THINK I'D GET TO SEE YOU AGAIN!
UM...
UM? YOUR SISTER, MIRANDA? DO I NEED TO KEEP REMINDING YOU?
SORRY. I'M A LITTLE SPACEY TODAY.
HOW ABOUT I MAKE YOU A CHICKEN SALAD SANDWICH?
YES, YES PLEASE VERY MUCH.
WHAT SORT OF BREAD DO YOU WANT?
GO FOR THE SPECIAL PALOUSE EIGHT-GRAIN WHEAT.
IF YOU CAN HANDLE IT.
MY STOMACH WELCOMES THE CHALLENGE.

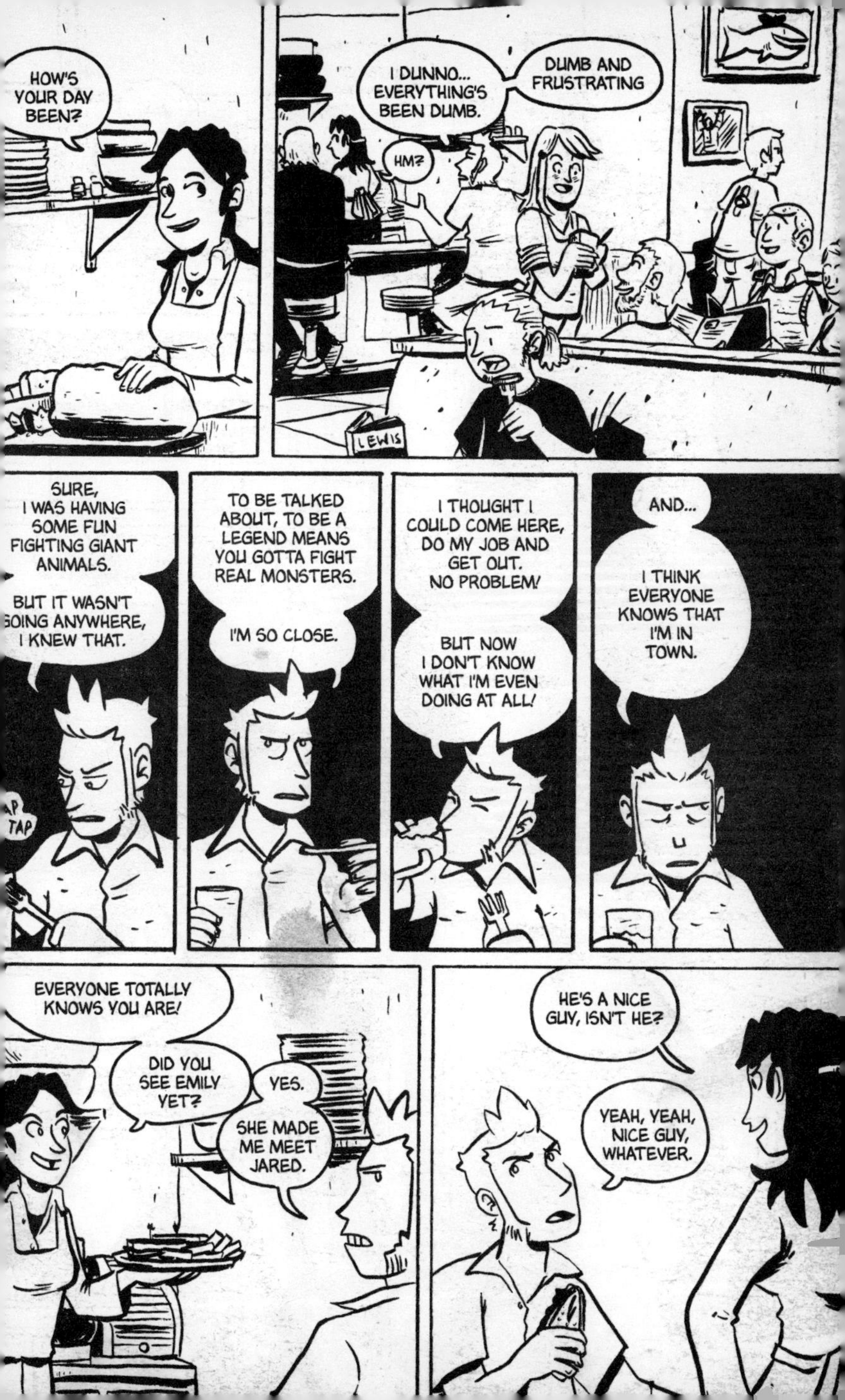
HOW'S YOUR DAY BEEN?
I DUNNO... EVERYTHING'S BEEN DUMB.
DUMB AND FRUSTRATING
HM?
LEWIS
SURE, I WAS HAVING SOME FUN FIGHTING GIANT ANIMALS.
BUT IT WASN'T GOING ANYWHERE, I KNEW THAT.
TAP TAP
TO BE TALKED ABOUT, TO BE A LEGEND MEANS YOU GOTTA FIGHT REAL MONSTERS.
I'M SO CLOSE.
I THOUGHT I COULD COME HERE, DO MY JOB AND GET OUT. NO PROBLEM!
BUT NOW I DON'T KNOW WHAT I'M EVEN DOING AT ALL!
AND...
I THINK EVERYONE KNOWS THAT I'M IN TOWN.
EVERYONE TOTALLY KNOWS YOU ARE!
DID YOU SEE EMILY YET?
YES.
SHE MADE ME MEET JARED.
HE'S A NICE GUY, ISN'T HE?
YEAH, YEAH, NICE GUY, WHATEVER.

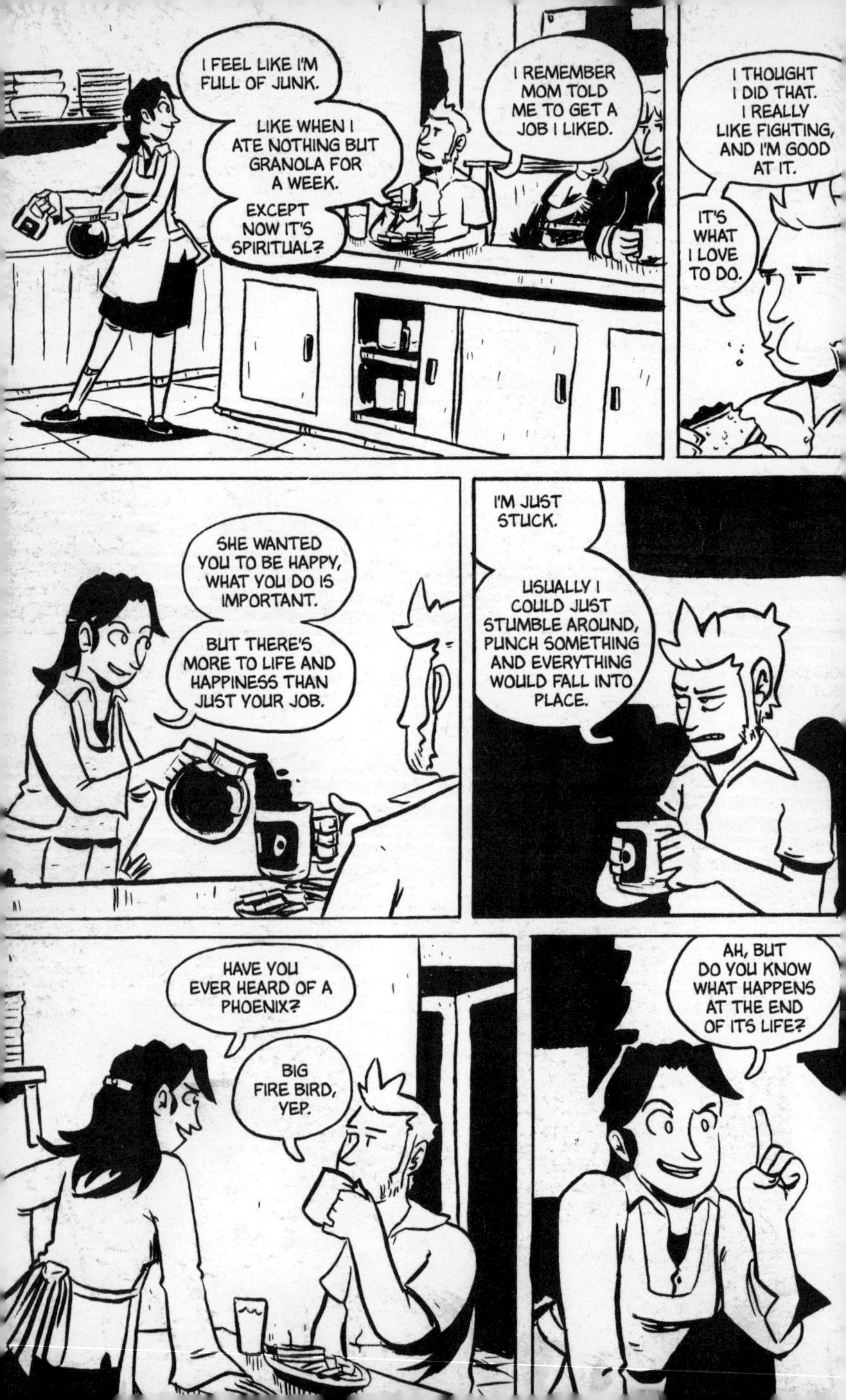
I FEEL LIKE I'M FULL OF JUNK.
LIKE WHEN I ATE NOTHING BUT GRANOLA FOR A WEEK.
EXCEPT NOW IT'S SPIRITUAL?
I REMEMBER MOM TOLD ME TO GET A JOB I LIKED.
I THOUGHT I DID THAT. I REALLY LIKE FIGHTING, AND I'M GOOD AT IT.
IT'S WHAT I LOVE TO DO.
SHE WANTED YOU TO BE HAPPY, WHAT YOU DO IS IMPORTANT.
BUT THERE'S MORE TO LIFE AND HAPPINESS THAN JUST YOUR JOB.
I'M JUST STUCK.
USUALLY I COULD JUST STUMBLE AROUND, PUNCH SOMETHING AND EVERYTHING WOULD FALL INTO PLACE.
HAVE YOU EVER HEARD OF A PHOENIX?
BIG FIRE BIRD, YEP.
AH, BUT DO YOU KNOW WHAT HAPPENS AT THE END OF ITS LIFE?

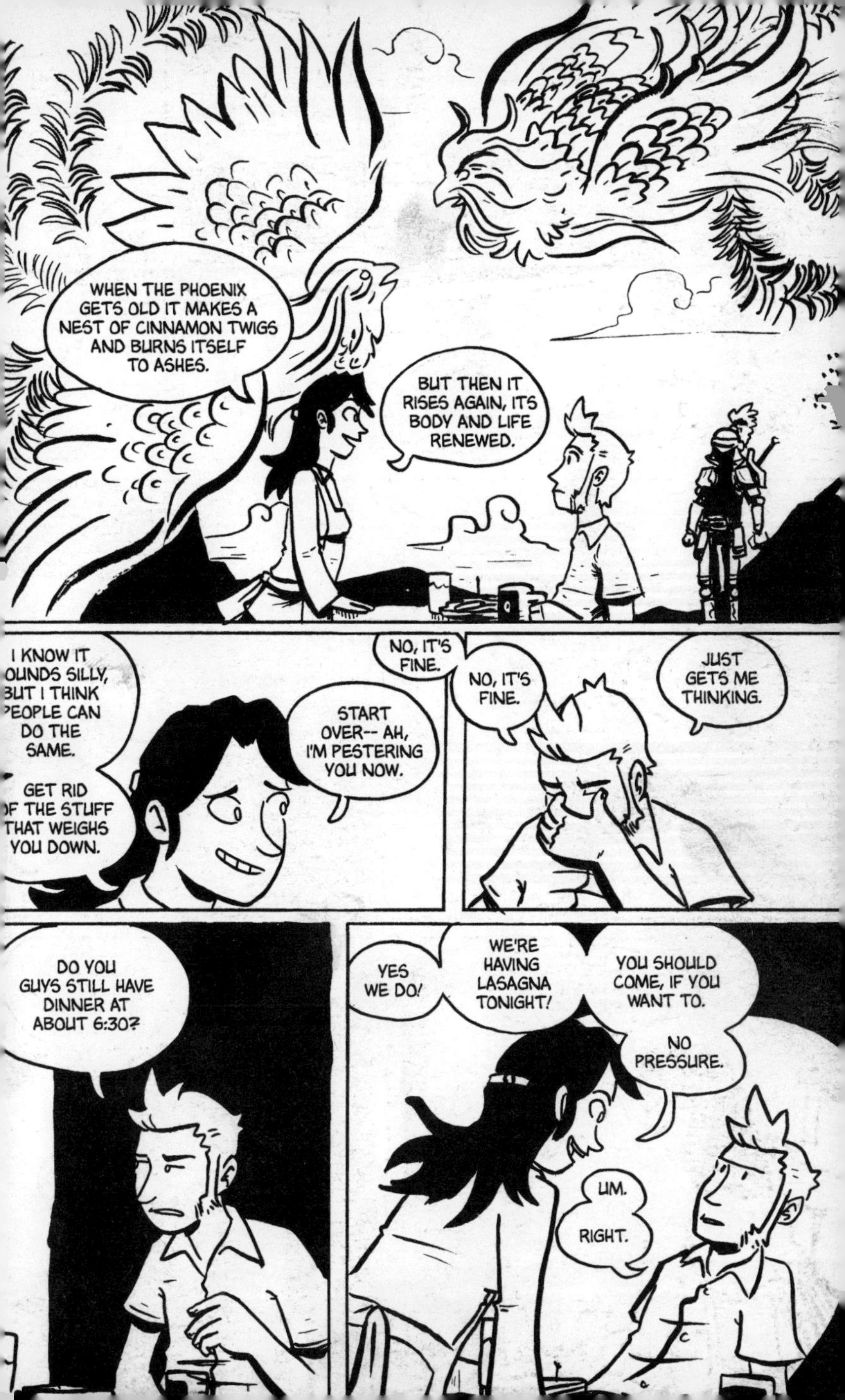
WHEN THE PHOENIX GETS OLD IT MAKES A NEST OF CINNAMON TWIGS AND BURNS ITSELF TO ASHES.
BUT THEN IT RISES AGAIN, ITS BODY AND LIFE RENEWED.
I KNOW IT SOUNDS SILLY, BUT I THINK PEOPLE CAN DO THE SAME.
GET RID OF THE STUFF THAT WEIGHS YOU DOWN.
START OVER-- AH, I'M PESTERING YOU NOW.
NO, IT'S FINE.
NO, IT'S FINE.
JUST GETS ME THINKING.
DO YOU GUYS STILL HAVE DINNER AT ABOUT 6:30?
YES WE DO!
WE'RE HAVING LASAGNA TONIGHT!
YOU SHOULD COME, IF YOU WANT TO.
NO PRESSURE.
UM.
RIGHT.

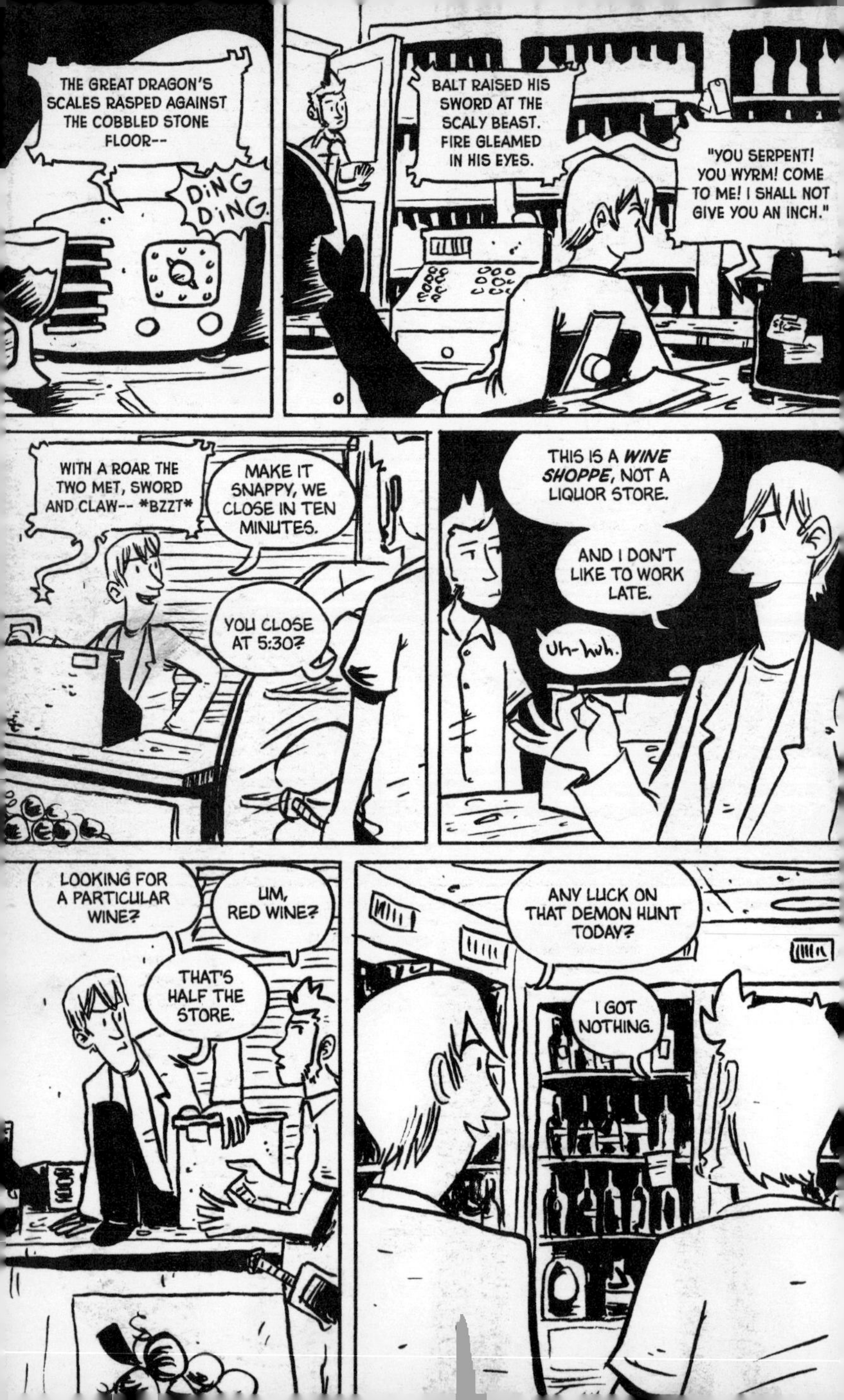
THE GREAT DRAGON'S SCALES RASPED AGAINST THE COBBLED STONE FLOOR--
DING DING
BALT RAISED HIS SWORD AT THE SCALY BEAST. FIRE GLEAMED IN HIS EYES.
"YOU SERPENT! YOU WYRM! COME TO ME! I SHALL NOT GIVE YOU AN INCH."
WITH A ROAR THE TWO MET, SWORD AND CLAW-- *BZZT*
MAKE IT SNAPPY, WE CLOSE IN TEN MINUTES.
YOU CLOSE AT 5:30?
THIS IS A *WINE SHOPPE*, NOT A LIQUOR STORE.
AND I DON'T LIKE TO WORK LATE.
Uh-huh.
LOOKING FOR A PARTICULAR WINE?
UM, RED WINE?
THAT'S HALF THE STORE.
ANY LUCK ON THAT DEMON HUNT TODAY?
I GOT NOTHING.

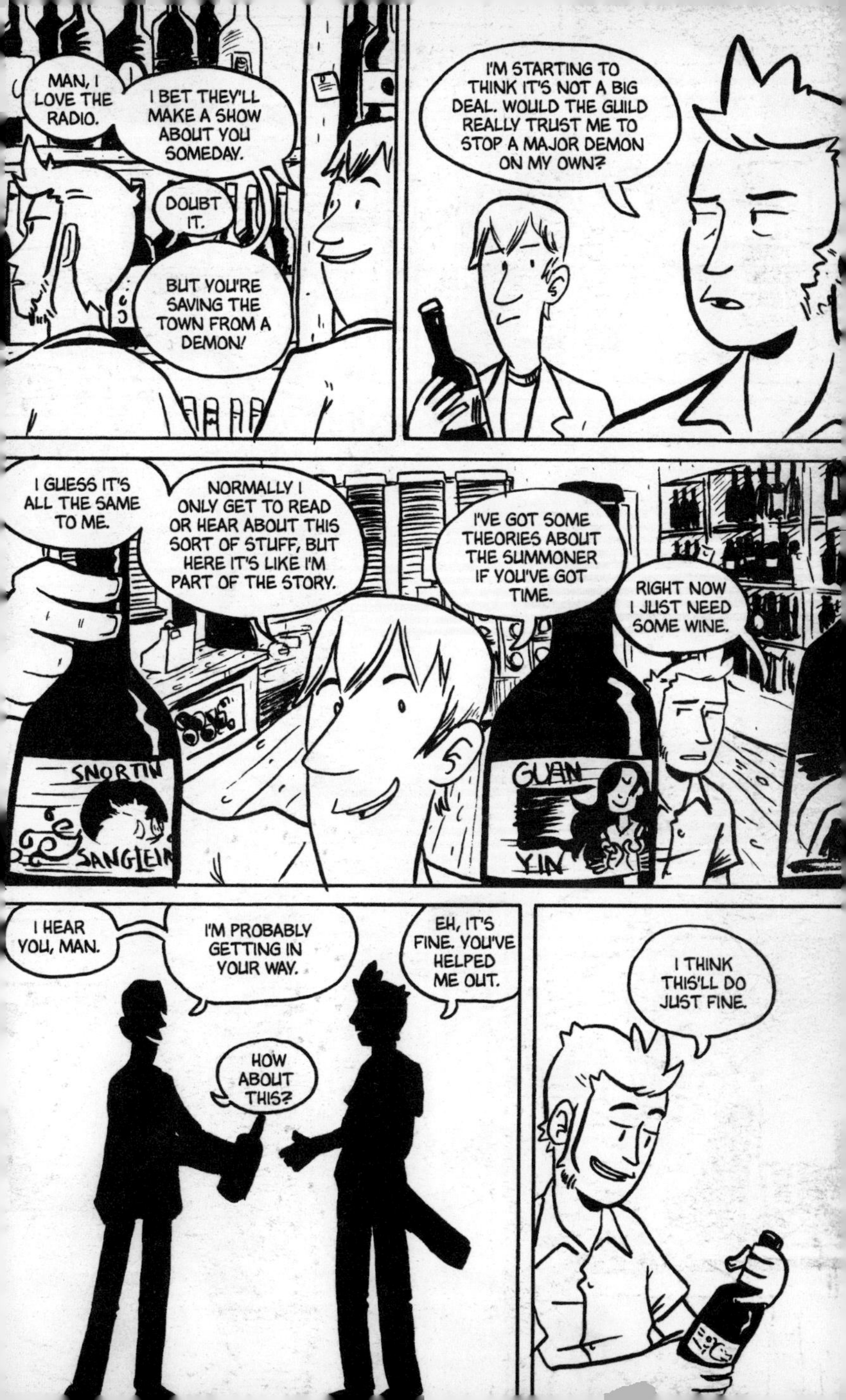
MAN, I LOVE THE RADIO.
I BET THEY'LL MAKE A SHOW ABOUT YOU SOMEDAY.
DOUBT IT.
BUT YOU'RE SAVING THE TOWN FROM A DEMON!
I'M STARTING TO THINK IT'S NOT A BIG DEAL. WOULD THE GUILD REALLY TRUST ME TO STOP A MAJOR DEMON ON MY OWN?
I GUESS IT'S ALL THE SAME TO ME.
NORMALLY I ONLY GET TO READ OR HEAR ABOUT THIS SORT OF STUFF, BUT HERE IT'S LIKE I'M PART OF THE STORY.
I'VE GOT SOME THEORIES ABOUT THE SUMMONER IF YOU'VE GOT TIME.
RIGHT NOW I JUST NEED SOME WINE.
SNORTIN
SANGLEIN
GUAN
YIN
I HEAR YOU, MAN.
I'M PROBABLY GETTING IN YOUR WAY.
EH, IT'S FINE. YOU'VE HELPED ME OUT.
HOW ABOUT THIS?
I THINK THIS'LL DO JUST FINE.

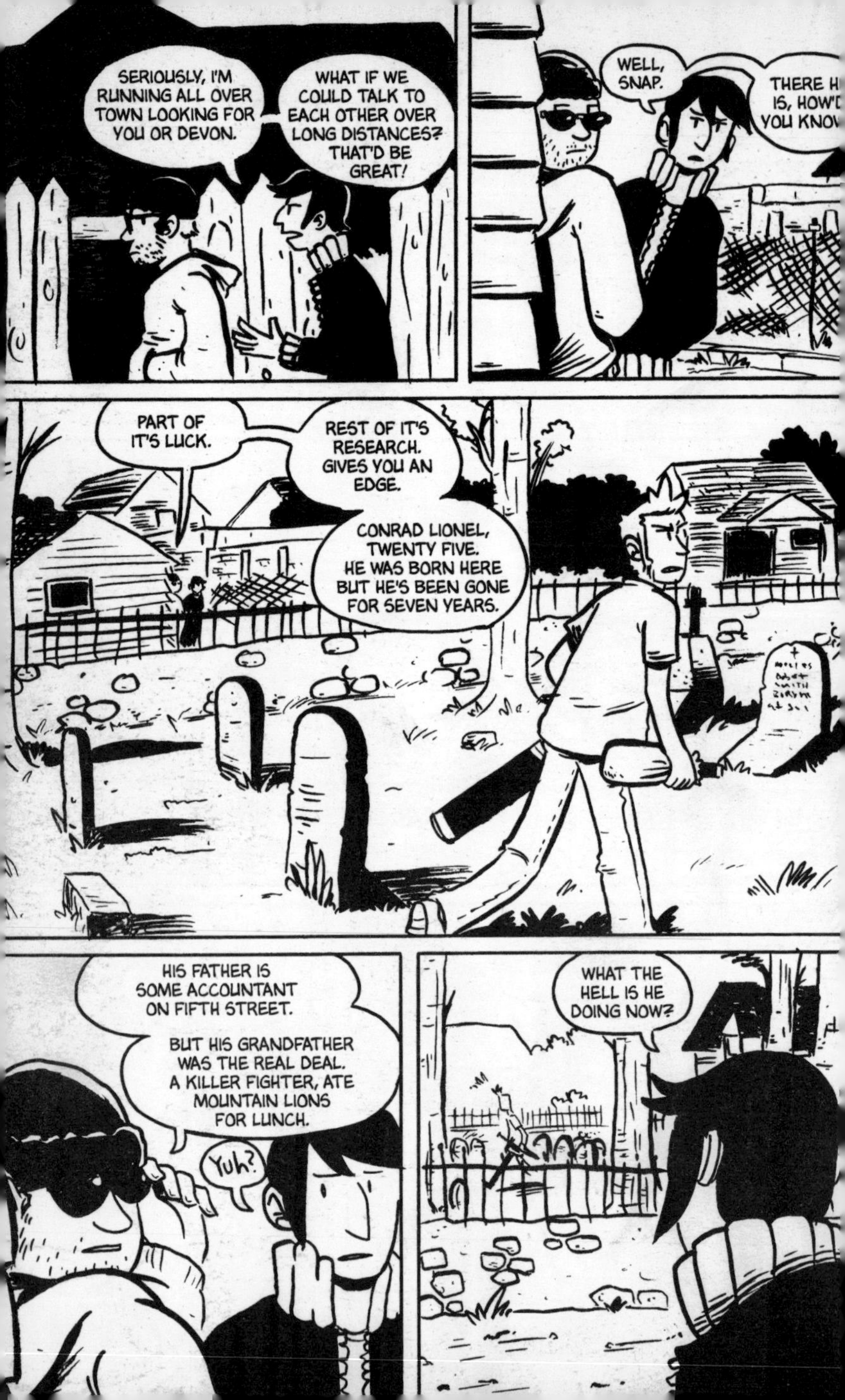
SERIOUSLY, I'M RUNNING ALL OVER TOWN LOOKING FOR YOU OR DEVON.
WHAT IF WE COULD TALK TO EACH OTHER OVER LONG DISTANCES? THAT'D BE GREAT!
WELL, SNAP.
THERE H IS, HOW'D YOU KNOW
PART OF IT'S LUCK.
REST OF IT'S RESEARCH. GIVES YOU AN EDGE.
CONRAD LIONEL, TWENTY FIVE. HE WAS BORN HERE BUT HE'S BEEN GONE FOR SEVEN YEARS.
HIS FATHER IS SOME ACCOUNTANT ON FIFTH STREET.
BUT HIS GRANDFATHER WAS THE REAL DEAL. A KILLER FIGHTER, ATE MOUNTAIN LIONS FOR LUNCH.
Yuh?
WHAT THE HELL IS HE DOING NOW?

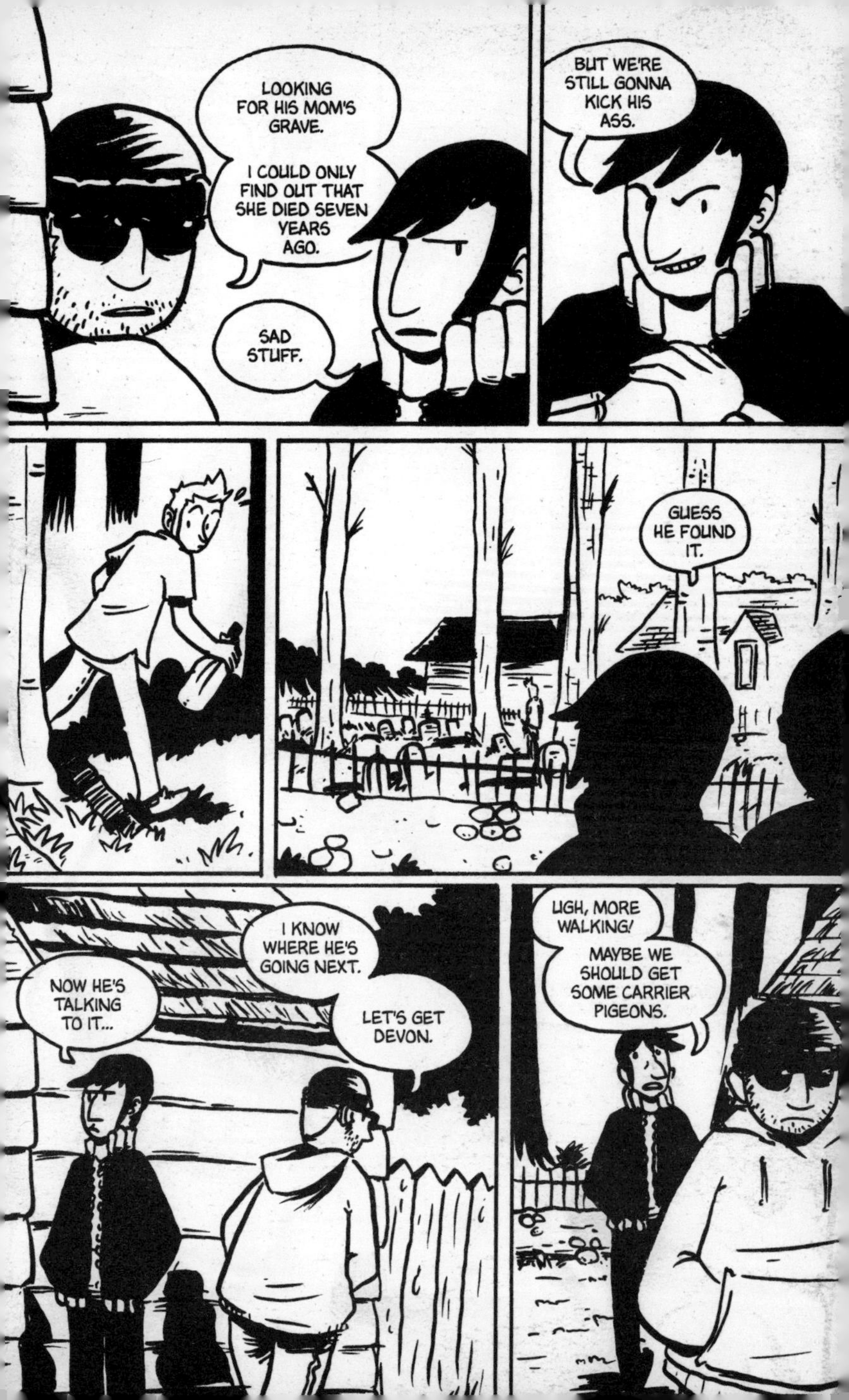
LOOKING FOR HIS MOM'S GRAVE.
I COULD ONLY FIND OUT THAT SHE DIED SEVEN YEARS AGO.
SAD STUFF.
BUT WE'RE STILL GONNA KICK HIS ASS.
GUESS HE FOUND IT.
NOW HE'S TALKING TO IT...
I KNOW WHERE HE'S GOING NEXT.
LET'S GET DEVON.
UGH, MORE WALKING!
MAYBE WE SHOULD GET SOME CARRIER PIGEONS.

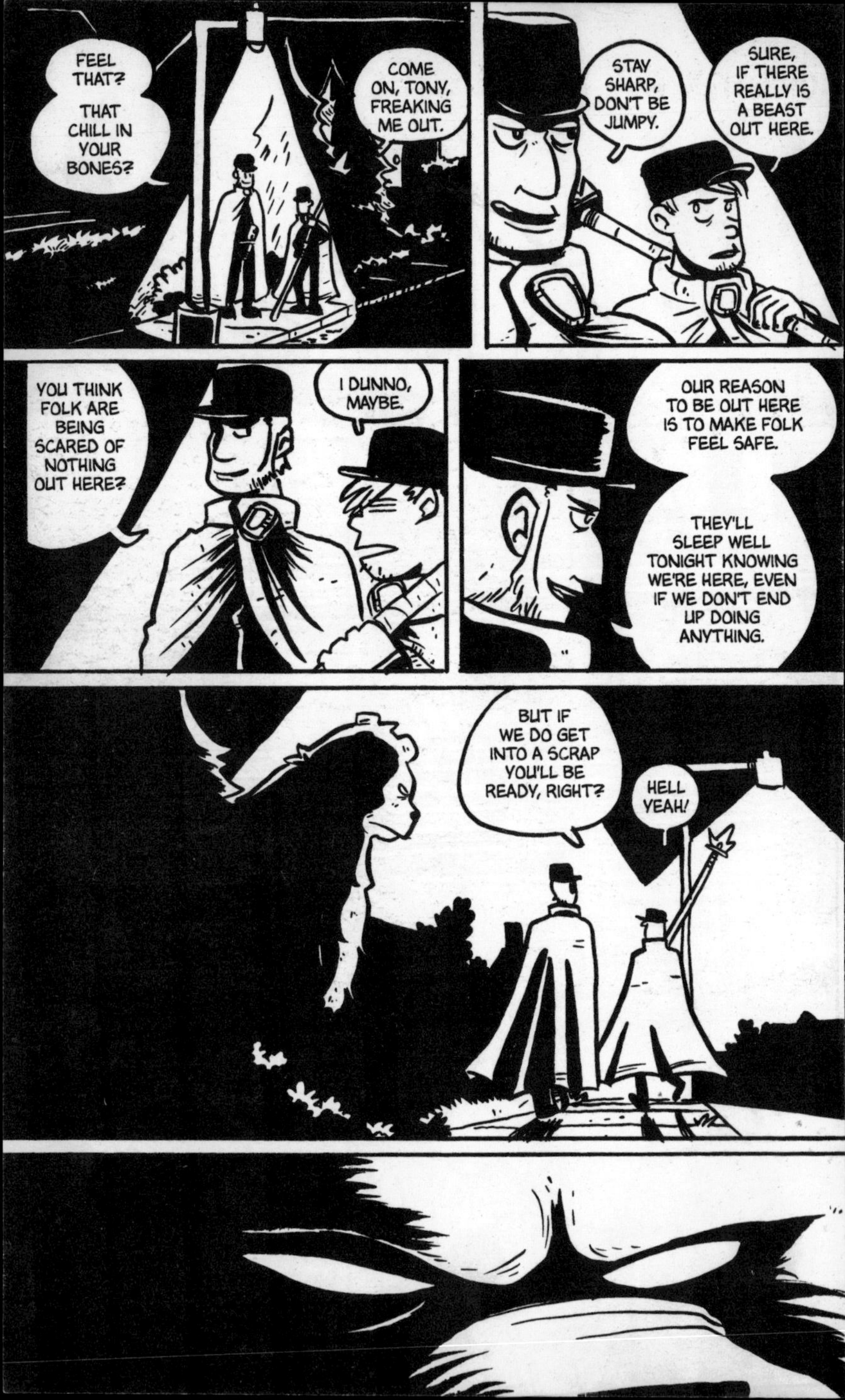
FEEL THAT? THAT CHILL IN YOUR BONES?
COME ON, TONY, FREAKING ME OUT.
STAY SHARP, DON'T BE JUMPY.
SURE, IF THERE REALLY IS A BEAST OUT HERE.
YOU THINK FOLK ARE BEING SCARED OF NOTHING OUT HERE?
I DUNNO, MAYBE.
OUR REASON TO BE OUT HERE IS TO MAKE FOLK FEEL SAFE.
THEY'LL SLEEP WELL TONIGHT KNOWING WE'RE HERE, EVEN IF WE DON'T END UP DOING ANYTHING.
BUT IF WE DO GET INTO A SCRAP YOU'LL BE READY, RIGHT?
HELL YEAH!

CHAPTER 6

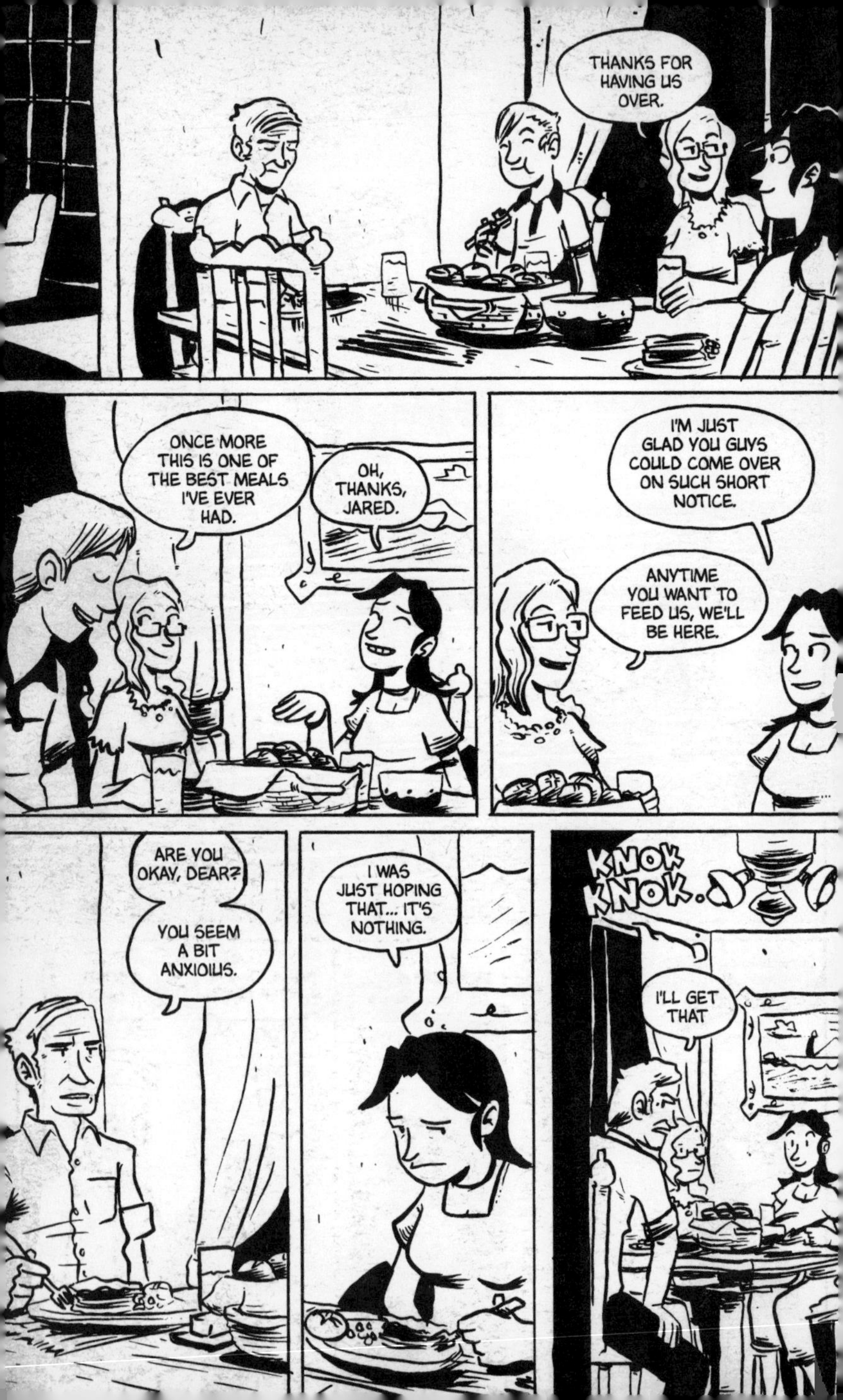
THANKS FOR HAVING US OVER.
ONCE MORE THIS IS ONE OF THE BEST MEALS I'VE EVER HAD.
OH, THANKS, JARED.
I'M JUST GLAD YOU GUYS COULD COME OVER ON SUCH SHORT NOTICE.
ANYTIME YOU WANT TO FEED US, WE'LL BE HERE.
ARE YOU OKAY, DEAR?
YOU SEEM A BIT ANXIOUS.
I WAS JUST HOPING THAT... IT'S NOTHING.
KNOK KNOK.
I'LL GET THAT

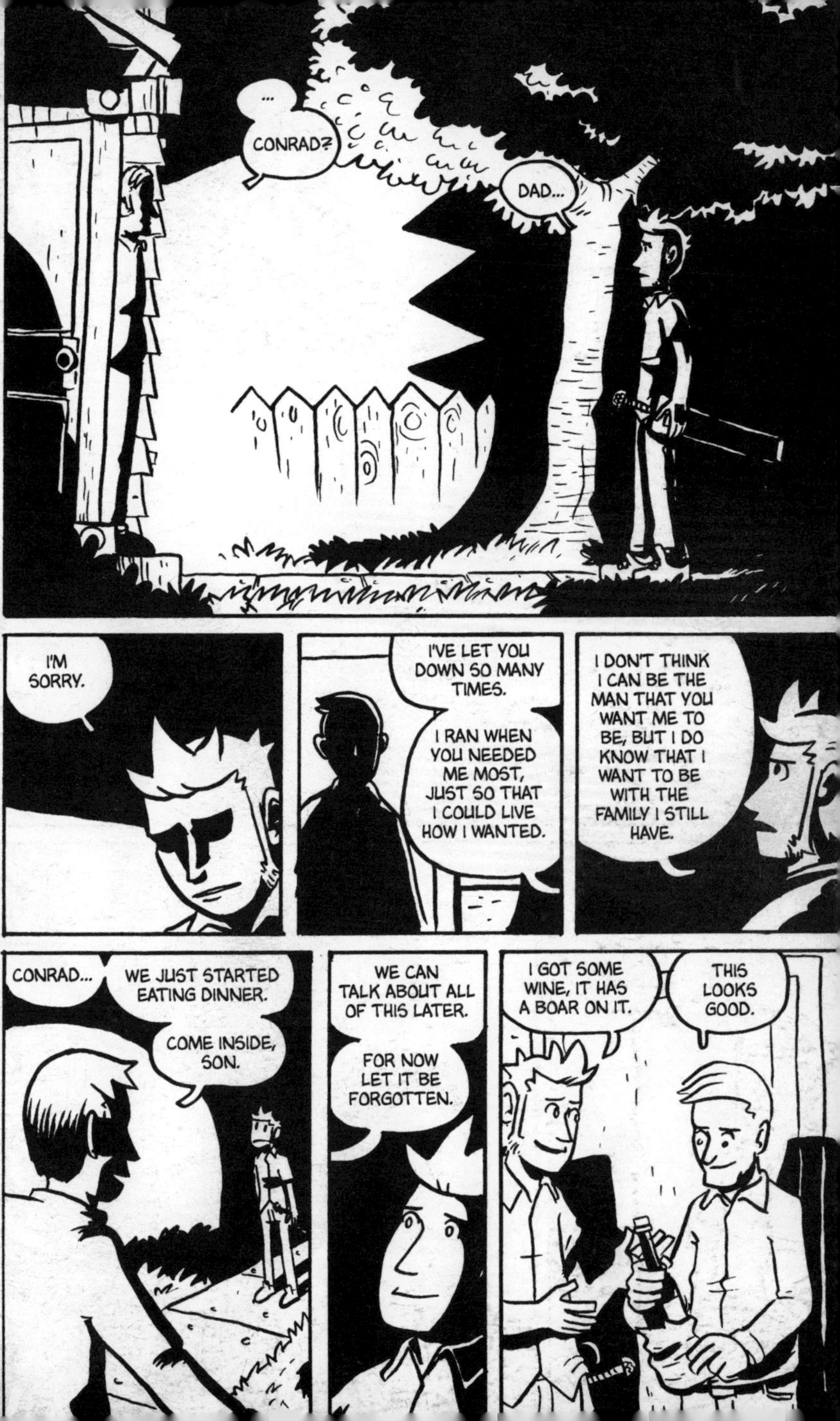
...
CONRAD?
DAD...
I'M SORRY.
I'VE LET YOU DOWN SO MANY TIMES.
I RAN WHEN YOU NEEDED ME MOST, JUST SO THAT I COULD LIVE HOW I WANTED.
I DON'T THINK I CAN BE THE MAN THAT YOU WANT ME TO BE, BUT I DO KNOW THAT I WANT TO BE WITH THE FAMILY I STILL HAVE.
CONRAD...
WE JUST STARTED EATING DINNER.
COME INSIDE, SON.
WE CAN TALK ABOUT ALL OF THIS LATER.
FOR NOW LET IT BE FORGOTTEN.
I GOT SOME WINE, IT HAS A BOAR ON IT.
THIS LOOKS GOOD.

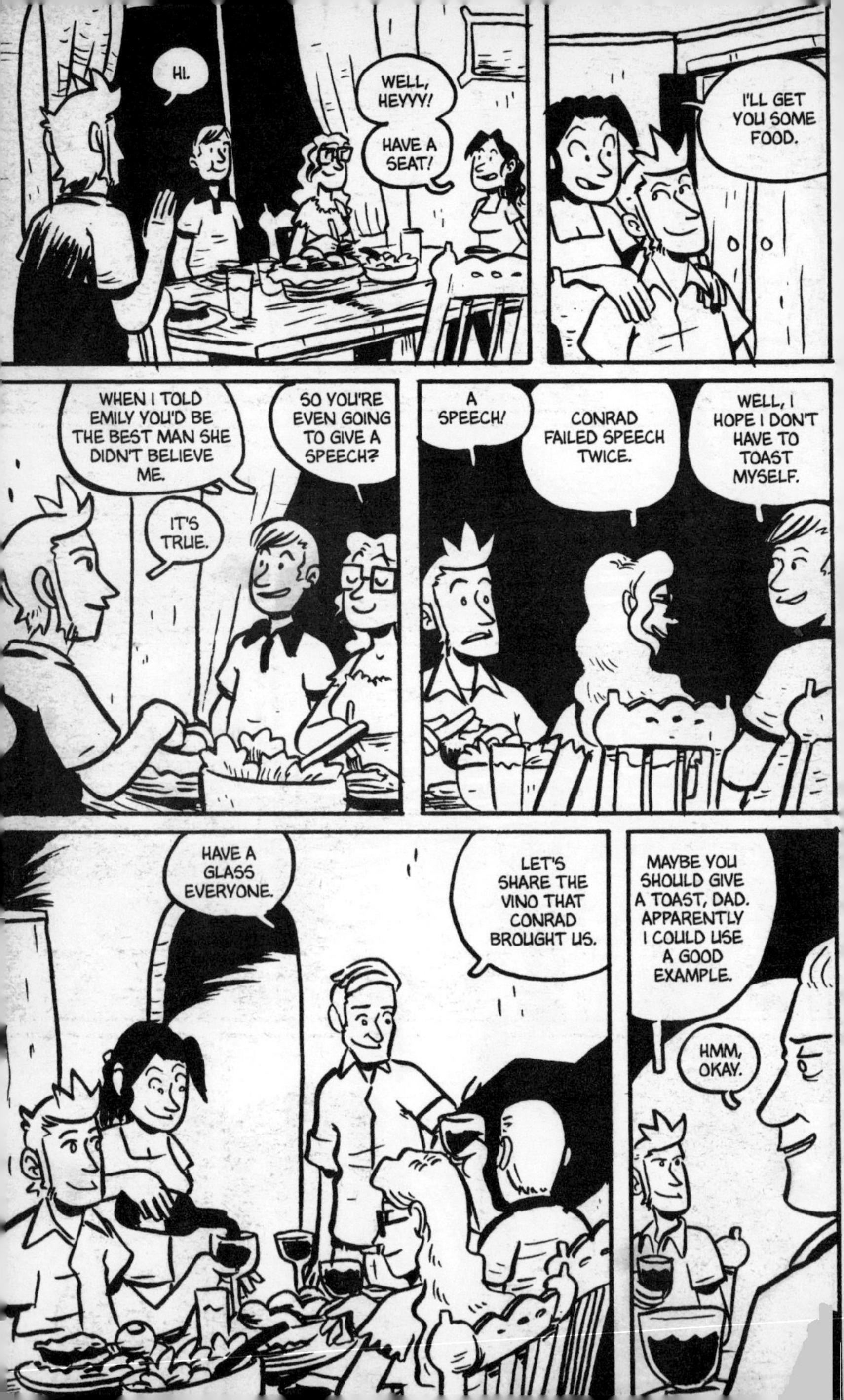
HI.
WELL, HEYYY!
HAVE A SEAT!
I'LL GET YOU SOME FOOD.
WHEN I TOLD EMILY YOU'D BE THE BEST MAN SHE DIDN'T BELIEVE ME.
IT'S TRUE.
SO YOU'RE EVEN GOING TO GIVE A SPEECH?
A SPEECH!
CONRAD FAILED SPEECH TWICE.
WELL, I HOPE I DON'T HAVE TO TOAST MYSELF.
HAVE A GLASS EVERYONE.
LET'S SHARE THE VINO THAT CONRAD BROUGHT US.
MAYBE YOU SHOULD GIVE A TOAST, DAD. APPARENTLY I COULD USE A GOOD EXAMPLE.
HMM, OKAY.

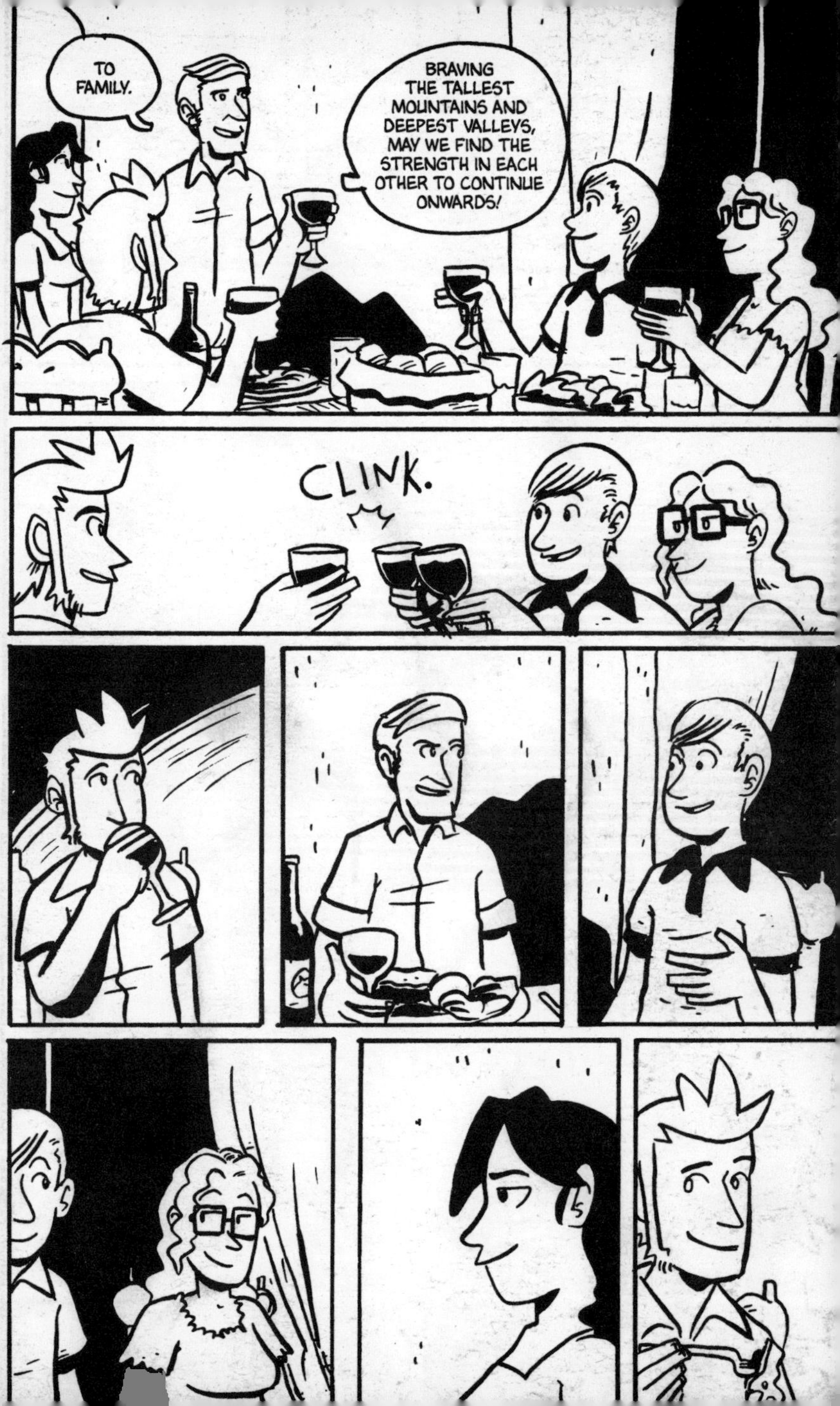
TO FAMILY.
BRAVING THE TALLEST MOUNTAINS AND DEEPEST VALLEYS, MAY WE FIND THE STRENGTH IN EACH OTHER TO CONTINUE ONWARDS!
CLINK.

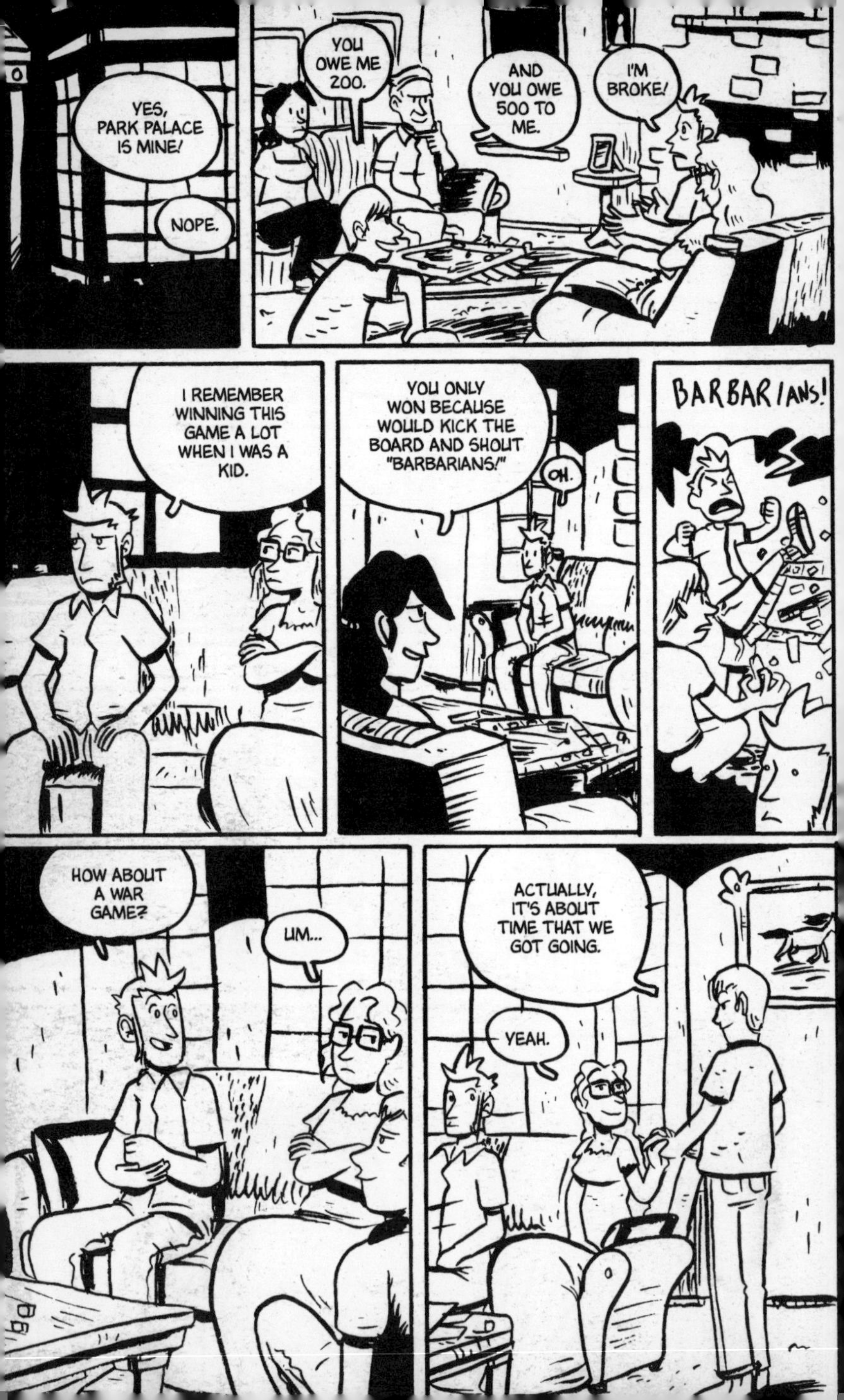
YES, PARK PALACE IS MINE!
NOPE.
YOU OWE ME 200.
AND YOU OWE 500 TO ME.
I'M BROKE!
I REMEMBER WINNING THIS GAME A LOT WHEN I WAS A KID.
YOU ONLY WON BECAUSE WOULD KICK THE BOARD AND SHOUT "BARBARIANS!"
OH.
BARBARIANS!
HOW ABOUT A WAR GAME?
UM...
ACTUALLY, IT'S ABOUT TIME THAT WE GOT GOING.
YEAH.

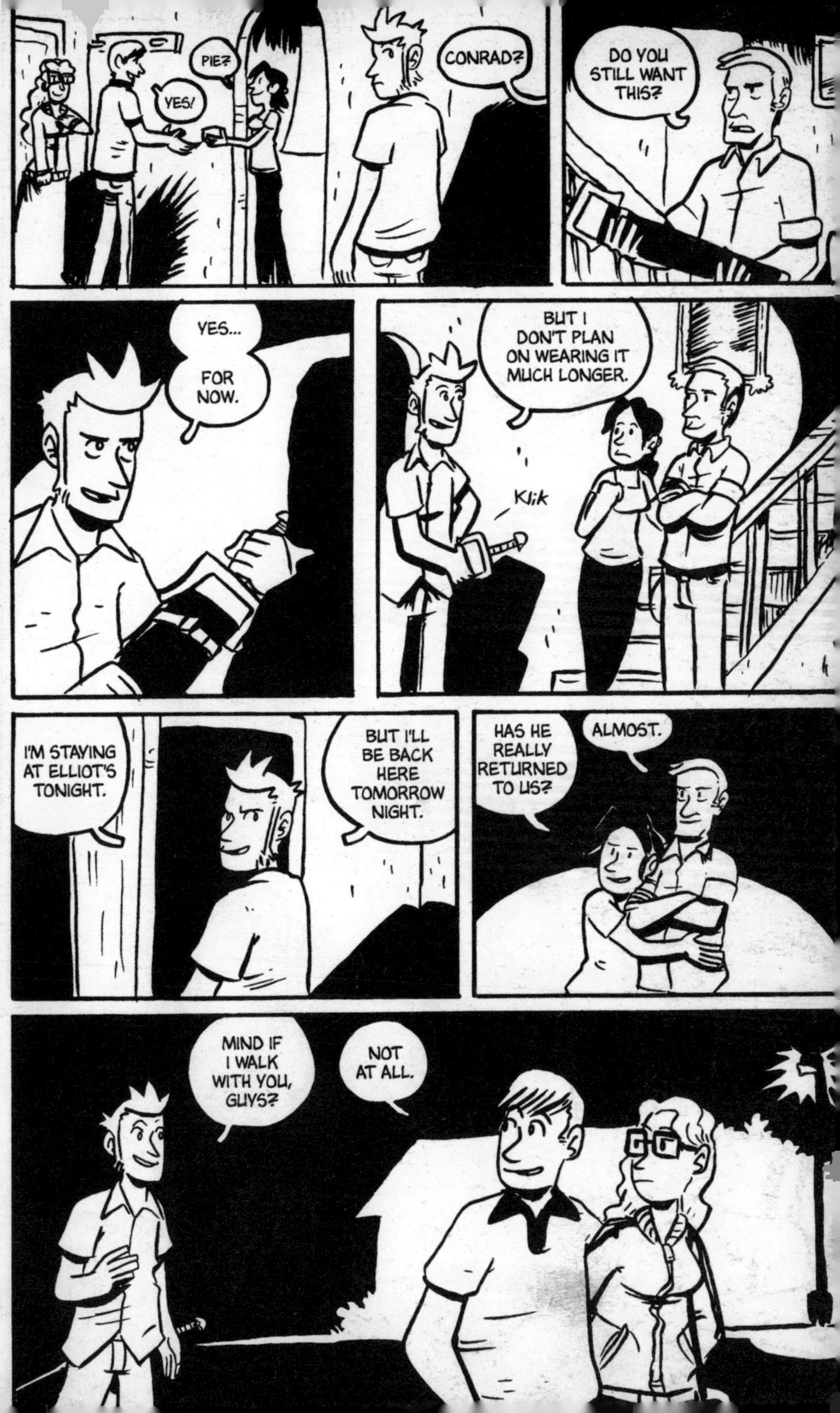
PIE?
YES!
CONRAD?
DO YOU STILL WANT THIS?
YES...
FOR NOW.
BUT I DON'T PLAN ON WEARING IT MUCH LONGER.
Klik
I'M STAYING AT ELLIOT'S TONIGHT.
BUT I'LL BE BACK HERE TOMORROW NIGHT.
HAS HE REALLY RETURNED TO US?
ALMOST.
MIND IF I WALK WITH YOU, GUYS?
NOT AT ALL.

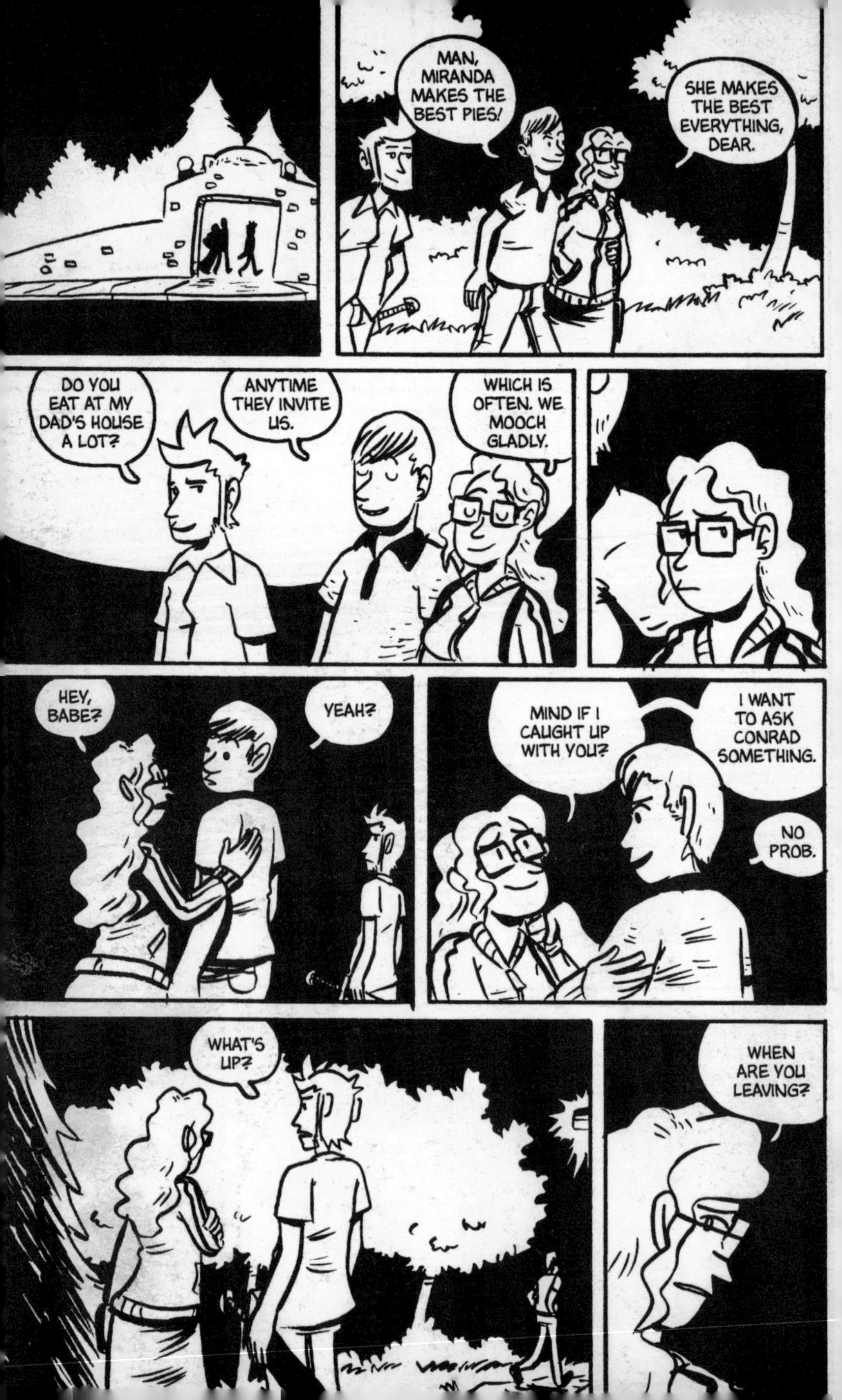
MAN, MIRANDA MAKES THE BEST PIES!
SHE MAKES THE BEST EVERYTHING, DEAR.
DO YOU EAT AT MY DAD'S HOUSE A LOT?
ANYTIME THEY INVITE US.
WHICH IS OFTEN. WE MOOCH GLADLY.
HEY, BABE?
YEAH?
MIND IF I CAUGHT UP WITH YOU?
I WANT TO ASK CONRAD SOMETHING.
NO PROB.
WHAT'S UP?
WHEN ARE YOU LEAVING?

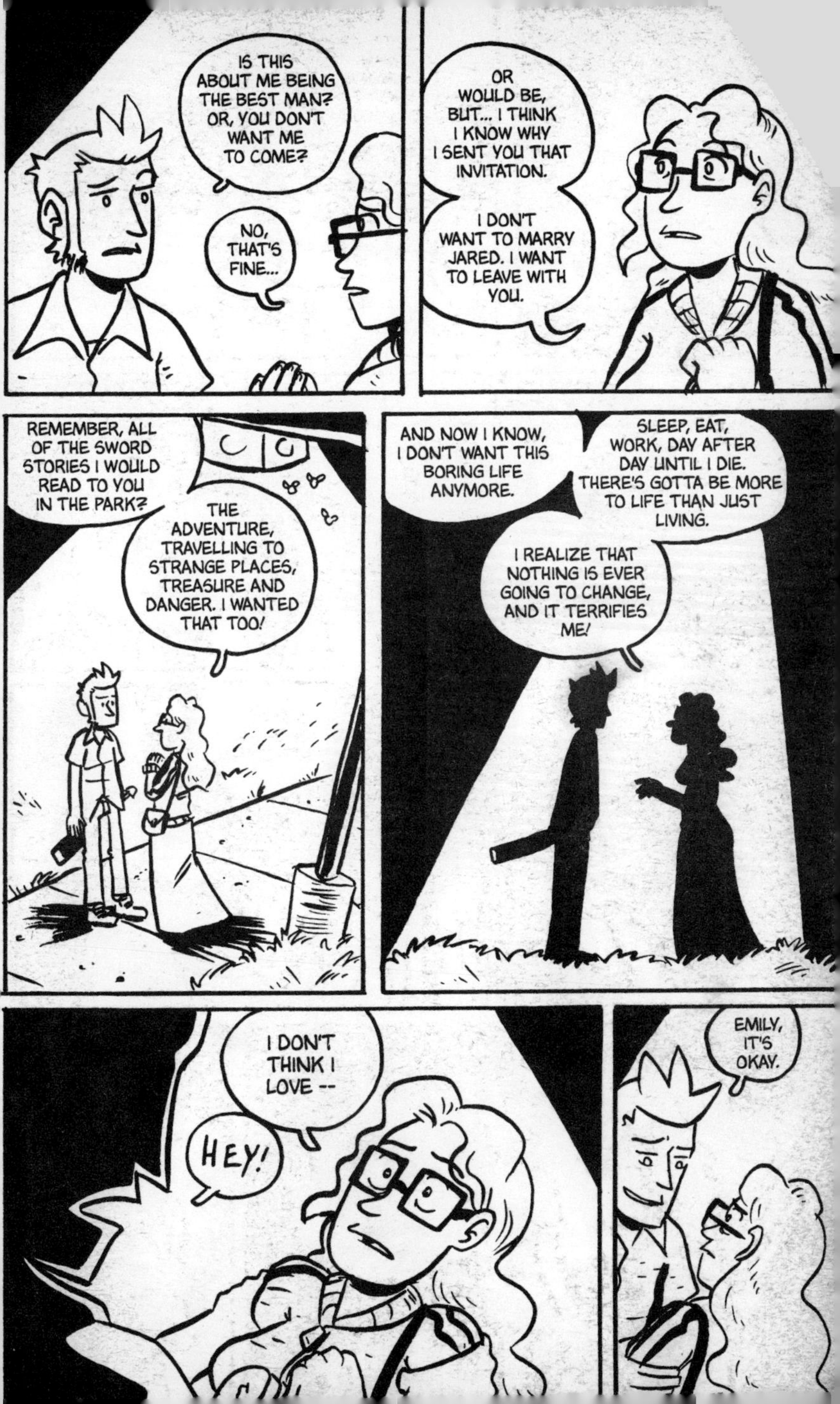
IS THIS ABOUT ME BEING THE BEST MAN? OR, YOU DON'T WANT ME TO COME?
NO, THAT'S FINE...
OR WOULD BE, BUT... I THINK I KNOW WHY I SENT YOU THAT INVITATION.
I DON'T WANT TO MARRY JARED. I WANT TO LEAVE WITH YOU.
REMEMBER, ALL OF THE SWORD STORIES I WOULD READ TO YOU IN THE PARK?
THE ADVENTURE, TRAVELLING TO STRANGE PLACES, TREASURE AND DANGER. I WANTED THAT TOO!
AND NOW I KNOW, I DON'T WANT THIS BORING LIFE ANYMORE.
SLEEP, EAT, WORK, DAY AFTER DAY UNTIL I DIE. THERE'S GOTTA BE MORE TO LIFE THAN JUST LIVING.
I REALIZE THAT NOTHING IS EVER GOING TO CHANGE, AND IT TERRIFIES ME!
I DON'T THINK I LOVE --
HEY!
EMILY, IT'S OKAY.

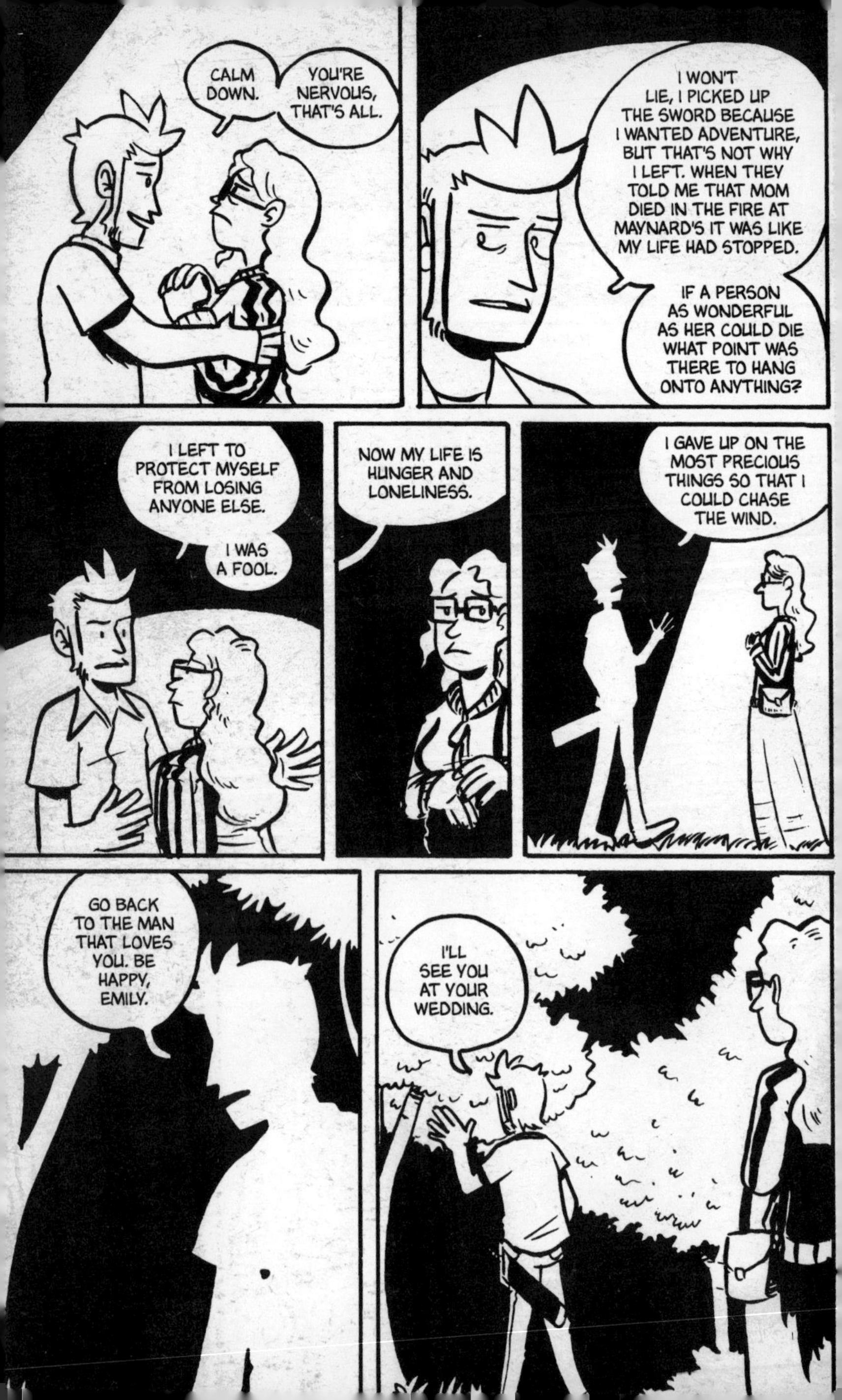
CALM DOWN.
YOU'RE NERVOUS, THAT'S ALL.
I WON'T LIE, I PICKED UP THE SWORD BECAUSE I WANTED ADVENTURE, BUT THAT'S NOT WHY I LEFT. WHEN THEY TOLD ME THAT MOM DIED IN THE FIRE AT MAYNARD'S IT WAS LIKE MY LIFE HAD STOPPED.
IF A PERSON AS WONDERFUL AS HER COULD DIE WHAT POINT WAS THERE TO HANG ONTO ANYTHING?
I LEFT TO PROTECT MYSELF FROM LOSING ANYONE ELSE.
I WAS A FOOL.
NOW MY LIFE IS HUNGER AND LONELINESS.
I GAVE UP ON THE MOST PRECIOUS THINGS SO THAT I COULD CHASE THE WIND.
GO BACK TO THE MAN THAT LOVES YOU. BE HAPPY, EMILY.
I'LL SEE YOU AT YOUR WEDDING.

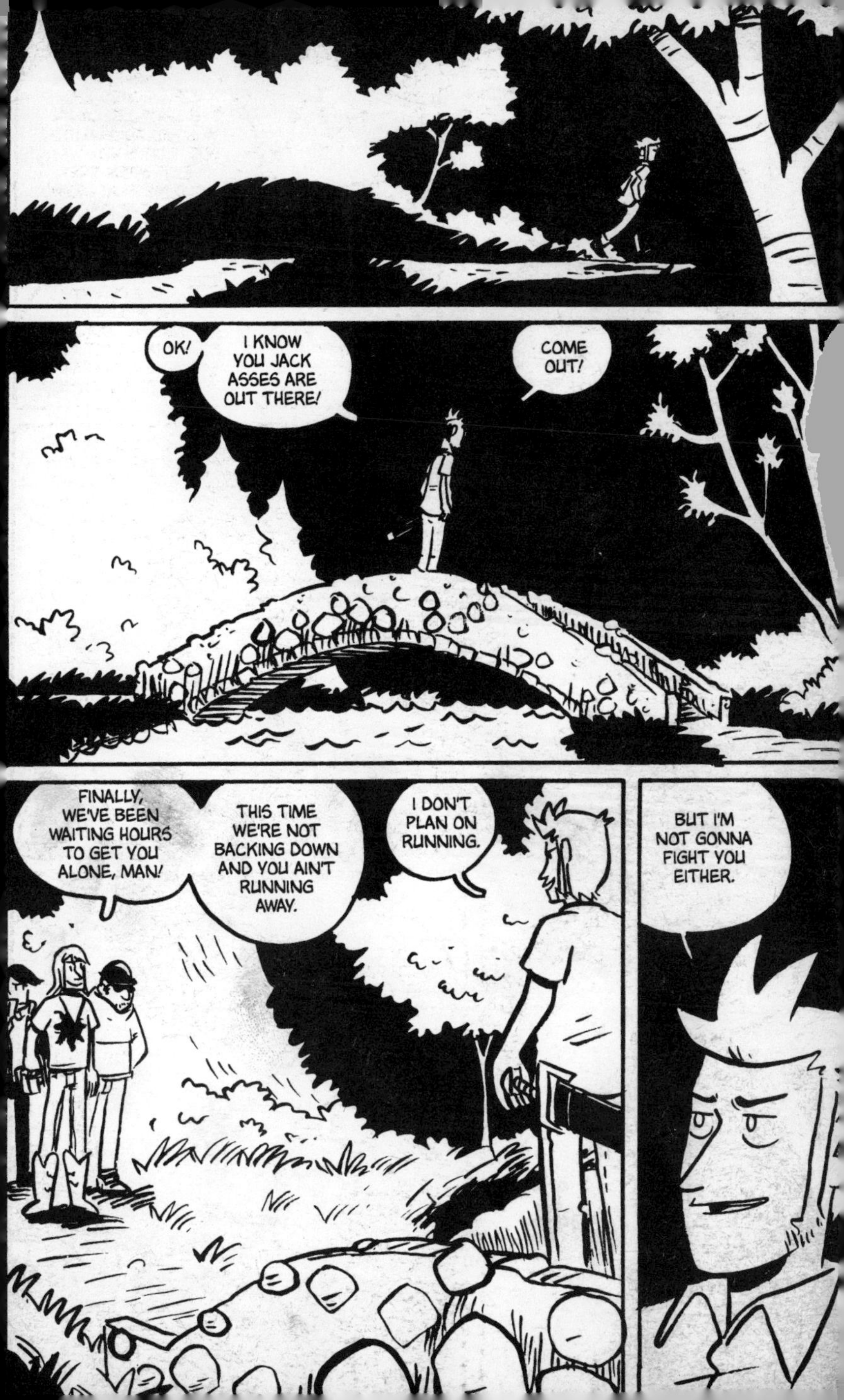
OK!
I KNOW YOU JACK ASSES ARE OUT THERE!
COME OUT!
FINALLY, WE'VE BEEN WAITING HOURS TO GET YOU ALONE, MAN!
THIS TIME WE'RE NOT BACKING DOWN AND YOU AIN'T RUNNING AWAY.
I DON'T PLAN ON RUNNING.
BUT I'M NOT GONNA FIGHT YOU EITHER.

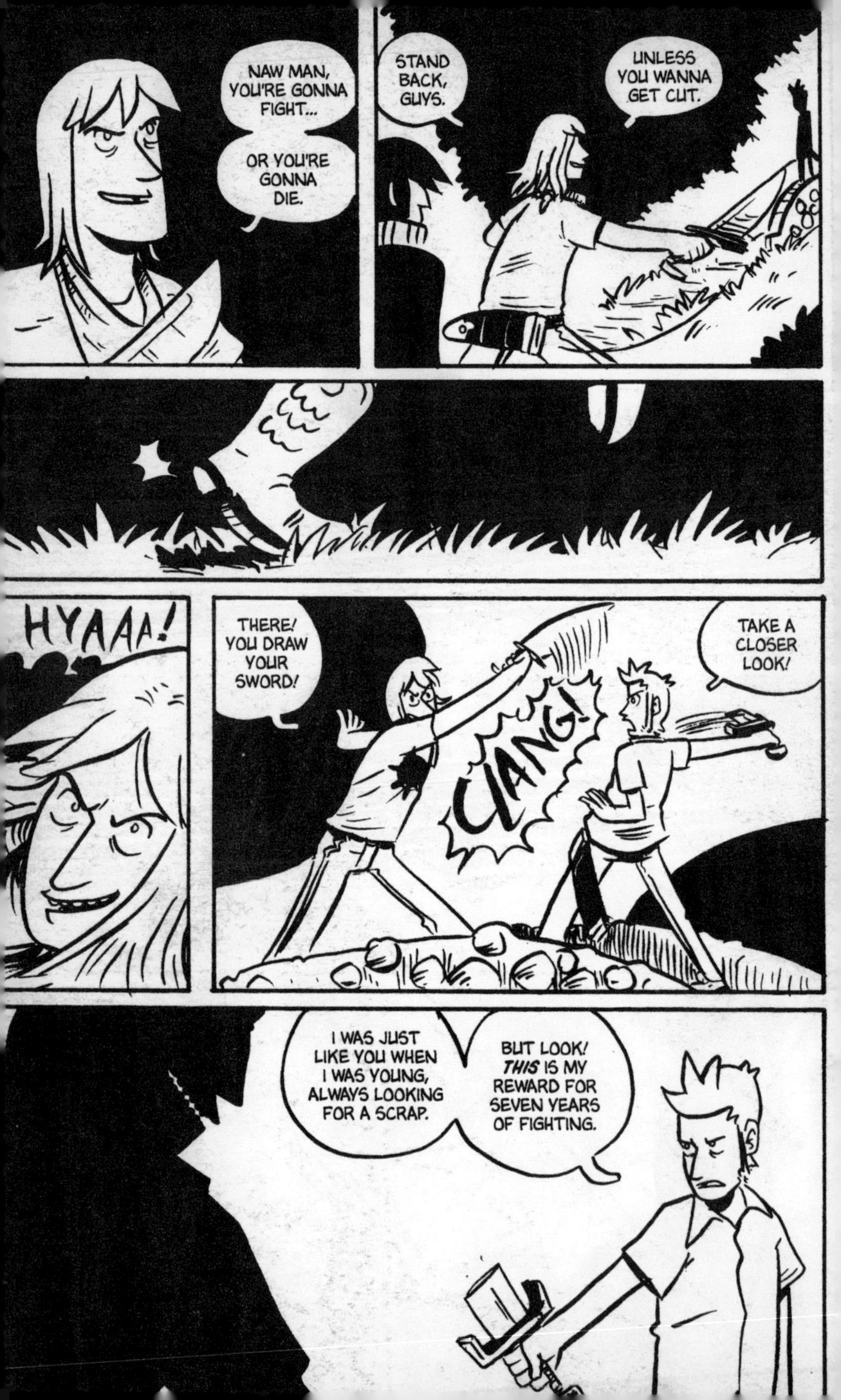

NAW MAN, YOU'RE GONNA FIGHT...
OR YOU'RE GONNA DIE.
STAND BACK, GUYS.
UNLESS YOU WANNA GET CUT.
HYAAA!
THERE! YOU DRAW YOUR SWORD!
CLANG!
TAKE A CLOSER LOOK!
I WAS JUST LIKE YOU WHEN I WAS YOUNG, ALWAYS LOOKING FOR A SCRAP.
BUT LOOK! *THIS* IS MY REWARD FOR SEVEN YEARS OF FIGHTING.

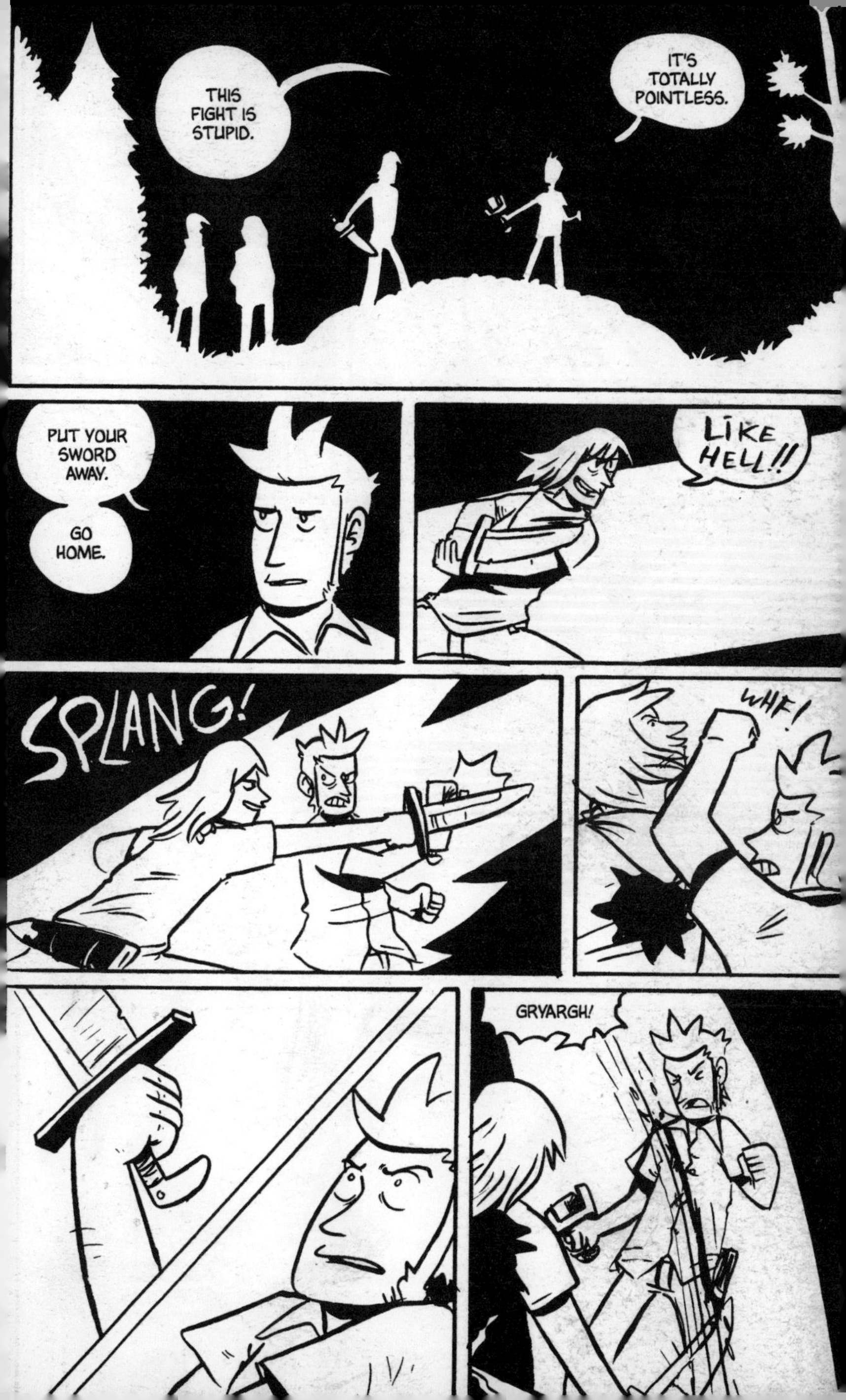
THIS FIGHT IS STUPID.
IT'S TOTALLY POINTLESS.
PUT YOUR SWORD AWAY.
GO HOME.
LIKE HELL!!
SPLANG!
WHF!
GRYARGH!

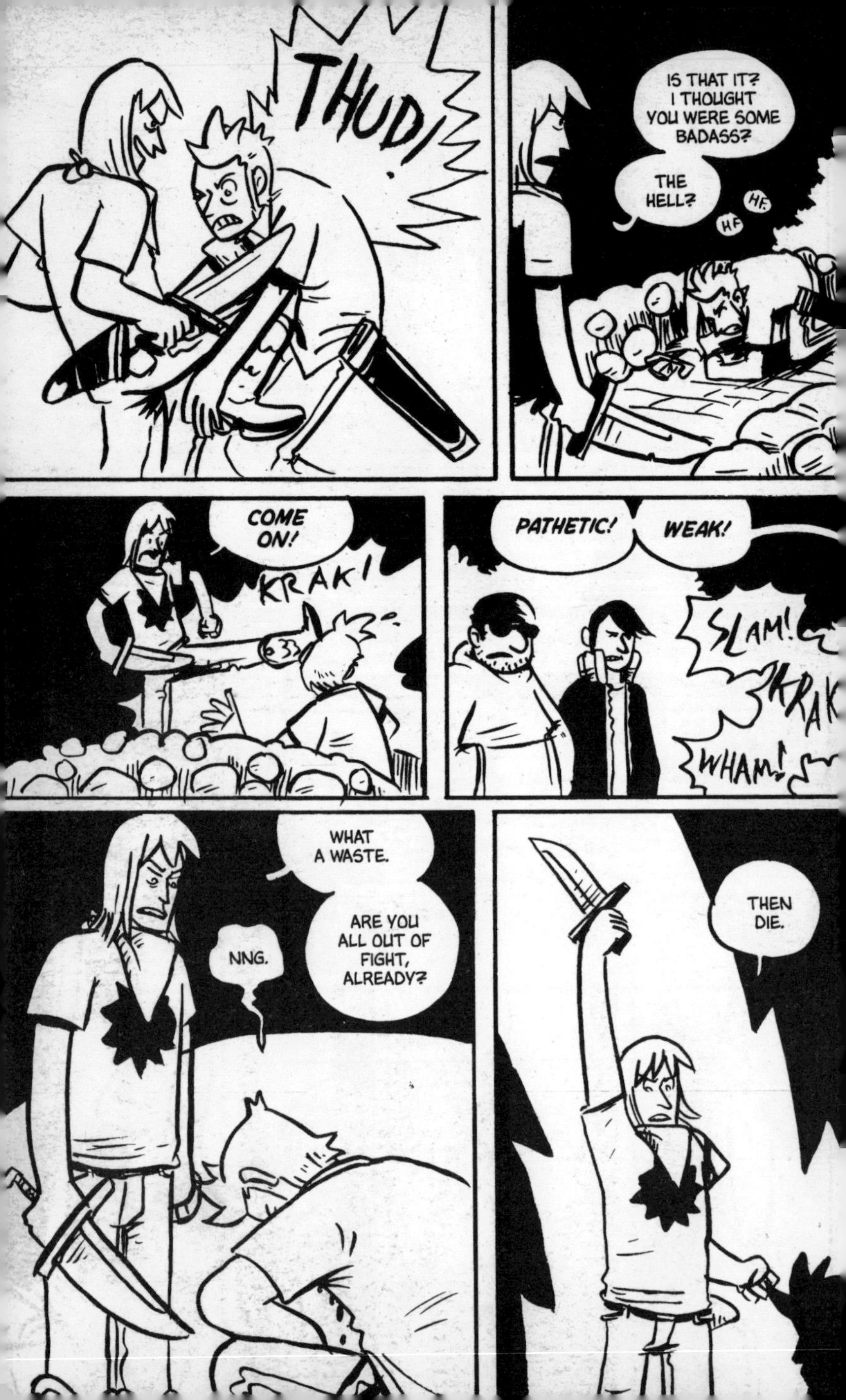
THUD!
IS THAT IT? I THOUGHT YOU WERE SOME BADASS?
THE HELL?
HF
HF
COME ON!
KRAK!
PATHETIC!
WEAK!
SLAM!
KRAK
WHAM!
WHAT A WASTE.
ARE YOU ALL OUT OF FIGHT, ALREADY?
NNG.
THEN DIE.

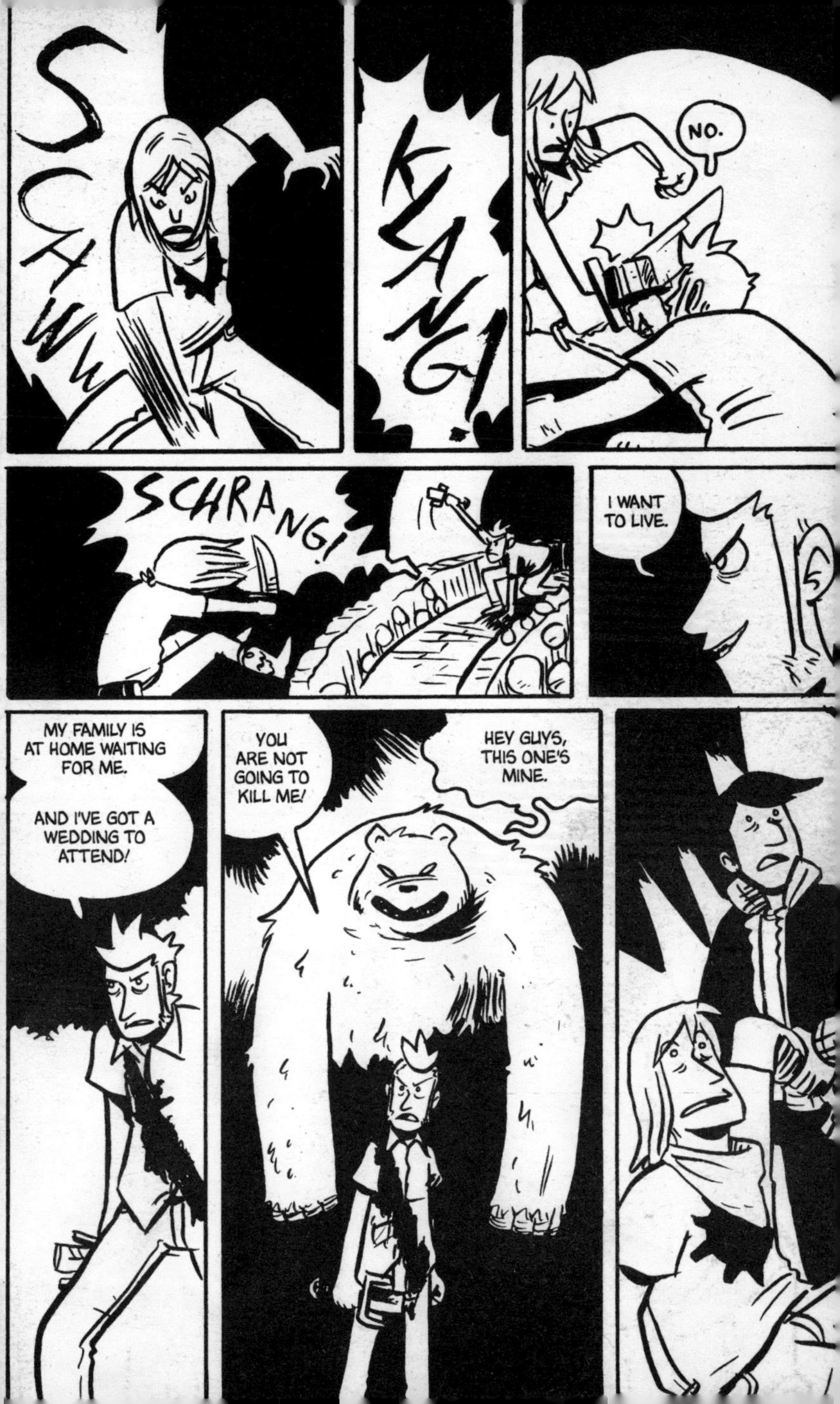
SCHWW
KLANG!
NO.
SCHRANG!
I WANT TO LIVE.
MY FAMILY IS AT HOME WAITING FOR ME.
AND I'VE GOT A WEDDING TO ATTEND!
YOU ARE NOT GOING TO KILL ME!
HEY GUYS, THIS ONE'S MINE.

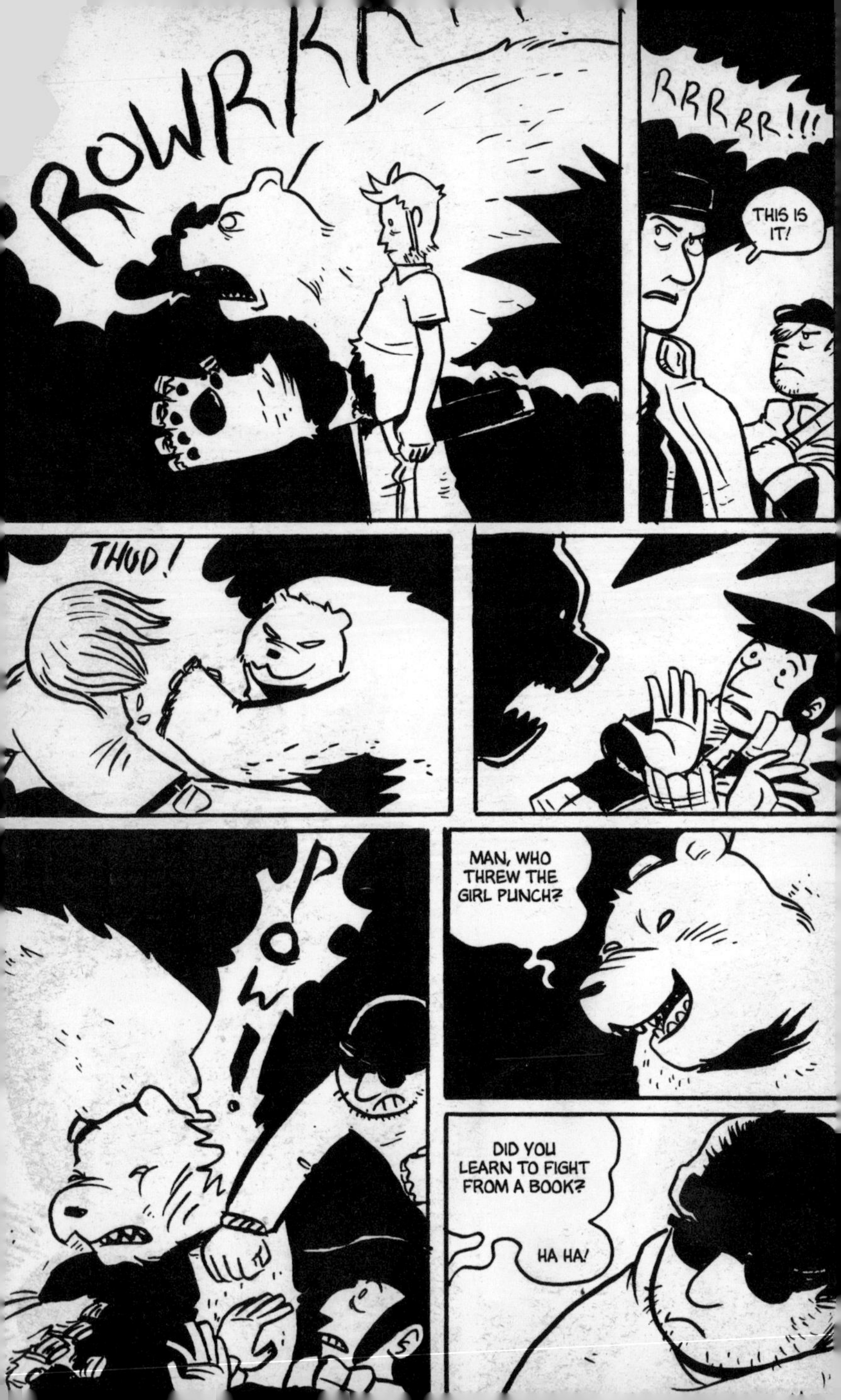
ROWRKK
RRRRRR!!!
THIS IS IT!
THUD!
POW!
MAN, WHO THREW THE GIRL PUNCH?
DID YOU LEARN TO FIGHT FROM A BOOK?
HA HA!

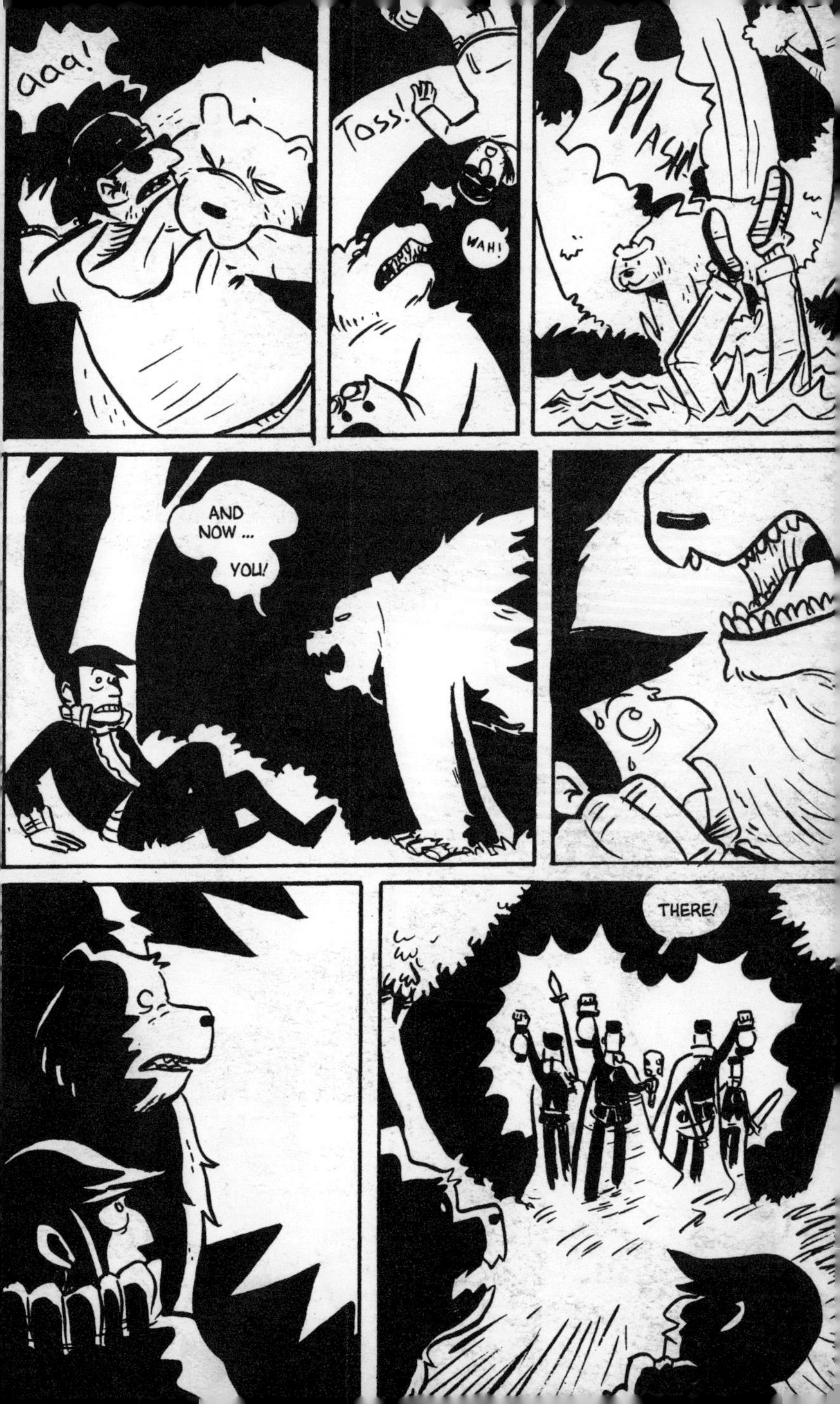
aaa!
Toss!
WAH!
SPLASH!
AND NOW ...
YOU!
THERE!

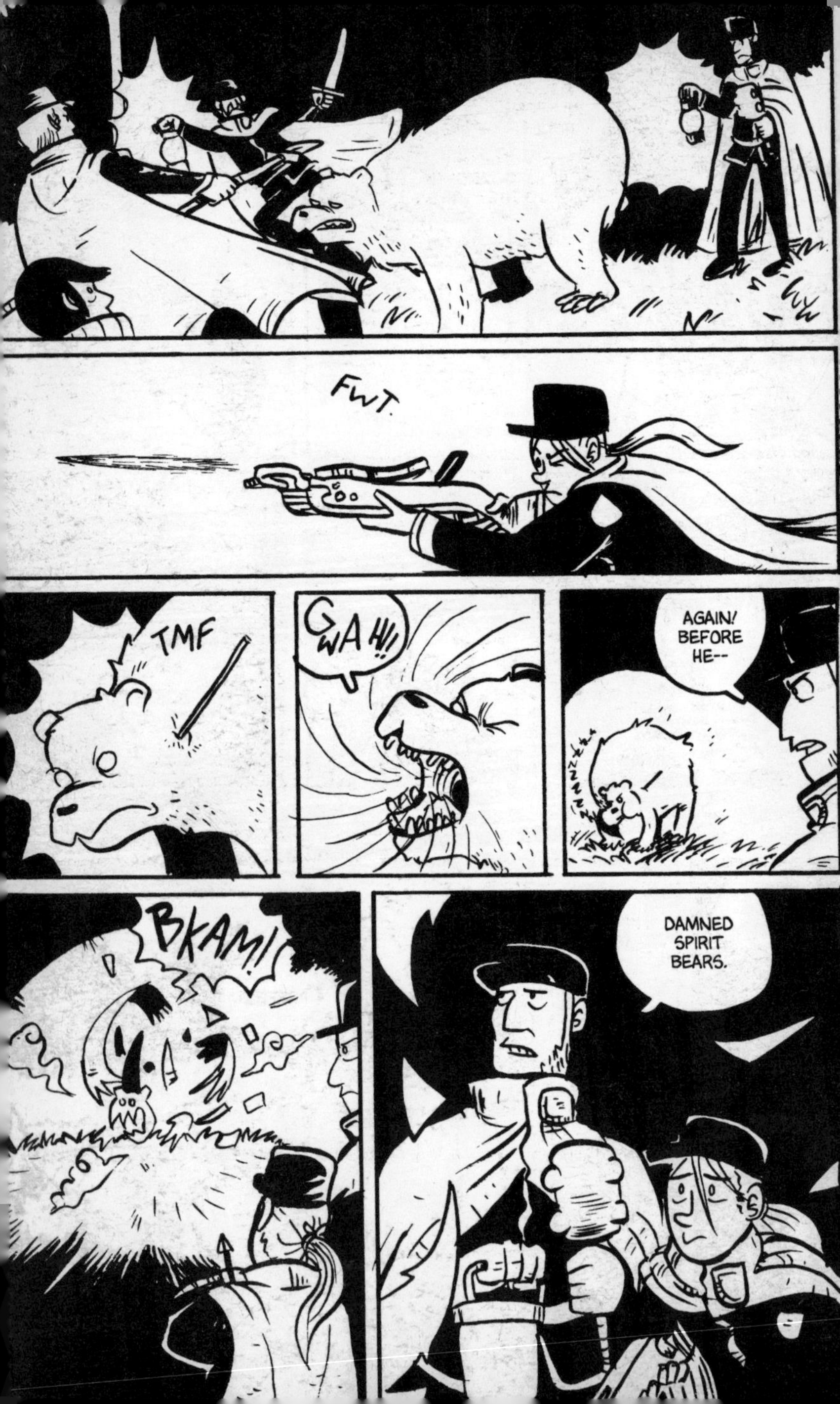
FWT.
TMF
GWAH!!
AGAIN! BEFORE HE--
BKAM!
DAMNED SPIRIT BEARS.

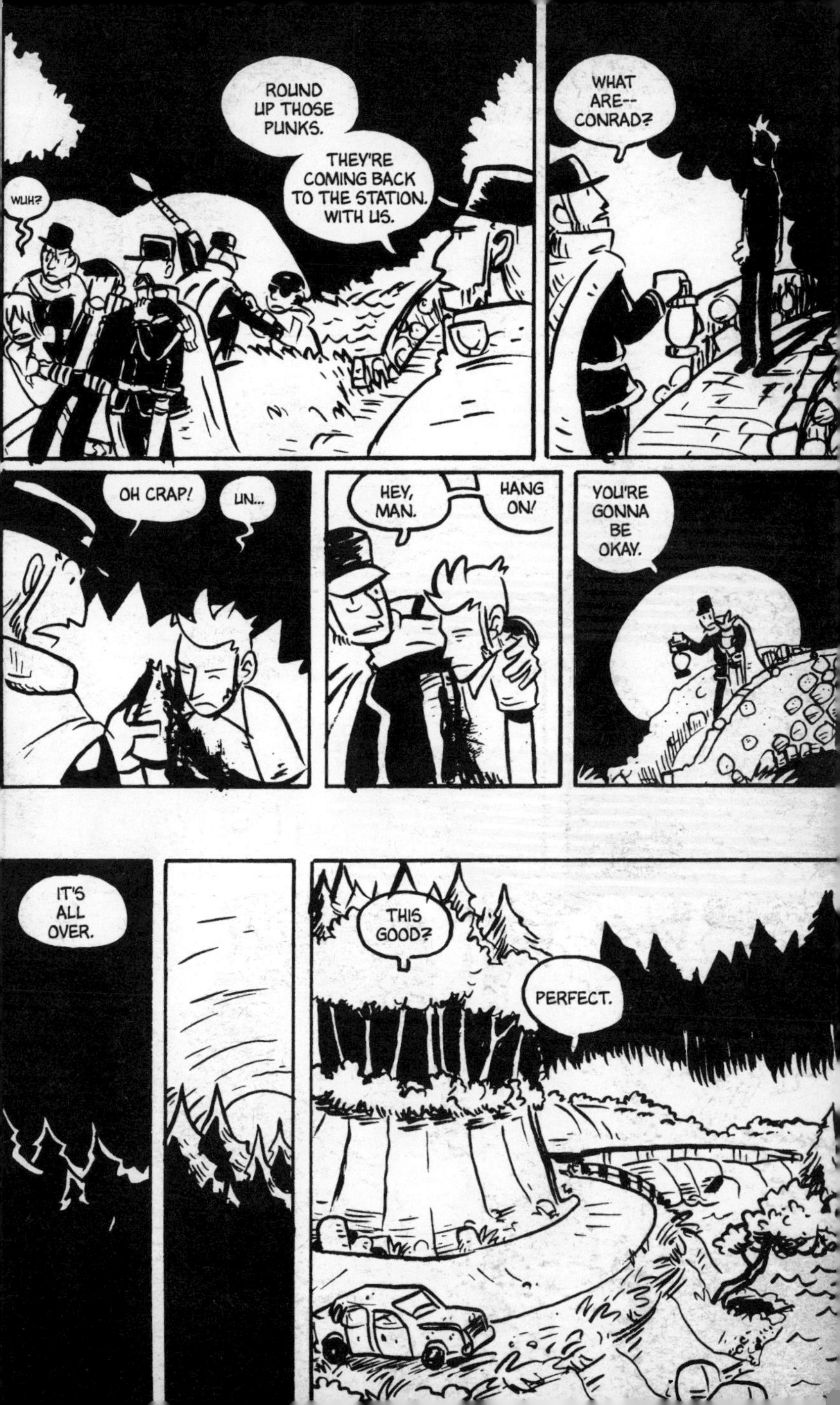
WUH?
ROUND UP THOSE PUNKS.
THEY'RE COMING BACK TO THE STATION. WITH US.
WHAT ARE-- CONRAD?
OH CRAP!
UN...
HEY, MAN.
HANG ON!
YOU'RE GONNA BE OKAY.
IT'S ALL OVER.
THIS GOOD?
PERFECT.

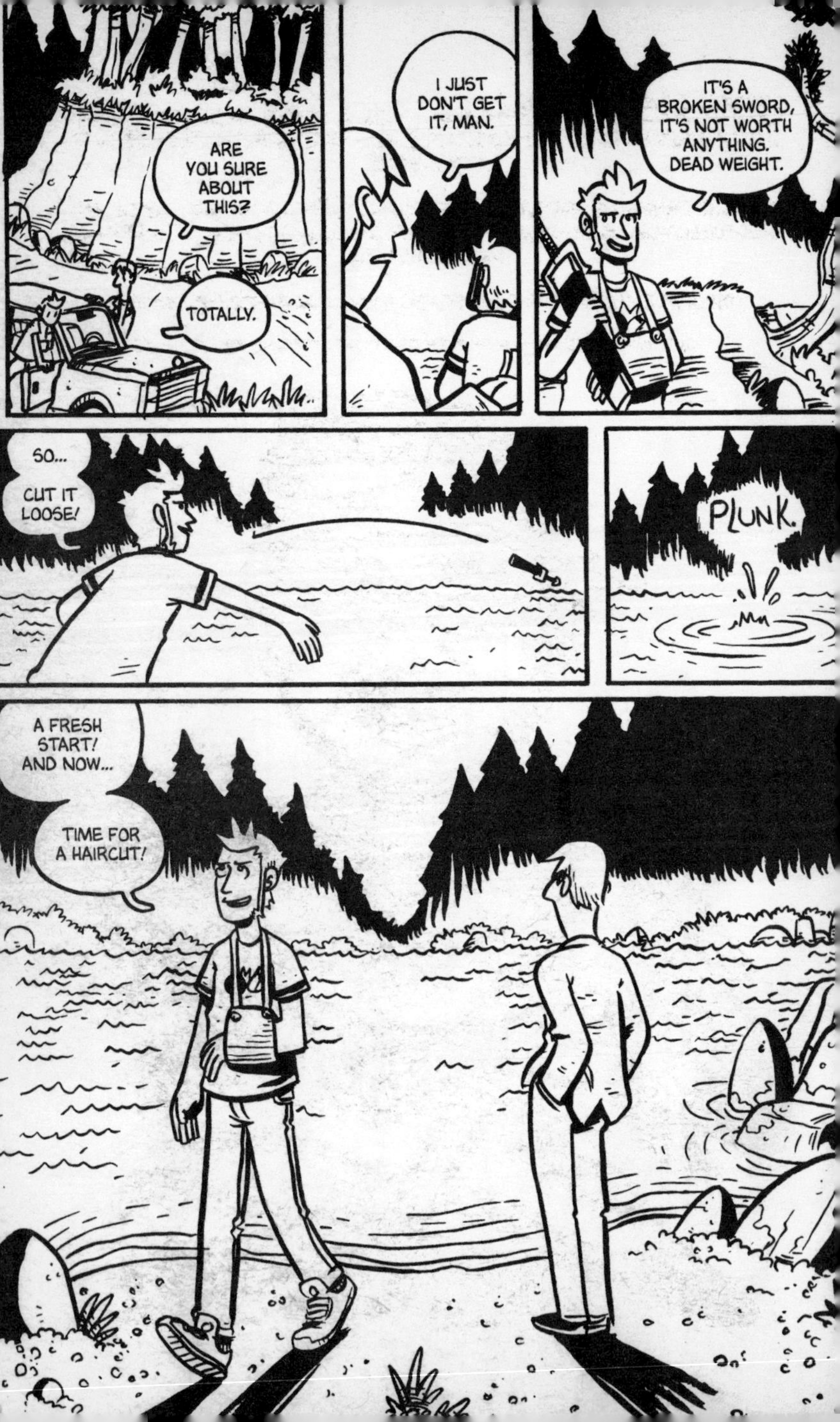
ARE YOU SURE ABOUT THIS?
TOTALLY.
I JUST DON'T GET IT, MAN.
IT'S A BROKEN SWORD, IT'S NOT WORTH ANYTHING. DEAD WEIGHT.
SO...
CUT IT LOOSE!
PLUNK.
A FRESH START! AND NOW...
TIME FOR A HAIRCUT!

ERIK LARS BROWN WAS BORN IN 1983. HE HAS BEEN WRITING, DRAWING, AND SELF-PUBLISHING HIS COMICS AND STORIES FOR SEVERAL YEARS. THIS IS HIS FIRST PUBLISHED GRAPHIC NOVEL.

THANKS TO AMANDA, KIEL, MATT, RUSS, J. FISH, BRYAN, COREY, BRANDON, JOHNO, JAMES, AND DOUG FOR ENCOURAGING ME, BELIEVING IN MY WORK AND FLIPPING THINGS BACK AT ME WHEN I WAS BEING STUPID.

OTHER *NORTH WORLD* STORIES CAN BE READ ONLINE AT NORTHWORLDONLINE.COM.

ILLUSTRATION BY LOUIE CHIN AT WEST-ATE.COM. INTERIOR COVER, CARVING BY LARS TJOETTA.

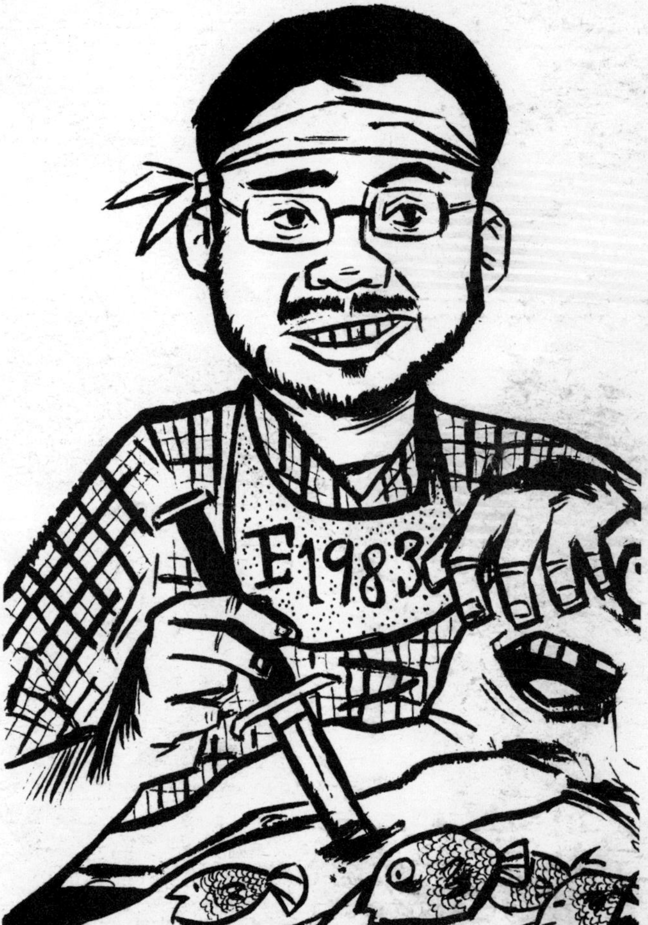
E1983

OTHER BOOKS FROM ONI PRESS

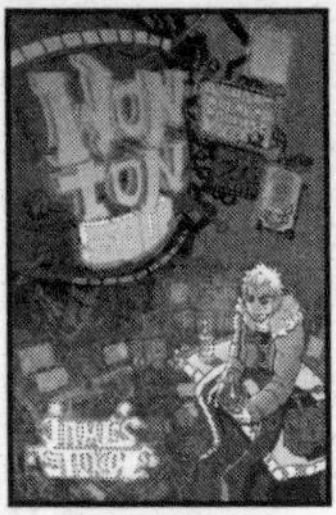

WONTON SOUP™
BY JAMES STOKOE
184 PAGES, BLACK+WHITE
$11.95 US
ISBN: 978-1-932664-60-7

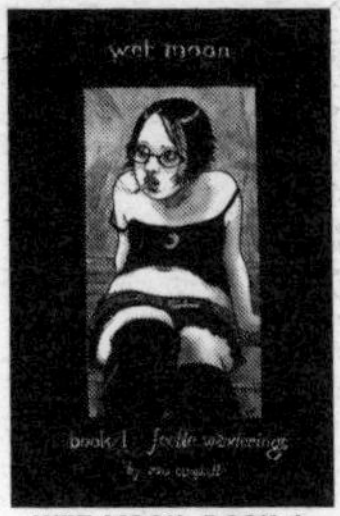
wet moon
book 1 feeble wanderings

WET MOON, BOOK 1: FEEBLE WANDERINGS™
BY ROSS CAMPBELL
176 PAGES, BLACK+WHITE
$14.95 US
ISBN 1-932664-07-6

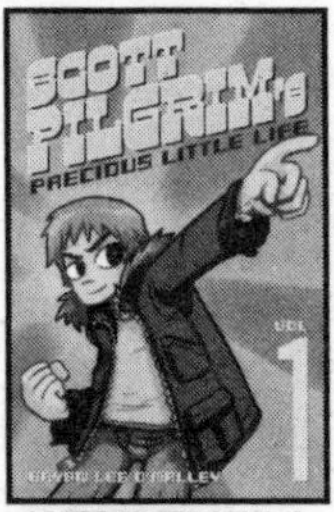
SCOTT PILGRIM'S
PRECIOUS LITTLE LIFE
VOL
1

SCOTT PILGRIM VOL 1: SCOTT PILGRIM'S PRECIOUS LITTLE LIFE™
BY BRYAN LEE O'MALLEY
168 PAGES, BLACK+WHITE
$11.95 US
ISBN 978-1-932664-08-9

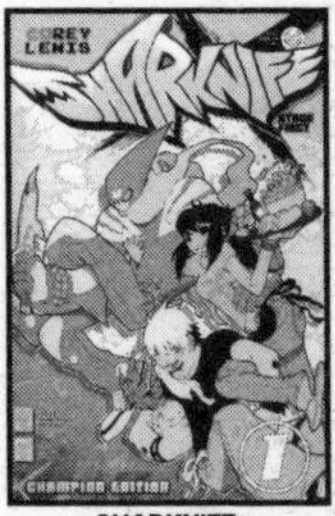
COREY LEWIS
CHAMPION EDITION

SHARKNIFE: STAGE FIRST™
BY COREY LEWIS
136 PAGES, BLACK+WHITE
$9.95 US
ISBN 978-1-932664-17-1

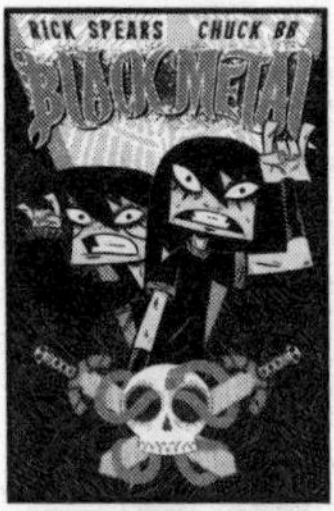
RICK SPEARS
CHUCK BB
BLACK METAL

BLACK METAL VOL. 1™
BY RICK SPEARS
+ CHUCK BB
160 PAGES, BLACK+WHITE
$11.95 US
ISBN 978-1-932664-72-0

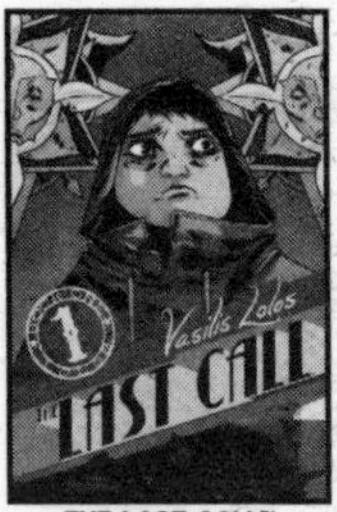
Vasilis Lolos
LAST CALL

THE LAST CALL™
BY VASILIS LOLOS
136 PAGES, BLACK+-WHITE
$11.95 US
ISBN 978-1-932664-69-0

AVAILABLE AT FINER COMICS SHOPS EVERYWHERE. FOR A COMICS STORE NEAR YOU, CALL 1-888-COMIC-BOOK OR VISIT WWW.THE-MASTER-LIST.COM. FOR MORE ONI PRESS TITLES AND INFORMATION VISIT WWW.ONIPRESS.COM.